Black American Fiction:

A Bibliography

by
CAROL FAIRBANKS
and
EUGENE A. ENGELDINGER

The Scarecrow Press, Inc.
Metuchen, N.J. & London
1978

Library of Congress Cataloging in Publication Data

Fairbanks, Carol, 1935-
    Black American fiction.

        Bibliography: p.
        1.   American fiction--Afro-American authors--Bibliography.
I.   Engeldinger, Eugene A., joint author.   II.   Title.
Z1229.N39F34   [PS153.N5]   016.813   √78-1351
ISBN 0-8108-1120-0

For Margaret and Gary

TABLE OF CONTENTS

v

ACKNOWLEDGMENTS

Caryl Laubach has typed over 2400 pages of manuscript for Scarecrow Press publications. This is an appropriate time, therefore, to acknowledge her expertise as typist and as editor, and to thank her for her enthusiastic assistance and support.

NOTE TO READERS

The purpose of this bibliography is to provide the user with a list of Black American authors, their fiction and criticism. Nonfiction has not been included, nor has children's literature or young adult fiction unless it is also of interest to more sophisticated readers.

Several categories are found under most authors: novels, short fiction, book reviews, and biography and criticism. As complete a citation as possible is included, based on Turabian's style manual, to assist both the casual student and the serious scholar in their research. Multiple sources for some works have been included when possible.

The attempt has been made to be as inclusive as possible, but it is often difficult to identify minor Black authors such as those who have written only a few short stories. Authors have been included only when there was proof that they were Black. The effect will undoubtedly be that worthy writers have been excluded due to lack of information regarding race. None were excluded intentionally, however.

Wherever possible, citations have been checked in the actual sources. In a few cases these sources were not available, so incomplete citations are included as we found them in other listings, believing that partial information is better than none.

A bibliography of general criticism is included at the end for those wishing overviews of Black American literature. However, many of these citations have been included under particular authors when they received sufficient treatment to warrant it. Abbreviated forms of anthologies including short fiction and novel excerpts are used throughout the author listing; the General Bibliography provides the complete citation.

Errors undoubtedly creep into works such as this. Our hope is that they will cause the reader no appreciable inconvenience.

AUTHORS (A-Z)

ABRAMSON, Dolores

Short Fiction

"A King in Search for a Queen." In Sanchez, Three Hundred and Sixty Degrees of Blackness Comin at You.

ADAMS, Alger LeRoy (Philip B. Kaye)

Novel

Taffy. New York: Crown, 1950; New York: Avon, 1951.

Biography and Criticism

Bone, Robert A. The Negro Novel in America. New Haven: Yale University Press, 1966.

Hughes, Carl M. The Negro Novelist 1940-1950. New York: Citadel Press, 1953.

Schraufnagel, Noel. From Apology to Protest: The Black American Novel. DeLand, Florida: Everett/Edwards, 1973.

Reviews

Taffy
    Lovell, John J. Journal of Negro Education 21 (Spring 1952): 177-179.

    Petry, Ann. Saturday Review of Literature, 23 December 1950, p. 21.

    Redding, Saunders. New York Herald Tribune Book Review. 19 November 1950, p. 18.

    Sullivan, Richard. New York Times, 5 November 1950, p. 32.

ADAMS, Alvin

Short Fiction

"Ice Tea." Negro Digest 15 (March 1966): 70-79.

ADAMS, Clayton

Novel

Ethiopia, The Land of Promise: The Book with a Purpose. New York: Cosmopolitan, 1917.

Biography and Criticism

Gloster, Hugh M. Negro Voices in American Fiction. Chapel Hill: University of North Carolina Press, 1948.

AIKEN, Aaron Eugene

Short Fiction

Exposure of Negro Society and Societies ... Twenty Stories Combined. New York: J. P. Wharton Printer, 1916.

ALBA, Nanina

Short Fiction

"The Satin-Back Crepe Dress." Negro Digest 14 (May 1965): 36-39.
"Scary Story." Negro Digest 15 (July 1966): 65-68.
"So Quaint." Negro Digest 13 (February 1964): 76-79.

Biography and Criticism

Emanuel, James A. and Theodore Gross, eds. Dark Symphony: Negro Literature in America. New York: Free Press, 1968.

ALLISON, Hughes

Short Fiction

"Imposture." Negro Digest 7 (March 1949): 79.
"Miss Hood Is Shocked." Challenge 1 (May 1935): 24-31.

AMINI, Johari (Jewel C. Latimore)

Short Fiction

"Wednesday." Black World 19 (June 1970): 54-56.

ANDERSON, Alston

Novel

All God's Children. Indianapolis: Bobbs-Merrill, 1965.

Short Fiction

(Collection): Lover Man: Stories of Blacks and Whites. Garden
    City, N.Y.: Doubleday, 1959; London: Cassell, 1959. Includes:
        "Big Boy."
        "Blueplate Special."
        "The Checker Board." Also in Hughes, The Best Short
            Stories by Negro Writers.
        "Comrad."
        "Dance of the Infidels."
        "The Dozens."
        "A Fine Romance."
        "Lover Man."
        "Old Man Maypeck."
        "Schooldays in North Carolina."
        "Signifying."
        "A Sound of Screaming."
        "Suzie Q."
        "Talisman."
        "Think."

Biography and Criticism

Schraufnagel, Noel. From Apology to Protest: The Black Ameri-
    can Novel. DeLand, Florida: Everett/Edwards, 1973.

Reviews

All God's Children
    Christian Century, 18 August 1964, p. 1013.
    Creekmore, Hubert, New York Times, 7 November 1965, p. 58.
    Kirkus, 1 June 1965, p. 544.
    Raines, C. A. Library Journal, 1 September 1965, p. 3471.
Lover Man
    Crisis 66 (November 1959): 580-581.

ANDERSON, Henry L. N.

Novel

No Use Cryin'. Los Angeles: Western, 1961.

ANDERSON, Mignon Holland (Mignon Holland)

Short Fiction

(Collection): Mostly Women Folk and a Man or Two: A Collection. Chicago: Third World Press, 1976.
"Gone After Jake." Black Creation 4 (Summer 1973): 22-23.
"November." Freedomways 11 (Second Quarter 1971): 260-263.

ANDERSON, S. E.

Short Fiction

"The Contraband." In Alhamisi and Wangara, Black Arts; King, Black Short Story Anthology.
"Soldier Boy." Black World 19 (June 1970): 88-92.

ANGELOU, Maya

Autobiographical Novels

Gather Together in My Name. New York: Random House, 1974; New York: Bantam, 1975.
I Know Why the Caged Bird Sings. New York: Random House, 1970; New York: Bantam, 1971. Excerpts in Harper's (February 1970); Exum, Keeping the Faith; Watkins and David, To Be a Black Woman.
Singin' and Swingin' and Gettin' Merry Like Christmas. New York: Random House, 1976.

Short Fiction

"All Day Long." In Clarke, Harlem.
"Glass Rain." Essence 1 (January 1971): 34-35.
"Steady Going Up." In Mayfield, Ten Times Black.

Biography and Criticism

Arensberg, Liliane K. "Death as Metaphor of Self in I Know Why the Caged Bird Sings." CLA Journal 20 (December 1976): 273-291.
"The Black Scholar Interviews: Maya Angelou." Black Scholar 8 (January-February 1977): 44-53.
Current Biography, 1974.
"I Know Why the Caged Bird Sings." Ebony 25 (April 1970): 62-64.
Julianelli, J. "Angelou: Interview." Harper's Bazaar (November 1972): 124.
Kent, George E. "Notes on the 1974 Black Literary Scene." Phylon 36 (June 1975): 182-203.
Smith, Sidonie Ann. "The Song of a Caged Bird: Maya Angelou's Quest for Self-Acceptance." Southern Humanities Review 7

(Fall 1973), 365-374.
Washington, Mary Helen. "Black Women Image Makers." Black
World 23 (August 1974): 10-18.
Weller, Sheila. "Work in Progress: Maya Angelou." Intellectual
Digest 3 (June 1973): 1.
Who's Who in America, 1974-75.

Reviews

Gather Together in My Name
    Adams, Phoebe. Atlantic 233 (June 1974): 114.
    Almeida, R. E. Library Journal, 1 June 1974, p. 1538.
    Booklist, 1 June 1974, pp. 1078, 1098.
    Choice 11 (September 1974): 920.
    Goode, Ann. Black Books Bulletin 2 (Fall 1974): 60-61.
    Gottlieb, Annie. New York Times Book Review, 16 June 1974,
        p. 16.
    Jones, Barbara. Freedomways 14 (Fourth Quarter 1974): 359-
        361.
    Kirkus, 1 April 1974, p. 394; 15 April 1974, p. 439.
    Minudri, Regina. Library Journal, 15 May 1974, p. 1494.
    New Republic, 6 July 1974, p. 32.
    New Yorker, 15 June 1974, p. 87.
    Publishers' Weekly, 1 April 1974, p. 54.
    Village Voice, 11 July 1974, p. 31.
I Know Why the Caged Bird Sings
    Booklist, 15 June 1970, p. 1256; 15 July 1970, p. 1399.
    Goode, Ann. Black Books Bulletin 2 (Fall 1974): 60-61.
    Gross, R. A. Newsweek, 2 March 1970, p. 90.
    Guiney, E. M. Library Journal, 15 March 1970, p. 1018.
    Kelly, E. B. Harvard Education Review 40 (November 1970):
        681.
    Life, 5 June 1970, p. 12.
    Minudri, Regina. Library Journal, 15 June 1970, p. 2320.
    Sepia 19 (June 1970): 23.
    Sutherland, Zena. Saturday Review, 9 May 1970, p. 70.
    Top of the News 27 (November 1970): 92.
    Wall Street Journal, 16 April 1970, p. 16; 8 December 1970,
        p. 22.
Singin' and Swingin' and Gettin' Merry Like Christmas
    Almeida, R. E. Library Journal, 1 September 1976, p. 1763.
    Booklist, 15 September 1976, p. 107.
    Evans, W. R. Best Sellers 36 (January 1977): 328-329.
    Jordan, June. Ms. 5 (January 1977): 40-41.
    Kirkus, 1 August 1976, p. 864; 15 August 1976, p. 912.
    National Observer, 2 October 1976, p. 21.
    Publishers' Weekly, 9 August 1976, p. 74.
    Saturday Review, 30 October 1976, p. 46.
    School Library Journal 23 (September 1976): 144.

ARNOLD, Ethel Nishua

Novel

She Knew No Evil. New York: Vantage, 1953.

ASHBY, William Mobile

Novel

Redder Blood. New York: Cosmopolitan, 1915.

Short Fiction

"Even the Blind." Opportunity 16 (November 1938): 329-330.

Biography and Criticism

Gloster, Hugh M. Negro Voices in American Fiction. Chapel
    Hill: University of North Carolina Press, 1948.
Hughes, Carl M. The Negro Novelist 1940-1950. New York:
    Citadel Press, 1953.
Mays, Benjamin E. The Negro's God as Reflected in His Litera-
    ture. Boston: Grimes & Chapman, 1938.

ASHLEY, Martin

Novel

Checkmate and Deathmate. New York: Vantage, 1973.

ATKINS, Russell

Short Fiction

(Collection): Maleficium. Cleveland: Free Lance, 1971.

Reviews

Maleficium
    Library Journal, 15 June 1972, p. 2191.

ATTAWAY, William

Novels

Blood on the Forge. New York: Doubleday, Doran, 1941; Chatham,
    N.J.: Chatham Booksellers, 1969; New York: Macmillan, 1970.
    Excerpt in Davis and Redding, Cavalcade.

Let Me Breathe Thunder. New York: Doubleday, Doran, 1939.
(Also published as Tough Kid. New York: Lion Books, 1952.)
Tough Kid see Let Me Breathe Thunder.

Short Fiction

"Tale of the Blackamoor." Challenge 1 (June 1936): 3-4.

Biography and Criticism

Bone, Robert A. The Negro Novel in America. New Haven: Yale University Press, 1966.

Davis, Arthur P. From the Dark Tower: Afro-American Writers 1900-1960. Washington, D.C.: Howard University Press, 1974.

Ellison, Ralph. "Transition." Negro Quarterly 1 (Spring 1942): 87-92.

Felgar, Robert. "William Attaway's Unaccommodated Protagonists." Studies in Black Literature 4 (Spring 1973): 1-3.

Gayle, Addison, Jr. The Way of the New World: The Black Novel in America. Garden City, N.Y.: Anchor Press/Doubleday, 1975.

Gloster, Hugh M. Negro Voices in American Fiction. Chapel Hill: University of North Carolina Press, 1948.

Harper, Clifford Doyl. "A Study of the Disunity Theme in the Afro-American Experience: An Examination of Five Representative Novels." Ph.D. Dissertation, Saint Louis University, 1972.

Klotman, Phyllis R. "An Examination of Whiteness in Blood on the Forge." CLA Journal 15 (June 1972): 459-464.

Margolies, Edward. Native Sons: A Critical Study of Twentieth-Century Negro American Authors. Philadelphia: J. P. Lippincott, 1968.

Schraufnagel, Noel. From Apology to Protest: The Black American Novel. DeLand, Florida: Everett/Edwards, 1973.

Simms, L. Moody, Jr. "In the Shadow of Richard Wright: William Attaway." Notes on Mississippi Writers 8 (Spring 1975): 13-18.

Vaughan, Philip. "From Pastoralism to Industrial Antipathy in William Attaway's Blood on the Forge." Phylon 36 (December 1975): 422-425.

Waldron, Edward E. "William Attaway's Blood on the Forge: The Death of the Blues." Negro American Literature Forum 10 (Summer 1976): 58-60.

Young, James O. Black Writers of the Thirties. Baton Rouge: Louisiana State University Press, 1973.

Reviews

Blood on the Forge
Books, 24 August 1941, p. 8.
de Kay, Drake. New York Times, 24 August 1941, p. 18.
Hopson, James O. Opportunity 19 (November 1941): 346-347.
New Yorker, 6 September 1941, p. 78.
Publishers' Weekly, 30 March 1970, p. 66.

Let Me Breathe Thunder
    Clark, Margaret. Boston Transcript, 1 July 1939, p. 1.
    Lee, Ulysses. Opportunity 17 (September 1939): 283-284.
    Marsh, F. T. New York Herald-Tribune Books, 25 June 1939,
       p. 10.
    New Republic, 30 August 1939, p. 112.
    New Yorker, 24 June 1939, p. 86.
    Young, Stanley. New York Times Book Review, 25 June 1939,
       p. 7.

AUSTIN, Edmund

Novel

The Black Challenge. New York: Vantage, 1958.

AWOONER, Kofi

Novel

This Earth, My Brother: An Allegorical Tale of Africa. Garden
    City, N.Y.: Doubleday, 1972.

Biography and Criticism

Achebe, Chinua. "Introduction." This Earth, My Brother. Garden
    City, N.Y.: Anchor Press/Doubleday, 1971.
Contemporary Authors, 29/32.
Duclos, Jocelyn-Robert. "'The Butterfly and the Pile of Manure':
    A Study of Kofi Awoonor, This Earth, My Brother." Canadian
    Journal of African Studies 9 no. 3 (1975): 511-522.
Lindfors, Bernth, et al. "Palaver: Interviews with Five African
    Writers in Texas." Monograph. Occasional Publications of the
    African and Afro-American Research Institute. Austin: Uni-
    versity of Texas, 1972.

Reviews

This Earth, My Brother
    Achebe, Chinua. Transition No. 41, p. 69.
    Choice 8 (July-August 1971): 682.
    Eddin, Mursi Saad. Lotus 19 (January 1974): 202-204.
    Kazin, Alfred. Saturday Review of Literature, 2 October 1971,
       p. 33.
    Kirkus, 1 February 1971, p. 127.
    New Statesman, 17 March 1972, p. 364.
    New York Times Book Review, 2 April 1972, p. 7.
    Observer, 26 March 1972, p. 37.
    Publishers Weekly, 22 February 1971, p. 139.
    Saturday Review of Literature, 27 November 1971, p. 46.
    Snyder, Emile. Saturday Review of Literature, 17 June 1971,

p. 23.
Thompson, John. New York Review of Books, 23 September
1971, p. 4.
Times Literary Supplement, 24 March 1972, p. 325.
Updike, John. New Yorker, 13 November 1971, p. 187.
Warner, J. M. Library Journal, 1 April 1971, p. 1286.

BALDWIN, James A.

Novels

Another Country. New York: Dial, 1962; New York: Dell, 1970.
　　Excerpts in Partisan Review 27 (Spring 1960): 282-294; The Dial:
　　An Annual of Fiction.
Giovanni's Room. New York: Dial, 1956; New York: New Ameri-
　　can Library, 1957, 1961; New York: William Morrow, 1962.
Go Tell It on the Mountain. New York: Knopf, 1953; New York:
　　New American Library, 1954; New York: Grosset, 1961; New
　　York: Dell, 1970; excerpts in American Mercury 75 (August
　　1962): 97-103; Clarke, American Negro Short Stories; Clarke,
　　Harlem; Davis and Redding, Cavalcade; Ford, Black Insights;
　　New World Writing, vol. 2.
If Beale Street Could Talk. New York: Dial, 1974.
Little Man, Little Man. New York: Dial, 1976.
Tell Me How Long the Train's Been Gone. New York: Dial, 1968;
　　New York: Dell, 1969.

Short Fiction

(Collection): Going to Meet the Man. New York: Dial, 1965; New
　　York: Dell, 1966.
"Caleb and Me." In Cooper and Chalpin, Achievements in Fiction.
"Come Out the Wilderness." Mademoiselle 46 (March 1958): 102-
　　104, 146-154; Negro Digest 10 (September 1961): 77-97; Abels
　　and Smith, 40 Best Stories from Mademoiselle, 1935-1960;
　　Abrahams, Fifty Years of the American Short Story; Angus,
　　The Trouble Is; Angus and Angus, Contemporary American
　　Short Stories; Baldwin, Going to Meet the Man; Casmier and
　　Souder, Coming Together; Dolan and Bennett, Introduction to
　　Fiction; Engle, Prize Stories, 1959; King, Black Short Story
　　Anthology; Sherrill and Robertson-Rose, Four Elements.
"Cornhill." Atlantic 206 (Spring 1961): 32-73.
"Death of the Prophet." Commentary 9 (March 1950): 257-261.
"Going to Meet the Man." In Baldwin, Going to Meet the Man;
　　Carpenter and Neumeyer, Elements of Fiction; Klotz and Ab-
　　carian, The Experience of Fiction; Peden, Short Fiction.
"The Man Child." In Baldwin, Going to Meet the Man; Boynton and
　　Mack, Introduction to the Short Story, rev. ed.; Hills and Hills,
　　How We Live; Turner, Black American Literature: Fiction.
"The Outing." New-Story (April 1951): 52-81; also in Baldwin, Going
　　to Meet the Man; Mills, Comparisons.
"Previous Condition." Commentary 6 (October 1948): 334-342; also

in Baldwin, Going to Meet the Man; Cooper and Chalpin, Achievements in Fiction; Gibson and Anselment, Black and White.
"The Rockpile." In Adams, Conn, and Slepian, Afro-American Literature: Fiction; Baldwin, Going to Meet the Man; Cooper and
Chalpin, Achievements in Fiction; Ravitz, The American Disinherited.
"Sonny's Blues." Partisan Review 24 (Summer 1957): 327-358; also
in Baldwin, Going to Meet the Man; Barksdale and Kinnamon,
Black Writers of America; Beaty, The Norton Introduction to
Literature; Berkley, The Short Story Reader, 3rd ed.; Cahill
and Cahill, Big City Stories; Casmier and Souder, Coming To-
gether; Emanuel and Gross, Dark Symphony; Flower, Counter-
parts; Foley and Burnett, Best American Short Stories, 1958;
Gasarch and Gasarch, Fiction: The Universal Elements; Gold,
Fiction of the Fifties; Gordon and Hills, New York, New York;
Hart, et al., Discovery and Response; Hills and Hills, How We
Live; Hollander, American Short Stories Since 1945; Huck and
Shanahan, The Modern Short Story; Kennedy, Stories East and
West; McKenzie, The Process of Fiction; Matthews, Archetypal
Themes in the Modern Story; Schulman, The Loners; Sherrill
and Robertson-Rose, Four Elements; Simonson, Quartet; Somer,
Narrative Experience; Timko, 29 Short Stories.
"Tell Me How Long the Train's Been Gone." In Foley, 200 Years
of Great American Short Stories; Hutrik and Yarber, An Intro-
duction to Short Fiction and Criticism; Foley and Burnett, The
Best American Short Stories, 1968; Perkins, Realistic Ameri-
can Short Fiction; Schneider, et al., The Range of Literature:
Fiction.
"This Morning, This Evening, So Soon." Atlantic 206 (Summer
1960): 34-52; Cornhill Magazine 172 (Spring 1961): 32-73; also
in Baldwin, Going to Meet the Man; Foley, Fifty Best American
Short Stories 1915-1965; Foley and Burnett, The Best American
Short Stories, 1961; Hughes, The Best Short Stories by Negro
Writers; Kissin, Stories in Black and White; McKenzie, The
Process of Fiction; Pickering, Fiction 100; Schneider, et al.,
The Range of Literature: Fiction; Scott, Studies in the Short
Story, alternate ed.

Biography and Criticism

Aldridge, John W. "The Fire Next Time?" Saturday Review/World,
15 June 1974, pp. 20, 24-25.
Alexander, Charlotte. "The 'Stink of Reality': Mothers and Whores
in James Baldwin's Fiction." Literature and Psychology 18
(1968): 9-26.
Allen, Shirley S. "Religious Symbolism and Psychic Reality in
Baldwin's Go Tell It on the Mountain." CLA Journal 19 (De-
cember 1975): 173-199.
Allen, Walter. The Modern Novel in Britain and the United States.
New York: Dutton, 1964.
Barksdale, Richard K. "Black America and the Mask of Comedy."
In The Comic Imagination in American Literature, pp. 349-360.
Edited by Louis D. Rubin, Jr. New Brunswick, N.J.: Rutgers

University Press, 1973.
_____. '"Temple of the Fire Baptized.'" Phylon 14 (1953):
326-327.
Bell, George E.   "The Dilemma of Love in Go Tell It on the Moun-
tain and Giovanni's Room. " CLA Journal 17 (March 1974):
397-406.
Bell, Pearl K.   "Blacks and the Blues. " New Leader, 27 May
1974, pp. 3-4.
Bennett, Joanne Spitznagel.   "James Baldwin: A Contemporary
Novelist of Manners. " Ph. D. Dissertation, Indiana University,
1974.
Bennett, Stephen B. and William W. Nichols.   "Violence in Afro-
American Fiction: An Hypothesis. " Modern Fiction Studies
17 (1971): 221-228.
Bigsby, C. W. E.   "The Committed Writer: James Baldwin as
Dramatist. " Twentieth Century Literature 13 (1967): 39-48.
Billingsley, R. G.   "Forging New Directions: The Burden of the
Hero in Modern Afro-American Literature. " Obsidian 1 (Winter
1975): 5-21.
Bingham, R. K.   "Two American Writers. " Reporter, 23 June
1953, pp. 38-39.
Black Authors.   Old Greenwich, Conn.: Listening Library, n. d.
(Filmstrip.)
"The Black Scholar Interview: James Baldwin. " Black Scholar 5
(December 1973-January 1974): 33-42.
Blaisdel, Gus.   "James Baldwin, the Writer. " Negro Digest 13
(January 1964): 61-68.
Bone, Robert A.   The Negro Novel in America.   New Haven: Yale
University Press, 1966.
_____.   "The Novels of James Baldwin. " Tri-Quarterly 2 (Win-
ter 1965): 3-20; also in Bone's The Negro Novel in America.
New Haven: Yale University Press, 1966.
Bonosky, Phillip.   "The Negro Writer and Commitment. " Main-
stream 15 (February 1962): 16-22.
Boyle, Kay.   "Introducing James Baldwin. " In Contemporary Amer-
ican Novelists.   Edited by Harry T. Moore.   Carbondale:
Southern Illinois University Press, 1964.
Bradford, Ernest Marvin.   "Biblical Metaphors of Bondage and Lib-
eration in Black Writing: A Study of the Evolution of Black Lib-
eration as Mediated in Writing Based on the Bible. " Ph. D.
Dissertation, The University of Nebraska-Lincoln, 1976.
Breaux, Elwyn Ellison.   "Comic Elements in Selected Prose Works
by James Baldwin, Ralph Ellison, and Langston Hughes. " Ed. D.
Dissertation, Oklahoma State University, 1971.
Breit, Harvey.   "James Baldwin and Two Footnotes. " In The Creative Present: Notes on Contemporary American Fiction, pp.
5-24.   Edited by Nona Balakian and Charles Simmons.   Garden
City, N. Y.: Doubleday, 1963.
Bryant, Jerry H.   "Wright, Ellison, Baldwin--Exorcising the De-
mon. " Phylon 37 (June 1976): 174-188.
Burke, William Martin.   "Modern Black Fiction and the Literature
of Oppression. " Ph. D. Dissertation, University of Oregon,
1971.

Charney, Maurice. "James Baldwin's Quarrel with Richard Wright."
American Quarterly 15 (1963): 65-75.
Collier, Eugenia W. "The Phrase Unbearably Repeated." Phylon
25 (1964): 288-296.
_____. "Thematic Patterns in Baldwin's Essays." Black World
21 (June 1972): 28-34.
Cosgrove, William. "Strategies of Survival: The Gimmick Motif
in Black Literature." Studies in the Twentieth Century 15
(Spring 1975): 109-127.
Cowan, Kathryn Osburn. "Black/White Stereotypes in the Fiction of
Richard Wright, James Baldwin, and Ralph Ellison." Ph.D.
Dissertation, St. Louis University, 1972.
Cox, C. B. and A. R. Jones. "After the Tranquillized Fifties:
Notes on Sylvia Plath and James Baldwin." Critical Quarterly
6 (1964): 107-122.
Dance, Daryl C. "You Can't Go Home Again: James Baldwin and
the South." CLA Journal 18 (1974): 81-90.
Daniels, Mark R. "Estrangement, Betrayal and Atonement: The
Political Theory of James Baldwin." Studies in Black Litera-
ture 7 (Autumn 1976): 10-13.
Davis, Arthur P. From the Dark Tower: Afro-American Writers
1900 to 1960. Washington, D.C.: Howard University Press,
1974.
Davis, Charles T. "The Heavenly Voice of the Black American."
Yearbook of Contemporary Criticism 4 (1971): 108-119.
Dickstein, Morris. "The Black Aesthetic in White America." Par-
tisan Review 38 (Winter 1971-1972): 376-395.
_____. "Wright, Baldwin, Cleaver." New Letters 38 (Winter
1971): 117-124.
Donlan, D. "Cleaver on Baldwin on Wright." Clearing House 48
(April 1974): 508-509.
Durham, Joyce Roberta. "The City in Recent American Literature:
A Study of Selected Writings of Bellow, Mailer, Ellison, Bald-
win, and Writers of the Black Aesthetic." Ph.D. Dissertation,
University of Maryland, 1974.
Eckman, Fern M. The Furious Passage of James Baldwin. New
York: M. Evans, 1966; New York: Popular Library, 1967.
Ellison, Curtis William. "Black Adam: The Adamic Assertion and
the Afro-American Novelist." Ph.D. Dissertation, University of
Minnesota, 1970.
Emerson, O. B. "Cultural Nationalism in Afro-American Litera-
ture." In The Cry of Home, pp. 227-230. Edited by H. Ernest
Lewald. Knoxville: University of Tennessee Press, 1972.
Fabre, Michel. "Fathers and Sons in James Baldwin's Go Tell It
on the Mountain." In Modern Black Novelists, pp. 88-104.
Edited by M. G. Cooke. Englewood Cliffs, N.J.: Prentice-
Hall, 1971.
Finn, James. "The Identity of James Baldwin." Commonweal, 26
October 1962, pp. 113-116.
Fischer, Russell G. "James Baldwin: A Bibliography, 1947-1962."
Bulletin of Bibliography 24 (January-April 1965): 127-130.

Foster, D. C. "'Cause My House Fell Down: The Theme of the Fall in Baldwin's Novels." Critique 13 no. 2 (1971): 50-62.

Gayle, Addison, Jr. "In Defense of James Baldwin." CLA Journal 10 (1967): 201-208.

_____. The Way of the New World: The Black Novel in America. Garden City, N.Y.: Anchor Press/Doubleday, 1975.

George, Felice. "Black Woman, Black Man." Harvard Journal of Afro-American Affairs 2 (1971): 1-17.

Gerard, Albert. "Humanism and Negritude: Notes on the Contemporary Afro-American Novel." Trans. S. Alexander. Diogenes, No. 37 (Spring 1962): 115-133.

_____. "The Sons of Ham." Studies in the Novel 3 (1971): 148-164.

Gibson, Donald B. "Ralph Ellison and James Baldwin." In The Politics of Twentieth-Century Novelists, pp. 307-320. Edited by George A. Panichas. New York: Hawthorn Books, 1971.

Giles, James R. "Religious Alienation and 'Homosexual Consciousness' in City of Night and Go Tell It on the Mountain." College English 36 (November 1974): 369-380.

Goldman, Suzy B. "James Baldwin's 'Sonny's Blues': A Message in Music." Negro American Literature Forum 8 (1974): 231-233.

Gross, Barry. "The 'Uninhabitable Darkness' of Baldwin's Another Country: Image and Theme." Negro American Literature Forum 6 (Winter 1972): 113-121.

Gross, Theodore L. The Heroic Ideal in American Literature. New York: Free Press, 1971.

_____. "The World of James Baldwin." Critique 7 (Winter 1964-65): 139-149.

Hagopian, John V. "James Baldwin: The Black and the Red-White-and-Blue." CLA Journal 7 (December 1963): 133-140.

Hall, John. "Interview." Transatlantic Review, nos. 37/38 (Autumn-Winter 1970-1971): 5-14.

Harper, Clifford Boyl. "A Study of the Disunity Theme in the Afro-American Experience: An Examination of Five Representative Novels." Ph.D. Dissertation, St. Louis University, 1972.

Harper, Howard M., Jr. Desperate Faith: A Study of Bellow, Salinger, Mailer, Baldwin, and Updike. Chapel Hill, University of North Carolina Press, 1967.

_____. "James Baldwin--Art or Propaganda." In The American Novel, pp. 551-555. Edited by Christof Weglin. New York: Free Press, 1972.

Hassan, Ihab. Contemporary American Literature 1945-1972: An Introduction. New York: Frederick Ungar, 1973.

_____. Radical Innocence: Studies in the Contemporary American Novel. Princeton, N.J.: Princeton University Press, 1961.

Hayashi, Susanna. "Dark Odyssey: Descent into the Underworld in Black American Fiction." Ph.D. Dissertation, Indiana University, 1971.

Hoerchner, Susan Jane. "'I Have to Keep the Two Things Separate'; Polarity in Women in the Contemporary American Novel." Ph.D. Dissertation, Emory University, 1973.

Holland, Thomas Richard. "Vestiges of African Culture in Afro-American Literature: A Preliminary Study." Ph.D. Dissertation, University of Nebraska-Lincoln, 1973.

Holloway, Clayton Glenn. "James Baldwin as a Writer of Short Fiction: An Evaluation." Ph.D. Dissertation, Bowling Green State University, 1975.

Howe, Irving. "Black Boys and Native Sons." Dissent 10 (Autumn 1963): 353-368.

Inge, M. Thomas. "James Baldwin's Blues." Notes on Contemporary Literature 2 (1972): 8-11.

Isaacs, H. R. "Five Writers and Their African Ancestors." Phylon 21 (Fall 1960): 243-265; (Winter 1960): 317-336.

Jackson, Jocelyn Eleanor Whitehead. "The Problem of Identity in the Essays and Selected Novels of James Baldwin." Ph.D. Dissertation, Emory University, 1973.

Jacobson, Dan. "James Baldwin as Spokesman." Commentary 32 (December 1961): 497-502.

Jarrett, Thomas D. "Search for Identity." Phylon 17 (First Quarter 1956): 87-88.

Jordan, Jennifer. "Cleaver vs. Baldwin: Icing the White Negro." Black Books Bulletin 1 (Winter 1972): 13-15.

Kazin, Alfred. "Brothers Crying Out for More Access to Life." Saturday Review, 2 October 1971, p. 33-35.

Kent, George. Blackness and the Adventure of Western Culture. Chicago: Third World Press, 1972.

_____. "Notes on the 1974 Black Literary Scene." Phylon 36 (June 1975): 182-203.

Killinger, John. The Fragile Presence: Transcendence in Modern Literature. Philadelphia: Fortress Press, 1973.

Kim, Kichung. "Wright, the Protest Novel, and Baldwin's Faith." CLA Journal 17 (March 1974): 387-396.

Kindt, Kathleen A. "James Baldwin: A Checklist, 1947-1962." Bulletin of Bibliography 24 (January-April 1965): 123-126.

Kinnamon, Keneth, ed. James Baldwin: A Collection of Critical Essays. Englewood Cliffs, N.J.: Prentice-Hall, 1974.

Lash, John S. "Baldwin Beside Himself: A Study in Modern Phallicism." CLA Journal 8 (December 1964): 132-140.

Leaks, Sylvester. "James Baldwin--I Know His Name." Freedomways 3 (Winter 1963): 102-105.

Lee, Brian. "James Baldwin: Caliban to Prospero." In The Black American Writer, vol. 1, pp. 169-179. Edited by C. W. E. Bigsby. DeLand, Fla.: Everett/Edwards, 1969.

Levin, David. "Baldwin's Autobiographical Essays: The Problem of Negro Identity." Massachusetts Review 5 (Winter 1964): 239-247.

Lottman, Herbert R. "It's Hard to Be James Baldwin: An Interview." Intellectual Digest 2 (July 1972): 67-68.

Love, Theresa R. "The Black Woman in Afro-American Literature." Paper presented at the Midwest Modern Language Association meeting, Chicago, November 1975. (Mimeographed.)

Macebuh, Stanley. James Baldwin: A Critical Study. New York: Third Press, 1973.

MacInnes, Colin. "Dark Angel: The Writings of James Baldwin." Encounter 21 (August 1963): 22-23.

Major, Clarence. The Dark and Feeling. New York: Third Press, 1974.

Marcus, Steven. "The American Negro in Search of Identity." Commentary 16 (November 1953): 456-463.

Margolies, Edward. Native Sons: A Critical Study of Twentieth-Century Negro American Authors. Philadelphia: J. B. Lippincott, 1968.

May, John R. "Ellison, Baldwin, and Wright: Vestiges of Christian Apocalypse." Toward a New Earth: Apocalypse in the American Novel. Notre Dame: University of Notre Dame Press, 1972.

Mayfield, Julian. "And Then Came Baldwin." Freedomways 3 (Spring 1963): 143-155.

Meserve, Walter. "James Baldwin's 'Agony Way.'" In The Black American Writer, vol. 2, pp. 171-186. Edited by C. W. E. Bigsby. DeLand, Fla.: Everett/Edwards, 1969.

Mikkelsen, Nina M. "A Redefinition of the International Novel: Studies in the Development of an American Genre." Ph.D. Dissertation, Florida State University, 1971.

Moller, Karin. "James Baldwin's Theme of 'Identity' and His 'Fall' Metaphor." Essays in Literature (Denver): 2 (March 1974): 34-50.

Murray, Albert. The Omni-Americans. New York: Outerbridge & Dienstfrey, 1970.

Neal, Lawrence P. "The Black Writer's Role: James Baldwin." Liberator (April 1966): 10-11, 18.

The Negro in American Culture. Los Angeles: Pacifica Tape Library, 1961. (95-minute tape.)

Noble, David W. The Eternal Adam and the New World Garden: The Central Myth in the American Novel Since 1830. New York: George Braziller, 1968.

O'Brien, Conor Cruise. "White Gods and Black Americans." New Statesman, 1 May 1964, pp. 681-682.

Ognibene, Elaine. "Black Literature Revisited: 'Sonny's Blues.'" English Journal 60 (January 1971): 36-37.

Peden, William. The American Short Story: Continuity and Change 1940-1975. Boston: Houghton Mifflin, 1975.

Pratt, Louis H. "James Baldwin and 'The Literary Ghetto.'" CLA Journal 20 (December 1976): 262-272.

"Ralph Ellison Talks about James Baldwin." Negro Digest 11 (September 1962): 61.

Ray, Robert. "James Baldwin's Insecurity." Books and Bookmen, September 1972, p. 61.

Reid, Kenneth Russell. "James Baldwin's Fiction: Literary Artistry in Special Pleading." Ph.D. Dissertation, Kansas State University, 1972.

Reilly, John M. "'Sonny's Blues': James Baldwin's Image of Black Community." Negro American Literature Forum 4 (1970): 56-60.

Ro, Sigmund. "The Black Musician as Literary Hero: Baldwin's 'Sonny's Blues' and Kelley's 'Cry for Me.'" American Studies in Scandinavia 7 no. 1 (1975): 17-48.

Roberts, John Willie. "The Uses and Functions of Afro-American Folk and Popular Music in the Fiction of James Baldwin." Ph.D. Dissertation, The Ohio State University, 1976.

Rosenblatt, Roger. Black Fiction. Cambridge: Harvard University Press, 1974.

Rupp, Richard H. Celebration in Postwar American Fiction, 1945-1967. Coral Gables: University of Miami, 1970.

Sayre, Robert F. "James Baldwin's Other Country." In Contemporary American Novelists, pp. 158-169. Edited by Harry T. Moore. Carbondale: Southern Illinois University Press, 1964.

Schorer, Mark. The Literature of America: Twentieth Century. New York: McGraw-Hill, 1970.

Schraufnagel, Noel. From Apology to Protest: The Black American Novel. DeLand, Fla.: Everett/Edwards, 1973.

Schrero, Elliot M. "Another Country and the Sense of Self." Black Academy Review, 1-2, pp. 91-100; also in Modern Black Literature, pp. 91-100. Edited by S. Okechukwu Mezu. Buffalo: Black Academy Press, 1971.

Scott, Nathan A., Jr. "Judgment Marked by a Cellar: The American Negro Writer and the Dialectic of Despair." Denver Quarterly 2 (Summer 1967): 5-35.

Scott, Robert. "Rhetoric, Black Power, and James Baldwin's Another Country." Journal of Black Studies 1 (September 1970): 21-34.

Seyersted, Per. "A Survey of Trends and Figures in Afro-American Fiction." American Studies in Scandinavia 6, nos. 1-2 (1973-1974): 67-86.

Simmons, Harvey G. "James Baldwin and the Negro Conundrum." Antioch Review 23 (Summer 1963): 250-255.

Singh, Raman K. "The Black Novel and Its Tradition." Colorado Quarterly 20 (Summer 1971): 23-29.

Smith, Cynthia Janis. "Escape and Quest in the Literature of Black Americans." Ph.D. Dissertation, Yale University, 1974.

Spender, Stephen. "James Baldwin: Voice of a Revolution." Partisan Review 30 (1963): 256-260.

Standley, Fred L. "Another Country, Another Time." Studies in the Novel 4 (Fall 1972): 504-512.

_____. "James Baldwin: A Checklist, 1963-1967." Bulletin of Bibliography 25 (May-August 1968): 135-137, 160.

_____. "James Baldwin: The Artist as Incorrigible Disturber of the Peace." Southern Humanities Review 4 (1970): 18-30.

_____. "James Baldwin: The Crucial Situation." South Atlantic Quarterly 65 (Summer 1966): 371-381.

Thelwell, Mike. "Another Country: Baldwin's New York Novel." In Bigsby, C. W. E., The Black American Writer, vol. 1, pp. 181-198. DeLand, Fla.: Everett/Edwards, 1969.

Thornton, Jerome Edward. "James Baldwin and the Christian Tradition." Ph.D. Dissertation, State University of New York at Buffalo, 1976.

Turner, Darwin. "Afro-American Authors: A Full House." College English 34 (January 1972): 15-19.

Vinson, James, ed. Contemporary Novelists. London and New York: St. James Press and St. Martin's Press, 1972.

Wakeman, John, ed. World Authors 1950-1970. New York: H. W. Wilson, 1975.

Walton, Martha R. "Major Concerns of the Black Novel in America in Relation to the American Mainstream." Ph.D. Dissertation, University of Denver, 1973.

Watson, Edward A. "The Novels of James Baldwin: Case-Book of a 'Lover's War' with the United States." Queen's Quarterly 72 (1965): 385-402.

Weatherby, W. J. Squaring Off: Mailer vs. Baldwin. New York: Mason Charter, 1977.

Whitlow, Roger. Black American Literature: A Critical History. Chicago: Nelson Hall, 1973.

Williams, Melvin G. "Snow White." Christianity and Literature 22 (Winter 1973): 29-34.

Williams, Sherley Ann. Give Birth to Brightness: A Thematic Study in Neo-Black Literature. New York: Dial, 1972.

Reviews

Another Country

Balliett, Whitney. New Yorker, 4 August 1962, p. 69.

Barret, William. Atlantic 210 (July 1962): 110.

Beck, Warren. Chicago Sunday Tribune, 24 June 1962, p. 3.

Curley, Thomas. Commonweal, 7 December 1962, p. 286.

Finkelstein, Sidney. Mainstream 15 (November 1962): 59-63.

Finn, James. Commonweal, 26 October 1962, p. 113.

Friedenberg, E. Z. New Republic, 27 August 1962, p. 23.

Goodman, Paul. New York Times Book Review, 24 June 1962, p. 5.

Hicks, Granville. Saturday Review, 7 July 1962, p. 21.

Hogan, William. San Francisco Chronicle, 28 June 1962, p. 35.

Kirkus, 1 June 1962, p. 478.

Maloff, Saul. Nation, 14 July 1962, p. 15.

Moon, Eric. Library Journal, 1 June 1962, p. 2154.

Nordell, Roderick. Christian Science Monitor, 19 July 1962, p. 11.

Root, Robert. Christian Century, 7 November 1962, p. 1354.

Spector, R. D. New York Herald Tribune Books, 17 June 1962, p. 3.

Southern, Terry. Nation, 17 November 1962, p. 331.

Taubman, Robert. New Statesman, 13 July 1962, p. 53.

Giovanni's Room

Algren, Nelson. Nation, 1 December 1956, p. 484.

Booklist, 1 December 1956, p. 174.

Esty, William. New Republic, 17 December 1956, p. 26.

Hicks, Granville. New York Times, 14 October 1956, p. 5.

Karp, David. Saturday Review, 1 December 1956, p. 34.

Rolo, C. J. Atlantic 198 (December 1956): 98.

San Francisco Chronicle, 2 December 1956, p. 24.

Sullivan, J. F. Commonweal, 21 December 1956, p. 318.
West, Anthony. New Yorker, 10 November 1956, p. 220.

Go Tell It on the Mountain

Barr, Donald. New York Times, 17 May 1953, p. 5.
Brunn, R. R. Christian Science Monitor, 23 May 1953, p. 11.
Byam, M. S. Library Journal, 15 May 1953, p. 916.
Cassidy, T. E. Commonweal, 23 May 1953, p. 186.
Hamilton, A. Books and Bookmen 10 (February 1965): 29.
Hughes, Riley. Catholic World 177 (August 1953): 393.
Kirkus, 1 April 1953, p. 231.
Nation, 6 June 1953, p. 488.
Ottley, Roi. Chicago Sunday Tribune, 12 July 1953, p. 7.
Raleigh, J. H. New Republic, 22 June 1953, p. 21.
Redding, J. S. New York Herald Tribune Book Review, 17
    May 1953, p. 5.
San Francisco Chronicle, 5 July 1953, p. 18.
Springfield Republican, 19 July 1953, p. 7D.
Time, 18 May 1963, p. 126.
Webster, H. C. Saturday Review, 16 May 1953, p. 14.
Yale Review 42 (Summer 1953): 10.

Going to Meet the Man

Booklist, 1 December 1965, p. 354.
Christian Century, 10 November 1965, p. 1385.
Donodio, S. Partisan Review 33 (Winter 1966): 136.
Donoghue, Denis. New York Review of Books, 9 December
    1965, p. 6.
Featherstone, Joseph. New Republic, 27 November 1965, p. 34.
Handlin, Oscar. Atlantic 216 (November 1965): 191.
Kauffmann, Stanley, New York Times Book Review, 12 December
    1965, p. 5.
Kennedy, W. National Observer, 15 November 1965, p. 23.
Kirkus, 15 August 1965, p. 852.
Krim, Seymour. Book Week, 7 November 1965, p. 5.
Leversohn, Alan. Christian Science Monitor, 18 November
    1965, p. 15.
Littlejohn, David. Nation, 13 December 1965, p. 478.
Mayne, Richard. New Statesman, 12 November 1965, p. 740.
Minerof, Arthur. Library Journal, 1 November 1965, p. 4804.
New Leader, 8 November 1965, p. 19.
Newsweek, 8 November 1965, p. 114.
Nye, R. Manchester Guardian, 2 December 1965, p. 12.
Observer, 31 October 1965, p. 28.
Schroth, R. A. America, 15 January 1966, p. 92.
Spectator, 26 November 1965, p. 706.
Stern, Daniel. Saturday Review, 6 November 1965, p. 32.
Times (London) Literary Supplement, 28 October 1965, p. 953.

If Beale Street Could Talk

Duffy, Martha. "All in the Family." Time, 10 June 1974,
    pp. 94, 96.
Edwards, Thomas R. New York Review of Books, 13 June
    1974, pp. 37-38.
Essence 5 (September 1974): 112.
Flamer, Merrianne. Freedomways 14 (Fourth Quarter 1974):

356-359.

Freedomways 14 (Second Quarter 1974): 169-170.
McCluskey, John. Black World 24 (December 1974): 51-52, 88-91.
Straub, Peter. "Happy Ends." New Statesman, 28 June 1974, p. 930.
Webster, Ivan. New Republic, 15 June 1974, pp. 25-26.
Tell Me How Long the Train's Been Gone
Algren, Nelson. Critic 27 (October 1968): 86.
Book World, 17 August 1969, p. 13.
Davenport, Guy. National Review, 16 July 1968, p. 701.
Gilman, Richard. New Republic, 17 August 1968, p. 27.
Hall, Stuart. New Statesman, 28 June 1968, p. 871.
Hicks, Granville. Saturday Review, 1 June 1968, p. 23.
Howe, I. Harpers 237 (September 1968): 92.
Jackson, K. G. Harpers 237 (July 1968): 104.
Llorens, D. Negro Digest 17 (August 1968), p. 51.
Long, R. E. Nation, 10 June 1968, p. 769.
McNamara, Eugene. America, 29 June 1968, p. 817.
Maloff, Saul. Newsweek, 3 June 1968, p. 92D.
Moon, Eric. Library Journal, 1 June 1968, p. 2256.
Morse, J. M. Hudson Review 21 (Autumn 1968): 529.
Murray, J. J. Best Seller, 1 July 1968, p. 138.
Publishers' Weekly, 26 May 1969, p. 57.
Puzo, Mario. New York Times Book Review, 23 June 1968, p. 5.
Richardson, Jack. New York Review of Books, 19 December 1968, p. 11.
Sheed, Wilfrid. Book World, 2 June 1968, p. 4.
Shrapnel, N. Manchester Guardian, 4 July 1968, p. 11.
Thompson, John. Commentary 45 (June 1968): 67.
Time, 7 June 1968, p. 104.
Times Literary Supplement, 4 July 1968, p. 697.
Toynbee, Philip. Atlantic 222 (July 1968): 91.
Williams, D. Punch, 3 July 1968, p. 34.

BALDWIN, Jo Ann

Short Fiction

"A Hole They Call a Grave." Black World 24 (June 1975): 70-3.

BAMBARA, Toni Cade (Toni Cade)

Short Fiction

(Collections):
Gorilla, My Love and Other Stories. New York: Random, 1972; New York: Pocket Books, 1973.
The Sea Birds Are Still Alive. New York: Random House, 1977.
"Basement." In Bambara, Gorilla, My Love.

"Blues Ain't No Mockin Bird. " In Bambara, Gorilla, My Love;
Sanchez, We Be Word Sorcerers.
"Gorilla, My Love. " In Bambara, Gorilla, My Love; Stadler, Out
of Our Lives.
"The Hammer Man. " Negro Digest 15 (February 1966): 54-60; al-
so in Bambara, Gorilla, My Love.
"Happy Birthday. " In Bambara, Gorilla, My Love.
"The Johnson Girls. " In Bambara, Gorilla, My Love.
"The Lesson. " In Bambara, Gorilla, My Love.
"The Long Night. " Black World 23 (June 1974): 54-60.
"Maggie of the Green Bottles. " In Bambara, Gorilla, My Love.
"Mama Hazel Takes to Her Bed. " Black World 20 (October 1971):
62-67; also in Exum, Keeping the Faith.
"Mississippi Ham Rider. " Massachusetts Review 5 (Summer 1964):
621; also in Bambara, Gorilla, My Love; Chametzky and Kaplan,
Black and White in American Culture.
"My Man Bovanne. " In Bambara, Gorilla, My Love; Rotter, Bit-
ches and Sad Ladies; Washington, Black-Eyed Susans.
"Playin with Punjab. " In Bambara, Gorilla, My Love.
"Raymond's Run. " In Bambara, Gorilla, My Love & Tales and Sto-
ries for Black Folks; Newman, Ethnic American Short Stories.
"The Survivor. " In Bambara, Gorilla, My Love.
"Sweet Town. " In Bambara, Gorilla, My Love.
"Talking bout Sonny. " In Bambara, Gorilla, My Love.
"Witchbird. " Essence 74 (August 1976): 52-54, 86, 88.

Biography and Criticism

Abrahams, Roger D. "Negotiating Respect: Patterns of Presenta-
tion among Black Women. " Journal of American Folklore 88
(January-March 1975): 58-80.
Contemporary Authors, 29/32.
Washington, Mary Helen. "Black Women Image Makers. " Black
World 23 (August 1974): 10-18.

Reviews

Gorilla, My Love
Black World 22 (July 1973): 80.
Book Week (Washington Post), 8 October 1972, p. 15.
Book World, 18 November 1973, p. 5.
Booklist, 1 December 1972, p. 327.
English Journal 63 (January 1974): 66.
Kirkus, 1 August 1972, p. 871.
Library Journal, 15 March 1973, p. 1021; 15 May 1973, p. 1656.
New York Times, 11 October 1972, p. 41.
New York Times Book Review, 15 October 1972, p. 31; 3 De-
cember 1972, p. 76.
Publishers' Weekly, 31 July 1972, p. 69; 13 August 1973, p. 57.
Saturday Review, 18 November 1972, p. 97; 2 December 1972,
p. 80.
Senior Scholastic, 18 November 1972, p. 97.
Village Voice, 12 April 1973, p. 39.

BANKS, Barbara

Short Fiction

"The Gypsies." In Exum, Keeping the Faith.

BANKS, Brenda

Short Fiction

"Like It Is." Black World 20 (June 1971): 53-57.
"Tender Root." Black World 22 (July 1973): 60-65.
"The Washtub." Black World 21 (July 1972): 70-75.

BARAKA, Imamu Amiri (Everett LeRoi Jones)

Collection

The System of Dante's Hell, The Dead Lecturer, and Tales. New
York: Grove, 1976.

Novel

The System of Dante's Hell. New York: Grove, 1965; excerpt in
Hill, Soon One Morning.

Short Fiction

(Collection): Tales. New York: Grove, 1967.
"The Alternative." Transatlantic Review 18 (Spring 1965): 46-60;
also in Jones, Tales.
"Answers in Progress." Umbra Anthology 3 (Winter 1967): 37-39;
Jones, Tales; Reed, 19 Necromancers from Now.
"A Chase (Alighieri's Dream)." Pa'Lante, 19 May 1962, pp. 91-
93; also in Jones, Tales.
"The Death of Horatio Alger." Evergreen Review 9 (June 1965):
28-29, 92-93; also in Jones, Tales; Ravitz, The American
Disinherited.
"God and Machine." In Sanchez, We Be Word Sorcerers.
"Going Down Slow." Evergreen Review 10 (October 1966): 41-43,
93-96; also in Jones, Tales.
"The Heretics." In Allen and Creeley, New American Story.
"Heroes Are Gang Leaders." In Jones, Tales.
"The Largest Ocean in the World." Yugen, 2 December 1962, pp.
58-59; also in Jones, Tales.
"New Spirit." In Jones, Tales.
"New-Sense." In Jones, Tales.
"No Body No Place." In Jones, Tales.
"Now and Then." In Jones, Tales.
"Round Trip." Mutiny 2 (Autumn 1959): 79-81.
"Salute." In Jones, Tales.
"The Screamers." Genesis West 2 (Fall 1963): 81-86;

also in Jones, Tales; Stadler, Out of Our Lives.
"Uncle Tom's Cabin: Alternate Ending." In Jones, Tales; Patterson, An Introduction to Black Literature in America.
"Unfinished." In Jones, Tales.
"Words." In Jones, Tales.

Biography and Criticism

"BBB Interviews Imamu Amiri Baraka." Black Books Bulletin 2 (Fall 1974): 35-43.

Baker, John. "Criteria for First Printings of LeRoi Jones." Yale University Library Gazette 49 (1974): 297-298.

Bell, Bernard W. The Folk Roots of Contemporary Afro-American Poetry. Detroit: Broadside, 1974.

Benston, Kimberly. Baraka: The Renegade and the Mask. New Haven: Yale University Press, 1976.

Bernard, Sidney. "An Interview with LeRoi Jones." Literary Times, May/June 1967, p. 19.

Brown, C. M. "Black Literature and LeRoi Jones." Black World 17 (June 1970): 24-31.

Brown, Cecil. "About LeRoi Jones." Evergreen Review 14 (February 1970): 65-70.

_____. "The Apotheosis of a Prodigal Son." Kenyon Review 30 (November 1968): 654-661.

Brown, Lloyd W. "Jones (Baraka) and His Literary Heritage in The System of Dante's Hell." Obsidian 1 (Spring 1975): 5-17.

_____. "LeRoi Jones as Novelist: Theme and Structure in The System of Dante's Hell." Negro American Literature Forum 7 (Winter 1974): 132-142.

Coleman, Larry. "Comic-Strip Heroes: LeRoi Jones and the Myth of American Innocence." Journal of Popular Culture 3 (Fall 1969): 191-204.

_____. "LeRoi Jones' Tales: Sketches of the Artist as a Young Man Moving Toward a Blacker Art." Black Lines 1 (Winter 1970): 17-26.

Conforti, J. M. "Nationalist from Newark." Society 9 (July 1972): 66.

Current Biography, 1970.

Dace, Letitia. LeRoi Jones (Imamu Amiri Baraka): A Checklist of Works by and about Him. London: Nether Press, 1971.

Davis, Arthur P. From the Dark Tower: Afro-American Writers 1900 to 1960. Washington, D. C.: Howard University Press, 1974.

Dennison, George. "The Demogogy of LeRoi Jones." Commentary 39 (February 1965): 67-70.

Dippold, Mary D. "LeRoi Jones: Tramp with Connections." Ph.D. Dissertation, University of Maryland, 1971.

Durham, Joyce Roberta. "The City in Recent American Literature: Black on White: A Study of Selected Writings of Bellow, Mailer, Ellison, Baldwin and Writers of the Black Aesthetic." Ph.D. Dissertation, University of Maryland, 1974.

Ellison, Curtis William. "Black Adam: The Adamic Assertion and the Afro-American Novelist." Ph.D. Dissertation, University of Minnesota, 1970.

Fischer, W. C. "Pre-Revolutionary Writing of Imamu Amiri Baraka." Massachusetts Review 14 (Spring 1973): 259-305.

Ford, Nick Aaron. "Review of From LeRoi Jones to Amiri Baraka by Theodore R. Hudson." CLA Journal 18 (September 1974): 127-130.

Fox, Robert Elliot. "The Mirrors of Caliban: A Study of the Fiction of LeRoi Jones (Imamu Amiri Baraka): Ishmael Reed and Samuel R. Delany." Ph. D. Dissertation, State University of New York at Buffalo, 1976.

Frost, David. The Americans. Chicago: Stein, 1970.

Fuller, Hoyt. "Contemporary Negro Fiction." Southwest Review 50 (Autumn 1965), 321-335.

_____. "The Negro Writer in the United States." Ebony 20 (November 1964): 126-128, 130-132, 134.

_____. "Perspectives." Negro Digest 13 (July 1964): 49-50, 87-92.

Gayle, Addison, Jr. The Way of the New World: The Black Novel in America. Garden City, N.Y.: Anchor Press/Doubleday, 1975.

Hayashi, Susanna. "Dark Odyssey: Descent into the Underworld in Black American Fiction." Ph. D. Dissertation, Indiana University, 1971.

Hentoff, Nat. "Uninventing the Negro." Evergreen Review 9 (November 1965): 34-36, 66-69.

Hudson, Theodore. From LeRoi Jones to Amiri Baraka: The Literary Work. Durham, N. C.: Duke University Press, 1973.

_____. "An Imamu Amiri Baraka (LeRoi Jones) Bibliography: A Keyed Guide to Selected Works By and About Him." Black Books Bulletin 2 (Fall 1974): 70-79.

Jackson, Esther M. "LeRoi Jones (Imamu Amiri Baraka): Form and the Progression of Consciousness." CLA Journal 17 (September 1973): 33-56.

Jackson, Kathryn. "LeRoi Jones and the New Black Writers of the Sixties." Freedomways 9 (Summer 1969): 232-247.

Joye, Barbara. "From Stereotype to Archetype." Phylon 28 (Spring 1967): 109-111.

Kauffmann, Stanley. "LeRoi Jones and the Tradition of the Fake." Dissent 12 (Spring 1965): 207-212.

Kazin, Alfred. "Brothers Crying Out for More Access to Life." Saturday Review, 2 October 1971, pp. 33-35.

Kempton, Murray. "Newark: Keeping Up with LeRoi Jones." New York Review of Books, 2 July 1970, pp. 21-23.

Killinger, John. The Fragile Presence: Transcendence in Modern Literature. Philadelphia: Fortress Press, 1973.

Klinkowitz, Jerome. Literary Disruptions: The Making of a Post-Contemporary American Fiction. Urbana: University of Illinois Press, 1975.

Lacey, Henry Clark. "A Study of the Poetry, Drama, and Fiction of Imamu Amiri Baraka (LeRoi Jones)." Ph. D. Dissertation, State University of New York at Binghamton, 1975.

Lhamon, W. T. "Baraka and the Bourgeois Figure." Studies in Black Literature 6 (Spring 1975): 18-21.

Llorens, David. "Ameer (LeRoi Jones) Baraka." Ebony 24 (August 1969): 75-78, 80-83.

Malkoff, Karl. Crowell's Handbook of Contemporary Poetry. New

York: T. Y. Crowell, 1973.

May, John R., S. J. "Images of Apocalypse in the Black Novel." Renascence 23 (1970): 31-45.

Menchise, Don N. "LeRoi Jones and a Case of Shifting Identities." CLA Journal 20 (December 1976): 232-234.

Munro, C. Lynn. "LeRoi Jones: A Man in Transition." CLA Journal 17 (September 1973): 57-78.

O'Brien, John. "Racial Nightmares and the Search for Self: An Explication of LeRoi Jones' 'A Chase: (Alighieri's Dream).'" Negro American Literature Forum 7 (Fall 1973): 89-90.

Pennington-Jones, Paulette. "From Brother LeRoi Jones Through The System of Dante's Hell to Imamu Ameer Baraka." Journal of Black Studies 4 (December 1973): 195-214.

Redding, J. Saunders. "The Problems of the Negro Writer." Massachusetts Review 6 (Autumn/Winter 1964-1965): 57-70.

Rich, Cynthia Jo. "Where's Baraka's Jones?" Black Times (Palo Alto) 4 (1974): 1, 6-7.

Riche, James. "The Politics of Black Modernism." Literature and Ideology No. 8 (1971): 85-90.

Schatt, Stanley. "LeRoi Jones: A Checklist to Primary and Secondary Sources." Bulletin of Bibliography 28 (April-June 1971): 55-57.

Schraufnagel, Noel. From Apology to Protest: The Black American Novel. DeLand, Florida: Everett/Edwards, 1973.

Seyersted, Per. "A Survey of Trends and Figures in Afro-American Fiction." American Studies in Scandinavia 6, Nos. 1-2 (1973-1974): 67-86.

Smith, Cynthia Janis. "Escape and Quest in the Literature of Black Americans." Ph.D. Dissertation, Yale University, 1974.

Sorrentino, Gilbert. "For the Floating Bear: Prose of Our Time." Floating Bear No. 30 (1964): 11-13.

Turner, Darwin T. "Afro-American Authors: A Full House." College English 34 (January 1972): 15-19.

Vickery, Olga W. "The Inferno of the Moderns." The Shaken Realist, pp. 147-164. Edited by Melvin J. Friedman and John B. Vickery. Baton Rouge: Louisiana State University, 1970.

Vinson, James, ed. Contemporary Novelists. New York: St. Martin's Press, 1972.

Wakeman, John, ed. World Authors--1950-1970. New York: H. W. Wilson, 1975. (Listed under Jones, LeRoi.)

Watkins, Mel. "Talk with LeRoi." New York Times Book Review, 27 June 1971, sec. 7, p. 4.

Weales, Gerald. "The Day LeRoi Jones Spoke on Penn Campus-- What Were the Blacks Doing in the Balcony?" New York Times Magazine, 4 May 1969, pp. 38-40.

Whitlow, Roger. Black American Literature: A Critical History. Chicago: Nelson Hall, 1973.

Williams, John A. "The Negro in Literature Today." Ebony 18 (September 1973): 73-76.

Reviews

The System of Dante's Hell

Adams, Phoebe. Atlantic 217 (January 1966): 122.

Antiquarian Bookman, 3 January 1966, p. 15.
Bergonzi, B. New York Review of Books, 20 January 1966, p. 22.
Capouya, E. New York Times Book Review, 28 November 1965, p. 4.
Choice 2 (February 1966): 860.
Daniel, J. Spectator, 16 September 1966, p. 356.
Fleischer, L. Publishers' Weekly, 8 August 1966, p. 61.
Gilman, R. Book Week, 26 December 1965, p. 9.
Mayne, R. New Statesman, 2 September 1966, p. 326.
Moon, Eric. Library Journal, 15 November 1965, p. 4999.
Newsweek, 22 November 1965, p. 114.
Randall, Dudley. Negro Digest 15 (March 1966): 52.
Saturday Review, 11 December 1965, p. 31.
Time, 19 November 1965, p. 140.
Times Literary Supplement, 1 September 1966, p. 777.
Van Duyn, M. Poetry 109 (February 1967): 332.

Tales
Bone, R. New York Times Book Review, 4 February 1968, p. 36.
Booklist, 15 January 1968, p. 584.
Choice 5 (March 1968): 50.
Elrod, J. M. Library Journal, 1 October 1967, p. 3445.
Graham, K. Listener, 4 September 1969, p. 319.
Hentoff, Nat. Commonweal, 6 December 1968, p. 359.
Kirkus, 1 September 1967, p. 1075.
Llorens, D. Negro Digest 17 (April 1968): 51.
London Magazine 9 (November 1969): 90.
Maloff, Saul. Newsweek, 4 December 1967, p. 103B.
Oberbeck, S. K. Book World, 24 December 1967, p. 7.
Observer, 31 August 1969, p. 21.
Publishers' Weekly, 4 September 1967, p. 51; 27 May, 1968, p. 60.
Raban, J. New Statesman, 5 September 1969, p. 315.
Resnick, H. S. Saturday Review, 7 December 1967, p. 28.
Times Literary Supplement, 11 September 1969, p. 993.

BARBER, John

Short Fiction

"Rites Fraternal." In Coombs, What We Must See.

BARKSDALE, Richard K.

Short Fiction

"The Last Supper." Phylon 27 (Spring 1966): 91-94.

BARRETT, Lindsay (Eseoghene)

Novel

Song for Mumu. London: Longmans, 1967; Washington, D. C.:
Howard University Press, 1974.

Short Fiction

"I Feel So Bad." Black World 2 (August 1971): 61-66.
"Ripe Times Will Pass." Black World 20 (December 1970): 73-79.

Reviews

Song for Mumu
A. B. Bookman's Weekly, 3 February 1975, p. 472.
Choice 11 (January 1975): 1626.
Levin, M. New York Times Book Review, 29 September 1974,
p. 40.
Library Journal, 15 December 1974, p. 3214.

BARRETT, Nathan

Novel

Bars of Adamant: A Tropical Novel. New York: Fleet, 1966.

Biography and Criticism

Contemporary Authors, 17/18.

Reviews

Bars of Adamant
Kirkus, 15 March 1966, p. 320.
Levin, M. New York Times Book Review, 21 August 1966,
p. 29.
Library Journal, 1 February 1966, p. 738; 15 May 1966,
p. 2516.
Shepard, R. F. New York Times, 6 July 1966, p. 47m.
Williams, R. Negro Digest 16 (January 1967): 94.

BARROW, Bari

Short Fiction

"The World Is Wide, The World Is Small." Black World 24 (May
1975): 54-61.

BATES, Arthenia J.   (Arthenia Bates Millican)

Short Fiction

(Collection): Seeds Beneath the Snow. New York: Greenwich,
    1969; Washington: Howard University Press, 1975.
"Home X and Me." Negro Digest 14 (September 1965):
    43-47.
"Wake Me Mama." Black World 2 (July 1971): 57-68.

Reviews

Seeds Beneath the Snow
        Atlantic 235 (February 1975): 122.
        Negro Digest 18 (August 1969): 94.

BATSON, Susan

Short Fiction

"Can't Hear the Drums Been Dreamin." In Sanchez, Three Hundred
    and Sixty Degrees of Blackness Comin at You.

BATTLE, Sol

Novel

Mélange in Black. New York: Panther House, 1970.

Biography and Criticism

Contemporary Authors, 25/28.
Who's Who in the East.

BATTLES, Jesse Moore

Novel

Somebody Please Help Me. New York: Pageant, 1965.

BEAUFORD, Fred

Short Fiction

"His Story." Black Creation 4 (Summer 1973): 4-6.

BECK, Robert (Iceberg Slim)

Novels

Mama Black Widow. Los Angeles, Calif.: Holloway, 1970.
Naked Soul of Iceberg Slim. Los Angeles, Calif.: Holloway, 1971.
    Excerpt in Young, Black Experience, Analysis and Synthesis
Pimp: The Story of My Life. Los Angeles, Calif.: Holloway,
    1967. Excerpts in Kochman, Rappin' and Stylin' Out; Robinson,
    Nommo; Young, Black Experience, Analysis and Synthesis.
Trick Baby. Los Angeles, Calif.: Holloway, 1967.

Biography and Criticism

Graham, D. B. "'Negative Glamour': The Pimp Hero in the Fic-
    tion of Iceberg Slim." Obsidian 1 (Summer 1975): 5-17.
"Portrait of an Ex-pimp Philosopher, Iceberg Slim." Los Angeles
    Free Press, 25 February 1972, p. 3.
Salaam, Kalamu ya. "The Psychology of the Pimp: Interview with
    Iceberg Slim." Black Collegian 5 (January-February 1975):
    33-37.

Reviews

Naked Soul of Iceberg Slim
    Black World, 21 (May 1972): 79.

BECKHAM, Barry

Novels

My Main Mother. New York: Walker, 1969; New York: New Amer-
    ican Library, 1971, 1972.
Runner Mack. New York: Morrow, 1972; New York: Popular Li-
    brary, 1973.

Short Fiction

"Cold Ben, New Castle." In Watkins, Black Review No. 1.

Biography and Criticism

Campenni, Frank. Contemporary Novelists. Edited by James Vin-
    son. New York: St. Martin's Press, 1976.
Contemporary Authors, 29/32.
Klotman, Phyllis Rauch. Another Man Gone: The Black Runner in
    Contemporary Afro-American Literature. Port Washington,
    N.Y.: Kennikat Press, 1977.
Pinsker, Sanford. "About Runner Mack: An Interview with Barry
    Beckham." Black Images 3 No. 3 (1974): 35-41.
    _____. "A Conversation with Barry Beckham." Studies in Black
    Literature 5 (Winter 1974): 17-20.

Reviews

My Main Mother
    Booklist, 15 January 1970, p. 598.
    Coombs, Orde. Negro Digest 19 (February 1970): 78.
    Kirkus, 15 August 1969, p. 880.
    Loprete, N. J. Best Seller, 15 December 1969, p. 372.
    Publishers' Weekly, 11 August 1969, p. 41.
    Rowley, Peter. New York Times Book Review, 30 November 1969, p. 64.
    Times Literary Supplement, 12 February 1971, p. 173.
Runner Mack
    Best Sellers, 15 September 1972, p. 276.
    Book World, 10 September 1972, p. 15.
    English Journal 63 (January 1974): 65.
    Kirkus, 1 July 1972, p. 737.
    Massachusetts Review 14 (Winter 1973): 190.
    New York Times Book Review, 17 September 1972, p. 3; 3 December 1972, p. 78.
    Publishers' Weekly, 17 July 1972, p. 111.
    Walker, Jim. Black Creation 4 (Winter 1973): 62-63.

BELLINGER, Claudia

Novel

Wolf Kitty. New York: Vantage, 1959.

BENNETT, Gwendolyn B.

Short Fiction

"Tokens." In Johnson, Ebony and Topaz.
"Wedding Day." Harlem 1 (1928); also in Huggins, Voices from the Harlem Renaissance.

BENNETT, Hal

Novels

The Black Wine. Garden City, N.Y.: Doubleday, 1968.
Lord of Dark Places. New York: Norton, 1970; New York: Bantam, 1971.
Seventh Heaven. Garden City, N.Y.: Doubleday, 1976.
Wait Until Evening. Garden City, N.Y.: Doubleday, 1974.
A Wilderness of Vines. Garden City, N.Y.: Doubleday, 1966; London: Cape, 1967; New York: Pyramid, 1970.

Short Fiction

"Also Known as Cassius. " Playboy 18 (August 1971): 72-74, 100, 194-198.
"Dotson Gerber Resurrected. " Playboy 17 (November 1970): 96-98, 178, 188-190; also in Foley and Burnett, The Best American Short Stories, 1971.
"Second Sunday. " Virginia Quarterly Review 52 (Summer 1976): 495-508.

Biography and Criticism

Walcott, Ronald. "The Novels of Hal Bennett. " Black World 23 (June 1974): 36-48, 89-97.

Reviews

The Black Wine
    Howe, I. Harper's 239 (December 1969): 130.
    Katz, B. Library Journal, 1 February 1969, p. 569.
    Library Journal, 15 April 1968, p. 1820.
    Kirkus, 15 December 1967, p. 1484.
    Publishers' Weekly, 4 December 1967, p. 42.
    Wright, C. New York Times Book Review, 5 May 1968, p. 36.
Lord of Dark Places
    Kirkus, 15 August 1970, p. 896.
    Library Journal, 1 November 1970, p. 3803.
    New Statesman, 1 October 1971, p. 449.
    New York Times, 6 October 1970, p. 49.
    Observer, 19 December 1971, p. 23.
    Publishers' Weekly, 17 August 1970, p. 48.
    Times Literary Supplement, 12 November 1971, p. 1427.
Seventh Heaven
    Griffin, L. W. Library Journal, 1 October 1976, p. 2082.
    Kirkus, 15 June 1976, p. 698.
    Publishers' Weekly, 14 June 1976, p. 101.
Wait Until Evening
    Kirkus, 1 July 1974, p. 694.
    Library Journal, 1 October 1974, p. 2498.
    New York Times Book Review, 22 September 1974, p. 14.
    Publishers' Weekly, 8 July 1974, p. 69.
A Wilderness of Vines
    Braybrooke, N. Spectator, 19 May 1967, p. 588.
    Buckman, P. Books and Bookmen 12 (August 1967): 38.
    Choice 4 (July-August 1967): 529.
    Katz, B. Library Journal 91 (July 1966): 3465.
    Kirkus, 1 June 1966, p. 550.
    Renek, Morris. Book Week, 2 October 1966, p. 8.
    Times Literary Supplement, 8 June 1967, p. 515.

BENNETT, John

Fiction

Madam Margot: A Grotesque Legend of Old Charleston. New York: Century, 1921.

BENNETT, Lerone

Short Fiction

"The Convert." Negro Digest 12 (January 1963): 61-73; also in Clarke, American Negro Short Stories; King, Black Short Story Anthology.

BENTLEY, Richard

Short Fiction

"The Farm." Negro Story 2 (December-January 1945): 3-9.
"Mrs. Clark." Negro Story 2 (April-May 1946): 6-9.
"The Night." Negro Story 2 (August-September 1945): 11-17.
"Old Mis' Cane." Negro Story 1 (May-June 1945): 43-48.
"The Slave." Negro Story 1 (March-April 1945): 21-30.
"Tomorrow." Negro Story 1 (December-January 1944-45): 31-39.

BERNARD, Ruth Thompson

Novel

What's Wrong with Lottery? Boston: Meador, 1943.

BETHUNE, Lebert

Short Fiction

"The Burglar." In Hughes, The Best Short Stories by Negro Writers.

BIBB, Eloise (Eloise Bibb Thompson)

Short Fiction

"Mademoiselle 'Tasie." Opportunity 3 (September 1925): 272-276.
"Masks." Opportunity 5 (October 1927): 300-302.

BLACK, Isaac J.

Short Fiction

"Rabbit, Rabbit You're Killing Me." Black World 24 (June 1975): 74-81.

BLACKSON, Lorenzo Dow

Novel

The Rise and Fall of the Kingdoms of Light and Darkness; or, The Reign of Kings Alpha and Abadon. Philadelphia: J. Nicholas, 1867.

Biography and Criticism

Loggins, Vernon. The Negro Author. Port Washington, N.Y.: Kennikat, 1964.
Williams, Kenny J. They Also Spoke. Nashville: Townsend, 1970.

BLACKWOOD, Granby

Novel

Un Sang Mal Mele. Paris: Editions Denoel, 1966.

BLAIR, John Paul

Novel

Democracy Reborn. New York: By the Author, 1947.

BLAND, Alden

Novel

Behold--A Cry. New York: Scribner, 1947; New York: AMS Press.

Short Fiction

"Beginnings." Negro Story 1 (July-August 1944): 42-44.
"Let's Go Visiting." Negro Story 1 (May-June 1944): 20-22.

Biography and Criticism

Fleming, Robert E. "Overshadowed by Richard Wright: Three Black Chicago Novelists." Negro American Literature Forum

7 (Fall 1973): 75-79.

Schraufnagel, Noel. From Apology to Protest: The Black American Novel. DeLand, Florida: Everett/Edwards, 1973.

Reviews

Behold--A Cry
  Booklist, 1 May 1947, p. 272.
  Burke, Arthur E. Crisis 54 (November 1947): 347.
  Butcher, Philip. Opportunity 25 (Fall 1947): 222.
  Cayton, Horace. Chicago Sun Book Week, 23 March 1947, p. 2.
  Kirkus, 15 February 1947, p. 105.
  Pratt, Theodore. New York Times, 25 March 1947, p. 18.
  Reddick, L. D. Library Journal, 1 March 1947, p. 72.
  Rosenberger, Coleman. New York Herald Tribune Weekly Book Review, 9 March 1947, p. 7.

BLUE, Cecil A.

Short Fiction

"The Flyer." Opportunity 6 (July 1928): 202-206.

Biography and Criticism

Perry, Margaret. Silence to the Drums: A Survey of the Literature of the Harlem Renaissance. Contributions in Afro-American and African Studies, no. 18. Westport, Conn.: Greenwood Press, 1976.

BOHANON, Wally

Short Fiction

Wally Bohanon: His Short Stories. New York: Amuru Press, 1973.

BOLES, Robert E.

Novels

Curling. Boston: Houghton-Mifflin, 1968.
The People One Knows. Boston: Houghton-Mifflin, 1964.

Short Fiction

"The Engagement Party." In Cooper and Chalpin, Achievements in Fiction; Gasarch and Gasarch, Fiction, The Universal Elements; Hughes, The Best Short Stories by Negro Writers; Patterson, An Introduction to Black Literature in America.

Biography and Criticism

"Black Writer's Views on Literary Lions and Values." Negro Digest 17 (January 1968): 28.

Schraufnagel, Noel. From Apology to Protest: The Black American Novel. DeLand, Florida: Everett/Edwards, 1973.

Reviews

Curling
  Cassill, C. V. Book World, 8 September 1968, p. 26.
  Christian Science Monitor, 18 April 1968, p. 11.
  Dempsey, David. New York Times Book Review, 3 March 1968, p. 40.
  Giovanni, Nikki. Negro Digest 17 (August 1968): 87.
  Greenya, John. Saturday Review, 17 February 1968, p. 38.
  Griffin, L. W. Library Journal 93 (February 1968): 569.
  Kirkus, 1 December 1967, p. 1432.
  Miller, T. C. Commonweal, 21 June 1968, p. 419.
  Publishers' Weekly, 4 December 1972, p. 42.
  Thompson, John. Commentary 45 (April 1968): 419.
  Watkins, M. New Leader, 8 April 1968, p. 25.
The People One Knows
  Book Week, 14 October 1964, p. 24.
  Fessler, A. L. Library Journal, 1 November 1964, p. 4388.
  Hicks, Granville. Saturday Review, 3 October 1974, p. 33.
  New Yorker, 20 February 1965, p. 163.
  Smith, W. J. Commonweal, 23 October 1964, p. 139.
  Sullivan, R. Books Today, 13 September 1964, p. 13.
  Woodford, J. Negro Digest 14 (May 1965): 52.

BONNER, Marita (Marita Bonner Occomy)

Short Fiction

"Black Fronts." Opportunity 16 (July 1938): 210.
"Drab Rambles." Crisis 34 (December 1927): 335-336, 354.
"The Hands." Opportunity 3 (August 1925): 235-237.
"Hongry Fire." Crisis 46 (December 1939): 360-362, 376.
"The Makin's." Opportunity 17 (January 1939): 18-21.
"Of Jimmie Harris." Opportunity 11 (August 1933): 242-244.
"One True Love." Crisis 48 (February 1941): 46-47, 58-59.
"Patch Quilt." Crisis 47 (March 1940): 71-72, 92.
"A Possible Triad on Black Notes." Opportunity 11 (July 1933): 205-217.
"A Sealed Pod." Opportunity 14 (March 1936): 88-91.
"Three Tales of Living." Opportunity 11 (September 1933): 269-271.
"Tin Can." Opportunity 12 (July 1934): 202-205; (August 1934): 236-240.
"The Whipping." Crisis 46 (June 1939): 172-174.

BONTEMPS, Arna

Novels

Black Thunder. New York: Macmillan, 1936; Berlin: Seven Seas
    Publishers, 1964; Boston: Beacon Press, 1968. Excerpts in
    Davis and Peplow, The New Negro Renaissance; Long and Col-
    lier, Afro-American Writing.
Drums at Dusk. New York: Macmillan, 1939.
God Sends Sunday. New York: Harcourt, Brace, 1931. (Drama-
    tized as St. Louis Woman, 1946.)

Short Fiction

(Collection): The Old South: "A Summer Tragedy" and Other Sto-
    ries of the Thirties. New York: Dodd, Mead, 1973.
"Barrel Staves." New Challenge 1 (March 1934): 16-24;
    also in Huggins, Voices from the Harlem Renaissance.
"Blue Boy." In Bontemps, The Old South.
"The Cure." In Bontemps, The Old South.
"The Devil Is a Conjurer." In Bontemps, The Old South.
"Heathen at Home." In Bontemps, The Old South.
"Hoppergrass Man." In Bontemps, The Old South.
"Let the Church Roll On." In Bontemps, The Old South.
"Lonesome Boy, Silver Trumpet." In Bontemps, The Old
    South.
"Mr. Kelso's Lion." In Bontemps, The Old South.
"Saturday Night." In Bontemps, The Old South.
"A Summer Tragedy." Opportunity 11 (June 1933): 174-
    177, 190; also in Anselm and Gibson, Black and White;
    Bontemps, The Old South; Chapman, Black Voices;
    Clarke, American Negro Short Stories; Davis and Wal-
    den, On Being Black; Ford, Black Insights; Hughes,
    The Best Short Stories by Negro Writers; James, From
    the Roots; Pickering, Fiction 100, Singh and Fellowes,
    Black Literature in America; Steinberg, et al., Insight:
    Literature of Imagination; Watkins, Anthology of Ameri-
    can Negro Literature.
"Talk to the Music." Cimarron Review (1971); also in Bon-
    temps, The Old South.
"Three Pennies for Luck." In Bontemps, The Old South.
"A Woman with a Mission." In Bontemps, The Old South.

Biography and Criticism

Alexander, Sandra Carlton. "The Achievement of Arna Bontemps."
    Ph.D. Dissertation, University of Pittsburgh, 1976.
Baker, Houston A., Jr. "Arna Bontemps: A Memoir." Black
    World 22 (September 1973): 4-9.
Bone, Robert. Down Home: A History of Afro-American Short
    Fiction from Its Beginnings to the End of the Harlem Renais-
    sance. New York: G. P. Putnam's Sons, 1975.
_____. The Negro Novel in America. New Haven: Yale Univer-

sity Press, 1966.

Brawley, Benjamin. The Negro in Literature and Art. New York: Duffield, 1930.

Brown, Lloyd W. "The Expatriate Consciousness in Black American Literature." Studies in Black Literature 3 (Summer 1972): 9-12.

Conroy, Jack. "Memories of Arna Bontemps: Friend and Colla- borator." Negro American Literature Forum 10 (Summer 1976): 53-57.

Contemporary Authors, 1R.

Davis, Arthur P. From the Dark Tower: Afro-American Writers 1900-1960. Washington, D.C.: Howard University Press, 1974.

Dreer, Herman. American Literature by Negro Authors. New York: Macmillan, 1950.

Gloster, Hugh M. Negro Voices in American Fiction. Chapel Hill: University of North Carolina Press, 1948.

Hemenway, Robert, ed. The Black Novelist. Columbus: Charles E. Merrill, 1970.

Holland, Thomas Richard. "Vestiges of African Culture in Afro- American Literature: A Preliminary Study." Ph.D. Disserta- tion, University of Nebraska-Lincoln, 1973.

Hughes, Carl M. The Negro Novelist 1940-1950. New York: Citadel Press, 1953.

Hughes, Langston. The Big Sea: An Autobiography. New York: Knopf, 1940.

Isani, Mukhtar Ali. "The Exotic and Protest in Earlier Black Lit- erature: The Use of Alien Setting and Character." Studies in Black Literature 5 (Summer 1974): 9-14.

Kent, George E. Blackness and the Adventure of Western Culture. Chicago: Third World, 1972.

O'Brien, John, ed. Interviews with Black Writers. New York: Liveright, 1973.

Perry, Margaret. Silence to the Drums: A Survey of the Litera- ture of the Harlem Renaissance. Contributions in Afro-Ameri- can and African Studies, no. 18. Westport, Conn.: Greenwood Press, 1976.

Schraufnagel, Noel. From Apology to Protest: The Black Ameri- can Novel. DeLand, Florida: Everett/Edwards, 1973.

Singh, Amritjit. "The Novels of the Harlem Renaissance: A Thé- matic Study." Ph.D. Dissertation, New York University, 1973.

_____. The Novels of the Harlem Renaissance: Twelve Black Writers 1923-1933. University Park: Pennsylvania State Uni- versity Press, 1976.

Tischler, Nancy M. Black Masks: Negro Characters in Modern Southern Fiction. University Park: Pennsylvania State Univer- sity Press, 1969.

Weil, Dorothy. "Folklore Motifs in Arna Bontemps' Black Thunder." Southern Folklore Quarterly 35 (March 1971): 1-14.

Williams, Melvin G. "Snow White." Christianity and Literature 22 (Winter 1973): 29-34.

Reviews

Black Thunder
>Booklist 32 (April 1936): 232.
>Brickell, Herschel. Review of Reviews 93 (March 1936): 19.
>Clark, Emily. Books, 2 February 1936, p. 3.
>Gruening, Martha. New Republic, 26 February 1936, p. 91.
>Saturday Review of Literature, 15 February 1936, p. 27.
>Tompkins, Lucy. New York Times, 2 February 1936, p. 7.
>Wright, Richard. Partisan Review and Anvil 3 (April 1936): 31.

Drums at Dusk
>Field, R. L. New York Herald Tribune Books, 7 May 1939, p. 16.
>New Republic, 24 May 1939, p. 84.
>New Yorker, 6 May 1939, p. 91.
>Owens, Olga. Boston Transcript, 6 May 1939, p. 1.
>Pratt Institute Quarterly (Autumn 1939): 27.
>Saturday Review of Literature, 13 May 1939, p. 12.
>Springfield Republican, 21 May 1939, p. 7e.
>Wallace, Margaret. New York Times Book Review, 7 May 1939, p. 7.

God Sends Sunday
>Bennett, G. B. Books, 22 March 1931, p. 16.
>Boston Transcript, 8 April 1931, p. 2.
>Du Bois, W. E. B. Crisis 38 (September 1931): 304.
>New York Times, 15 March 1931, p. 7.
>Saturday Review of Literature, 2 May 1931, p. 801.
>Springfield Republican, 12 April 1931, p. 7e.

The Old South: "A Summer Tragedy" and Other Stories of the Thirties
>Best Sellers, 1 December 1973, p. 285.
>Kirkus, 1 June 1973, p. 616.
>Publishers' Weekly, 18 June 1973, p. 66.
>Simms, A. G. Library Journal, 1 September 1973, p. 2462.
>Tyms, J. D. New Republic, 14 January 1974, p. 27.
>Wilson Library Bulletin 48 (March 1974): 538.
>Yardley, Jonathan. New York Times Book Review, 23 December 1973, p. 11.

BOOKER, Simeon, Jr.

Short Fiction

"She Never Knew?" In Ford and Faggett, Best Short Stories by Afro-American Writers.

BOSWORTH, William

Novel

The Long Search. Great Barrington, Mass.: Advance, 1957.

BRADLEY, David

Novel

South Street. New York: Grossman, 1975.

Reviews

South Street
    Allen, Bruce. Library Journal, 15 October 1975, p. 1946.
    Bianco, David. Best Sellers 35 (December 1975): 265.
    Black Scholar 7 (December 1975): 49.
    Booklist, 15 December 1975, p. 550.
    Charyn, J. New York Times Book Review, 28 September 1975,
        p. 30.
    Choice 12 (December 1975): 1305.
    Kirkus, 1 July 1975, p. 724.
    Progressive 39 (December 1975): 60.
    Publishers' Weekly, 2 June 1975, p. 48.
    Watkins, Mel. New York Times, 4 October 1975, p. 25.

BRAGG, Linda Brown see Brown, Linda

BRAITHWAITE, William Stanley Beaumont

Novels

The Canadian, a Novel. Boston: Small, Maynard, 1901.
Going over Tindel, a Novel. Boston: Brimmer, 1924.

Biography and Criticism

Brawley, Benjamin. The Negro Genius. New York: Dodd, Mead,
    1940.
Clairmonte, Glenn. "He Made American Writers Famous." Phylon
    30 (Summer 1969): 184-190.
Cromwell, Otelia, Lorenzo Dow Turner, and Eva B. Dykes, eds.
    Readings from Negro Authors. New York: Harcourt, Brace,
    1931.

BRANCH, Edward

Novel

The High Places. New York: Exposition, 1957.

BRAWLEY, Benjamin

Short Fiction

"The Baseball." Crisis 12 (July 1916): 145-147; reprinted Crisis
77 (December 1970): 409-410; also in Fagin, America Through
the Short Story; Hibbard, Stories of the South.

Biography and Criticism

Journal of Negro History 24 (April 1939): 242-243.
Parker, John W. "Phylon Profile, XIX: Benjamin Brawley--Teach-
er and Scholar." Phylon 10 (First Quarter 1949): 15-23.
Rush, Theressa Gunnels, Carol Fairbanks Myers, and Esther Spring
Arata. Black American Writers Past and Present: A Biographical and Bibliographical Dictionary. Metuchen, N.J.: Scarecrow Press, 1975.
Thorpe, Earl E. Black Historians. New York: Wm. Morrow,
1971.

BRAY, Rosemary

Short Fiction

"Water." Essence 7 (November 1976): 90, 122, 124.

BRIDGEFORTH, Med

Novel

Another Chance. New York: Exposition, 1951. (Published in 1927
under the title: God's Law and Man's.)

BRIGHT, Hazel

Short Fiction

"Mama Pritchett." Black World 22 (October 1973): 54-58.
"When You Dead, You Aint Done." Black World 22 (January 1973):
60-65.

BROADUS, Robert Deal

Novel

Spokes for the Wheel. Muncie: Kingsman Press, 1961.

BROCKET, Joshua Arthur

Novel

Zipporah, the Maid of Midian. Zion, Ill.: Zion Printing & Publishing House, 1926.

BROOKS, Gwendolyn

Novel

Maud Martha. New York: Harper, 1953. Excerpts in Adams, Conn, and Slepian, Afro-American Literature; Hill, Soon One Morning; Hughes, The Best Short Stories by Negro Writers; Patterson, An Introduction to Black Literature in America from 1746 to the Present; Stanford, I, Too, Sing America; Washington, Black-Eyed Susans.

Short Fiction

"Chicago Portraits." Negro Story 1 (May-June 1944): 49-50.
"Helen." In Schneiderman, By and About Women.
"Home." In Murray and Thomas, Major Black Writers.
"The Life of Lincoln West." In Gibson and Anselment, Black and White; Hill, Soon One Morning.
"Maud Martha and New York." In Adoff, Brothers and Sisters.
"The Rise of Maud Martha." Chicago (February 1955); also in Sanchez, We Be Word Sorcerers.

Biography and Criticism

Authors in the News, vol. 1. Detroit: Gale Research Co., 1976.
Baker, Houston A., Jr. "The Achievement of Gwendolyn Brooks." CLA Journal 16 (September 1972): 23-31.
Barrow, William. "Five Fabulous Females." Negro Digest 12 (July 1963): 78-83.
Brooks, Gwendolyn. Report from Part One. Detroit: Broadside, 1972.
_____, and Ida Lewis. "Conversation." Essence 1 (April 1971): 26-31.
Contemporary Authors, 1R.
Davis, Arthur P. From the Dark Tower: Afro-American Writers 1900-1960. Washington, D.C.: Howard University Press, 1974.
Kent, George E. Blackness and the Adventure of Western Culture. Chicago: Third World, 1972.
Lee, Don L. "The Achievement of Gwendolyn Brooks." Black Scholar 3 (Summer 1972): 32-41.
Miller, Ronald Baxter. Gwendolyn Brooks and Langston Hughes: A Reference Guide. Boston: G. K. Hall, 1977.
Rush, Theressa Gunnels, Carol Fairbanks Myers, Esther Spring Arata. Black American Writers Past and Present. Metuchen,

N.J.: Scarecrow Press, 1975.
Schraufnagel, Noel. From Apology to Protest: The Black American Novel. DeLand, Florida: Everett/Edwards, 1973.
Stravos, George. "An Interview with Gwendolyn Brooks." Contemporary Literature 12 (Winter 1970): 1-20.
Washington, Mary Helen. "Black Women Image Makers." Black World 23 (August 1974): 10-18.
Whitlow, Roger. Black American Literature: A Critical History. Chicago: Nelson Hall, 1973.

Reviews

Maud Martha
　　Booklist, 15 July 1953, p. 365; 15 October 1953, p. 78.
　　Butcher, Fanny. Chicago Sunday Tribune, 4 October 1953, p. 11.
　　Creekmore, Hubert. New York Times, 4 October 1953, p. 4.
　　Kirkus, 15 July 1953, p. 458.
　　New York Herald Tribune Book Review, 18 October 1953, p. 4.
　　New Yorker, 10 October 1953, p. 153.
　　Rivers, Gertrude B. Journal of Negro Education 23 (Spring 1954): 156.
　　Saturday Review of Literature, 31 October 1953, p. 41.
　　Wisconsin Library Bulletin 49 (November 1953): 259.

BROWN, Cecil M.

Novel

The Life and Loves of Mr. Jiveass Nigger. New York: Farrar, Straus, Giroux, 1970; New York: Fawcett, 1971. Excerpts in Chapman, New Black Voices; Hicks, Cutting Edges; Reed, 19 Necromancers from Now.

Short Fiction

"A Few Hypes You Should Be Hip Too by Now." Black Scholar 6 (June 1975): 21-29.

Biography and Criticism

Klotman, Phyllis R. "The White Bitch Archetype in Contemporary Black Fiction." Bulletin of the Midwest Modern Language Association 6 (Spring 1973): 96-110.
Rosenblatt, Roger. Black Fiction. Cambridge: Harvard University Press, 1974.
Schraufnagel, Noel. From Apology to Protest: The Black American Novel. DeLand, Florida: Everett/Edwards, 1973.
Sullivan, Philip. "Buh Rabbit: Going Through the Changes." Studies in Black Literature 4 (Summer 1973): 28-32.
Wiggins, William H., Jr. "The Trickster as Literary Hero: Cecil Brown's The Life and Loves of Mr. Jiveass Nigger." New York

Folklore Quarterly 29 (December 1973): 269-286.

Reviews

The Life and Loves of Mr. Jiveass Nigger
 Adams, Phoebe. Atlantic 225 (February 1970): 120.
 Antioch Review 29 (Winter 1969-70): 588.
 Elder, Lonne III. Black World 19 (June 1970): 51.
 Griffin, L. W. Library Journal, 15 December 1969, p. 4538.
 Howard, M. Partisan Review 37 (Fall 1970): 564.
 Hudson Review 23 (Spring 1970): 166.
 Kirkus, 1 November 1969, p. 1168.
 Kuehl, Linda. Commonweal, 23 October 1970, p. 105.
 Moore, Kenneth. Essence 1 (June 1970): 7.
 New Leader, 16 March 1970, p. 19.
 New York Times, 14 January 1970, p. 45.
 New York Times Book Review, 7 June 1970, p. 2.
 Observer, 21 June 1970, p. 30.
 Publishers' Weekly, 3 November 1969, p. 48; 4 December 1970,
  p. 40.
 Reynolds, Stanley. New Statesman, 19 July 1970, p. 892.
 Rhodes, Richard. New York Times Book Review, 1 February
  1970, p. 4.
 Rotondaro, Fred. Best Sellers, 15 January 1970, p. 394.
 Time, 2 February 1970, p. 72.
 Times Literary Supplement, 31 July 1970, p. 845.

BROWN, Charlotte Hawkins (Mrs. Edward S.)

Novel

Mammy. Boston: Pilgrims Press, 1919.

Biography and Criticism

Brawley, Benjamin. Negro Builders and Heroes. Chapel Hill:
 University of North Carolina Press, 1937.
Dannett, Sylvia G. Liebovitz. Profiles of Negro Womanhood. 2
 vols. Yonkers: Educational Heritage, 1964.
Who's Who in Colored America, 1927.

BROWN, Claude

Autobiographical Novels

The Children of Ham. Briar Cliff Manor, N.Y.: Stein & Day,
 1976.
Manchild in the Promised Land. New York: Macmillan, 1965;
 New York: New American Library. Excerpts in Austin, Fenderson and Nelson, The Black Man and the Promise of America; Davis and Redding, Cavalcade; Demarest and Landin, The

Ghetto Reader; Faderman and Bradshaw, Speaking for Ourselves; Ford, Black Insights; Gross, A Nation of Nations; Simmons et al., Black Culture; Watkins and David, To Be a Black Woman.

Biography and Criticism

Baker, Houston A., Jr. "The Environment as Enemy in a Black Autobiography: Manchild in the Promised Land." Phylon 32 (Spring 1971): 53-59.

Brown, Claude. "In Consequence of Manchild." In Yardbird Reader, vol. 1. Berkeley: Yardbird, 1972.

Current Biography, 1966.

Goldman, Robert M. and William D. Crano. "Black Boy and Manchild in the Promised Land." Journal of Black Studies 7 (December 1976): 169-180.

Klotman, Phyllis Rauch. Another Man Gone: The Black Runner in Contemporary Afro-American Literature. Port Washington, N.Y.: Kennikat Press, 1977.

Murray, Albert. The Omni-Americans. New York: Outerbridge, 1970.

Rosenblatt, Roger. Black Fiction. Cambridge: Harvard University Press, 1974.

Reviews

The Children of Ham

Davis, George. New York Times Book Review, 15 August 1976, p. 24.

Edwards, A. O. Library Journal, 15 April 1976, p. 993.

Harris, Jessica. Essence 7 (August 1976): 32.

Rampersad, Arnold. New Republic, 8 May 1976, p. 25.

Manchild in the Promised Land

Aaron, D. New Statesman, 5 August 1966, p. 204.

Balliett, Whitney. New Yorker, 13 November 1965, p. 242.

Bannon, B. A. Publishers' Weekly, 29 August 1966, p. 346.

Beckinsale, M. Books and Bookmen 11 (September 1955): 26.

Bernstein, Abraham. Teachers College Record 61 (June 1966): p. 311.

Booklist, 1 September 1965, p. 10.

Bouise, O. A. Best Sellers, 1 September 1965, p. 225.

Choice 2 (December 1965): 736.

Christian Century, 18 August 1965, p. 1013.

Daniels, Guy. New Republic, 25 September 1965, p. 26.

Dennison, George. Commentary 41 (January 1966): 82.

Economist, 24 September 1966, p. 1259.

Fremont-Smith, E. New York Times, 14 August 1965, p. 21.

Godsell, Geoffrey. Christian Science Monitor, 11 November 1965, p. 11.

Goodman, Paul. New York Review of Books, 26 August 1965, p. 8.

Grennen, J. American Scholar 37 (Summer 1968): 528.

Hays, F. Carleton Miscellany 6 (Fall 1965): 69.

Hentoff, Nat. Book Week, 22 August 1965, p. 5.

Kirkus, 1 June 1965, p. 561.
Kugler, R. F. Library Journal 90 (August 1965): 3277.
Lester, A. Observer, 12 June 1966, p. 26.
Linney, Romulus. New York Times Book Review, 22 August
    1965, p. 1.
Llorens, D. Negro Digest 15 (January 1966): 49.
Maloff, S. Commonweal, 3 December 1965, p. 288.
Mathes, W. Antioch Review 25 (Fall 1965): 456.
Miller, Warren. Saturday Review of Literature, 28 August
    1965, p. 49.
Newsweek, 16 August 1965, p. 81; 27 December 1965, p. 78.
Peterson, C. Books Today, 23 October 1966, p. 15.
Reporter, 4 November 1965, p. 53.
Ross, F. E. New York Times Book Review, Part 2, 26 Feb-
    ruary 1967, p. 33.
Saturday Review, 17 December 1966, p. 38.
Schaap, D. New York Herald Tribune Book Review, 17 August
    1965, p. 17.
Semple, R. B., Jr. National Observer, 30 August 1965, p. 19.
Shelton, F. Harvard Educational Review 36 (Spring 1966):
    p. 216.
Short, C. Punch, 22 June 1966, p. 924.
Time, 27 August 1965, p. 86.
Times Literary Supplement, 11 August 1966, p. 723.
Tucker, Martin. Commonweal, 24 September 1965, p. 700.

BROWN, Frank London.

Novels

The Myth Makers. Chicago: Path Press, 1969.
Trumbull Park. Chicago: Regnery, 1959.

Short Fiction

"McDougal." In Margolies, A Native Sons Reader.
"A Matter of Time." In Clarke, American Negro Short Stories.
"Singing Dinah's Song." In Adams, Conn, and Slepian, Afro-Amer-
    ican Literature; Hill, Soon, One Morning; Hughes, The Best
    Short Stories by Negro Authors.
"The Whole Truth." In Beier, Black Orpheus.

Biography and Criticism

Fleming, Robert E. "Overshadowed by Richard Wright: Three
    Black Chicago Novelists." Negro American Literature Forum
    7 (Fall 1973): 75.
"Frank London Brown: Courageous Author." Sepia 8 (June 1960):
    26-30.
Hughes, Carl M. The Negro Novelist 1940-1950. New York:
    Citadel Press, 1953.
Major, Clarence. "Frank London Brown: Reckless Enough to Be a

Man. " In The Dark and Feeling, pp. 99-103. New York: Third Press, 1974; Nickel Review, 26 September 1969.

Rush, Theressa, Carol Fairbanks Myers, and Esther Spring Arata, Black American Writers Past and Present. Metuchen, N.J.: Scarecrow Press, 1975.

Schraufnagel, Noel. From Apology to Protest: The Black American Novel. DeLand, Florida: Everett/Edwards, 1973.

Stuckey, Sterling. "Frank London Brown." In Black Voices, pp. 669-676. Edited by Abraham Chapman. New York: New American Library, 1968.

Reviews

Trumbull Park
    Booklist, 1 May 1959, p. 476.
    Byam, M. S. Library Journal, 15 March 1959, p. 861.
    Christian Century, 15 April 1959, p. 454.
    Golden, Harry. Nation, 16 May 1959, p. 456.
    Hughes, Langston. New York Herald Tribune Book Review, 5 July 1959, p. 5.
    Kirkus, 1 February 1959, p. 110.
    Paton, Alan. Chicago Sunday Tribune, 12 April 1959, p. 1.
    Sepia 8 (June 1960): 26-30.

BROWN, Lloyd Louis

Novel

Iron City. New York: Masses & Mainstream, 1951.

Short Fiction

"Cousin Oscar. " Masses and Mainstream 6 (December 1953): 14-19.

"The Glory Train. " Masses & Mainstream 3 (December 1950): 22-41.

"God's Chosen People. " Masses & Mainstream 1 (April 1948): 57-63.

"Jericho, USA. " New Masses, 29 October 1946, pp. 15-16.

"Wanamaker's and the Three Bears. " Masses & Mainstream 1 (December 1948): 35-37.

Biography and Criticism

Schraufnagel, Noel. From Apology to Protest: The Black American Novel. DeLand, Florida: Everett/Edwards, 1973.

Reviews

Iron City
    Butcher, Margaret Just. Phylon 12 (September 1951): 294-296.
    Lawson, John Howard. Masses & Mainstream 4 (July 1951): 90-96.

BROWN, Martha

Short Fiction

"The Red Hat." In Ford and Faggett, Best Short Stories by Afro-American Writers.

BROWN, Mattye Jeanette

Novel

The Reign of Terror. New York: Vantage, 1962.

BROWN, Samn

Short Fiction

"Winona Young Is a Faceless Person." Black World 2 (August 1971) 53-59.

BROWN, Sterling

Short Fiction

"And/Or." Phylon 7 (1946): 269-272; also in Clarke, American Negro Short Stories.

Biography and Criticism

Brawley, Benjamin. The Negro Genius. New York: Dodd, Mead, 1940.
Henderson, Stephen A. "A Strong Man Called Sterling Brown." Black World 19 (September 1970): 5-12.
Huggins, Nathan Irvin. Harlem Renaissance. New York: Oxford University Press, 1971.
Rowell, Charles H. "Sterling A. Brown and the Afro-American Folk Tradition." Studies in the Literary Imagination 7 (1974): 131-152.

BROWN, Tyki

Short Fiction

"Brother, Where Are You?" Black Creation 3 (Winter 1972): 26-27.
"Mother Wit Versus the Sleet Medallion Fleet." In Sanchez, Three Hundred and Sixty Degrees of Blackness Comin at You; Sanchez, We Be Word Sorcerers.
"Put Ya Feet in a Rock!" In Sanchez, We Be Word Sorcerers.

BROWN, William Wells

Novels

Clotel; or, The President's Daughter: A Narrative of Slave Life in
the United States. London: Partridge & Oakey, 1853; With an
introduction by Arthur Davis, New York: Collier Books, 1970;
With an introduction and notes by William Edward Farrison,
New York: Citadel Press, 1969; With a sketch of the author's
life, Upper Saddle River, N.J.: Gregg Press, 1969. Excerpts
in Barksdale and Kinnamon, Black Writers of America; Patterson, An Introduction to Black Literature in America.
Clotelle: A Tale of the Southern States. Boston: J. Redpath,
1864; Philadelphia: A. Saifer, 1955.
Clotelle; or, The Colored Heroine. A Tale of the Southern States.
Boston: Lee & Shepard, 1857.
Miralda; or, The Beautiful Quadroon. Serialized in Anglo-African,
1860-1861.

Biography and Criticism

Bell, Bernard W. "Literary Sources of the Early Afro-American
Novel." CLA Journal 18 (September 1974): 29-43.
Bone, Robert A. The Negro Novel in America. New Haven: Yale
University Press, 1966.
Brawley, Benjamin. Early Negro American Writers. Freeport,
N.Y.: Books for Libraries, 1968.
Brown, Josephine. Biography of an American Bondsman. Boston:
Walcutt, 1855.
Davis, Arthur P. From the Dark Tower: Afro-American Writers
1900-1960. Washington, D.C.: Howard University Press,
1974.
Ellison, Curtis William. "Black Adam: The Adamic Assertion and
the Afro-American Novelist." Ph.D. Dissertation, University
of Minnesota, 1970.
Farrison, W. Edward. "Clotel, Thomas Jefferson, and Sally
Hemings." CLA Journal 17 (December 1973): 147-174.
_____. "A Flight Across Ohio: The Escape of William Wells
Brown from Slavery." Ohio State Archeological and Historical
Quarterly 61 (1952): 272-282.
_____. "One Ephemerer After Another." CLA Journal 13 (De-
cember 1969): 192-197.
_____. "The Origin of Brown's Clotel." Phylon 15 (1954): 347-
354.
_____. "Phylon Profile, XVI: William Wells Brown." Phylon
9 (1948): 13-23.
_____. William Wells Brown, Author and Reformer. Chicago:
University of Chicago Press, 1969.
_____. "William Wells Brown, Social Reformer." Journal of
Negro Education 18 (1949): 29-39.
Fleming, Robert E. "Humor in the Early Black Novel." CLA

Journal 17 (December 1973): 250-262.

Gloster, Hugh M. Negro Voices in American Fiction. Chapel Hill: University of North Carolina Press, 1948.

Heermance, J. Noel. William Wells Brown and Clotelle: A Portrait of the Artist in the First Negro Novel. Hamden, Conn.: Archon Books, 1969. (Includes facsimile reprint of the 1864 ed. Clotelle, published by J. Redpath.)

Hughes, Carl M. The Negro Novelist 1940-1950. New York: Citadel Press, 1953.

Isani, Mukhtar. "The Exotic and Protest in Earlier Black Literature: The Use of Alien Setting and Character." Studies in Black Literature 5 (Summer 1974): 9-14.

Klotman, Phyllis Rauch. Another Man Gone: The Black Runner in Contemporary Afro-American Literature. Port Washington, N.Y.: Kennikat Press, 1977.

Ramsey, Priscilla. "A Study of Black Identity in 'Passing' Novels of the Nineteenth and Early Twentieth Centuries." Studies in Black Literature 7 (Winter 1976): 1-7.

Schraufnagel, Noel. From Apology to Protest: The Black American Novel. DeLand, Florida: Everett/Edwards, 1973.

Sloss, Phyllis Ann. "Hierarchy, Irony, and the Thesis of Death in William Wells Brown's Clotel; or, The President's Daughter." Ph.D. Dissertation, State University of New York at Buffalo, 1976.

Whitlow, Roger. "Black Literature and American Innocence." Studies in Black Literature 5 (Summer 1974): 1-4.

BROWNE, Benjamin A.

Short Fiction

"The Last Volume." Harlem Quarterly 1 (Winter 1949-50): 36-41.

BRUCE, John Edward (pseud., "Grit")

Novel

The Awakening of Hezekiah Jones. Hopkinsville, Ky.: Philip H. Brown, 1916.

Biography and Criticism

Rush, Theressa Gunnels, Carol Fairbanks Myers, and Esther Spring Arata. Black American Writers Past and Present. Metuchen, N.J.: Scarecrow Press, 1975.

BRUCE, Richard

Short Fiction

"Smoke, Lilies and Jade." In Huggins, Voices from the Harlem
    Renaissance.

BULLINS, Ed

Novel

The Reluctant Rapist. New York: Harper & Row, 1973.

Short Fiction

(Collection): The Hungered One: Early Writings. New York:
    Morrow, 1971.
"The Absurd One." In Bullins, The Hungered One.
"The Ancient One." In Bullins, The Hungered One.
"Dandy; or Astride the Funky Finger of Lust." In Bullins,
    The Hungered One; King, Black Short Story Anthology;
    Sanchez, We Be Word Sorcerers.
"The Drive." In Bullins, The Hungered One.
"The Enemy." In Bullins, The Hungered One.
"The Excursion." In Bullins, The Hungered One.
"The Harlem Mice." Black World 24 (June 1975): 54-55.
"He Couldn't Say Sex." In Bullins, The Hungered One.
"The Helper." In Bullins, The Hungered One.
"The Hungered One." In Bullins, The Hungered One.
"In New England Winter." In Bullins, The Hungered One.
"In the Wine Time." In Bullins, The Hungered One.
"Loneliest Man in the Universe." Negro Digest 15 (August
    1966): 21-25.
"The Messenger." In Bullins, The Hungered One.
"Mister Newcomer." In Bullins, The Hungered One.
"Moon Writer." In Bullins, The Hungered One.
"The Rally; or, Dialect Determinism." In Bullins, The
    Hungered One.
"The Real Me." In Bullins, The Hungered One.
"The Reason Why." In Bullins, The Hungered One.
"The Reluctant Voyage." In Bullins, The Hungered One.
"The Saviour." In Bullins, The Hungered One.
"The Storekeeper." Negro Digest 16 (May 1967): 55-58.
"Support Your Local Police." Negro Digest 17 (November
    1967): 53-58; also in Bullins, The Hungered One.
"Travel from Home." In Bullins, The Hungered One; Wat-
    kins, Black Review No. 1.

Biography and Criticism

Jackson, Kennell, Jr. "Notes on the Works of Ed Bullins and The
    Hungered One." CLA Journal 18 (1974): 292-299.

O'Brien, John. "Interview with Ed Bullins." Negro American Literature Forum 7 (Fall 1973): 108.

Reviews

The Hungered One
 Black Scholar 3 (February 1972): 59.
 Choice 8 (December 1971): 1328.
 Kirkus, 15 February 1971, p. 187.
 Library Journal, 15 May 1971, p. 1726.
 National Observer, 9 August 1971, p. 23.
 New York Times Book Review, 20 June 1971, p. 4; 5 December
  1971, p. 83.
 Publishers' Weekly, 22 March 1971, p. 46.
The Reluctant Rapist
 Book World, 30 September 1973, p. 15.
 Booklist, 1 September 1973, p. 29.
 Choice 10 (January 1974): 1715.
 Kirkus, 1 August 1973, p. 827.
 Library Journal 98 (August 1973): 2331.
 McClain, Ruth Rambo. Black World 24 (December 1974): 92-94.
 Nation, 21 November 1973, p. 501.
 New York Times Book Review, 30 September 1973, p. 24.
 New Yorker, 15 October 1973, p. 186.
 Publishers' Weekly, 30 July 1973, p. 59.
 Village Voice, 25 October 1973, p. 33.

BULLOCK, Clifton

Short Fiction

(Collection): Baby Chocolate and Other Stories: Aspects of the
 Black Experience. New York: William-Frederick Press, 1975.
 Includes:
  "Baby Chocolate."
  "Darkest Destiny."
  "The Disturbance."
  "Escape into What?"
  "Family Affair."
  "He Took Three."
  "The Last Letter."
  "Lust for a Crippled Girl."
  "Penitentiary Love Affair."
  "The Rise and the Fall."
  "The Tragedy."
  "The Tryout."
  "White Menace."

Reviews

Baby Chocolate and Other Stories
 Black Scholar 4 (December 1975): 49.

BURROUGHS, Margaret Taylor Goss

Short Fiction

"Eric Was Eric." Negro Digest 13 (November 1963): 54-63.
"Party in Hyde Park." Negro Digest 12 (December 1962): 53-60.
"'Strawberry Blonde', That Is." Black World 19 (July 1970): 78-81.

Biography and Criticism

Rush, Theressa Gunnels, Carol Fairbanks Myers, and Esther Spring
Arata. Black American Writers Past and Present. Metuchen,
N.J.: Scarecrow Press, 1975.

BUSTER GREENE

Novel

Brighter Sun: An Historical Account of the Struggles of a Man to
Free Himself and His Family from Human Bondage, By His
Grandson. New York: Pageant, 1954.

CADE, Toni see Bambara, Toni Cade

CAIN, George

Novel

Blueschild Baby. New York: McGraw-Hill, 1971; New York: Dell,
1972; excerpt in Gerald and Blecher, Survival Prose.

Biography and Criticism

Baker, Houston A., Jr. Singers of Daybreak: Studies in Black
American Literature. Washington, D.C.: Howard University
Press, 1974.
Billingsley, R. G. "Forging New Directions: The Burden of the
Hero in Modern Afro-American Literature." Obsidian 1 (Win-
ter 1975): 5-21.
Kent, George. "Struggle for the Image: Selected Books by or
about Blacks during 1971." Phylon 33 (Winter 1972): 304-323.
Seyersted, Per. "A Survey of Trends and Figures in Afro-American
Fiction." American Studies in Scandinavia 6, nos. 1-2 (1973-
74): 67-86.

Reviews

Blueschild Baby
American Libraries, 2 September 1971, p. 897.
Best Sellers, 1 April 1972, p. 24.

Black World 20 (September 1971): 93; 22 (July 1973): 51.
Booklist, 1 March 1971, p. 544.
Essence 2 (August 1971): 26.
Freedomways 11 no. 2 (1971): 27-28.
Gayle, Addison. New York Times Book Review, 17 January 1971, p. 4.
Kirkus, 1 November 1970, p. 1209.
Library Journal, 15 December 1970, p. 4279.
Major, Clarence. Essence 2 (August 1971): 26; also in Major, The Dark and Feeling, pp. 55-56.
New York Times, 28 December 1970, p. 29.
New York Times Book Review, 6 June 1971, p. 3; 5 December 1971, p. 82.
Publishers' Weekly, 23 November 1970, p. 37.
Rafalko, Robert. Best Sellers, 15 January 1971, p. 435.
Trickett, Rachel. Yale Review 61 (October 1971): 121.

CAIN, Johnnie Mae

Fiction

White Bastards. New York: Vantage, 1973.

CALDWELL, Lewis A. H. (Abe Noel)

Novel

The Policy King. Chicago: New Vistas, 1945.

Biography and Criticism

Schraufnagel, Noel. From Apology to Protest: The Black American Novel. DeLand, Florida: Everett/Edwards, 1973.

CAMPBELL, Bebe

Short Fiction

"Shopping Trip!" Essence 7 (October 1976): 78-79, 124-127.

CAMPBELL, James E.

Short Fiction

"Enfranchisement--A Short Story." Freedomways 2 (Spring 1962): 181-185.

CANNON, Steve

Novel

Groove, Bang, and Jive Around. New York: Olympia, 1971. Excerpt in Reed, 19 Necromancers from Now.

Biography and Criticism

Rush, Theressa Gunnels, Carol Fairbanks Myers, and Esther Spring Arata. Black American Writers Past and Present. Metuchen, N.J.: Scarecrow Press, 1975.

CARRERE, Mentis

Novel

Man in the Cane. New York: Vantage, 1956.

CARVALHO, Grimaldo

Novel

The Negro Messiah. New York: Vantage, 1969.

Biography and Criticism

Rush, Theressa Gunnels, Carol Fairbanks Myers, and Esther Spring Arata. Black American Writers Past and Present. Metuchen, N.J.: Scarecrow Press, 1975.

CHANTRELLE, Seginald

Novel

Not Without Dust. New York: Exposition, 1954.

CHERRY, Eileen

Short Fiction

"The Crossing." Black World 24 (November 1974): 55-69.

CHESNUTT, Charles Waddell

Novels

The Colonel's Dream. New York: Doubleday, Page, 1905; Free-

port, N.Y.: Books for Libraries; New York: Gregg, 1969;
Miami: Mnemosyne; Westport, Conn.: Negro Universities
Press.

The House Behind the Cedars. Boston: Houghton Mifflin, 1900;
serialized in Self-Culture Magazine 11 (August 1900); 12 (February 1901); New York: Gregg, 1968.

The Marrow of Tradition. Boston: Houghton Mifflin, 1901; Freeport, N.Y.: Books for Libraries; New York: AMS Press;
New York: Arno; New York: Gregg; Ann Arbor: University
of Michigan Press, 1969.

Short Fiction

(Collections):
The Conjure Woman. Boston: Houghton, Mifflin, 1899; Cambridge: Riverside Press, 1899; New York: Gregg, 1968;
Ann Arbor: University of Michigan Press, 1969.

The Short Fiction of Charles W. Chesnutt. Edited by Sylvia
Lyons Render. Washington, D.C.: Howard University
Press, 1974.

The Wife of His Youth and Other Stories of the Color Line.
Boston: Houghton, Mifflin, 1899; New York: Gregg, 1967;
Ann Arbor: University of Michigan Press, 1968.

"Appreciation." Puck, 20 April 1887, p. 128.

"Aunt Lucy's Search." Family Fiction, 16 April 1887; also in Render, The Short Fiction of Charles W. Chesnutt.

"Aunt Mimy's Son." Youth's Companion, 1 March 1900, pp. 104-105; also in Render, The Short Fiction of Charles W. Chesnutt.

"The Averted Strike." In Render, The Short Fiction of Charles W. Chesnutt.

"A Bad Night." Atlanta Constitution, 2 August 1886, p. 5, cols. 1-3; also in Render, The Short Fiction of Charles W. Chesnutt.

"Baxter's Procrustes." Atlantic Monthly 93 (June 1904): 823-830;
also in Render, The Short Fiction of Charles W. Chesnutt.

"The Bouquet." Atlantic Monthly 84 (November 1899): 648-654;
also in Chesnutt, The Wife of His Youth; Walser, North Carolina
in the Short Story.

"The Bunch of Yellow Roses." Living Age, 7 April 1900, pp. 63-66
(same as "The Bouquet").

"A Busy Day in a Lawyer's Office." Tid-Bits, 15 January 1887.

"Cartwright's Mistake." Cleveland News and Herald, 19 September
1888; also in Render, The Short Fiction of Charles W. Chesnutt.

"A Cause Célèbre." Puck, 14 January 1891, p. 354.

"Cicely's Dream." In Chesnutt, The Wife of His Youth; Walser,
Short Stories from the Old North State.

"Concerning Father." Crisis 37 (May 1930): 153-155, 175; also in
Render, The Short Fiction of Charles W. Chesnutt.

"The Conjurer's Revenge." Overland Monthly 13 (June 1889): 623-629; also in Chesnutt, The Conjure Woman; Simpson, The Local
Colorists.

"Dave's Neckliss." Atlantic Monthly 64 (October 1889): 500-508;
also in Render, The Short Fiction of Charles W. Chesnutt.

"A Deep Sleeper." Two Tales, 11 March 1893, pp. 1-8; also in

Render, The Short Fiction of Charles W. Chesnutt.

"The Doctor's Wife." Chicago Ledger, 1 June 1887; also in Render, The Short Fiction of Charles W. Chesnutt.

"The Doll." Crisis 3 (April 1912): 248-252; also in Render, The Short Fiction of Charles W. Chesnutt.

"A Doubtful Success." Cleveland News and Herald, 17 February 1888.

"The Dumb Witness." In Render, The Short Fiction of Charles W. Chesnutt.

"An Eloquent Appeal." Puck, 6 June 1888, p. 246.

"The Exception." In Render, The Short Fiction of Charles W. Chesnutt.

"The Fall of Adam." Family Fiction, 25 December 1886; also in Render, The Short Fiction of Charles W. Chesnutt.

"A Fatal Restriction." Puck, 1 May 1889, p. 166.

"A Fool's Paradise." Family Fiction, 24 November 1888; also in Render, The Short Fiction of Charles W. Chesnutt.

"The Goophered Grapevine." Atlantic Monthly 60 (August 1887): 254-260; also in Barksdale and Kinnamon, Black Writers of America; Chesnutt, The Conjure Woman; Clarke, American Negro Short Stories; Davis and Redding, Cavalcade; Emanuel and Gross, Dark Symphony; Long and Collier, Afro-American Writing.

"A Grass Widow." Family Fiction, 14 May 1887; also in Render, The Short Fiction of Charles W. Chesnutt.

"Gratitude." Puck, 26 December 1888, p. 300.

"The Gray Wolf's Ha'nt." In Chesnutt, The Conjure Woman.

"Her Virginia Mammy." In Chesnutt, The Wife of His Youth.

"Hot-Foot Hannibal." Atlantic Monthly 83 (January 1899): 49-56; also in Chesnutt, The Conjure Woman; Cromwell, Turner and Dykes, Readings from Negro Authors for Schools and Colleges.

"How a Good Man Went Wrong." Puck, 28 November 1888, p. 214.

"How Dasdy Came Through." Family Fiction, 12 February 1887; also in Render, The Short Fiction of Charles W. Chesnutt.

"How He Met Her." In Render, The Short Fiction of Charles W. Chesnutt.

"Jim's Romance." In Render, The Short Fiction of Charles W. Chesnutt.

"The Kiss." In Render, The Short Fiction of Charles W. Chesnutt.

"A Limb of Satan." In Render, The Short Fiction of Charles W. Chesnutt.

"Lonesome Ben." Southern Workman 29 (March 1900): 137-145; also in Render, The Short Fiction of Charles W. Chesnutt.

"McDugald's Mule." Family Fiction, 15 January 1887; also in Render, The Short Fiction of Charles W. Chesnutt.

"The March of Progress." Century 61 (January 1901): 422-428; also in Render, The Short Fiction of Charles W. Chesnutt.

"The Marked Tree." Crisis 29 (December-January 1925): 59-64, 110-113; also in Render, The Short Fiction of Charles W. Chesnutt.

"Mars Jeems's Nightmare." In Chesnutt, The Conjure Woman.

"A Matter of Principle." In Chesnutt, The Wife of His Youth.
"A Metropolitan Experience." Chicago Ledger, 15 June 1887; also
    in Render, The Short Fiction of Charles W. Chesnutt.
"A Midnight Adventure." New Haven Register, 6 December 1887;
    also in Render, The Short Fiction of Charles W. Chesnutt.
"A Miscarriage of Justice." In Render, The Short Fiction of
    Charles W. Chesnutt.
"Mr. Taylor's Funeral." Crisis 9 (April 1915): 313-316; 10 (May
    1915): 34-37; reprinted 77 (November 1970): 357-361; also in
    Render, The Short Fiction of Charles W. Chesnutt.
"The Origin of the Hatchet Story." Puck, 24 April 1889, p. 132.
"An Original Sentiment." n.p., n.d.
"The Partners." Southern Workman 30 (May 1901): 271-278; also
    in Render, The Short Fiction of Charles W. Chesnutt.
"The Passing of Grandison." In Barksdale and Kinnamon, Black
    Writers of America; Chesnutt, The Wife of His Youth; Perkins,
    Realistic American Short Fiction.
"Po' Sandy." Atlantic Monthly 61 (May 1888): 605-611; also in
    Baro, After Appomattox; Chesnutt, The Conjure Woman; Mar-
    golies, A Native Sons Reader; Turner, Black American Litera-
    ture: Fiction.
"The Prophet Peter." Hathaway-Brown Magazine, 1 April 1906,
    pp. 51-66; also in Render, The Short Fiction of Charles W.
    Chesnutt.
"A Roman Antique." Puck, 17 July 1889, p. 351.
"A Secret Ally." New Haven Register, 6 December 1886; also
    Render, The Short Fiction of Charles W. Chesnutt.
"The Shadow of My Past." In Render, The Short Fiction of Charles
    W. Chesnutt.
"She Reminded Him." Puck, 21 September 1887, p. 58.
"The Sheriff's Children." Independent, 7 November 1889, pp. 30-32;
    also in Chesnutt, The Wife of His Youth; Hughes, The Best
    Short Stories by Negro Writers; Kissin, Stories in Black and
    White; Taylor, The Short Story: Fiction in Transition.
"Sis' Becky's Pickaninny." In Chesnutt, The Conjure Woman; Foley
    and Gentles, America in Story; Hibbard, Stories of the South;
    Warfel and Orians, American Local-Color Stories.
"A Soulless Corporation." Tid-Bits, 16 April 1887.
"Stryker's Waterloo." In Render, The Short Fiction of Charles W.
    Chesnutt.
"The Sway-Backed House." Outlook 66 (November 1900): 588-593;
    also in Render, The Short Fiction of Charles W. Chesnutt.
"A Tight Boot." Cleveland News and Herald, 30 January 1886; also
    in Render, The Short Fiction of Charles W. Chesnutt.
"Tobe's Tribulations." Southern Workman 29 (November 1900):
    656-664; also in Render, The Short Fiction of Charles W. Ches-
    nutt.
"Tom's Warm Welcome." Family Fiction, 27 November 1886; also
    in Render, The Short Fiction of Charles W. Chesnutt.
"Uncle Peter's House." Cleveland News and Herald, December
    1885; also in Render, The Short Fiction of Charles W. Chesnutt.
"Uncle Wellington's Wives." In Chesnutt, The Wife of His Youth.
"A Victim of Heredity; or, Why the Darkey Loves Chicken." Self-

Culture Magazine 11 (July 1900): 404-409; also in Render, The Short Fiction of Charles W. Chesnutt.

"A Virginia Chicken. " Household Realm, August 1887; also in Render, The Short Fiction of Charles W. Chesnutt.

"Walter Knox's Record. " In Render, The Short Fiction of Charles W. Chesnutt.

"The Web of Circumstance. " In Chesnutt, The Wife of His Youth; Hall, The Realm of Fiction.

"White's Weeds. " In Render, The Short Fiction of Charles W. Chesnutt.

"The Wife of His Youth. " Atlantic Monthly 82 (July 1898): 55-61; also in Barksdale and Kinnamon, Black Writers in America; Chesnutt, The Wife of His Youth; Cromwell, Turner and Dykes, Readings from Negro Authors for Schools and Colleges; Davis and Redding, Cavalcade; Ford, Black Insights; Nagel, Vision and Value; Stanford, I, Too, Sing America.

"Wine and Water. " Family Fiction, 23 April 1887; also in Render, The Short Fiction of Charles W. Chesnutt.

Biography and Criticism

Ames, Russell. "Social Realism in Charles Chesnutt. " Phylon 14 (1953): 199-206.

Andrews, William L. "Charles Waddell Chesnutt: An Essay in Bibliography. " Resources for American Literary Study 6 (Spring 1976): 3-22.

_____ . "Chesnutt's Patesville: The Presence and Influence of the Past in The House Behind the Cedars. " CLA Journal 15 (March 1972): 284-294.

_____ . "The Fiction of Charles W. Chesnutt. " Ph. D. Dissertation, University of North Carolina, 1974.

_____ . "A Reconsideration of Charles Waddell Chesnutt: Pioneer of the Color Line. " CLA Journal 19 (December 1975): 136-151.

_____ . "The Significance of Charles W. Chesnutt's Conjure Stories. " Southern Literary Journal 7 (Fall 1974): 78-99.

_____ . "Two New Books on Charles W. Chesnutt. " Mississippi Quarterly 28 (Fall 1975): 511-520.

_____ . "The Works of Charles W. Chesnutt: A Checklist. " Bulletin of Bibliography 33 (January 1976): 45-47, 52.

Arden, Eugene. "The Early Harlem Novel. " Phylon 20 (Spring 1959): 25-31.

Baldwin, R. E. "The Art of The Conjure Woman. " American Literature 43 (November 1971): 385-398.

Bell, Bernard W. "Afro-American Poetry as Folk Art. " Black World 22 (March 1973): 16-26, 74-83.

_____ . "Literary Sources of the Early Afro-American Novel. " CLA Journal 18 (September 1974): 29-43.

Bone, Robert. Down Home: A History of Afro-American Short Fiction from Its Beginnings to the End of the Harlem Renaissance. New York: G. P. Putnam's Sons, 1975.

_____ . The Negro Novel in America. New Haven: Yale University Press, 1966.

Boswell, Jackson C. "A Black Grimm. " New Republic, 1 March

1975, p. 31.

Brawley, Benjamin. The Negro Genius. New York: Dodd, Mead, 1940.

_____. The Negro in Literature and Art. New York: Duffield, 1930.

Britt, David D. "Chesnutt's Conjure Tales: What You See Is What You Get." CLA Journal 15 (March 1972): 269-283.

Brown, Sterling. "In Memorium: Charles Chesnutt." Opportunity 10 (December 1932): 387.

_____. The Negro in American Fiction. Washington, D.C.: Associates in Negro Folk Education, 1937.

Chamberlain, John. "The Negro as Writer." Bookman 70 (February 1930): 603-611.

Chesnutt, Helen M. Charles Waddell Chesnutt: Pioneer of the Color Line. Chapel Hill: University of North Carolina Press, 1952.

Cunningham, Dorothy Joan. "The Published Fiction of Charles Waddell Chesnutt: A Critical Analysis." Ph.D. Dissertation, Florida State University, 1974.

_____. "Secondary Studies on the Fiction of Charles W. Chesnutt." Bulletin of Bibliography 33 (January 1976): 48-52.

_____. "The Uncollected Short Stories of Charles Waddell Chesnutt." Negro American Literature Forum 9 (Summer 1975): 57-58.

Davis, Arthur P. From the Dark Tower: Afro-American Writers 1900 to 1960. Washington, D.C.: Howard University Press, 1974.

Davis, Elrick B. "Reading and Writing." Cleveland Press, 2 February 1929, p. 3.

Dixon, Melvin. "The Teller as Folk Trickster in Chesnutt's The Conjure Woman." CLA Journal 18 (December 1974): 186-197.

Dreer, Herman. American Literature by Negro Authors. New York: Macmillan, 1950.

Du Bois, W. E. B. "Chesnutt." Crisis 40 (January 1933): 20.

Ellison, Curtis W. and E. W. Metcalf, Jr. Charles W. Chesnutt: A Reference Guide. Boston: G. K. Hall, 1977.

Farnsworth, Robert M. "A New Introduction to The Marrow of Tradition." Ann Arbor: University of Michigan Press, 1969.

_____. "Testing the Color Line--Dunbar and Chesnutt." In The Black American Writer, vol. 1, pp. 111-124. Edited by C. W. E. Bigsby. DeLand, Florida: Everett/Edwards, 1969.

Foster, Charles William. "The Representation of The Conjure Woman." Ph.D. Dissertation, University of Alabama, 1969.

Gartner, Carol B. "Charles W. Chesnutt: Novelist of a Cause." Markham Review 1 (October 1968): [5-12].

Gayle, Addison, Jr., ed. Black Expression. New York: Weybright & Talley, 1969.

_____. The Way of the New World: The Black Novel in America. Garden City, N.Y.: Doubleday, 1974.

Gecau, James Kimani. "Charles W. Chesnutt and His Literary Crusade." Ph.D. Dissertation, State University of New York at Buffalo, 1975.

Giles, James R. "Chesnutt's Primus and Annie: A Contemporary

View of The Conjure Woman. " Markham Review 3 (May 1972): 46-49.

Gloster, Hugh M. "Charles W. Chesnutt: Pioneer in the Fiction of Negro Life. " Phylon 2 (First Quarter 1941): 57-66.

Gross, Theodore L. The Heroic Ideal in American Literature. New York: Free Press, 1971.

Harper, Clifford Doyl. "A Study of the Disunity Theme in the Afro-American Experience: An Examination of Five Representative Novels. " Ph. D. Dissertation, Saint Louis University, 1972.

Harris, Trudier. "The Tie that Binds: The Function of Folklore in the Fiction of Charles Waddell Chesnutt, Jean Toomer and Ralph Ellison. " Ph. D. Dissertation, Ohio State University, 1973.

Haslam, Gerald W. "'The Sheriff's Children': Chesnutt's Tragic Racial Parable. " Negro American Literature Forum 2 (Summer 1968): 21-26.

Heermance, J. Noel. Charles W. Chesnutt: America's First Great Black Novelist. Hamden, Conn. : Archon Books, 1974.

_____ . "Charles W. Chesnutt: The Artist, the Man, and His Times. " Ph. D. Dissertation, Howard University, 1970.

Hemenway, Robert. "'Baxter's Procrustes': Irony and Protest. " CLA Journal 18 (December 1974): 172-185.

_____ . The Black Novelist. Columbus: Charles E. Merrill, 1970.

_____ . "Gothic Sociology: Charles Chesnutt and the Gothic Mode. " Studies in the Literary Imagination 7 (Spring 1974): 101-119.

Holland, Thomas Richard. "Vestiges of African Culture in Afro-American Literature: A Preliminary Study. " Ph. D. Dissertation, University of Nebraska-Lincoln, 1973.

Hovit, Theodore R. "Chesnutt's 'The Goophered Grapevine' as Social Criticism. " Negro American Literature Forum 7 (Fall 1973): 86-90.

Howells, William Dean. "Charles W. Chesnutt's Stories. " Atlantic Monthly 85 (May 1900): 699-701; Current Literature 28 (June 1900): 277-278.

_____ . Psychological Counter-Current in Recent Fiction. " North American Review 173 (December 1901): 872-888.

Hughes, Carl M. The Negro Novelist 1940-1950. New York: Citadel Press, 1953.

Hugley, G. "Charles Waddell Chesnutt. " Negro History Bulletin 19 (December 1955): 54-55.

Jackson, Blyden. "The Negro's Image of the Universe as Reflected in His Fiction. " CLA Journal 4 (September 1960): 23-31.

Jackson, Wendell. "Charles W. Chesnutt's Outrageous Fortune. " CLA Journal 20 (December 1976): 195-204.

Jarrett, D. C. "A Negro Novelist Remembered. " Negro Digest 13 (October 1964): 38-45.

Jaskoski, Helen. "Power Unequal to Man: The Significance of Conjure in Works by Five Afro-American Authors. " Southern Folklore Quarterly 38 (June 1974): 91-108.

Keller, Dean H. "Charles Waddell Chesnutt (1858-1932). " American Literary Realism 3 (Summer 1968): 1-4.

Kent, George. Blackness and the Adventure of Western Culture.

Chicago: Third World Press, 1972.

Klotman, Phyllis Rauch. Another Man Gone: The Black Runner in Contemporary Afro-American Literature. Port Washington, N.Y.: Kennikat Press, 1977.

Lee, A. Robert. "'The Desired State of Feeling': Charles Waddell Chesnutt and Afro-American Literary Tradition." Durham University Journal 35 (1974): 163-170.

Locke, Alain. "The Negro in American Literature." New World Library: First Mentor Selection. New York: New Library of World Literature, 1952.

Mabie, Hamilton Wright. "Two Novelists." Outlook, 24 February 1900, pp. 440-441.

Masare, Julian D., Jr. "Charles W. Chesnutt as Southern Author." Mississippi Quarterly 20 (1967): 77-89.

Mason, Julian. "The Stories of Charles W. Chesnutt." Southern Literary Journal 1 (Autumn 1968): 89-94.

Mays, Benjamin E. The Negro's God as Reflected in His Literature. New York: Negro Universities Press, 1969.

Mebane, Mary Elizabeth. "The Family in the Works of Charles W. Chesnutt and Selected Works of Richard Wright." Ph.D. Dissertation, University of North Carolina at Chapel Hill, 1973.

Moon, Bucklin. "Fighter Against Bias." New York Times Book Review, 19 June 1952, p. 4.

Muhlenfeld, Elisabeth. "Charles Waddell Chesnutt." American Literary Realism 8 (Summer 1975): 220-222.

Nelson, John H. "Negro Characters in American Literature." Humanistic Studies at the University of Kansas, vol. 4. Lawrence, Ka.: University Publishers, 1932.

Parker, John W. "Chesnutt as a Southern Town Remembered Him." Crisis 56 (July 1949): 205-206, 221.

Ramsey, Priscilla. "A Study of Black Identity in 'Passing' Novels of the Nineteenth and Early Twentieth Centuries." Studies in Black Literature 7 (Winter 1976): 1-7.

Redding, J. Saunders. To Make a Poet Black. Chapel Hill: University of North Carolina Press, 1939.

Rees, Robert A., and Earl N. Harbert, eds. Fifteen American Authors Before 1900. Madison: University of Wisconsin Press, 1971.

Reilly, J. M. "Dilemma in Chesnutt's The Marrow of Tradition." Phylon 32 (Spring 1971): 31-38.

Render, Sylvia Lyons. "Eagle with Clipped Wings: Form and Feeling in the Fiction of Charles Waddell Chesnutt." Ph.D. Dissertation, George Peabody College for Teachers, 1963.

_____. "North Carolina Dialect: Chesnutt Style." North Carolina Folklore 15 (1967): 67-76.

_____. "Tar Heelia in Chesnutt." CLA Journal 9 (September 1965): 39-50.

Rosenblatt, Roger. Black Fiction. Cambridge: Harvard University Press, 1974.

Rush, Theressa Gunnels, Carol Fairbanks Myers, and Esther Arata. Black American Writers Past and Present. Metuchen, N.J.: Scarecrow Press, 1975.

Sedlack, Robert P. "The Evolution of Charles Chesnutt's The House

Behind the Cedars. " CLA Journal 19 (December 1975): 125-135.

Shipman, Carolyn. "The Author of The Conjure Woman, Charles W. Chesnutt. " Critic 35 (July 1899): 632-634.

Sillen, Samuel. "Charles W. Chesnutt: A Pioneer Negro Novelist. " Masses & Mainstream 6 (February 1953): 8-14.

Simon, Myron. Ethnic Writers in America. New York: Harcourt Brace Jovanovich, 1972.

Smith, Robert A. "Note on the Folktales of Charles W. Chesnutt. " CLA Journal 5 (March 1962): 229-232.

──────. "A Pioneer Black Writer and the Problems of Discrimination and Miscegenation. " Costerus 9 (1973): 181-185.

Sochen, June. "Charles Waddell Chesnutt and the Solution to the Race Problem. " Negro American Literature Forum 3 (Summer 1969): 52-56.

Stepto, Robert Burns. "From Behind the Veil: Afro-American Reform Literature at the Turn of the Century. " Ph.D. Dissertation, Stanford University, 1974.

Taxel, Joel. "Charles Waddell Chesnutt's Sambo: Myth and Reality. " Negro American Literature Forum 9 (Winter 1975): 105-108.

Teller, Walter. "Charles W. Chesnutt's Conjuring and Color Line Stories. " American Scholar 42 (Winter 1972-1973): 125-127.

Terry, Eugene. "A Critical Analysis of Charles Waddell Chesnutt's The Conjure Woman and The Wife of His Youth and Other Stories of the Color Line. " Ph.D. Dissertation, University of Massachusetts, 1975.

Turner, D. "Introduction" to Charles Chesnutt's The House Behind the Cedars. Toronto: Collier-Macmillan, 1969.

──────. "The Negro Novel in America: In Rebuttal. " CLA Journal 10 (December 1966): 122-134.

Walcott, R. "Chesnutt's 'The Sheriff's Children' as Parable. " Negro American Literature Forum 7 (Fall 1973): 84-85.

Wideman, John. "Charles W. Chesnutt: The Marrow of Tradition. " American Scholar 42 (Winter 1972-1973): 128-134.

Williams, Kenny J. They Also Spoke. Nashville: Townsend, 1970.

Winkelman, Donald M. "Three American Authors as Semi-Folk Artists. " Journal of American Folklore 78 (April-June 1965): 130-135.

Wintz, Cary D. "Race and Realism in the Fiction of Charles W. Chesnutt. " Ohio History 81 (1972): 122-130.

Yates, Elizabeth. "Pioneer of Color Line. " Christian Science Monitor, 31 July 1952, p. 11.

Reviews

The Colonel's Dream
    Athenaeum, 13 January 1906, p. 43.
    Independent, 5 October 1905, p. 816.
    New York Times Book Review, 16 September 1905, p. 605.
    Outlook, 30 September 1905, p. 278.
The Conjure Woman
    Black World 21 (December 1971): 95.

The Critic 35 (July 1899): 646.
Morgan, Florence. Bookman 9 (June 1899): 373.
Nation, 28 February 1901, p. 182.
Publishers' Weekly, 4 August 1969, p. 50.
The Marrow of Tradition
  Bookman 14 (January 1902): 533.
  Nation, 2 March 1902, p. 232.
  Spectator, 16 August 1969, p. 210.
The Short Fiction of Charles W. Chesnutt
  American Literature 47 (May 1975): 280.
  Choice 12 (March 1975): 68.
  New Republic, 1 March 1975, p. 31.
The Wife of His Youth
  Banks, N. H. Bookman 10 (February 1900): 597-598.
  Southern Literary Journal (Autumn 1968): 89.
  Spectator, 21 March 1969, p. 374.

CHILDRESS, Alice

Short Fiction

(Collection): Like One of the Family: Conversations from a Domes-
  tic's Life. Brooklyn, N.Y.: Independence, 1956.
"The Pocketbook Game." In Childress, Like One of the Family;
  Hughes, The Best Short Stories by Negro Writers; Olsen and
  Swinburne, Dreamers of Dreams; Stanford, I, Too, Sing Ameri-
  ca.

Biography and Criticism

"Conversation with Alice Childress and Toni Morrison." Black
  Creation 6 (Annual 1974-1975): 90-92.
Rush, Theressa Gunnels, Carol Fairbanks Myers, and Esther Spring
  Arata. Black American Writers Past and Present. Metuchen,
  N.J.: Scarecrow Press, 1975.

Review

Like One of the Family
  Davis, Helen. Mainstream 9 (July 1956): 50-51.

CLARKE, John Henrik

Short Fiction

"The Boy Who Painted Christ Black." Opportunity 18 (September
  1940): 264-266; also in Adoff, Brothers and Sisters; Beck and
  Clowers, Understanding American History Through Fiction, vol.
  2; Clarke, American Negro Short Stories; Gibson and Anselment,
  Black and White; Larson, Prejudice; Murray and Thomas, The
  Journey; Sanchez, We Be Word Sorcerers.

"The Bridge. " Harlem Quarterly 1 (Winter 1949-50): 2-8.
"Leader of the Mob. " Opportunity 17 (October 1939): 301-303.
"Prelude to an Education. " Opportunity 18 (November 1940): 335-
    350.
"Return of the Askia. " Harlem Quarterly 1 (Spring 1950): 45-48.
"Return to the Inn. " Crisis 48 (September 1941): 288; also in
    Freedomways 4 (Summer 1964): 405-407.
"Revolt of the Angels. " Freedomways 3 (Summer 1963): 355-360.
"Santa Claus Is a White Man. " Opportunity 17 (December 1939):
    365-367; also in Hughes, The Best Short Stories by Negro
    Writers.

Biography and Criticism

Authors in the News, vol. 1.   Detroit: Gale Research Co. , 1976.
Cruse, Harold.   The Crisis of the Negro Intellectual.   New York:
    Morrow, 1967.

CLARKE, Sebastian

Short Fiction

"Sun and Flesh. " In Sanchez, We Be Word Sorcerers.

CLEAVER, Eldridge

Short Fiction

"Black Moochie. " Ramparts 8 (October 1969): 21-24; (November
    1969): 8.
"The Flashlight. " Playboy (December 1969); also in Abrahams,
    Prize Stories 1971: The O'Henry Awards; Angus, The Trouble
    Is: Stories of Social Dilemma; Foley and Burnett, The Best
    American Short Stories, 1970; Pickering, Fiction 100.

Biography and Criticism

Contemporary Authors 21/22.
Current Biography 1970.
Rush, Theressa, Carol Fairbanks Myers, and Esther Spring Arata.
    Black American Writers Past and Present.   Metuchen, N.J. :
    Scarecrow Press, 1976.
Who's Who Among Black Americans 1975-1976.

CLIFFORD, Carrie William

Short Fiction

"Love's Way (A Christmas Story). " Alexander's Magazine 1 (Janu-
    ary 1906): 55-58.

CLINTON, Dorothy Randle

Novel

The Maddening Scar: A Novel. Boston: Christopher, 1962.

COLEMAN, Anita Scott

Short Fiction

"The Little Grey House." Half Century 13 (July-August 1922): 4,
  17, 19; (September-October 1922): 4, 21.
"The Nettleby's New Year." Half Century 8 (January 1920): 4,
  14-15.
"Rich Man, Poor Man." Half Century 8 (May 1920): 6, 14.
"Three Dogs and a Rabbit." Crisis 31 (January 1926): 118-122.
"El Tisico." Crisis 19 (March 1920): 252-253.
"Two Old Women A-Shopping Go." Crisis 40 (May 1933): 109-110.

COLEMAN, Wanda

Short Fiction

"Watching the Sunset." Negro Digest 19 (February 1970): 53-54.

Biography and Criticism

Rush, Theressa Gunnels, Carol Fairbanks Myers, and Esther Spring
  Arata. Black American Writers Past and Present. Metuchen,
  N.J.: Scarecrow Press, 1975.

COLLIER, Eugenia

Short Fiction

"Marigolds." Negro Digest 19 (November 1969): 54-62; also in
  Adoff, Brothers and Sisters.
"Ricky." Black World 24 (August 1975): 54-75.
"Sinbad the Cat." Black World 2 (July 1971): 53-55.
"Sweet Potato Pie." Black World 21 (August 1972): 54-62.

Biography and Criticism

Rush, Theressa Gunnels, Carol Fairbanks Myers, and Esther Spring
  Arata. Black American Writers Past and Present. Metuchen,
  N.J.: Scarecrow Press, 1975.

COLTER, Cyrus

Novels

The Hippodrome.   Chicago: Swallow, 1973.
Rivers of Eros.   Chicago: Swallow, 1972; Philadelphia: Curtis, 1973.

Short Fiction

(Collection): The Beach Umbrella. Iowa City: University of Iowa Press, 1970; Chicago: Swallow, 1971.
"After the Ball." In Colter, The Beach Umbrella.
"The Beach Umbrella." In Adams, Conn, and Slepian, Afro-American Literature: Fiction; Colter, The Beach Umbrella; Gasarch and Gasarch, Fiction: The Universal Elements; Hardy, The Modern Talent; Hill, Soon, One Morning; Hughes, The Best Short Stories by Negro Writers; Smart, Women & Men & Women.
"Black for Dinner." In Colter, The Beach Umbrella; Stadler, Out of Our Lives.
"A Chance Meeting." In Colter, The Beach Umbrella.
"The Frog Hunters." Chicago Review 25 no. 1 (1973-1974): 100-118.
"A Gift." In Colter, The Beach Umbrella.
"Girl Friend." In Colter, The Beach Umbrella.
"The Lookout." In Colter, The Beach Umbrella.
"A Man in the House." In Colter, The Beach Umbrella.
"The March." Black World 2 (June 1971): 58-68.
"Mary's Convert." Chicago Review 17 (1965): 169-178; also in Chapman, New Black Voices; Colter, The Beach Umbrella.
"Moot." In Colter, The Beach Umbrella.
"Overnight Trip." Epoch 11 (Fall 1961): 146-156; also in Colter, The Beach Umbrella.
"The Panther Is at Long Last No Pseudoevent." Chicago Review 22 (Autumn 1970): 88-91.
"Rapport." Epoch 13 (Winter 1964): 155-166; also in Colter, The Beach Umbrella.
"The Rescue." Epoch 11 (Winter 1962): 231-243; also in Colter, The Beach Umbrella.
"An Untold Story." In Colter, The Beach Umbrella.

Biography and Criticism

"Black Writer's Views on Literary Lions and Values." Negro Digest 17 (January 1968): 34.
O'Brien, John. "Forms of Determinism in the Fiction of Cyrus Colter." Studies in Black Literature 4 (Summer 1973): 24-28.
_____. Interviews with Black Writers. New York: Liveright, 1973.
Peden, William. The American Short Story: Continuity and Change 1940-1975. Boston: Houghton Mifflin, 1975.
Perry, Joan Ellen. "Visions of Reality: Values and Perspectives in the Prose of Carlos Castaneda, Robert M. Pirsig, Ursula

K. LeGuin, James Purdy, Cyrus Colter, and Sylvia Plath. "
Ph. D. Dissertation, The University of Wisconsin-Madison,
1976.
Reilly, John M. *Contemporary Novelists.* Edited by James Vinson.
New York: St. Martin's Press, 1976.
Rush, Theressa Gunnels, Carol Fairbanks Myers, and Esther Spring
Arata. *Black American Writers Past and Present.* Metuchen,
N.J.: Scarecrow Press, 1975.

Reviews

The Beach Umbrella
    Library Journal, 1 October 1970, p. 3303.
    Nation, 26 November 1973, p. 570.
    Randall, Dudley. Black World 20 (November 1970): 67.
    Saturday Review of Literature, 22 August 1970, p. 55.
The Hippodrome
    Antioch Review 32 (Summer 1972): 699.
    Best Sellers, 1 June 1973, p. 102.
    Black World 23 (February 1974): 78.
    Book World, 29 April 1973, p. 15.
    Kirkus, 15 February 1973, p. 205.
    Library Journal, 1 April 1973, p. 1190.
    Prairie Schooner 48 (Spring 1974): 77.
    Publishers' Weekly, 5 March 1973, p. 73.
The Rivers of Eros
    Booklist, 15 July 1972, p. 971.
    Bryant, J. H. Nation, 5 June 1972, p. 727.
    Choice 10 (March 1973): 90.
    Contemporary Literature 15 (Autumn 1974): 539.
    Davis, George. New York Times Book Review, 17 September
      1972, p. 48.
    Donald, Miles. New Statesman, 23 June 1972, p. 878.
    Holbert, Cornelia. Best Seller, 1 June 1972, p. 102.
    Kirkus, 15 February 1972, p. 216.
    Library Journal, 15 April 1972, p. 1459.
    National Observer, 8 July 1972, p. 21.
    New Statesman, 23 June 1972, p. 878.
    Publishers' Weekly, 21 February 1972, p. 1105.
    Watkins, Mel. New York Times, 14 July 1972, p. 28.

COOMBS, Orde

Short Fiction

"Another Life." Essence 7 (June 1976): 56-57, 85-86.
"Letter to My Lost Love." Essence 3 (October 1972): 28-29.
"Zinza, A Memoir." Essence 2 (May 1971): 62-63.

Biography and Criticism

Rush, Theressa Gunnels, Carol Fairbanks Myers, and Esther Spring

Arata. <u>Black American Writers Past and Present</u>. Metuchen,
N.J.: Scarecrow Press, 1975.

COOPER, Alvin Carlos

Novel

<u>Stroke of Midnight</u>. Nashville, Tenn.: Hemphill, 1949.

COOPER, Clarence L., Jr.

Novels

<u>Black! Two Short Novels</u>. Evanston, Ill.: Regency, 1963.
<u>The Dark Messenger</u>. Evanston, Ill.: Regency, 1962.
<u>The Farm</u>. New York: Crown, 1967; New York: Universal Pub-
    lishing & Distributing Corp., 1970.
<u>The Scene</u>. New York: Crown, 1960.
<u>Weed</u>. Evanston, Ill.: Regency, 1961.

Short Fiction

"Not We Many." In King, <u>Black Short Story Anthology</u>.

Reviews

<u>The Farm</u>
    Bannon, B. A. <u>Publishers' Weekly</u>, 30 January 1967, p. 107.
    Barrow, W. <u>Negro Digest</u> 17 (May 1968): 94.
    Gambee, R. R. <u>Library Journal</u>, 15 March 1967, p. 1176.
    <u>Kirkus</u>, 1 February 1967, p. 151.
    LaFore, L. <u>New York Times Book Review</u>, 1 May 1967, p. 32.
    <u>Publishers' Weekly</u>, 20 April 1970, p. 63.
    Scannell, V. <u>New Statesman</u>, 5 April 1968, p. 455.
<u>The Scene</u>
    Bullock, F. H. <u>New York Herald Tribune Book Review</u>, 28
        February 1960, p. 13.
    Byam, M. <u>Library Journal</u>, 1 December 1959, p. 3790.
    Gleason, R. J. <u>San Francisco Chronicle</u>, 14 February 1960,
        p. 17.
    <u>New Yorker</u>, 30 January 1960, p. 105.
    Richardson, Maurice. <u>New Statesman</u>, 3 September 1960, p.
        317.
    <u>Times Literary Supplement</u>, 16 September 1960, p. 59.

COOPER, John L.

Novel

<u>Opus One</u>. New York: Maelstrom, 1966.

COOPER, William

Novel

Thank God for a Song: A Novel of Negro Church Life in the Rural
South. New York: Exposition, 1962.

Review

Thank God for a Song
    Abernathy, Dorothy. Community 23 (October 1963): 11.

CORBO, Dominic R., Jr.

Novel

Hard Ground. New York: Vantage, 1954.

CORNELL, Adrienne

Short Fiction

"Because of the King of France." In Beier, Black Orpheus.

CORROTHERS, James David

Short Fiction

"A Man They Didn't Know." Crisis 7 (December 1913): 85; (Janu-
    ary 1914): 136.

Biography and Criticism

"J. D. Corrothers." Crisis 9 (January 1915): 116.
Barton, Rebecca C. Witnesses for Freedom. New York: Harper,
    1948.
Brawley, Benjamin. The Negro Genius. New York: Dodd, Mead,
    1940.
Rush, Theressa Gunnels, Carol Fairbanks Myers, and Esther Spring
    Arata. Black American Writers Past and Present. Metuchen,
    N.J.: Scarecrow Press, 1975.

COTTER, Joseph Seamon, Sr.

Short Fiction

(Collection): Negro Tales. New York: Cosmopolitan Press, 1912;
    Freeport, N.Y.: Books for Libraries. Includes:
        "Boy and the Ideal."

"Caleb. "
"Can and the Umbrella. "
"Faith in White Folks. "
"How Mr. Rabbit Secures a Pretty Wife and Rich Father-in-
   Law. "
"Jackal and the Lion. "
"King's Shoes. "
"'Kotchin' de Nines. '"
"Little Boy and Mister Dark. "
"Negro and the Automobile. "
"Observation. "
"Regnan's Anniversary. "
"Rodney. "
"Rustic Comedy. "
"Stump of a Cigar. "
"Tesney, the Deceived. "
"Town Sketch. "

Biography and Criticism

Crisis 19 (January 1920): 126.
Gloster, Hugh M. Negro Voices in American Fiction. Chapel Hill:
   University of North Carolina Press, 1948.
Rush, Theressa Gunnels, Carol Fairbanks Myers, and Esther Spring
   Arata. Black American Writers Past and Present. Metuchen,
   N.J.: Scarecrow Press, 1975.

COTTON, Ella Earls

Novel

Queen of Persia: The Story of Esther Who Saved Her People. New
   York: Exposition, 1960.

COUSINS, Linda

Short Fiction

"A Fairy Tale?" In Sanchez, Three Hundred Sixty Degrees of Blackness Comin at You.

COX, Joseph Mason Andrew

Novel

The Search. New York: Daniel S. Mead, 1960.

Biography and Criticism

Rush, Theressa Gunnels, Carol Fairbanks Myers, and Esther Spring

Arata. Black American Writers Past and Present. Metuchen, N.J.: Scarecrow Press, 1975.

CRAWFORD, Marc

Short Fiction

"Willie T. Washington's Blues." Black World 21 (May 1972): 54-66.

CRAYTON, Pearl

Short Fiction

"Cotton Alley." In Adoff, Brothers and Sisters.
"The Day the World Came to an End." Negro Digest 14 (August 1965): 54-60; also in Bambara, Tales and Stories for Black Folks; Gasarch and Gasarch, Fiction: The Universal Elements; Hughes, The Best Short Stories by Negro Writers.
"The Gold Fish Monster." In Stadler, Out of Our Lives.

CRITTENDEN, Annie R.

Short Fiction

"Love Know." Essence 3 (June 1972): 48-49.

CROSS, June

Short Fiction

"The Lovers." Harvard Advocate 107 no. 4 (1974): 54, 62.

CRUMP, George Peter, Jr.

Novel

From Bondage They Came. New York: Vantage, 1954.

CRUMP, Paul

Novel

Burn, Killer, Burn. Excelsior, Mn.: Melvin McCosh Bookseller, 1962; excerpt in Negro Digest 11 (October 1962): 37-42.

Biography and Criticism

Crump, Paul. "Fifteen Dates with the Electric Chair." Ebony 17 (July 1962): 31-34.
_____. "How a Prisoner Became a Writer." Ebony 18 (November 1962): 88-90.
"Justification for Living." Negro Digest 11 (October 1962): 50.
Nizer, Louis. The Jury Returns. Garden City, N.Y.: Doubleday, 1966.
Schraufnagel, Noel. From Apology to Protest: The Black American Novel. DeLand, Florida: Everett/Edwards, 1973.

Reviews

Burn, Killer, Burn
    Chicago Jewish Forum (Fall 1963): 54.
    Chicago Sunday Tribune, 27 January 1963, p. 10.
    Library Journal, 15 December 1962, p. 4559.
    Nation, 8 December 1962, p. 409.
    Time, 21 December 1962, p. 81.

CULLEN, Countée Porter

Novel

One Way to Heaven. New York: Harper, 1932; New York: AMS Press. Excerpt in Clarke, Harlem.

Short Fiction

"The Frenchman's Bath." The Magpie 21 (November 1921): 30-32.
"Invictus." The Magpie 21 (October 1921): 22.
"Modernized Myths." The Magpie 21 (December 1921): 15-17.

Biography and Criticism

Arden, Eugene. "The Early Harlem Novel." Phylon 20 (Spring 1959): 25-31.
Baldwin, James. "Rendezvous with Life: An Interview with Countée Cullen." The Magpie 26 (Winter 1942): 19-21.
Bone, Robert A. The Negro Novel in America. New Haven: Yale University Press, 1966.
Bontemps, Arna. The Harlem Renaissance Remembered. New York: Dodd, Mead, 1972.
Brown, Martha Hursey. "Images of Black Women: Family Roles in Harlem Renaissance Literature." D.A. Dissertation, Carnegie-Mellon University, 1976.
Calvin, Floyd J. "Countée Cullen Tells How He Writes." Pittsburgh Courier, 18 June 1927, sec. 2, p. 4.
Chamberlain, John. "The Negro as Writer." Bookman 70 (February 1930): 609-610.
Dodson, Owen. "Countée Cullen (1903-1946)." Phylon 7 (First

Quarter 1946): 19-21.

Ferguson, Blanche. Countée Cullen and the Negro Renaissance. New York: Dodd, Mead, 1966.

Gloster, Hugh M. Negro Voices in American Fiction. Chapel Hill: University of North Carolina, 1948.

Huggins, Nathan Irvin. Harlem Renaissance. New York: Oxford University Press, 1971.

Jackson, Blyden. "The Harlem Renaissance." In The Comic Imagination in American Literature, pp. 295-303. Edited by Louis D. Rubin, Jr. New Brunswick, N.J.: Rutgers University Press, 1973.

Larson, Charles R. "Three Harlem Novels of the Jazz Age." Critique 11 No. 3 (1969): 66-78.

Lomax, Michael L. "Countée Cullen: A Key to the Puzzle." Studies in the Literary Imagination 7 (Fall 1974): 39-48.

_____. "Fantasies of Affirmation: The 1920's Novel of Life." CLA Journal 16 (December 1972): 232-246.

Perry, Margaret. A Bio-Bibliography of Countée P. Cullen, 1903-1946. Westport, Conn.: Greenwood, 1971.

_____. Silence to the Drums: A Survey of the Literature of the Harlem Renaissance. Contributions in Afro-American and African Studies, no. 18. Westport, Conn.: Greenwood Press, 1976.

Reiss, Winold. "Countée Cullen." Survey, 1 June 1925, p. 299.

Robb, Izetta W. "From the Darker Side." Opportunity 4 (December 1926): 381-382.

Rosenblatt, Roger. Black Fiction. Cambridge: Harvard University Press, 1974.

Rush, Theressa Gunnels, Carol Fairbanks Myers, and Esther Spring Arata. Black American Writers Past and Present. Metuchen, N.J.: Scarecrow Press, 1975.

Schraufnagel, Noel. From Apology to Protest: The Black American Novel. DeLand, Florida: Everett/Edwards, 1973.

Singh, Amritjit. "The Novels of the Harlem Renaissance: A Thematic Study." Ph.D. Dissertation, New York University, 1973.

_____. The Novels of the Harlem Renaissance: Twelve Black Writers, 1923-1933. University Park: The Pennsylvania State University Press, 1976.

Starke, Catherine Juanita. Black Portraiture in American Fiction: Stock Characters, Archetypes, and Individuals. New York: Basic Books, 1971.

Van Doren, Carl. "The Younger Generation of Negro Writers." Opportunity 2 (May 1924): 144-145.

Young, James O. Black Writers in the Thirties. Baton Rouge: Louisiana State University Press, 1973.

Reviews

One Way to Heaven
     Booklist 28 (April 1932): 349.
     Boston Transcript, 12 March 1932, p. 3.
     Brown, Elizabeth. New York Times, 28 February 1932, p. 7.
     Fisher, Rudolph. Books, 28 February 1932, p. 3.

Gruening, Martha. Saturday Review of Literature, 12 March 1932, p. 585.
Pittsburgh Monthly Bulletin 37 (May 1932): 35.
Root, E. M. Christian Century, 4 May 1932, p. 582.
Times Literary Supplement, 22 December 1932, p. 976.
Wisconsin Library Bulletin 28 (May 1932): 163.

CUNNINGHAM, George, Jr.

Novel

Lily-Skin Lover: His Passion for Light-Complexioned Women Leads Him to Destruction. New York: Exposition, 1960.

CUTHBERT, Marion

Short Fiction

"Mob Madness." Crisis 43 (April 1936): 108-114.

DALY, Victor

Novel

Not Only War: A Story of Two Great Conflicts. Boston: Christopher, 1932; New York: AMS Press, 1970; Washington, D.C.: McGrath, 1969.

Short Fiction

"Goats, Wildcats and Buffalo." Crisis 39 (March 1932): 91.
"Private Walker Goes Patrolling." Crisis 37 (June 1930): 199-201, 213.
"Still Five More." Crisis 41 (February 1934): 44-45.

Biography and Criticism

Gloster, Hugh M. Negro Voices in American Fiction. Chapel Hill: University of North Carolina Press, 1948.
Schraufnagel, Noel. From Apology to Protest: The Black American Novel. DeLand, Florida: Everett/Edwards, 1973.

DAVIS, A. L.

Short Fiction

"Suffer Little Children." Essence 5 (May 1974): 46-47, 81-82, 84.

DAVIS, Arthur P.

Short Fiction

"How John Boscoe Outsung the Devil." In Clarke, American Negro
Short Stories; Gibson and Anselment, Black and White; Murray
and Thomas, The Scene.

Biography and Criticism

Rush, Theressa Gunnels, Carol Fairbanks Myers, and Esther Spring
Arata. Black American Writers Past and Present. Metuchen,
N.J.: Scarecrow Press, 1975.

DAVIS, Charles

Novel

Two Weeks to Find a Killer. New York: Carlton, 1966.

DAVIS, Gene

Short Fiction

"Amateur Night in Harlem." In Ford and Faggett, The Best Short
Stories by Afro-American Writers.

DAVIS, George B.

Novel

Coming Home. New York, Dell, 1975.

Short Fiction

"Ben (Parts 1 & 2)." In Karlin, et al., Free Fire Zone.
"Coming Home." In Cowan, et al., Three for Show.
"Home Is Much Too Far to Go." In Watkins, Black Review No. 1.
"Like a Piece of Blues." Negro Digest 16 (July 1967): 55-63; also
in King, Black Short Story Anthology.

Biography and Criticism

Beauford, Fred. "Conversation with George Davis." Black Creation
3 (Spring 1972): 16-17.
Kent, George E. "Struggle for the Image: Selected Books by or
About Blacks during 1971." Phylon 33 (Winter 1972): 304-323.
Klotman, Phyllis Rauch. Another Man Gone: The Black Runner in
Contemporary Afro-American Literature. Port Washington,
N.Y.: Kennikat Press, 1977.

Reviews

Coming Home
   Black World 22 (January 1973): 79.
   Booklist, 15 April 1972, p. 701.
   Bryant, J. H. Nation, 6 March 1972, p. 311.
   Choice 9 (September 1972): 810.
   Dillon, R. T. Library Journal, 15 January 1972, p. 214.
   Kirkus, 1 November 1971, p. 1171.
   New Outlook, 27 May 1972, p. 21.
   New York Times Book Review, 4 June 1972, p. 22; Dec. 1972.
   Publishers' Weekly, 1 November 1971, p. 49.
   Rand, Peter. New York Times Book Review, 9 Jan. 1972, p. 7.

DAVIS, Gloria

Short Fiction

"The Wall. " Negro Digest 15 (August 1966): 59-62.

DAVIS, John P.

Short Fiction

"The Overcoat. " Opportunity 6 (December 1928): 366-367; also in
   Carson and Carson, The Impact of Fiction; Clarke, American
   Negro Short Stories.
"Ruth Trent Cries. " Opportunity 7 (January 1929): 19-20.
"Verisimilitude. " In Clarke, Harlem.
"The Waters of Megara. " Opportunity 5 (November 1927): 326+, 343.

DAVIS, Joseph

Novel

Black Bondage: A Novel of a Doomed Negro in Today's South. New
   York: Exposition, 1959.

DAVIS, Nolan

Novel

Six Black Horses. New York: Putnam, 1971.

Biography and Criticism

Land, I. S. "First Novelists. " Library Journal, 1 October 1971,
   p. 3164-3165.
Rush, Theressa Gunnels, Carol Fairbanks Myers, and Esther Spring
   Arata. Black American Writers Past and Present. Metuchen,
   N.J.: Scarecrow Press, 1975.

Reviews

Six Black Horses
 Allen, Bruce. Library Journal, 1 December 1972, p. 4029.
 Booklist, 15 December 1971, p. 352.
 Catholic Library World 43 (May 1972): 532.
 Cavallini, Joanne. Library Journal, 15 May 1972, p. 1933.
 Cooper, Arthur. Newsweek, 6 December 1971, p. 114B.
 English Journal 63 (January 1974): 65.
 Essence 2 (February 1972): 62.
 Kinlery, Paul. Best Sellers, 15 November 1971, p. 380.
 Kirkus, 15 August 1971, p. 890.
 New York Times, 27 November 1971, p. 29.
 Publishers' Weekly, 16 August 1971, p. 55.
 Sutherland, Zena. Saturday Review of Literature, 15 January
  1972, p. 47.

DAVIS, Russell F.

Novel

Anything for a Friend. New York: Crown, 1963.

Reviews

Anything for a Friend
 Gasnick, Roy M. America, 20 April 1963, p. 586.
 Jackson, R. B. Library Journal, 1 May 1963, p. 1900.

DEAN, Corinne

Short Fiction

(Collection): Cocoanut Suite: Stories of the West Indies. Boston:
 Meador, 1944.
"Plantation Stain." Crisis 47 (January 1940): 16-18.
"Thorns & Tails." Crisis 47 (July 1940): 202-204, 210.

DELANY, Martin R.

Fiction

Blake, or the Huts of America; A Tale of the Mississippi Valley,
 the Southern United States and Cuba. Boston: Beacon, 1970.
 Excerpt in Davis and Redding, Cavalcade.

Biography and Criticism

Austin, Allan D. "The Significance of Martin Robison Delany's
 Blake, or The Huts of America." Ph.D. Dissertation, Univer-

sity of Massachusetts, 1975.

Bell, Bernard W. "Literary Sources of the Early Afro-American Novel." CLA Journal 18 (September 1974): 29-43.

Bone, Robert A. The Negro Novel in America. New Haven: Yale University Press, 1966.

Brawley, Benjamin. Early Negro American Writers. Freeport, N.Y.: Books for Libraries, 1968.

Butcher, Margaret Just. The Negro in American Culture. New York: Mentor, 1971.

Fleming, Robert E. "Delany's Blake." Negro History Bulletin 36 (February 1973): 37-40.

Gayle, Addison, Jr. "Politics of Revolution: Afro-American Literature." Black World 21 (June 1972): 4-12.

_____. The Way of the New World: The Black Novel in America. Garden City, N.Y.: Anchor Press/Doubleday, 1975.

Gloster, Hugh M. Negro Voices in American Fiction. Chapel Hill: University of North Carolina Press, 1948.

Hite, Roger W. "'Stand Still and See the Salvation': The Rhetorical Design of Martin Delany's Blake." Journal of Black Studies 5 (December 1974): 192-202.

Loggins, Vernon. The Negro Author: His Development in America to 1900. Port Washington, N.Y.: Kennikat Press, 1964.

Malveaux, Julianne. "Revolutionary Themes in Martin Delany's Blake." Black Scholar 4 (July-August 1973): 52-56.

"Negro Novelists Blazing the Way in Fiction." Negro History Bulletin 3 (December 1938): 17.

Pfeiffer, John. "Black American Speculative Literature: A Checklist." Extrapolation 17 (December 1975): 35-43.

Rollins, Frank A. Life and Public Services of Martin R. Delany. Boston: Lee & Shepard, 1883.

Rush, Theressa Gunnels, Carol Fairbanks Myers, and Esther Spring Arata. Black American Writers Past and Present. Metuchen, N.J.: Scarecrow Press, 1975.

Schraufnagel, Noel. From Apology to Protest: The Black American Novel. DeLand, Florida: Everett/Edwards, 1973.

Takaki, Ronald T. Violence in the Black Imagination. New York: Putnam's Sons, 1972.

Ullman, Victor. Martin Delany: The Beginning of Black Nationalism. Boston: Beacon Press, 1971.

Williams, Walter L. "A Review of the African Dream: Martin R. Delany and the Emergence of Pan-African Thought by Cyril E. Griffith." Journal of Ethnic Studies 3 (Winter 1976): 120-121.

Yellin, Jean Fagan. The Intricate Knot: The Negro in American Literature, 1776-1863. New York: New York University Press, 1971.

Yeugner, John. "A Note on Martin Delany's Blake and Black Militancy." Phylon 32 (Spring 1971): 98-105.

Reviews

Blake
    Booklist, 15 December 1970, p. 327.
    Choice 8 (September 1971): 830.

Kirkus, 1 August 1970, p. 819.
Library Journal, 1 November 1970, p. 3804.
Publishers' Weekly, 31 August 1970, p. 281.

DELANY, Samuel R.

Novels

Babel-17. London: V. Gollancz, 1966; New York: Ace, 1973.
The Ballad of Beta-2, 1965; New York: Ace, 1971.
Captives of the Flame. New York: Ace, 1963.
City of a Thousand Suns. New York: Ace, 1965; London: Sphere
     Books, 1969. (Vol. 3 of The Fall of the Towers.)
Dhalgren. New York: Bantam, 1975.
Driftglass: Ten Tales of Speculative Fiction. New York: New
     American Library, 1971.
The Einstein Intersection. London: V. Gollancz, 1967; New York:
     Ace, 1971.
Empire Star. New York: Ace, 1966.
The Fall of the Towers. New York: Ace, 1972. (Originally pub-
     lished in three volumes: Out of the Dead City. London:
     Sphere, 1968; The Towers of Toron. New York: Ace, 1964;
     City of a Thousand Suns. London: Sphere, 1969.)
Galaxies. New York: Bantam, forthcoming.
The Jewels of Aptor. London: V. Gollancz, 1968; New York: Ace,
     1962.
Nova. Garden City, N.Y.: Doubleday, 1968.
Out of the Dead City. London: Sphere Books, 1968. (Vol. 1 of
     The Fall of the Towers.)
The Tides of Lust. New York: Lancer, 1973.
The Towers of Toron. New York: Ace, 1964; London: Sphere
     Books, 1968. (Vol. 2 of The Fall of the Towers.)
Triton. New York: Bantam, 1976.

Short Fiction

"Corona." In Ferman, The Best from Fantasy and Science Fiction,
     17th Series.
"Driftglass." In Allison et al., Survival Printout: Total Effect;
     Clareson, A Spectrum of Worlds; Wollheim and Carr, World's
     Best Science Fiction, 4th Series.
"Empire Star." In Wollheim, Ace Science Fiction Reader.
"Time Considered as a Helix of Semi-Precious Stones." In Asi-
     mov, The Hugo Winners, vol. 2; Fiedler, In Dreams Awake;
     Wollheim and Carr, World's Best Science Fiction, 1969.

Biography and Criticism

Alterman, Peter S. "The Surreal Translations of Samuel R. De-
     lany." Science-Fiction Studies 4 (March 1977): 25-34.
Barbour, Douglas. "Multiplex Misdemeanors: The Figures of the
     Artist and the Criminal in the Science Fiction Novels of Samuel

R. Delany." In Khatru #2. Edited by Jeffrey D. Smith. Baltimore, Md.: n.p., 1975.

Brunner, John. "One Sense of Wonder, Slightly Tarnished." Books and Bookmen 12 (July 1967): 19-20.

Clareson, Thomas D., ed. A Spectrum of Worlds. New York: Doubleday, 1972.

Delany, Samuel. "Thickening the Plot." In Those Who Can: A Science Fiction Reader, pp. 70-77. Edited by Robin Scott Wilson. New York: New American Library, 1974.

Fox, Robert Elliot. "The Mirrors of Caliban: A Study of the Fiction of LeRoi Jones (Imamu Amiri Baraka), Ishmael Reed and Samuel R. Delany." Ph.D. Dissertation, State University of New York at Buffalo, 1976.

Miesel, Sandra. "Samuel R. Delany's Use of Myth in Nova." Extrapolation 12 (May 1971): 86-93.

Russ, Joanna. "A Boy and His Dog: The Final Solution." Frontiers: A Journal of Women Studies 1 (Fall 1975): [153]-162.

_____. "Communique from the Front: Teaching and the State of Art." Colloquy 4 (May 1971): 28-31.

Schweitzer, Darrell. "An Interview with Samuel R. Delany." Algol 13 (Summer 1976): 16-20.

Scobie, Stephen. "Different Mazes: Mythology in Samuel R. Delaney's [sic] The Einstein Intersection." Riverside Quarterly 5 (1971): 12-18.

Sheppard, R. Z. "Future Grok." Time, 29 March 1971, pp. 86, 88-89.

Shippey, T. A. In Contemporary Novelists. Edited by James Vinson. New York: St. Martin's Press, 1976.

Reviews

Babel-17
  Analog 80 (December 1967): 163-164.
  Ballard, J. G. Manchester Guardian, 4 January 1968, p. 11.
  Magazine of Fantasy and Science Fiction 31 (December 1966): 35-36.
  New Worlds No. 167 (October 1966): 153-154.
  Nightingale, B. Observer, 17 December 1967, p. 21.
  Punch, 22 November 1967, p. 797.
  SF Commentary 20 (April 1971): 23-24.

The Ballad of Beta-2
  Magazine of Fantasy and Science Fiction 29 (November 1965): 18-19.

Captives of the Flame
  Analog 72 (November 1963): 90-91.

City of a Thousand Suns
  Analog 79 (June 1967): 167-168.

Dhalgren
  Book World, 17 January 1975, p. 2; 14 September 1975, p. 5.
  Booklist, 1 June 1975, p. 991.
  Commonweal, 5 December 1975, p. 599.
  Jonas, G. New York Times Book Review, 16 February 1975, p. 27.

Library Journal, 15 March 1975, p. 604.
Publishers' Weekly, 25 November 1974, p. 47.
Driftglass
    Algol 19 (November 1972): 29.
    Analog 89 (July 1972): 167-168.
    Kliatt Paperback Book Guide 6 (April 1972): 87.
The Einstein Intersection
    Analog 81 (April 1968): 163-164.
    Books and Bookmen 13 (June 1968): 35.
    Fantastic Stories 18 (October 1968): 136-137.
    Galaxy 26 (October 1967): 193-194.
    Merril, J. Magazine of Fantasy and Science Fiction 33 (November 1967): 34-36.
    New Worlds No. 173 (July 1967): 63.
    SF Commentary 1 (January 1969): 16.
    Times Literary Supplement, 30 May 1968, p. 560.
    Young, B. A. Observer, 12 June 1968, p. 865.
Empire Star
    Magazine of Fantasy and Science Fiction 31 (December 1966): 35-36.
    New Worlds No. 163 (June 1966): 143-144.
The Fall of the Towers
    Luna Monthly 40 (September 1972): 24.
The Jewels of Aptor
    Analog 71 (August 1963): 91-92.
    Punch, 1 January 1969, p. 35.
    Tablet (London), 4 January 1969, p. 12.
    Times Literary Supplement, 28 November 1968, p. 1346.
Nova
    Analog 82 (November 1968): 166-167.
    Books and Bookmen 14 (July 1969): 38.
    Galaxy 27 (January 1969): 189-192.
    Kirkus, 1 June 1968, p. 622.
    Library Journal, 1 October 1968, p. 3576; 15 October 1968, p. 3995.
    Merril, J. Magazine of Fantasy and Science Fiction 35 (November 1968): 43-46.
    New Worlds No. 185 (December 1968): 61.
    Publishers' Weekly, 20 May 1968, p. 61.
    SF Commentary 13 (July 1970): 9-10; 14 (August 1970): 7-10; 17 (November 1970): 38-41.
    Son of WSFA Journal 54 (May 1972): 3.
    Speculation 3 (January 1970): 17-20.
The Tides of Lust
    Publishers' Weekly, 19 February 1973, p. 82.
The Towers of Toron
    Analog 74 (November 1964): 88.
Triton
    Booklist, 1 June 1976, p. 1393.
    New York Times Book Review, 28 March 1976, p. 30.

DEMBY, William

Novels

Act of Outrage see Beetlecreek
Beetlecreek. New York: Rinehart, 1950; Chatham, N.J.: Chatham
Bookseller, 1972; New York: Avon, 1967; also published as
Act of Outrage, New York: Lion Books, 1955; excerpts in Da-
vis and Redding, Cavalcade; Hill, Soon One Morning; Miller,
Blackamerican Literature.
The Catacombs. New York: Pantheon Books, 1965; New York:
Perennial, 1970. Excerpts in Margolies, A Native Sons Read-
er.

Short Fiction

"The Table of Wishes Come True." In Barksdale and Kinnamon,
Black Writers of America.

Biography and Criticism

Bayliss, John F. "Beetlecreek: Existential or Human Document."
Negro Digest 19 (November 1969): 70-74.
Bigsby, C. W. E. "From Protest to Paradox: The Black Writer
at Mid-Century." In The Fifties, pp. 217-240. Edited by Nor-
man Podhoretz. New York: Farrar, Straus, 1964.
Bone, Robert. The Negro Novel in America. New Haven: Yale
University Press, 1966.
_____. "William Demby's Dance of Life." Tri-Quarterly 9
(1969): 127-141.
Brown, Lloyd L. "Separate Paths." Masses & Mainstream 3
(April 1950): 88-90.
Hassan, Ihab. Contemporary American Literature 1945-1972: An
Introduction. New York: Frederick Ungar, 1973.
Hoffman, Nancy Y. "The Annunciation of William Demby." Studies
in Black Literature 2 (Spring 1972): 8-13.
_____. "Technique in Demby's The Catacombs." Studies in
Black Literature 2 (Summer 1971): 10-13.
Johnson, Joe. "Interview with William Demby." Black Creation 3
(Spring 1972): 18-21.
Klinkowitz, Jerome. Literary Disruptions: The Making of a Post-
Contemporary American Fiction. Urbana: University of Illinois
Press, 1975.
Littlejohn, David. Black on White: A Critical Survey of Writing by
American Negroes. New York: Grossman, 1966.
O'Brien, John. Interviews with Black Writers. New York: Live-
right, 1973.
Rosenblatt, Roger. Black Fiction. Cambridge: Harvard University
Press, 1974.
Schraufnagel, Noel. From Apology to Protest. DeLand, Fla.:
Everett/Edwards, 1973.
Singh, Raman K. "The Black Novel and Its Tradition." Colorado
Quarterly 20 (Summer 1971): 23-29.

Whitlow, Roger. <u>Black American Literature</u>. Chicago: Nelson Hall, 1973.

Reviews

<u>Beetlecreek</u>
  Cayton, Horace. <u>New York Times</u>, 26 February 1950, p. 4.
  Conroy, Jack. <u>Chicago Sun</u>, 23 March 1950, p. 6.
  Derleth, August. <u>Chicago Sunday Tribune</u>, 12 February 1950, p. 4.
  Fleischer, L. <u>Publishers' Weekly</u>, 28 November 1966, p. 63.
  Fuller, Edmund. <u>Saturday Review of Literature</u>, 4 March 1950, p. 17.
  Hansen, Harry. <u>Survey</u> 86 (March 1950): 156.
  Jones, Ernest. <u>Nation</u>, 11 February 1950, p. 138.
  <u>Kirkus</u>, 15 December 1949, p. 674.
  <u>New York Herald Tribune Book Review</u>, 12 February 1950, p. 13.
  <u>New Yorker</u>, 11 February 1950, p. 93.
  <u>San Francisco Chronicle</u>, 5 March 1950, p. 18.
The <u>Catacombs</u>
  Buitenhuis, Peter. <u>New York Times</u>, 11 July 1965, p. 4.
  <u>Kirkus</u>, 1 April 1965, p. 400.
  <u>Library Journal</u>, 15 June 1965, p. 2870.
  Rennert, Maggie. <u>Book Week</u>, 27 June 1965, p. 22.

DE RAMUS, Betty

Short Fiction

"The Addict." <u>Black World</u> 19 (June 1970): 74-77.
"The Fake Picasso." <u>Black World</u> 21 (June 1972): 66-69.
"Waiting for Beale." <u>Essence</u> 74 (May 1976): 73, 83.

DIXON, Edwina

Short Fiction

"Pa Sees Again." In Ford and Faggett, <u>Best Short Stories by Afro-American Writers</u>.

DODSON, Owen

Novels

<u>Boy at the Window</u>. New York: Farrar, Straus & Young, 1951. (Also published as <u>When Trees Were Green</u>. New York: Popular Library, 1951.) Excerpt in Davis and Redding, <u>Cavalcade</u>.
<u>Come Home Early, Child</u>. New York: Popular Library, 1977.
<u>When Trees Were Green</u> see <u>Boy at the Window</u>.

Short Fiction

"Come Home Early, Chile." In Hill, Soon, One Morning; Hughes,
    The Best Short Stories by Negro Writers.
"The Summer Fire." In Best Short Stories from The Paris Review.

Biography and Criticism

Bone, Robert A. The Negro Novel in America. New Haven: Yale
    University Press, 1966.
Long Look, Owen Dodson. Los Angeles: Pacifica Tape Library,
    1975. (102-minute tape.)
O'Brien, John. Interviews with Black Writers. New York: Live-
    right, 1973.
Rush, Theressa Gunnels, Carol Fairbanks Myers, and Esther Spring
    Arata. Black American Writers Past and Present. Metuchen,
    N.J.: Scarecrow Press, 1975.
Schraufnagel, Noel. From Apology to Protest. DeLand, Fla.:
    Everett/Edwards, 1973.

Reviews

Boy at the Window
    Booklist, 1 April 1951, p. 273.
    Bourjaily, Vance. New York Herald Tribune Book Review, 25
        February 1951, p. 14.
    Christian Science Monitor, 8 March 1951, p. 15.
    Engle, Paul. Chicago Sunday Tribune, 1 April 1951, p. 5.
    Kirkus, 15 December 1950, p. 732.
    McDonald, G. D. Library Journal, 15 February 1951, p. 325.
    New Yorker, 17 March 1951, p. 129.
    Redding, J. S. New York Times Book Review, 18 February
        1951, p. 4.
    Smallwood, Osborn T. Journal of Negro Education 21 (Spring
        1952): 175-176.
Come Home Early, Child
    Publishers' Weekly, 27 December 1976, p. 58.

DOLAN, Harry

Short Fiction

"Crazy Nigger." In Schulberg, From the Ashes.
"I Remember Papa." In Schulberg, From the Ashes; Somerville,
    Intimate Relationships.
"The Sand-Clock Day." In Schulberg, From the Ashes.

DORSEY, John T.

Novel

The Lion of Judah. Chicago: Fouche Co., 1924.

DOWNING, Henry Francis

Novel

The American Cavalryman: A Liberian Romance. New York:
    Neale, 1917; Washington, D.C.: McGrath, 1969; New York:
    AMS Press, 1969.

Biography and Criticism

Bone, Robert A. The Negro Novel in America. New Haven: Yale
    University Press, 1966.
Gloster, Hugh M. Negro Voices in American Fiction. Chapel Hill:
    University of North Carolina Press, 1948.

Reviews

The American Cavalryman
    Crisis 15 (February 1918): 186.
    Hunt, Ida Gibbs. Journal of Negro History 3 (October 1918):
        444-445.

DRAKE, Sandra

Short Fiction

"A Windy Day in May." In Mayfield, Ten Times Black.

DREER, Herman

Novels

The Immediate Jewel of His Soul. St. Louis, Mo.: Argus, 1919;
    Washington, D.C.: McGrath, 1969; New York: AMS Press,
    1969.
The Tie That Binds. Boston: Meador, 1958.

Biography and Criticism

Bone, Robert A. The Negro Novel in America. New Haven: Yale
    University Press, 1966.
Gloster, Hugh M. Negro Voices in American Fiction. Chapel Hill:
    University of North Carolina Press, 1948.
Hughes, Carl M. The Negro Novelist 1940-1950. New York: Cita-

del Press, 1953.
Rees, Robert A. and Earl N. Harbert, eds. Fifteen American
Authors Before 1900. Madison: University of Wisconsin
Press, 1971.
Yenser, Thomas, ed. Who's Who in Colored America, 3rd ed.
New York: Yenser, 1930-31-32.

DU BOIS, David Graham

Novel

. . . And Bid Him Sing. Palo Alto, Ca.: Ramparts, 1975.

Reviews

. . . And Bid Him Sing
Bouise, O. A. Best Sellers 35 (August 1975): 121.
Choice 12 (September 1975): 840.
Griffin, L. W. Library Journal, 15 May 1975, p. 1008.
Levin, M. New York Times Book Review, 29 June 1975, p. 28.
New Yorker, 9 May 1975, p. 127.
Publishers' Weekly, 17 March 1975, p. 51.
Wilson, Francille Rusan. Black Scholar 6 (July-August 1975):
52-53.

DU BOIS, William Edward Burghardt

Novels

The Black Flame: A Trilogy. New York: Mainstream, 1957,
1959, 1961. (Book One: The Ordeal of Mansart, 1957; excerpt
in Masses and Mainstream 8 (February 1955): 21-29. Book
Two: Mansart Builds a School, 1959. Book Three: Worlds of
Color, 1961.)
Dark Princess: A Romance. New York: Harcourt, Brace, 1928;
New York: AMS Press; excerpt in Long and Collier, Afro-
American Writing.
The Quest of the Silver Fleece: A Novel. Chicago: McClurg, 1911;
Freeport, N.Y.: Books for Libraries; New York: Arno, 1969;
Westport, Conn.: Negro Universities Press, 1969; New York:
AMS Press; Washington, D.C.: McGrath, 1969; Miami: Mnemo-
syne, 1969.

Short Fiction

"Miralda or the Beautiful Octoroon." Anglo-African Magazine (December 1960).
"The Princess of the Hither Isles." Crisis 6 (October 1913): 285,
288-289.

Biography and Criticism

Amann, Clarence A. "Three Negro Classics--An Estimate." Negro American Literature Forum 4 (Winter 1970): 113-119.

Aptheker, Herbert. "Du Bois: The Final Years." Journal of Human Relations 14 (First Quarter 1966): 149-155.

Bone, Robert A. The Negro Novel in America. New Haven: Yale University Press, 1966.

Brawley, Benjamin. The Negro in Literature and Art. New York: Duffield, 1930.

Broderick, Francis L. W. E. B. Du Bois, Negro Leader at a Time of Crisis. Stanford, Ca.: Stanford University Press, 1959.

Clarke, John Henrik, et al. Black Titan: W. E. B. Du Bois, an Anthology by the Editors of Freedomways. Boston: Beacon Press, 1970.

Davis, Arthur P. From the Dark Tower: Afro-American Writers 1900 to 1960. Washington, D. C.: Howard University Press, 1974.

Elder, Arlene A. "Swamp Versus Plantation: Symbolic Structure in W. E. B. Du Bois' The Quest of the Silver Fleece." Phylon 34 (December 1973): 358-367.

Finkelstein, Sidney. "W. E. B. Du Bois' Trilogy: A Literary Triumph." Mainstream 14 (October 1961): 6-17.

Gayle, Addison, Jr. The Way of the New World: The Black Novel in America. Garden City, N. Y.: Anchor Press/Doubleday, 1975.

Gipson, Carolyn Renee. "Intellectual Dilemmas in the Novels of W. E. B. Du Bois." Ph. D. Dissertation, University of Michigan, 1971.

Gloster, Hugh M. Negro Voices in American Fiction. Chapel Hill: University of North Carolina Press, 1948.

Graham, Shirley. His Day Is Marching On: A Memoir of W. E. B. Du Bois. Philadelphia: Lippincott, 1971.

Green, Dan. "W. E. B. Du Bois: Black Yankee." Connecticut Review 6 (October 1972): 46-56.

Harding, Vincent. "W. E. B. Du Bois and the Black Messianic Vision." Freedomways 9 (Winter 1969): 44-58.

Isani, Mukhtar Ali. "The Exotic and Protest in Earlier Black Literature: The Use of Alien Setting and Character." Studies in Black Literature 5 (Summer 1974): 9-14.

Kent, George. Blackness and the Adventure of Western Culture. Chicago: Third World Press, 1972.

Kostelanetz, Richard. "Fiction of a Negro Politics: The Neglected Novels of W. E. B. Du Bois." Xavier University Studies 7 (1968): 5-39.

Lester, Julius, ed. The Seventh Son: The Thought and Writings of W. E. B. Du Bois. New York: Random House, 1971.

Logan, Rayford Whittingham, ed. W. E. B. Du Bois: A Profile. New York: Hill & Wang, 1971.

Mays, Benjamin E. The Negro's God as Reflected in His Literature. New York: Negro Universities Press, 1969.

Mootry, Maria Katella. "Studies in Black Pastoral: Five Afro-

American Writers. " Ph. D. Dissertation, Northwestern University, 1974.

Newsome, Elaine M. "W. E. B. Du Bois' 'Figure in the Carpet': A Cyclical Pattern in the Belletristic Prose. " Ph. D. Dissertation, University of North Carolina at Chapel Hill, 1971.

Pfeiffer, John. "Black American Speculative Literature: A Checklist. " Extrapolation 17 (December 1975): 35-43.

Pugh, Wesley C. "The Inflated Controversy: Du Bois vs. Washington. " Crisis 81 (April 1974): 132-133.

Rampersad, Arnold. The Art and Imagination of W. E. B. Du Bois. Cambridge: Harvard University Press, 1976.

Rosenblatt, Roger. Black Fiction. Cambridge: Harvard University Press, 1974.

Rush, Theressa Gunnels, Carol Fairbanks Myers, and Esther Spring Arata. Black American Writers Past and Present. Metuchen, N.J.: Scarecrow Press, 1975.

Schraufnagel, Noel. From Apology to Protest. DeLand, Fla.: Everett/Edwards, 1973.

Singh, Amritjit. "The Novels of the Harlem Renaissance: A Thematic Study. " Ph. D. Dissertation, New York University, 1973.
———. The Novels of the Harlem Renaissance: Twelve Black Writers, 1923-1933. University Park: Pennsylvania State University Press, 1976.

Stepto, Robert Burns. "From Behind the Veil: Afro-American Reform Literature at the Turn of the Century. " Ph. D. Dissertation, Stanford University, 1974.

Turner, Darwin T. "W. E. B. Du Bois and the Theory of a Black Aesthetic. " Studies in the Literary Imagination 7 (Fall 1974): 1-21.

Whitlow, Roger. Black American Literature: A Critical History. Chicago: Nelson Hall, 1973.

Reviews

Dark Princess; A Romance
Boston Transcript, 14 July 1928, p. 5.
Cleveland Open Shelf (September 1928): 105.
Davis, Allison. Crisis 35 (October 1928): 339-340.
Locke, Alain. Books (New York Herald Tribune), 20 May 1928, p. 12.
New Republic, 22 August 1928, p. 27.
New York Evening Post, 12 May 1928, p. 9.
New York Times, 13 May 1928, p. 19.
Reitell, Jane. American Academy of Political and Social Science Annals 140 (November 1928): 347.
Springfield Republican, 28 May 1928, p. 6.
Whipple, Leon. Opportunity 6 (August 1928): 244.
World Tomorrow 11 (November 1928): 473.

Mansart Builds a School
Butcher, Philip. Journal of Negro Education 29 (Spring 1960): 156.
Cooke, Marvel. Mainstream 13 (April 1960): 54-56.

The Ordeal of Mansart
> Butcher, Philip. Journal of Negro Education 26 (Fall 1957): 479-480.
> Crisis 64 (August-September 1957): 454-455.
> Rubinstein, Annette. Mainstream 10 (June 1957): 52-55.

The Quest of the Silver Fleece
> Braithwaite, William S. Crisis 3 (December 1911): 77-78.
> Opportunity 6 (August 1928): 244.

Worlds of Color
> Graham, Lorenz. Freedomways 1 (Summer 1961): 211-214.
> Ivy, J. W. Crisis 68 (June-July 1961): 378-379.
> Library Journal 86 (September 1961): 2815.

DUBOSE, Janet

Novel

A Cry from a Child of the Ghetto. New York: Vantage Press, 1974.

DUMAS, Henry

Novel

Jonoah and the Green Stone. New York: Random House, 1976.

Short Fiction

(Collection): "Ark of Bones" and Other Stories. Edited by Hale Chatfield and Eugene Redmond. Carbondale: Southern Illinois University Press, 1970; new ed., edited by Eugene Redmond. New York: Random House, 1974.

"Ark of Bones." In Dumas, "Ark of Bones"; Hicks, Cutting Edges.

"A Bowl of Roses." In Dumas, "Ark of Bones."

"The Crossing." Negro Digest 15 (November 1965): 80-86; also in Dumas, "Ark of Bones."

"Double Nigger." In Dumas, "Ark of Bones."

"Echo Tree." In Dumas, "Ark of Bones."

"Fon." In Dumas, "Ark of Bones."

"A Harlem Game." In Dumas, "Ark of Bones."

"Rain God." Negro Digest 17 (January 1968): 54-57.

"Strike and Fade." In Dumas, "Ark of Bones."

"Thalia." Black Scholar 6 (June 1975): 63-66.

"Will the Circle Be Unbroken?" Negro Digest 16 (November 1966): 76-80; also in Dumas, "Ark of Bones."

Biography and Criticism

Rush, Theressa Gunnels, Carol Fairbanks Myers, and Esther Spring Arata. Black American Writers Past and Present. Metuchen, N.J.: Scarecrow Press, 1975.

Reviews

"Ark of Bones" and Other Stories
A. B. Bookmen's Weekly, 25 January 1971, p. 237.
Black World 24 (January 1975): 51.
Choice 12 (March 1975): 70.
Kirkus, 15 June 1974, p. 648.
Library Journal, 1 June 1971, p. 2008.
New York Times Book Review, 20 October 1974, p. 36.
New Yorker, 6 January 1975, p. 81.
Publishers' Weekly, 24 June 1974, p. 54.
Saturday Review/World, 7 September 1974, p. 23.
Jonoah and the Green Stone
Best Sellers 36 (September 1976): 181.
Kirkus, 15 March 1976, p. 341.
Library Journal 101 (August 1976): 1656.
New Yorker, 10 May 1976, p. 142.
Publishers' Weekly, 15 March 1976, p. 49.
Toney, Richard. San Francisco Review of Books 2 (September 1976): 14, 18.

DUNBAR, Paul Laurence

Novels

The Fanatics. New York: Dodd, Mead, 1901; Freeport, N.Y.:
Books for Libraries, 1971; Boston: Gregg, 1971; Miami:
Mnemosyne; New York: Negro Universities Press.
The Love of Landry. New York: Dodd, Mead, 1900; Freeport,
N.Y.: Books for Libraries; Boston: Gregg, 1970; Miami:
Mnemosyne; Westport, Conn.: Negro Universities Press.
The Sport of the Gods. New York: Dodd, Mead, 1902; Lippincott's
Magazine 67 (May 1901): 515-594; Freeport, N.Y.: Books for
Libraries; New York: Macmillan; New York: AMS Press;
Miami: Mnemosyne.
The Uncalled. New York: Dodd, Mead, 1898; Lippincott's Maga-
zine 64 (May 1898): 579-669; Freeport, N.Y.: Books for Li-
braries; New York: AMS Press; Boston: Gregg; Washington,
D.C.: McGrath, 1969; Miami: Mnemosyne; New York: Panther
House; Westport, Conn.: Negro Universities Press.

Short Fiction

(Collections):
The Best Stories of Paul Laurence Dunbar. Edited by B. G.
Brawley. New York: Dodd, Mead, 1938.
Folks from Dixie. New York: Dodd, Mead, 1898: London:
J. Bowden; Freeport, N.Y.: Books for Libraries; Boston:
Gregg; Westport, Conn.: Negro Universities Press.
The Heart of Happy Hollow. New York: Dodd, Mead, 1904;
Freeport, N.Y.: Books for Libraries; Westport, Conn.:
Negro Universities Press.

In Old Plantation Days. New York: Dodd, Mead, 1903; West-
port, Conn.: Negro Universities Press.
The Paul Laurence Dunbar Reader. Edited by Jay Martin and
Gossie Hudson. New York: Dodd, Mead, 1974.
The Strength of Gideon and Other Stories. New York: Dodd,
Mead, 1900; Freeport, N.Y.: Books for Libraries;
New York: Arno.
"Anner 'Lizer's Stumblin' Block." In Davis and Redding, Cavalcade;
Dunbar, Best Stories; Dunbar, Folks from Dixie.
"Ash-Cake Hannah and Her Ben." In Dunbar, In Old Plantation
Days.
"At Shaft 11." In Dunbar, Best Stories; Dunbar, Folks from Dixie;
Dunbar, The Paul Laurence Dunbar Reader.
"Aunt Mandy's Investment." In Dunbar, Best Stories; Dunbar, Folks
from Dixie.
"Aunt Tempe's Revenge." In Dunbar, In Old Plantation Days.
"Aunt Tempe's Triumph." In Dunbar, Best Stories.
"Blessed Deceit." In Dunbar, In Old Plantation Days.
"Boy and the Bayonet." In Dunbar, Best Stories; Dunbar, The
Heart of Happy Hollow.
"Brief Cure of Aunt Fanny." In Dunbar, In Old Plantation Days.
"Cahoots." In Dunbar, The Heart of Happy Hollow.
"Case of 'Ca'line.'" In Dunbar, Best Stories; Dunbar, The Strength
of Gideon.
"The Churching of Grandma Pleasant." Lippincott's, March 1905;
also in Dunbar, The Paul Laurence Dunbar Reader.
"Colonel's Awakening." In Cromwell, Turner, and Dykes, Readings
from Negro Authors; Dunbar, Folks from Dixie.
"Conjuring Contest." In Dunbar, In Old Plantation Days.
"Council of State." In Dunbar, The Paul Laurence Dunbar Reader;
Dunbar, The Strength of Gideon.
"Dandy Jim's Conjure Scare." In Dunbar, In Old Plantation Days.
"Defection of Maria Ann Gibbs." In Dunbar, In Old Plantation Days.
"Defender of the Faith." In Dunbar, The Heart of Happy Hollow.
"Deliberation of Mr. Dunkin." In Dunbar, Folks from Dixie.
"Dizzy-Headed Dick." In Dunbar, In Old Plantation Days.
"Easter Wedding." In Dunbar, In Old Plantation Days.
"The Emancipation of Evalina Jones." People's Monthly, April
1900.
"Faith Cure Man." In Dunbar, Best Stories; Dunbar, The Strength
of Gideon.
"Family Feud." In Dunbar, Best Stories; Dunbar, Folks from Dixie.
"Finding of Martha." In Dunbar, In Old Plantation Days.
"Finding of Zach." In Dunbar, The Strength of Gideon.
"The Finish of Patsy Barnes." In Dunbar, The Strength of Gideon;
Gold, Point of Departure.
"Fruitful Sleeping of the Rev. Elisha Edwards." In Dunbar, The
Paul Laurence Dunbar Reader; Dunbar, The Strength of Gideon.
"The Gambler's Wife." Dayton Tattler, 13, 20, 27 December 1890.
(Published anonymously.)
"His Bride of the Tombs." Dayton Tattler, 13, 20, 27 December
1890. (Pseud. Philip Louis Denterley.)
"His Failure in Arithmetic." Dayton Tattler, 20 December 1890.

(Published anonymously.)

"Home-Coming of 'Rastus Smith. " In Dunbar, The Heart of Happy Hollow.

"How Brother Parker Fell from Grace. " In Dunbar, In Old Plantation Days.

"In a Circle. " Metropolitan Magazine, October 1901; also in Dunbar, The Paul Laurence Dunbar Reader.

"The Independence of Silas Bollender. " Lippincott's, September 1901; also in Dunbar, The Paul Laurence Dunbar Reader.

"The Ingrate. " In Dunbar, Best Stories; Dunbar, The Strength of Gideon.

"Interference of Patsy Ann. " In Dunbar, The Heart of Happy Hollow.

"Intervention of Peter. " In Dunbar, Folks from Dixie; Hart and Perry, Representative Short Stories.

"Jethro's Garden. " The Literary Era, July 1902; also in Dunbar, The Paul Laurence Dunbar Reader.

"Jim's Probation. " In Dunbar, The Strength of Gideon.

"Jimsella. " In Dunbar, Best Stories; Dunbar, Folks from Dixie; Olsen and Swinburne, Dreamers of Dreams.

"Johnsonham, Junior. " In Dunbar, The Strength of Gideon.

"Judgement of Paris. " In Dunbar, Best Stories; Dunbar, In Old Plantation Days.

"Lady Slipper. " In Dunbar, In Old Plantation Days.

"Lafe Halloway's Two Fights. " New York Independent, 7 September 1899; also in Dunbar, The Paul Laurence Dunbar Reader.

"Last Fiddling of Mordaunt's Jim. " In Dunbar, Best Stories; Dunbar, In Old Plantation Days.

"The Lion Tamer. " Smart Set, January 1901; also in Dunbar, The Paul Laurence Dunbar Reader.

"Little Billy. " A. N. Kellogg Newspaper Co., ca 1891.

"The Lynching of Jube Benson. " In Clarke, American Negro Short Stories; Dunbar, Best Stories; Dunbar, The Heart of Happy Hollow.

"Mammy Peggy's Pride. " In Dunbar, The Strength of Gideon.

"Matter of Doctrine. " In Dunbar, Best Stories; Dunbar, The Heart of Happy Hollow.

"Memory of Martha. " In Dunbar, In Old Plantation Days.

"A Mess of Pottage. " In Dunbar, The Paul Laurence Dunbar Reader; Dunbar, The Strength of Gideon.

"The Minority Committee. " Lippincott's, November 1901; also in Dunbar, The Paul Laurence Dunbar Reader.

"Mission of Mr. Scatters. " In Dunbar, Best Stories; Dunbar, The Heart of Happy Hollow.

"Mister Cornelius Johnson, Office-Seeker. " In Dunbar, The Paul Laurence Dunbar Reader; Dunbar, The Strength of Gideon; Turner, Black American Literature: Fiction.

"Mr. Groby's Slippery Gift. " In Dunbar, In Old Plantation Days.

"The Mortification of the Flesh. " Lippincott's, August 1901; also in Dunbar, The Paul Laurence Dunbar Reader; Turner, Black American Literature: Fiction.

"Mount Pisgah's Christmas 'Possum. " In Dunbar, Folks from Dixie; Hibbard, Stories of the South.

"Nelse Hatton's Vengence." In Dunbar, Folks from Dixie; Dunbar,
  The Paul Laurence Dunbar Reader.
"Old Abe's Conversion." In Dunbar, Best Stories; Dunbar, The
  Heart of Happy Hollow.
"Old-Time Christmas." In Dunbar, The Strength of Gideon.
"One Christmas at Shiloh." In Dunbar, The Heart of Happy Hollow.
"One Man's Fortunes." In Dunbar, The Paul Laurence Dunbar
  Reader; Dunbar, The Strength of Gideon.
"Ordeal of Mt. Hope." In Dunbar, Best Stories; Dunbar, The Folks
  from Dixie; Dunbar, The Paul Laurence Dunbar Reader; Hey-
  drick, Americans All.
"The Promoter." In Dunbar, The Heart of Happy Hollow.
"Race Question." In Dunbar, The Heart of Happy Hollow.
"The Scapegoat." In Dunbar, Best Stories; Dunbar, The Heart of
  Happy Hollow; Dunbar, The Paul Laurence Dunbar Reader;
  Hughes, Best Short Stories by Negro Writers; Murray and Tho-
  mas, Major Black Writers; Patterson, An Introduction to Black
  Literature in America; Rockowitz, Life Styles.
Schwalliger's Philanthropy." In Dunbar, Best Stories; Dunbar, The
  Heart of Happy Hollow.
"Silas Jackson." In Dunbar, The Strength of Gideon.
"Silent Sam'el." In Dunbar, In Old Plantation Days.
"Sister Jackson's Superstitions." In Dunbar, The Paul Laurence
  Dunbar Reader.
"Stanton Coachman." In Dunbar, In Old Plantation Days.
"Strength of Gideon." In Dunbar, The Strength of Gideon.
"Supper by Proxy." In Dunbar, In Old Plantation Days.
"The Tenderfoot." A. N. Kellogg Newspaper Co., ca 1891.
"Tragedy at Three Forks." In Dunbar, The Strength of Gideon.
"Trial Sermons on Bull-Skin." In Dunbar, Best Stories; Dunbar,
  Folks from Dixie.
"Triumph of Ol' Mis' Pease." In Dunbar, The Heart of Happy Hol-
  low.
"Trouble About Sophiny." In Dunbar, In Old Plantation Days.
"The Trousers." In Dunbar, In Old Plantation Days.
"Trustfulness of Polly." In Dunbar, The Strength of Gideon.
"Uncle Simon's Sundays Out." In Dunbar, The Strength of Gideon.
"The Vindication of Jared Hargot." Lippincott's, March 1904; also
  in Dunbar, The Paul Laurence Dunbar Reader.
"Viney's Free Papers." In Dunbar, The Strength of Gideon.
"The Visiting of Mother Danbury." Lippincott's, December 1901;
  also in Dunbar, The Paul Laurence Dunbar Reader.
"Walls of Jericho." In Dunbar, Best Stories; Dunbar, In Old Plan-
  tation Days.
"The Way of Love." Lippincott's, January 1905; also in Dunbar,
  The Paul Laurence Dunbar Reader.
"The White Counterpane." Lippincott's, October 1901; also in Dun-
  bar, The Paul Laurence Dunbar Reader.
"Who Stands for the Gods." In Dunbar, In Old Plantation Days.
"Wisdom of Silence." In Dunbar, The Heart of Happy Hollow.

Biography and Criticism

Arden, Eugene. "The Early Harlem Novel." Phylon 20 (September 1959): 25-31.

Arnold, Edward F. "Some Personal Reminiscences of Paul Laurence Dunbar." Journal of Negro History 17 (October 1932): 400-408.

Baker, Houston A., Jr. "Paul Laurence Dunbar: An Evaluation." Black World 21 (November 1971): 30-37.

_____. "Report on a Celebration: Paul Laurence Dunbar's One-Hundredth Year." Black World 22 (February 1973): 81-85.

_____. Singers of Daybreak: Studies in Black American Literature. Washington, D.C.: Howard University Press, 1974.

Bell, Bernard W. "Literary Sources of the Early Afro-American Novel." CLA Journal 18 (September 1974): 29-43.

Bone, Robert. Down Home: A History of Afro-American Short Fiction from Its Beginnings to the End of the Harlem Renaissance. New York: G. P. Putnam's Sons, 1975.

_____. The Negro Novel in America. New Haven: Yale University Press, 1966.

Brawley, Benjamin. Negro Builders and Heroes. Chapel Hill: University of North Carolina Press, 1937.

_____. Negro Genius. New York: Dodd, Mead, 1940.

_____. The Negro in Literature and Art. New York: Duffield, 1930.

_____. Paul Laurence Dunbar: Poet of His People. Chapel Hill: University of North Carolina Press, 1936.

Candela, Gregory L. "We Wear the Mask: Irony in Dunbar's The Sport of the Gods." American Literature 48 (March 1976): 60-72.

Daniel, T. W. "Paul Laurence Dunbar and the Democratic Ideal." Negro History Bulletin 6 (June 1943): 206-208.

Davis, Arthur P. From the Dark Tower: Afro-American Writers 1900 to 1960. Washington, D.C.: Howard University Press, 1974.

Dreer, Herman, ed. American Literature by Negro Authors. New York: Macmillan, 1950.

Dunbar, Alice, W. C. Scarborough, and Reverdy C. Ransom. Paul Laurence Dunbar: Poet Laureate of the Negro Race. Philadelphia: A. M. E. Church Review, 1914.

Gayle, Addison, Jr. Oak and Ivy. New York: Doubleday, 1971.

_____. The Way of the New World: The Black Novel in America. Garden City, N.Y.: Anchor Press/Doubleday, 1975.

Gross, Theodore L. The Heroic Ideal in American Literature. New York: Free Press, 1971.

Hughes, Carl M. The Negro Novelists 1940-1950. New York: Citadel Press, 1953.

Larsen, Charles R. "The Novels of Paul Laurence Dunbar. Phylon 29 (Fall 1968): 257-271.

Lawson, Victor. Dunbar Critically Examined. Washington, D.C.: Associated, 1941.

Lee, A. Robert. "The Fiction of Paul Laurence Dunbar." Negro American Literature Forum 8 (1974): 166-172.

Lucas, Doris Marie. "Patterns of Accommodation and Protest in the Fiction of Paul Laurence Dunbar." Ph.D. Dissertation, University of Illinois at Urbana-Champaign, 1973.

Martin, Jay. "'Jump Back Honey': Paul Laurence Dunbar and the Rediscovery of American Political Traditions." The Bulletin of the Midwest Modern Language Association 7 (Spring 1974): 40-51.

_____, ed. A Singer in the Dawn: A Reinterpretation of Paul Laurence Dunbar. New York: Dodd, Mead, 1974.

Metcalf, Eugene W., Jr. "The Letters to Paul and Alice Dunbar: A Private History." Ph.D. Dissertation, University of California, Irvine, 1974.

_____. Paul Laurence Dunbar: A Bibliography. Metuchen, N.J.: Scarecrow Press, 1975.

Mootry, Maria Katella. "Studies in Black Pastoral: Five Afro-American Writers." Ph.D. Dissertation, Northwestern University, 1974.

New York Times, 10 February 1906, sec. 1, p. 4. (Obituary.)

Rosenblatt, Roger. Black Fiction. Cambridge: Harvard University Press, 1974.

Rush, Theressa Gunnels, Carol Fairbanks Myers, and Esther Spring Arata. Black American Writers Past and Present. Metuchen, N.J.: Scarecrow Press, 1975.

Schraufnagel, Noel. From Apology to Protest: The Black American Novel. DeLand, Florida: Everett/Edwards, 1973.

Wiggins, Linda Keck. "Den of a Literary Lion." Voice of the Negro 3 (January 1905): 50-53.

_____. The Life and Works of Paul Laurence Dunbar. New York: Dodd, Mead, 1907.

Reviews

The Sport of the Gods
    Publishers' Weekly, 10 August 1970, p. 58.

DUNBAR-NELSON, Alice Moore (Alice Ruth [Moore] Dunbar Nelson)

Short Fiction

(Collections):
    The Goodness of St. Rocque and Other Stories. New York: Dodd, Mead, 1899. Gaithersburg, Md.: Consortium Press; Freeport, N.Y.: Books for Libraries. Includes:
        "By the Bayou St. John."
        "A Carnival Jangle."
        "The Fisherman of Pass Christian."
        "The Goodness of Saint Rocque."
        "La Juanita."
        "Mr. Baptiste."
        "M'Sieu Fortier's Violin."
        "Odalie."
        "The Praline Woman."

> "Sister Josepha."
> "TiTee."
> "Tony's Wife."
> "When the Bayou Overflows."

Violets and Other Tales. Boston: The Monthly Review, 1895.
"The Ball Dress." Leslie's Weekly, 12 December 1901.
"Hope Deferred." Crisis 8 (September 1914): 238-242.
"The Little Mother." Brooklyn Standard Union, 7 March 1900.
"Science in Frenchtown--A Short Story." Saturday Evening Mail,
Magazine Section, 7 December 1912, pp. 8-9, 26, 27.

Biography and Criticism

"Alice Dunbar-Nelson." Negro History Bulletin 31 (April 1968):
5-6.
"Biography of Alice Dunbar-Nelson." Negro History Bulletin 31
(April 1968): 5.
Ford, Nick Aaron. "Alice Dunbar-Nelson." In Notable American
Women, 1660-1950. Edited by Edward T. James. Cambridge,
Mass.: Harvard-Belknap Series, 1971.
Gayle, Addison, Jr. Oak and Ivy. New York: Doubleday, 1971.
Holly, Allie Miller. "Alice Ruth Moore Dunbar-Nelson: The In-
dividual." Biographical Sketch presented at the Delta Sigma
Theta Conference, New Orleans, 2-5 June 1968.
_____. "The Vision Has Lighted the World." Delta 60 (Novem-
ber 1972): 46-47.
Journal of Negro History 21 (January 1936): 95-96. (Obituary.)
"Mrs. Alice Ruth Dunbar-Nelson." Who's Who in Colored America,
1933-37.
Rush, Theressa Gunnels, Carol Fairbanks Myers, and Esther Spring
Arata. Black American Writers Past and Present. Metuchen,
N.J.: Scarecrow Press, 1975.
Williams, Ora. "Works by and about Alice Ruth (Moore) Dunbar-
Nelson: A Bibliography." CLA Journal 19 (March 1976):
322-326.

Reviews

Violets and Other Tales
The Monthly Review 3 (July 1895): 157-158.

DUNCAN, Pearl

Short Fiction

"Rendezvous with G. T." Essence 5 (April 1975): 42-43, 87.

DUNHAM, Katherine

Novels

Kasamance. Chicago: Third Press, 1974.

A Touch of Innocence. New York: Harcourt Brace, 1959; London:
Cassell, 1960; New York: Harcourt Brace Jovanovich, 1969.
Excerpt in Hill Soon One Morning.

Short Fiction

"Afternoon Into Night." In Hughes, The Best Short Stories of Negro
Writers.

Biography and Criticism

Biemiller, Ruth. "Black Academy of Arts and Letters." Black
World 21 (November 1971): 68-71.
Ebony 2 (January 1947): 14-18, 3 (March 1948): 36; 10 (December
1954): 83-86.
"Katherine Dunham." Crisis 57 (June 1950): 344.
Mazer, Gwen. "Katherine Dunham." Essence 7 (December 1976):
69, 116, 119-120.
Rush, Theressa Gunnels, Carol Fairbanks Myers, and Esther Spring
Arata. Black American Writers Past and Present. Metuchen,
N.J.: Scarecrow Press, 1975.

Reviews

Kasamance
Dance Magazine 49 (October 1975): 83.
Ebony 30 (February 1975): 26.
Kirkus, 15 December 1974, p. 1303.
Publishers' Weekly, 20 May 1974, p. 64.
School Library Journal 21 (January 1975): 44.
A Touch of Innocence
Booklist, 1 September 1959, p. 10; 15 November 1959, p. 179.
Bookmark 19 (November 1959): 33.
Butcher, Fanny. Chicago Sunday Tribune, 25 October 1959,
p. 4.
Farjeon, Annabel. Dance Magazine 35 (March 1961): 22.
_____ . New Statesman, 29 October 1960, p. 657.
Guardian, 18 November 1960, p. 6.
Hughes, Langston. New York Herald Tribune Book Review, 25
October 1959, p. 9.
Janeway, Elizabeth. New York Times Book Review, 8 Novem-
ber 1959, p. 54.
Kirkus, 15 August 1959, p. 624.
Mayer, G. L. Library Journal, 1 October 1959, p. 3026.
Mortimer, John. Spectator, 25 November 1960, p. 852.
New Yorker, 17 October 1959, p. 227.
Times Literary Supplement, 25 November 1960, p. 764.
Todd, Arthur. Saturday Review of Literature, 5 December 1959,
p. 38.
Winslow, Henry F. Crisis 67 (February 1960): 118.

DURANT, E. Elliott

Novel

The Princess of Naragpur, or a Daughter of Allah. New York: Grafton Press, 1928.

DURHAM, John S.

Novelette

"Diane: Princess of Haiti." Lippincott's Monthly Magazine, April 1902.

Biography and Criticism

Rush, Theressa Gunnels, Carol Fairbanks Myers, and Esther Spring Arata. Black American Writers Past and Present. Metuchen, N.J.: Scarecrow Press, 1975.

EARLE, Victoria (Victoria Earle Matthews)

Novel

Aunt Lindy, A Story Founded on Real Life. New York: Press of J. J. Little, 1893.

ECHEWA, T. Obinkaram

Short Fiction

"Return of Tarkwa." Essence 7 (October 1976): 76-77, 121, 123-124.

EDWARDS, Junius

Novel

If We Must Die. New York: Doubleday, 1963; excerpt in Adams, Conn, and Slepian, Afro-American Literature: Fiction.

Short Fiction

"Duel with the Clock." In Hughes, The Best Short Stories by Negro Writers.
"Liars Don't Qualify." King, Black Short Story Anthology.
"Mother Dear and Daddy." In Adams, Conn and Slepian, Afro-American Literature: Fiction; Margolies, A Native Sons Reader; Williams, Beyond the Angry Black.

Biography and Criticism

Schraufnagel, Noel. From Apology to Protest. DeLand, Fla.:
Everett/Edwards, 1973.

Reviews

If We Must Die
Berry, Faith. Crisis 70 (October 1963): 508-509.
Christian Century, 7 August 1963, p. 983.
Donoghue, D. New Statesman, 2 July 1965, p. 19.
Elman, Richard. New York Herald Tribune Books, 11 August
1963, p. 4.
Friedman, Joseph. New York Times Book Review, 4 August
1963, p. 4.
Giles, Louise. Library Journal, 1 September 1963, p. 3101.
Hicks, Granville. Saturday Review, 3 August 1963, p. 17.
Interracial Review 36 (Summer 1963): 177.
Observer, 23 May 1965, p. 27.
Show 3 (August 1963): 39.
Times Literary Supplement, 1 July 1965, p. 563.

EDWARDS, S. W. see SUBLETTE, Walter

ELLIS, George Washington

Novel

The Leopard's Claw. New York: International Author's Assoc.,
1917; New York: AMS Press, 1970.

ELLISON, Ralph Waldo

Novel

Invisible Man. New York: Random, 1952; New York: Modern Li-
brary, 1963. Excerpts in Horizon 93 (October 1947): 104-117;
The Magazine of the Year 2 (January 1948): 14-32; Angus and
Angus, Contemporary American Short Stories; Boynton and Mack,
Introduction to the Short Story, rev. ed.; Chapman, Black
Voices; Coyle, The Young Man in American Literature; Davis
and Redding, Cavalcade; Dietrich and Sundell, The Art of Fic-
tion, 2nd ed.; Ford, Black Insights; Gold, The Human Commit-
ment; Gold and Stevenson, Stories of Modern America; Gross,
A Nation of Nations; Karl and Hamalian, the naked i; Long and
Collier, Afro-American Writing; Margolies, A Native Sons
Reader; Miller, Blackamerican Literature; Mizener, Modern
Short Stories; Patterson, An Introduction to Black Literature in
America; Scholes, Some Modern Writers; Stein and Walters,
The Southern Experience in Short Fiction; Warren and Erskine,
A New Southern Harvest; Williams, The Angry Black.

Short Fiction

"Afternoon." In Negro Story Magazine 1 (March-April 1945): 3-8;
  Partisan Review 19 (January 1952): 31-40.
"And Hickman Arrives." Noble Savage 1 (1956): 5-29; also in
  Barksdale and Kinnamon, Black Writers of America.
"The Birthmark." New Masses, 2 July 1940, pp. 16-17; Negro
  World Digest 1 (November 1940): 61-65; Negro Story Magazine,
  1945; O'Brien, The Best Short Stories, 1941.
"Cadillac Flambé." In Solotaroff, American Review 16.
"A Coupla Scalped Indians." New World Writing, No. 9. New
  York: The New American Library of World Literature, 1956;
  also in King, Black Short Story Anthology.
"Did You Ever Dream Lucky?" New World Writing, No. 5. New
  York: The New American Library of World Literature, 1954;
  also in Flower, Counterparts.
"Flying Home." In Adams, Conn and Slepian, Afro-American Lit-
  erature: Fiction; Casmier and Souder, Coming Together; Da-
  vis, Ten Modern Masters, 3rd. ed.; Fenton, Best Short Stories
  of World War II; Gibson and Anselment, Black and White;
  Hughes, The Best Short Stories by Negro Writers; Kissin, Sto-
  ries in Black and White; Nagel, Vision and Value; Schneider, et
  al., The Range of Literature: Fiction, 3rd ed.; Seaver, Cross-
  Section; Sherrill and Robertson-Rose, Four Elements; Somer,
  Narrative Experience; Stanford, I, Too, Sing America; Stein
  and Walters, The Southern Experience in Short Fiction; Timko,
  29 Short Stories.
"In a Strange Country." Tomorrow 3 (July 1944): 41-44; also in
  Murray and Thomas, Major Black Writers; Sterling, I Have
  Seen War.
"It Always Breaks Out." Partisan Review 30 (Spring 1963): 13-28.
"Juneteenth." Quarterly Review of Literature 13 (1965): 262-276.
"King of the Bingo Game." Tomorrow 4 (November 1944): 29-33;
  also in Adams, Conn and Slepian, Afro-American Literature:
  Fiction; Albrecht, The World of Short Fiction; Antico and Hazel-
  rigg, Insight through Fiction; Carson and Carson, The Impact of
  Fiction; Casmier and Souder, Coming Together; Goldstone, et al.,
  Points of Departure; Klein and Pack, Short Stories; Minor and
  Wilson, Three Stances of Modern Fiction; Morse, The Choices
  of Fiction; Pickering, Fiction 100; Stansbury, Impact; Tytell and
  Jaffe, Affinities.
"Mister Toussan." New Masses, 4 November 1941, pp. 19-20;
  Negro Story 1 (July-August 1944): 37-41; also in Turner,
  Black American Literature: Fiction.
"The Roof, the Steeple and the People." Quarterly Review of Lit-
  erature 10 (September 1960): 115-128.
"Slick Gonna Learn." Direction 2 (September 1939): 10-11, 14, 16.
"Song of Innocence--Excerpt from a Novel in Progress." Iowa Re-
  view 1 (Spring 1970): 30-40.
"That I Had the Wings." Common Ground 3 (Summer 1943): 30-37.

Biography and Criticism

(Collections):

Cooke, M. G., ed. Modern Black Novelists: A Collection of Critical Essays. Englewood Cliffs, N.J.: Prentice-Hall, 1971.

Gibson, Donald B., ed. Five Black Writers. New York: New York University Press, 1970.

Gottesman, Ronald, ed. Studies in "Invisible Man." Columbus, Ohio: Charles E. Merrill, 1971.

Hemenway, Robert, ed. The Black Novelist. Columbus: Charles E. Merrill, 1970.

Hersey, John, ed. Ralph Ellison: A Collection of Critical Essays. Englewood Cliffs, N.J.: Prentice-Hall, 1974.

Reilly, John M., ed. Twentieth Century Interpretations of "Invisible Man": A Collection of Critical Essays. Englewood Cliffs, N.J.: Prentice-Hall, 1970.

Allen, Michael. "Some Examples of Faulknerian Rhetoric in Ellison's Invisible Man." In The Black American Writer, vol. 1, pp. 143-151. Edited by C. W. E. Bigsby, DeLand, Fla.: Everett/Edwards, 1969.

Alter, Robert. "The Apocalyptic Temper." Commentary 41 (June 1966): 61-66.

Anderson, J. "Profiles." New Yorker, 22 November 1976, pp. 55-56.

Ashour, Radwa M. "The Search for a Black Poetics: A Study of Afro-American Critical Writings." Ph.D. Dissertation, University of Massachusetts, 1975.

Baker, Houston A., Jr. "Forgotten Prototype." Virginia Quarterly 49 (Summer 1973): 433-449.

_____. Singers of Daybreak: Studies in Black American Literature. Washington, D.C.: Howard University Press, 1974.

Barksdale, Richard K. "Black America and the Mask of Comedy." In The Comic Imagination in American Literature, pp. 349-360. Edited by Louis Rubin, Jr. New Brunswick, N.J.: Rutgers University Press, 1973.

Baumbach, Jonathan. "Nightmare of a Native Son: Ellison's Invisible Man." Critique 6 (Spring 1963): 48-65; also in Cooke, Modern Black Novelists; Gibson, Five Black Writers; Reilly, Twentieth Century Interpretations.

Bell, Bernard W. The Folk Roots of Contemporary Afro-American Poetry. Detroit: Broadside Press, 1974.

Bell, J. D. "Ellison's Invisible Man." Explicator 29 (1970): Item 19.

Bellow, Saul. "Man Underground." In Hersey, Ralph Ellison.

Bennett, John Z. "The Race and the Runner: Ellison's Invisible Man." Xavier University Studies 5 (March 1966): 12-26.

Bennett, Stephen B., and William W. Nichols. "Violence in Afro-American Fiction: An Hypothesis." Modern Fiction Studies 17 (Summer 1971): 221-228; also in Hersey, Ralph Ellison.

Bloch, Alice. "Sight Imagery in Invisible Man." English Journal 55 (November 1966): 1019-21, 1024.

Bone, Robert A. The Negro Novel in America. New Haven: Yale

University Press, 1966.

_____. "Ralph Ellison and the Uses of Imagination." Tri-Quar-
terly 6 (1966): 39-54; also in Cooke, Modern Black Novelists;
Gottesman, Studies in "Invisible Man"; Reilly, Twentieth Century Interpretations of "Invisible Man".

Bontemps, Arna. "Recent Writing by Negroes." In Literature in
the Modern World, pp. 119-122. Edited by William Griffin.
Nashville, Tenn.: George Peabody College for Teachers, 1954.

Boskin, Joseph. "The Life and Death of Sambo: Overview of an
Historical Hang-up." Journal of Popular Culture 4 (Winter
1971): 647-657.

Boulgar, James D. "Puritan Allegory in Four Modern Novels."
Thought 44 (Autumn 1969): 413-432.

Breaux, Elwyn Ellison. "Comic Elements in Selected Prose Works
by James Baldwin, Ralph Ellison, and Langston Hughes."
Ed.D. Dissertation, Oklahoma State University, 1971.

Britt, David Dobbs. "The Image of the White Man in the Fiction
of Langston Hughes, Richard Wright, James Baldwin, and Ralph
Ellison." Ph.D. Dissertation, Emory University, 1968.

Brown, L. L. "The Deep Pit." In Reilly, Twentieth Century Interpretations of "Invisible Man."

Brown, Lloyd W. "Black Entitles: Names as Symbols in Afro-
American Literature." Studies in Black Literature 1 (September 1970): 16-44.

_____. "Ralph Ellison's Exhorters: The Role of Rhetoric in
Invisible Man." CLA Journal 13 (March 1970): 289-303.

Brumm, Ursula. "The Figure of Christ in American Literature."
Partisan Review 24 (1957): 403-413.

Bryant, Jerry H. "Wright, Ellison, Baldwin--Exorcising the De-
mon." Phylon 37 (June 1976): 174-188.

Bucco, Martin. "Ellison's Invisible West." Western American Literature 10 (November 1975): 237-238.

Burke, William Martin. "Modern Black Fiction and the Literature
of Oppression." Ph.D. Dissertation, University of Oregon,
1971.

Callow, James T., and Robert J. Reilly. Guide to American Literature from Emily Dickinson to the Present. New York:
Barnes & Noble, 1977.

Cannon, Steve, Lennox Raphael and James Thompson. "A Very
Stern Discipline." Harper's Magazine 234 (March 1967): 76-95.

Carson, David Loeser. "Ralph Ellison: His Fiction and Its Background." Ph.D. Dissertation, University of Delaware, 1974.

_____. "Ralph Ellison Twenty Years After." Studies in Ameri-
can Fiction 1 (Spring 1973): 1-23. (Interview.)

Cash, Earl A. "The Narrators in Invisible Man and Notes from
Underground: Brothers in Spirit." CLA Journal 16 (June 1973):
505-507.

Chaffee, Patricia. "Slippery Ground: Ralph Ellison's Bingo Player."
Negro American Literature Forum 10 (Spring 1976): 23-24.

Chargois, Josephine Asbury. "Two Views of Black Alienation: A
Comparative Study of Chinua Achebe and Ralph Ellison." Ph.D.
Dissertation, Indiana University, 1974.

Cheshire, Ardner R., Jr. "Invisible Man and the Life of Dialogue."

CLA Journal 20 (September 1976): 19-34.

Chester, Alfred, and Vilma Howard. "The Art of Fiction: An Interview." Paris Review No. 8 (Spring 1955): 54-71; also in Writers at Work, pp. 316-334. Edited by George Plimpton. New York: Viking Press, 1963; Ellison's Shadow and Act, pp. 167-183. New York: Random House, 1964.

Chisolm, Lawrence Washington. "Signifying Everything." In Hersey, Ralph Ellison.

Christian, Barbara. "Ralph Ellison: A Critical Study." In Black Expression, pp. 353-365. Edited by Addison Gayle, Jr. New York: Weybright and Talley, 1969; also in The American Novel: Background Readings and Criticism, pp. 512-525. Edited by Christof Wegelin. New York: Free Press, 1972.

Clarke, John Henrik. "The Visible Dimensions of Invisible Man." Black World 20 (December 1970): 27-30.

Clipper, Lawrence J. "Folklore and Mythic Elements in Invisible Man." CLA Journal 13 (March 1970): 229-241.

Collier, Eugenia W. "The Nightmare Truth of an Invisible Man." Black World 20 (December 1970): 12-19.

Contemporary Authors, 11/12.

Cooke, Michael G. "The Descent into the Underworld and Modern Black Fiction." Iowa Review 5 (1974): 72-90.

Corry, John. "An American Novelist Who Sometimes Teaches." The New York Times Sunday Magazine, 20 November 1966, pp. 54-55, 179-180.

_____. "Profile of an American Novelist." Black World 20 (December 1970): 116-125.

Covo, Jacqueline. The Blinking Eye: Ralph Waldo Ellison and His American, French, German, and Italian Critics, 1952-1971. Metuchen, N.J.: Scarecrow Press, 1974.

Cowan, Kathryn Osburn. "Black/White Stereotypes in the Fiction of Richard Wright, James Baldwin and Ralph Ellison." Ph.D. Dissertation, St. Louis University, 1972.

Cowley, Malcolm. The Literary Situation. New York: Viking Press, 1954.

Current Biography Yearbook, 1968.

Daiches, David. "Writers' Shop Talk." Saturday Review, 16 November 1957, pp. 19-20.

Davis, Arthur P. From the Dark Tower: Afro-American Writers 1900 to 1960. Washington, D.C.: Howard University Press, 1974.

Deutsch, Leonard J. "Affirmation in the Works of Ralph Waldo Ellison." Ph.D. Dissertation, Kent State University, 1972.

_____. "Ellison's Early Fiction." Negro American Literature Forum 7 (Summer 1973): 53-59.

Doyle, Mary Ellen. "In Need of Folk: The Alienated Protagonists of Ralph Ellison's Short Fiction." CLA Journal 19 (December 1975): 165-172.

Durham, Joyce Roberta. "The City in Recent American Literature: Black on White: A Study of Selected Writings by Bellow, Mailer, Ellison, Baldwin, and Writers of the Black Aesthetic." Ph.D. Dissertation, University of Maryland, 1974.

Eisinger, Chester E. Fiction of the Forties. Chicago: The University of Chicago Press, 1963.

Ellison, Ralph. "February." Saturday Review 38 (1 January 1955): 25.

_____. 'On Initiation Rites and Power: Ralph Ellison Speaks at West Point." Edited by Robert H. Moore. Contemporary Literature 15 (Spring 1974): 165-186.

_____. "'Tell It Like It Is, Baby.'" Nation 20 (September 1965): 129-136.

_____. "The World and the Jug." In Ellison's Shadow and Act. New York: Random House, 1974; also in Gibson, Five Black Writers.

_____, William Styron, Robert Penn Warren, and C. Van Woodward. "The Uses of History in Fiction." Southern Literary Journal 1 (Spring 1969): 57-90.

Emerson, O. B. "Cultural Nationalism in Afro-American Literature." In The Cry of Home, pp. 222-227. Edited by H. Ernest Lewald. Knoxville: University of Tennessee Press, 1972.

Fabre, Michael. The Unfinished Quest of Richard Wright. New York: Morrow, 1973.

Fass, Barbara. "Rejection of Paternalism: Hawthorne's 'My Kinsman Major Molineaux' and Ellison's Invisible Man." CLA Journal 14 (March 1971): 317-323.

Fischer, Russell G. "Invisible Man as History." CLA Journal 17 (1974): 338-367.

Fontaine, William T. "The Negro Continuum from Dominant Wish to Collective Act." African Forum 3 (Spring and Summer 1968): 63-96.

Ford, Nick Aaron. "The Ambivalence of Ralph Ellison." Black World 20 (December 1970): 5-9.

_____. "Four Popular Negro Novelists." Phylon 15 (March 1954): 29-39.

Forrest, Leon. "A Conversation with Ralph Ellison." Muhammad Speaks, 15 December 1972, pp. 29-31.

_____. "Racial History as a Clue to the Action in Invisible Man." Muhammad Speaks, 15 September 1972, pp. 28-30.

Foster, Frances S. "The Black and White Masks of Frantz Fanon and Ralph Ellison." Black Academy Review 1 (1970): 46-58.

Fraiberg, Selma. "Two Modern Incest Heroes." Partisan Review 28 (September-October 1961): 646-661; also in Reilly, Twentieth Century Interpretations of 'Invisible Man."

Frohock, Wilbur M. Strangers to This Ground: Cultural Diversity in Contemporary American Writing. Dallas: Southern Methodist University Press, 1961.

Furay, Michael. "Négritude--a Romantic Myth." New Republic, 2 July 1966, pp. 32-35.

Gayle, Addison, Jr. The Way of the New World: The Black Novel in America. Garden City, N.Y.: Anchor Press/Doubleday, 1975.

Geismar, Maxwell. "The Postwar Generation in Arts and Letters." Saturday Review, 14 March 1953, pp. 11-12. Reprinted, with slight modification, in Geismar's American Moderns: From Rebellion to Conformity. New York: Hill & Wang, 1958.

Geller, Allen. "An Interview with Ralph Ellison." Tamarack Re-

view no. 32 (Summer 1964): 3-24; also in Bigsby's The Black
American Writer, vol. 1. DeLand, Fla.: Everett/Edwards,
1969.

_____. "Ralph Ellison and James Baldwin." In The Politics of
the Twentieth Century Novelists, pp. 307-320. Edited by George
A. Panichas. New York: Hawthorn Books, 1971.

Glicksberg, Charles I. "The Symbolism of Vision." Southwest Review 39 (1954): 259-265; also in Reilly, Twentieth Century Interpretations of "Invisible Man."

Goede, William. "On Lower Frequencies: The Buried Men in
Wright and Ellison." Modern Fiction Studies 15 (Winter 1969-
1970): 483-501.

Graham, John and George Garrett. The Writer's Voice: Conversations with Contemporary Writers. New York: Morrow, 1973.

Gray, Valerie Bonita. "Invisible Man's Literary Heritage: Benito
Cereno and Moby Dick." Ph. D. Dissertation, The Ohio State
University, 1976.

Greenberg, Alvin. "Ironic Alternatives in the World of the Contemporary Novel." In American Dreams, American Nightmares, pp.
177-186. Edited by David Madden. Carbondale: Southern Illinois University Press, 1970.

Griffin, Edward N. "Notes from a Clean, Well-Lighted Place:
Ralph Ellison's Invisible Man." Twentieth Century Literature
15 (October 1969): 129-144.

Griffith, Patricia Anne Thomas. "The Technoscape in the Modern
Novel: Aleksandr Solzhenitsyn's The First Circle and Ralph El-
lison's Invisible Man." Ph. D. Dissertation, University of
Southern California, 1976.

Gross, Theodore L. The Heroic Ideal in American Literature.
New York: Oxford University Press, 1971.

_____. "The Idealism of Negro Literature in America." Phylon
30 (Spring 1969): 5-10.

Grow, Lynn M. "The Dream Scenes of Invisible Man." Wichita
State University Bulletin 50 (1974): 3-12.

Guttman, Allen. "Focus on Ralph Ellison's Invisible Man." In
American Dreams, American Nightmares, pp. 188-196.
Edited by David Madden. Carbondale: Southern Illinois University Press, 1970; London and Amsterdam: Feffer & Simons,
1970.

Gvereschi, Edward. "Anticipations of Invisible Man: Ralph Ellison's
'King of the Bingo Game.'" Negro American Literature Forum
6 (Winter 1972): 122-124.

Gysin, Fritz. The Grotesque in American Negro Fiction. The
Cooper Monographs on English and American Literature no. 22.
Basel, Switzerland: Francke Verlag Bern, 1975.

Haslam, Gerald W. "Two Traditions in Afro-American Literature."
Research Studies 37 (September 1969): 183-193.

Hassan, Ihab. Contemporary American Literature 1945-1972: An
Introduction. New York: Frederick Ungar, 1973.

_____. "The Novel of Outrage: A Minority Voice in Postwar
American Fiction." American Scholar 34 (Spring 1965): 239-
253. Also in The American Novel Since World War II, pp.
196-209. Edited by Marcus Klein. New York: Fawcett, 1969.

_____. Radical Innocence: Studies in the Contemporary Novel.
Princeton, N.J.: Princeton University Press, 1961.
Havemann, Carol. "The Fool as Mentor in Modern American Para-
bles of Entrapment: Ken Kesey's One Flew Over the Cuckoo's
Nest, Joseph Heller's Catch-22 and Ralph Ellison's Invisible
Man." Ph.D. Dissertation, Rice University, 1971.
Hayashi, Susanna. "Dark Odyssey: Descent into the Underworld in
Black American Fiction." Ph.D. Dissertation, Indiana Univer-
sity, 1971.
Hays, Peter L. "The Incest Theme in Invisible Man." Western
Humanities Review 23 (Autumn 1969): 142-159.
_____. The Limping Hero: Grotesques in Literature. New
York: New York University, 1971.
Hedin, Anne Miller. "The Self as History: Studies in Adam,
Faulkner, Ellison, Belyj, Pasternak." Ph.D. Dissertation,
University of Virginia, 1975.
Heermance, J. Noel. "A White Critic's Viewpoint: The Modern
Negro Novel." Negro Digest 13 (May 1964): 66-76.
Hoffman, Frederick J. The Modern Novel in America, rev. ed.
Chicago: Henry Regnery, 1963.
Horowitz, Ellin. "The Rebirth of the Artist." In On Contemporary
Literature, pp. 330-346. Edited by Richard Kostelanetz. New
York: Avon, 1964; also in Reilly's Twentieth Century Interpre-
tation of "Invisible Man."
Horowitz, Floyd R. "Enigma of Ellison's Intellectual Man." CLA
Journal 7 (December 1963): 126-132.
_____. "An Experimental Confession from a Reader of Invisible
Man." CLA Journal 13 (March 1970): 304-314.
_____. "Ralph Ellison's Modern Version of Brer Bear and Brer
Rabbit in Invisible Man." Midcontinental American Studies Jour-
nal 4 (Fall 1963): 21-27; also in Reilly's Twentieth Century In-
terpretations of "Invisible Man."
Howard, David C. "Points in Defense of Ellison's Invisible Man."
Notes on Contemporary Literature 1 (January 1971): 13-14.
Howe, Irving. "Black Boys and Native Sons." Dissent 10 (1963):
353-368; also in Gibson's Five Black Writers; Hersey, Ralph
Ellison; Reilly, Twentieth Century Interpretations of "Invisible
Man."
_____. "A Reply to Ralph Ellison." New Leader 3 (February
1964): 12-14.
Hughes, Carl. The Negro Novelist: A Discussion of the Writings
of American Negro Novelists 1940-1950. New York: Citadel
Press, 1953.
Hux, Samuel Holland. "American Myth and Existential Vision: The
Indigenous Existentialism of Mailer, Bellow, Styron, and Elli-
son." Ph.D. Dissertation, University of Connecticut, 1965.
Hyman, Stanley Edgar. "The Folk Tradition." Partisan Review 25
(Spring 1958): 197-211; also in Hyman's The Promised End.
New York: World, 1963.
Isaacs, Harold R. "Five Writers and Their African Ancestors."
Part II. Phylon 21 (Winter 1960): 317-322.
Jackson, Blyden. "A Golden Mean for the Negro Novel." CLA
Journal 3 (September 1959): 81-87.

Johnson, Abby Arthur. "Birds of Passage: Flight Imagery in Invisible Man." Studies in the Twentieth Century No. 14 (Fall 1974): 91-104.

Kaiser, Ernest. "A Critical Look at Ellison's Fiction and at Social and Literary Criticism By and About the Author." Black World 20 (December 1970): 53-97.

Kazin, Alfred. "Absurdity as Contemporary Style." Mediterranean Review 1 (Spring 1971): 39-46.

_____. "Brothers Crying Out for More Access to Life." Saturday Review, 2 October 1971, pp. 33-35.

_____. Contemporaries. Boston: Little, Brown, 1962.

Kent, George E. Blackness and the Adventure of Western Culture. Chicago: Third World Press, 1972.

_____. "Ethnic Impact in American Literature: Reflections on a Course." CLA Journal 11 (September 1967): 24-37.

_____. "Ralph Ellison and Afro-American Folk and Cultural Tradition." CLA Journal 13 (March 1970: 265-276; also in Hersey, Ralph Ellison; Kent, Blackness and the Adventure of Western Culture.

Killinger, John. The Fragile Presence: Transcendence in Modern Literature. Philadelphia: Fortress Press, 1973.

Kist, E. M. "A Langian Analysis of Blackness in Ralph Ellison's Invisible Man." Studies in Black Literature 7 (Spring 1976): 19-23.

Klotman, Phyllis Rauch. Another Man Gone: The Black Runner in Contemporary Afro-American Literature. Port Washington, N.Y.: Kennikat Press, 1977.

_____. "The Running Man as Metaphor in Ellison's Invisible Man." CLA Journal 13 (March 1970): 277-288.

Knox, George. "The Totentanz in Ellison's Invisible Man." Fabula 12 (1971): 168-178.

Kochanek, Patricia Sharpe. "In Pursuit of Proteus: A Piagetian Approach to the Structure of the Grotesque in American Fiction of the Fifties." Ph.D. Dissertation, The Pennsylvania State University, 1972.

Kostelanetz, Richard. "The Politics of Ellison's Booker: Invisible Man as Symbolic History." Chicago Review 19 (1967): 5-26; also in Hemenway, The Black Novelist.

_____. "Ralph Ellison: Novelist as Brown-Skinned Aristocrat." Shenandoah 20 (Summer 1969): 56-77; also in Kostelanetz' Master Minds: Portraits of Contemporary Artists and Intellectuals. New York: Macmillan, 1969.

Kugelmass, Harold. "The Search for Identity: The Development of the Protean Model of Self in Contemporary American Fiction." Ph.D. Dissertation, University of Oregon, 1973.

Lane, James B. "Underground to Manhood: Ralph Ellison's Invisible Man." Negro American Literature Forum 7 (Summer 1973): 64.

LeClaire, Thomas. "The Blind Leading the Blind: Wright's Native Son and a Brief Reference to Ellison's Invisible Man." CLA Journal 13 (March 1970): 315-320.

Lee, A. Robert. "Sight and Mask: Ralph Ellison's Invisible Man." Negro American Literature Forum 4 (March 1970): 22-23.

Lee, L. L. "The Proper Self: Ralph Ellison's Invisible Man."
Descant 10 (Spring 1966): 38-48.
Lehan, Richard. A Dangerous Crossing. Carbondale: Southern
Illinois University, 1973.
_____. "Existentialism in Recent American Fiction: The Demo-
nic Quest." Texas Studies in Literature and Language 1 (Sum-
mer 1959): 181-202.
_____. "The Strange Silence of Ralph Ellison." California Eng-
lish Journal 1 (Spring 1965): 63-68; partly reprinted in Reilly,
Twentieth Century Interpretations of "Invisible Man."
Levant, Howard. "Aspiraling We Should Go." Midcontinent Ameri-
can Studies Journal 4 (Fall 1963): 3-20.
Lewis, Richard W. B. The American Adam. Chicago: University
of Chicago Press, 1955.
_____. "Recent Fiction: Picaro and Pilgrim." In A Time of
Harvest, pp. 144-153. Edited by Robert E. Spiller. New
York: Hill & Wang, 1962.
_____. Trials of the Word: Essays in American Literature and
the Humanistic Tradition. New Haven: Yale University Press,
1965.
Lieber, T. M. "Ralph Ellison and the Metaphor of Invisibility in
Black Literary Tradition." American Quarterly 24 (March
1972): 86-100.
Lieberman, Marcia R. "Moral Innocents: Ellison's Invisible Man
and Candide." CLA Journal 15 (September 1971): 64-79.
Lillard, Stewart. "Ellison's Ambitious Scope in Invisible Man."
English Journal 58 (September 1969): 833-839.
Lindberg, J. "Black Aesthetic: Minority or Mainstream?" North
American Review 260 (Winter 1975): 48-52.
Littlejohn, David. Black on White: A Critical Survey of Writing
by American Negroes. New York: Viking Press, 1966.
Long, Madeleine J. "Sartrean Themes in Contemporary American
Literature." Ph.D. Dissertation, Columbia University, 1967.
Ludington, Charles T., Jr. "Protest and Anti-Protest: Ralph El-
lison." Southern Humanities Review 4 (Winter 1970): 31-39.
Ludwig, Jack B. Recent American Novelists. University of Min-
nesota Pamphlets on American Writers, no. 22. Minneapolis:
University of Minnesota Press, 1962.
McCarthy, Colman. "Thinkers and Their Thoughts (III): Ralph El-
lison and the Value of Tradition and Culture." The Washington
Post, 21 November 1970, p. A14.
McConnell, Frank D. "Black Words and Black Becoming." Yale
Review 63 (Winter 1974): 193-210.
McPherson, James Alan. "Indivisible Man." Atlantic 226 (Decem-
ber 1970): 45-60 (Interview); also in Hersey, Ralph Ellison.
Major, Clarence. "Open Letters: A Column" American Poetry
Review 2 (November/December 1973): 17.
Marcus, Steven. "American Negro in Search of Identity." Com-
mentary 16 (November 1953): 456-463.
Margolies, Edward. Native Sons: A Critical Study of Twentieth-
Century Negro American Authors. Philadelphia, Pa.: J. B.
Lippincott, 1968.
Mason, Clifford. "Ralph Ellison and the Underground Man." Black

World 20 (December 1970): 20-26.
Maund, Alfred. "The Negro Novelist and the Contemporary Scene."
   Chicago Jewish Forum 12 (Fall 1954): 28-34.
Maxwell, Joan Lovell Bauerly. "Themes of Redemption in Two Ma-
   jor American Writers, Ralph Ellison and Richard Wright."
   Ph. D. Dissertation, University of Oregon, 1976.
May, John R. "Images of Apocalypse in the Black Novel." Rena-
   scence 23 (Autumn 1970): 31-45.
_____. Toward a New Earth: Apocalypse in the American Novel.
   Notre Dame: University of Notre Dame, 1972.
Mengeling, Marvin E. "Whitman and Ellison: Older Symbols in a
   Modern Mainstream." Walt Whitman Review 12 (September
   1966): 67-70.
Miller, Stuart. The Picaresque Novel. Cleveland, Ohio: Case
   Western Reserve University, 1967.
Mitchell, Louis D. "Invisibility: Permanent or Resurrective."
   CLA Journal 17 (1974): 379-386.
_____, and Henry J. Stauffenberg. "Ellison's B. P. Rinehart:
   'Spiritual Technologist.'" Negro American Literature Forum 9
   (Summer 1975): 51-52.
Mitra, Barun. "The Art of Ralph Ellison." Indian Journal of Eng-
   lish Studies 13 (1972): 155-160.
Mootry, Maria Katella. "Studies in Black Pastoral: Five Afro-
   American Writers." Ph. D. Dissertation, Northwestern Univer-
   sity, 1974.
Mueller, William R. Celebration of Life: Studies in Modern Fic-
   tion. New York: Sheed & Ward, 1972.
Murray, Albert. The Omni-Americans: New Perspectives on Black
   Experience and American Culture. New York: Outerbridge &
   Dienstfrey, 1970.
Myers, Carol Fairbanks. "Invisible Man as Existentialist Rebel."
   M. A. Thesis, University of Wisconsin-Eau Claire, 1971.
Nash, Russell W. "Stereotypes and Social Types in Ellison's In-
   visible Man." Sociological Quarterly 6 (Autumn 1965): 349-360.
Neal, Larry. "Ellison's Zoot Suit." Black World 20 (December
   1970): 31-52; also in Hersey, Ralph Ellison.
Nettlebeck, C. W. "From Inside Destitution: Céline's Bardamer and
   Ellison's Invisible Man." Southern Review: An Australian Jour-
   nal of Literary Studies 7 (1974): 246-253.
Nichols, William W. "Ralph Ellison's Black American Scholar."
   Phylon 31 (Spring 1970): 70-75.
Nower, Joyce. "The Tradition of Negro Literature in the United
   States." Negro American Literature Forum 3 (Spring 1969):
   5-12.
O'Brien, John. Interviews with Black Writers. New York: Live-
   right, 1973.
O'Daniel, Thurman B. "Image of Man as Portrayed by Ralph Elli-
   son." CLA Journal 10 (June 1967): 277-284; also in Gibson,
   Five Black Writers; Reilly, Twentieth Century Interpretations of
   "Invisible Man."
Olderman, Raymond M. "Ralph Ellison's Blues and Invisible Man."
   Wisconsin Studies in Contemporary Literature 7 (Summer 1966):
   142-159.

Palmo, Rosemary Helen Grebin. "The Double Motif in Literature: From Origins to an Examination of Three Modern American Novels." Ph.D. Dissertation, University of Wisconsin, 1972.

Parks, Gordon. "A Man Becomes Invisible: Invisible Man translated into Pictures by Gordon Parks with help from Ellison." Life, 25 August 1952, pp. 9-11.

Parrish, Paul A. "Writing as Celebration: The Epilogue of Invisible Man." Renascence 26 (Spring 1974): 152-157.

Pearce, Richard. Stages of the Clown: Perspectives on Modern Fiction from Dostoevsky to Beckett. Carbondale: Southern Illinois University, 1970.

Phillips, Elizabeth C. Ralph Ellison's Invisible Man. Monarch Notes. New York: Monarch Press, 1971.

_____. "Two Underground Men: Richard Wright's 'The Man Who Lived Underground' and Ralph Ellison's Invisible Man." Paper presented at the Tennessee Philological Association, Memphis State University, March 1971. Abstract in Tennessee Philological Bulletin 8 (July 1971): 27-28.

Powell, Grosvernor E. "Role and Identity in Ralph Ellison's Invisible Man." In Private Dealings: Eight Modern American Writers, pp. 95-105. Edited by David J. Burrows, et al. Stockholm: Almqvist and Wiksell, 1970.

Pryse, Marjorie. "Ralph Ellison's Heroic Fugitive." American Literature 46 (March 1974): 1-15.

Pugh, Griffith T., Fred L. Standley, Charles T. Ludington, and Darwin T. Turner. "Three Negro Novelists: Protest and Anti-Protest--a Symposium;" Southern Humanities Review 4 (Winter 1970): 17-50.

Radford, Frederick L. "The Journey Towards Castration: Interracial Sexual Stereotypes in Ellison's Invisible Man." Journal of American Studies 4 (February 1971): 227-231.

"Ralph Ellison Fiction Winner." Crisis 60 (March 1953): 154-156.

Reilly, John M. In Contemporary Novelists. Edited by James Vinson. New York: St. Martin's Press, 1976.

Riche, James. "The Politics of Black Modernism." Literature and Ideology. No. 8 (1971): 85-90.

Rocard, Marcienne. "Homme Invisible, pour qui joues-tu?" Caliban 9 (1973): 67-76.

Rodnon, Stewart. "The Adventures of Huckleberry Finn and Invisible Man: Thematic and Structural Comparisons." Negro American Literary Forum 4 (July 1970): 45-51.

_____. "Invisible Man: Six Tentative Approaches." CLA Journal 12 (March 1969): 244-256; also in Gottesman, Studies in "Invisible Man."

Rollins, Ronald G. "Ellison's Invisible Man." Explicator 30 (November 1971): Item 22.

Rosenblatt, Roger. Black Fiction. Cambridge: Harvard University Press, 1974.

Rovit, Earl H. "Ralph Ellison and the American Comic Tradition." Wisconsin Studies in Contemporary Literature 1 (Fall 1960): 34-42; also in Gibson, Five Black Writers; Hersey, Ralph Ellison; Reilly's Twentieth Century Interpretations of "Invisible Man."

Rubin, Steven J. "Richard Wright and Ralph Ellison: Black Existential Attitudes." Ph.D. Dissertation, University of Michigan, 1969.

Ruotolo, Lucio P. Six Existential Heroes: The Politics of Faith. Cambridge, Mass.: Harvard University Press, 1973.

Rupp, Richard H. Celebration of Postwar American Fiction 1945-1967. Coral Gables, Fla.: University of Miami Press, 1970.

Rush, Theressa Gunnels, Carol Fairbanks Myers, and Esther Spring Arata. Black American Writers Past and Present. Metuchen, N.J.: Scarecrow Press, 1975.

Ruzicka, Dolores Ann. "Ralph Ellison's Invisible Man as a Repository of Major Elements from Principal Western Literary Traditions." Ph.D. Dissertation, University of Southern California, 1973.

Samstag, N. A. and Ted Cohen. "An Interview with Ralph Ellison." Phoenix (Fall 1961): 4-10.

Sanders, Archie D. "Odysseus in Black: An Analysis of the Structure of Invisible Man." CLA Journal 13 (March 1970): 217-228.

Saunders, Pearl I. "Symbolism in Ralph Ellison's 'King of the Bingo Game.'" CLA Journal 20 (September 1976): 35-39.

Schafer, William J. "Irony from Underground: Satiric Elements in Invisible Man." Satire Newsletter 7 (Fall 1969): 22-28; also in Reilly, Twentieth Century Interpretations of "Invisible Man."

_____. "Ralph Ellison and the Birth of the Anti-Hero." Critique 10 no. 2 (1968): 81-93; also in Gottesman, Studies in "Invisible Man"; Hersey, Ralph Ellison.

Schor, Edith. "The Early Fiction of Ralph Ellison: The Genesis of Invisible Man." Ph.D. Dissertation, Columbia University, 1973.

Schraufnagel, Noel. From Apology to Protest. DeLand, Fla.: Everett/Edwards, 1973.

Scott, Nathan A., Jr. "Judgment Marked by a Cellar: The American Negro Writer and the Dialectic of Despair." University of Denver Quarterly 2 (Summer 1967): 5-35.

Scruggs, Charles W. "Ralph Ellison's Use of The Aeneid in Invisible Man." CLA Journal 17 (March 1974): 368-378.

Selke, Hartmut K. "An Allusion to Sartre's The Flies in Ralph Ellison's Invisible Man." Notes on Contemporary Literature 4 (1974): 3-4.

_____. "'The Education at College of Fools': References to Emerson's 'Self-Reliance' in Invisible Man." Notes on Contemporary Literature 4 (1974): 13-15.

Sequeira, Isaac. "The Uncompleted Initiation of the Invisible Man." Studies in Black Literature 6 (Spring 1975): 9-13.

Seyersted, Per. "A Survey of Trends and Figures in Afro-American Fiction." American Studies in Scandinavia 6, nos. 1-2 (1973-74): 67-86.

Singh, Raman K. "The Black Novel and Its Tradition." Colorado Quarterly 20 (Summer 1971): 23-29.

Singleton, M. K. "Leadership Mirages as Antagonists in Invisible Man." Arizona Quarterly 22 (Summer 1966): 157-171; also in Reilly, Twentieth Century Interpretations of "Invisible Man."

Skerrett, Joseph Taylor, Jr. "Take My Burden Up: Three

Studies in Psychobiographical Criticism and Afro-American Fiction. " Ph. D. Dissertation, Yale University, 1975.

Smith, Jane Schur. "Identity as Change: The Protean Character in Nineteenth- and Twentieth-Century Fiction. " Ph. D. Dissertation, Yale University, 1974.

Stanford, Raney. "The Return of Trickster: When a Not-a-Hero Is a Hero. " Journal of Popular Culture 1 (Winter 1967): 228-242.

Stark, John. "Invisible Man: Ellison's Black Odyssey. " Negro American Literature Forum 7 (Summer 1973): 60-63.

Starke, Juanita G. "Symbolism of the Negro College in Three Recent Novels. " Phylon 17 (December 1956): 365-373.

Steele, Shelby. "Ralph Ellison's Blues. " Journal of Black Studies 7 (December 1976): 151-168.

Steinbrink, Jeffrey. "Toward a Vision of Infinite Possibility: A Reading of Invisible Man. " Studies in Black Literature 7 (Autumn 1976): 1-5.

Sylvander, Carolyn W. "Ralph Ellison's Invisible Man and Female Stereotypes. " Paper presented at the MLA Meeting, New York City, December 1976.

Tenenbaum, Elizabeth Brody. "Concepts of the Self in the Modern Novel. " Ph. D. Dissertation, Stanford University, 1972.

Thomas, Gwendolyn A. "The Craft of Ralph Ellison: An Analysis of Invisible Man. " Ph. D. Dissertation, University of Denver, 1974.

Tischler, Nancy. Black Masks: Negro Characters in Modern Southern Fiction. University Park, Pa. : Pennsylvania State University Press, 1969.

_____. "Negro Literature and Classic Form. " Contemporary Literature 10 (Summer 1969): 252-265.

Trimmer, Joseph F. "Ralph Ellison's 'Flying Home.'" Studies in Short Fiction 9 (Spring 1972): 175-182.

Turner, Darwin T. "Afro-American Authors: A Full House. " College English 34 (January 1972): 15-19.

_____. "Invisible Man (Ralph Ellison)." The Twentieth Century American Novel Series. DeLand, Fla.: Everett/Edwards, n.d. (Cassette).

_____. "Sight in Invisible Man. " CLA Journal 13 (March 1970): 258-264.

"Visible Man. " Newsweek, 12 August 1963, pp. 81-82.

Vogler, T. A. "An Ellison Controversy. " Contemporary Literature 11 (Winter 1970): 130-135; also in Gottesman, Studies in "Invisible Man. "

_____. "Invisible Man: Somebody's Protest Novel. " Iowa Review 1 (Spring 1970): 64-82; also in Hersey, Ralph Ellison.

Walcott, Ronald. "Ellison, Gordone and Tolson: Some Notes on the Blues, Style and Space. " Black World 22 (December 1972): 4-29.

Walker, James. "What Do You Say Now, Ralph Ellison?" Black Creation 1 (Summer 1970): 16-18.

Walling, William. "'Art' and 'Protest': Ralph Ellison's Invisible Man Twenty Years After. " Phylon 34 (June 1973): 120-134.

_____. "Ralph Ellison's Invisible Man: 'It Goes a Long Way Back, Some Twenty Years.'" Phylon 34 (March 1973): 4-16.

Walton, Martha R. "Major Concerns of the Black Novel in America in Relation to the American Mainstream." Ph. D. Dissertation, University of Denver, 1973.

Waniek, Marilyn Nelson. "The Space Where Sex Should Be: Toward a Definition of the Black American Literary Tradition." Studies in Black Literature 6 (Fall 1975): 7-13.

Warren, Robert Penn. "The Unity of Experience." Commentary 39 (May 1965): 91-96; also in Hersey, Ralph Ellison.

_____. Who Speaks for the Negro? New York: Random House, 1965.

Wasserman, Jerry. "Embracing the Negative: Native Son and Invisible Man." Studies in American Fiction 4 (Spring 1976): 93-104.

Weinstein, Sharon R. "Comedy and Nightmare: The Fiction of John Hawkes, Kurt Vonnegut, Jr., Jerzy Kosinski, and Ralph Ellison." Ph. D. Dissertation, University of Utah, 1971.

_____. "Comedy and the Absurd in Ellison's Invisible Man." Studies in Black Literature 3 (Autumn 1972): 12-16.

Whitlow, Roger. Black American Literature: A Critical History. Chicago: Nelson Hall, 1973.

Wicks, Ulrich. "Onlyman." Mosaic 8 (Spring 1975): 21-47.

Williams, John A. "Ralph Ellison and Invisible Man: Their Place in American Letters." Black World 20 (December 1970): 10-11.

Williams, Phillip G. "A Comparative Approach to Afro-American and Neo-African Novels: Ellison and Achebe." Studies in Black Literature 7 (Winter 1976): 15-18.

Williams, Sherley Anne. Give Birth to Brightness: A Thematic Study in Neo-Black Literature. New York: Dial, 1972.

Wilner, Eleanor R. "The Invisible Black Thread: Identity and Nonentity in Invisible Man." CLA Journal 13 (March 1970): 242-257.

Witham, W. Tasker. The Adolescent in the American Novel 1920-1960. New York: Frederick Ungar, 1964.

Zietlow, Edward R. "Wright to Hansberry: The Evolution of Outlook in Four Negro Writers." Ph. D. Dissertation, University of Washington, 1967.

Reviews

Invisible Man

Barrett, William. American Mercury 74 (June 1952): 100-104.

Bellow, Saul. Commentary 13 (June 1952): 608-610.

Berry, Abner W. The Worker, 1 June 1952, sec. 2, p. 7.

Booklist, 15 July 1952, p. 378.

Brown, Lloyd L. Masses & Mainstream 5 (June 1952): 62-64.

Byam, Milton S. Library Journal, 15 April 1952, pp. 716-717.

Cartwright, Marguerite D. Amsterdam News, 7 March 1953, p. 14.

_____. Amsterdam News, 14 March 1953, p. 16. Reprinted with preceding article in abbreviated form as a letter to the editor: "Descendants of Bigger Thomas." Phylon 14 (March 1953): 116-118.

Cassidy, T. E. Commonweal, 2 May 1952, pp. 99-100.
Chase, Richard. Kenyon Review 14 (Autumn 1952): 678-684.
Curtis, Constance. Amsterdam News, 14 March 1953, p. 16.
Daiches, David. Saturday Review, 16 November 1957, pp. 19-20.
Hedden, Worth T. New York Herald Tribune Book Review, 13
    April 1952, p. 5.
Howe, Irving. Nation, 10 May 1952, p. 454.
Hughes, Langston. New York Age, 28 February 1953, p. 12.
Killens, John O. Freedom (June 1952): 7.
Kirkus, 1 February 1952, p. 94.
Langbaum, Robert. Furioso (Carleton College) 7 no. 4 (1952):
    58.
Lewis, Richard W. B. Hudson Review 6 (Spring 1953): 144-
    150.
Locke, Alain. Phylon 14 (March 1953): 34-44.
Martin, Gertrude. Chicago Defender, 19 April 1952, p. 11.
Mayberry, George. New Republic 21 (April 1952): 19.
Morris, Wright. New York Times Book Review, 13 April 1952,
    p. 5.
Murray, Florence. Amsterdam News, 28 March 1953.
Ottley, Roi. Chicago Sunday Tribune, 11 May 1952, p. 4.
Prattis, P. L. Pittsburgh Courier, 4 April 1953, p. 7.
Prescott, Orville. New York Times, 16 April 1952, p. 25.
Redding, Saunders. Baltimore Afro-American, 10 May 1952,
    Afro-Magazine Section, p. 10.
Rolo, Charles J. Atlantic 190 (July 1952): 84.
Schwartz, Delmore. Partisan Review 19 (May-June 1952):
    354-359.
Smith, Lucymae. New York Age, 26 April 1952, p. 8.
Time, 1 February 1963, p. 84; 14 April 1952, p. 112.
W. H. B. San Francisco Chronicle, 27 July 1952, p. 12.
Webster, Harvey C. Saturday Review, 12 April 1952, pp. 22-
    23.
West, Anthony. New Yorker, 31 May 1952, pp. 93-96; also in
    West's Principles and Persuasions. New York: Harcourt,
    Brace, 1957.
Winslow, Henry F. Crisis 59 (June-July 1952): 397-398.
Yaffe, James. Yale Review, n. s. 41 (Summer 1952): viii.

ENGLISH, Rubynn M. , Sr.

Novel

Citizen U. S. A. New York: Pageant, 1957.

EVANS, Don

Short Fiction

"Love Song on South Street. " Essence 4 (November 1973): 60-61,
    86, 88.

Biography and Criticism

Rush, Theressa Gunnels, Carol Fairbanks Myers, and Esther Spring
Arata. Black American Writers Past and Present. Metuchen,
N.J.: Scarecrow Press, 1975.

EVANS, Mari

Short Fiction

"The Third Stop in Caraway Park." Black World 26 (March 1975):
54-62.

FAGGETT, H. L.

Short Fiction

"Chatter-Stick Sermon." In Ford and Faggett, Best Short Stories
by Afro-American Writers.

FAIR, Ronald L.

Novels

Cornbread, Earl and Me see Hog Butcher
Hog Butcher. New York: Harcourt Brace Jovanovich, 1966; New
York: Bantam, 1973. Also published as Cornbread, Earl and
Me. New York: Bantam, 1975.
Many Thousand Gone: An American Fable. New York: Harcourt,
1965; Chatham, N.J.: Chatham Bookseller, 1973; excerpt in
Ebony (April 1965): 57-58.
We Can't Breathe. New York: Harper-Row, 1971; excerpts in
Chapman, New Black Voices, Reed, 19 Necromancers from Now.
World of Nothing: Two Novellas. New York: Harper & Row, 1970;
Chatham, N.J.: Chatham Bookseller, 1970.

Short Fiction

"Just a Little More Glass." Essence 2 (July 1971): 40-41.
"Life with Redtop." Negro Digest 14 (July 1965): 65-72; also in
Jones and Neal, Black Fire; Ravitz, The American Disinherited.
"Miss Luhester Gives a Party." In Hughes, The Best Short Stories
by Negro Writers.
"Thank God It Snowed." American Scholar 39 (Winter 1969-1970):
105-108.
"We Who Came After." In Chapman, New Black Voices.

Biography and Criticism

Booth, Martha F. "Black Ghetto Life Portrayed in Novels for the

Adolescent." Ph.D. Dissertation, University of Iowa, 1971.
Fleming, Robert E. "The Novels of Ronald L. Fair." CLA Journal 15 (June 1972): 477-487.
Kent, George E. "Struggle for the Image: Selected Books by or about Blacks During 1971." Phylon 33 (Winter 1972): 304-322.
Klotman, Phyllis Rauch. Another Man Gone: The Black Runner in Contemporary Afro-American Literature. Port Washington, N.Y.: Kennikat Press, 1977.
_____. "The Passive Resistant in A Different Drummer, Day of Absence, and Many Thousand Gone." Studies in Black Literature 3 (Autumn 1972): 7-11.
Pfeiffer, John. "Black American Speculative Literature: A Checklist." Extrapolation 17 (December 1975): 35-43.
Schraufnagel, Noel. From Apology to Protest. DeLand, Fla.: Everett/Edwards, 1973.

Reviews

Hog Butcher
    Archer, W. H. Best Sellers 26 (September 1966): 207.
    Best Sellers, 1 May 1973, p. 70.
    Booklist, 1 November 1966, p. 300.
    Catholic Library World 38 (November 1966): 209.
    Christian Century, 31 August 1966, p. 1057.
    Conroy, J. Books Today, 11 September 1966, p. 10.
    Fuller, H. W., Jr. Negro Digest 15 (October 1966): 85.
    Gardner, J. Southern Review 5 (Winter 1969): 224.
    Greenya, J. J. Saturday Review of Literature, 3 September 1966, p. 36.
    Kirkus, 15 June 1966, p. 602; 1 July 1966, p. 636.
    Kitching, J. Publishers' Weekly, 20 June 1966, p. 77.
    Library Journal 91 (August 1966): 3764; (November 1966): 5701.
    Newsweek, 5 September 1966, p. 89A.
    Revel, Morris. Book Week, 2 October 1966, p. 8.
Many Thousand Gone: An American Fable
    Booklist, 15 May 1965, p. 61.
    Choice 2 (July/August 1965): 296.
    Christian Century, 13 January 1965, p. 56.
    Fremont-Smith, E. New York Times, 20 January 1965, p. 41M.
    Hill, W. B. America, 8 May 1965, p. 678.
    Janeway, Elizabeth. Christian Science Monitor, 4 February 1965, p. 11.
    Levin, Martin. New York Times Book Review, 10 January 1965, p. 10.
    MacGillivray, Arthur. Best Sellers, 1 February 1965, p. 418.
    Macmanus, Patricia. Book Week, 24 January 1965, p. 14.
    Midstream 11 (March 1965): 109.
    Negro Digest 14 (March 1965): 51.
    New Yorker, 30 January 1965, p. 123.
    Shrapnel, N. Manchester Guardian, 9 September 1965, p. 11.
    Times Literary Supplement, 21 October 1965, p. 942.
    Young, B. A. Punch, 15 September 1965, p. 407.

We Can't Breathe
  Booklist, 15 November 1971, p. 272.
  Bryant, J. H. Nation, 21 February 1972, p. 253.
  Choice 9 (July 1972): 644.
  Cooke, Michael. Yale Review 61 (June 1972): 599.
  Davis, George. New York Times Book Review, 6 February
    1972, p. 6.
  English Journal 62 (December 1973): 1300; 63 (January 1974):
    65.
  Kirkus, 15 October 1971, p. 1139.
  Library Journal, 1 December 1971, p. 4029.
  Marsh, Pamela. Christian Science Monitor, 30 December
    1971, p. 6.
  New Yorker, 5 February 1972, p. 103.
  Publishers' Weekly, 18 October 1971, p. 42.
  Saturday Review, 19 February 1972, p. 74.
  Top of the News 29 (April 1973): 257.
World of Nothing
  Booklist, 15 November 1970, p. 253.
  Choice 8 (March 1971): 64.
  Kirkus, 15 June 1970, p. 653.
  Library Journal 95 (August 1970): 2715.
  Publishers' Weekly, 8 June 1970, p. 177.
  Ryan, S. P. Best Sellers, 15 September 1970, p. 223.
  Stevens, Shane. New York Times Book Review, 23 August
    1970, p. 28.

FAIRLEY, Ruth Ann

Novel

Rocks and Roses. New York: Vantage, 1970.

Biography and Criticism

Rush, Theressa Gunnels, Carol Fairbanks Myers, and Esther Spring
  Arata. Black American Writers Past and Present. Metuchen,
  N.J.: Scarecrow Press, 1975.

FARRELL, John T.

Novel

The Naked Truth. New York: Vantage, 1961.

FAULKNER, Blanche

Fiction

The Lively House. Los Angeles: Crescent Publications, 1975.

FAUSET, Arthur

Short Fiction

"Jumby. " In Johnson, Ebony and Topaz.
"Safe in the Arms of Jesus. " Opportunity 7 (April 1929): 124-128,
133.
"Symphonesque. " Opportunity 4 (June 1926): 178-180, 198-200; al-
so in O'Brien, Best American Short Stories, 1926; Williams,
Prize Stories of 1926.
"A Tale of the North Carolina Woods. " Crisis 2 (January 1922):
111-113.

Biography and Criticism

Huggins, Nathan Irvin. Harlem Renaissance. New York: Oxford
University Press, 1971.
Opportunity 4 (June 1926): 189.
Perry, Margaret. Silence to the Drums: A Survey of the Litera-
ture of the Harlem Renaissance. Contributions in Afro-Ameri-
can and African Studies, no. 18. Westport, Conn.: Greenwood
Press, 1976.
Shockley, Ann Allen and Sue P. Chandler. Living Black American
Authors. New York: Bowker, 1973.

FAUSET, Jessie Redmond

Novels

The Chinaberry Tree: A Novel of American Life. New York:
Stokes, 1931; New York: AMS Press, 1969; Washington, D.C.:
McGrath, 1969; New York: Negro Universities Press, 1969.
Comedy: American Style. New York: Stokes, 1933; New York:
AMS Press; Washington, D.C.: McGrath, 1969; New York:
Negro Universities Press, 1969.
Plum Bun, A Novel Without a Moral. London: E. Mathews &
Marrot Ltd. , 1928; New York: Stokes, 1929.
There Is Confusion. New York: Boni & Liveright, 1924. Excerpts
in Brown, Davis and Lee, Negro Caravan; Calverton, An An-
thology of American Negro Literature; Davis and Peplow. The
New Negro Renaissance; Davis and Redding, Cavalcade; Ken-
dricks and Levitt, Afro-American Voices.

Short Fiction

"Double Trouble. " Crisis 26 (August 1923): 155-159; (September
1923): 205-209.
"Emmy. " Crisis 5 (December 1912): 79-87; (January 1913): 134-
142.
"Mary Elizabeth. " Crisis 19 (December 1919): 51-56.
"My House and a Glimpse of My Life Therein. " Crisis 8 (July
1914: 143-145.

"The Sleeper Wakes, a novelette in three installments." <u>Crisis</u> 20
(August 1920; 168-173; (September 1920): 226-229; (October
1920): 267-274.
"'There Was One Time.' A Story of Spring." <u>Crisis</u> 13 (April
1917): 272-277; 14 (May 1917): 11-15.

Biography and Criticism

Bone, Robert A. <u>The Negro Novel in America</u>. New Haven: Yale
University Press, 1966.
Bontemps, Arna. <u>The Harlem Renaissance Remembered</u>. New
York: Dodd, Mead, 1972.
Braithwaite, William S. "The Novels of Jessie Fauset." <u>Opportuni</u>-
ty 12 (January 1934): 24-28; also in Hemenway, <u>The Black</u>
<u>Novelist</u>.
Brawley, Benjamin. <u>The Negro in Literature and Art</u>. New York:
Duffield, 1930.
Brown, Martha Hursey. "Images of Black Women: Family Roles
in Harlem Renaissance Literature." D.A. Dissertation, Car-
negie-Mellon University, 1976.
Dannett, Sylvia. <u>Profiles of Negro Womanhood</u>, vol. 2. Yonkers,
N.Y.: Educational Heritage, 1964.
Davis, Arthur P. <u>From the Dark Tower</u>. Washington, D.C.:
Howard University Press, 1974.
Doyle, Sister Mary Ellen. "The Heroine of Black Novels." In
<u>Perspectives on Afro-American Women</u>, pp. 112-125. Edited
by Willa D. Johnson and Thomas L. Green. Washington, D.C.:
ECCA Publications, 1975.
Edwards, Lee R. and Arlyn Diamond. "Introduction." <u>American</u>
<u>Voices, American Women</u>. New York: Avon, 1973.
Fauset, Arthur Huff. <u>For Freedom; a Biographical Story of the</u>
<u>American Negro</u>. Philadelphia: Franklin, 1929.
Feeney, Joseph J. "Greek Tragic Patterns in a Black Novel:
Jessie Fauset's The Chinaberry Tree." <u>CLA Journal</u> 18 (De-
cember 1974): 211-215.
Gayle, Addison, Jr. <u>The Way of the New World: The Black Novel</u>
<u>in America</u>. Garden City, N.Y.: Anchor Press/Doubleday,
1975.
Gloster, Hugh M. <u>Negro Voices in American Fiction</u>. Chapel Hill:
University of North Carolina Press, 1948.
Gruening, Martha. "The Negro Renaissance." <u>Hound and Horn</u> 5
(1932): 504-514.
Hemenway, Robert. <u>The Black Novelist</u>. Columbus, Ohio: Charles
E. Merrill, 1970.
Huggins, Nathan Irvin. <u>Harlem Renaissance</u>. New York: Oxford
University Press, 1971.
Hughes, Langston. <u>The Big Sea: An Autobiography</u>. New York:
Knopf, 1940.
Jackson, Blyden. "The Harlem Renaissance." In <u>The Comic Ima</u>-
<u>gination in American Literature</u>, pp. 295-303. Edited by Louis
D. Rubin, Jr. New Brunswick, N.J.: Rutgers University
Press, 1973.
"Jessie Fauset." <u>Negro History Bulletin</u> 2 (December 1938): 19.

Klotman, Phyllis Rauch. Another Man Gone: The Black Runner in
 Contemporary Afro-American Literature. Port Washington,
 N.Y.: Kennikat Press, 1977.
Locke, Alain. The New Negro: An Interpretation. New York:
 Albert Charles Boni, 1925; New York: Arno, 1968.
Perry, Margaret. Silence to the Drums: A Survey of the Litera-
 ture of the Harlem Renaissance. Contributions in Afro-Ameri-
 can and African Studies, no. 18. Westport, Conn.: Greenwood
 Press, 1976.
Ramsey, Priscilla Barbara Ann. "A Study of Black Identity in
 'Passing' Novels of the Nineteenth and Early Twentieth Centu-
 ries." Ph.D. Dissertation, The American University, 1975.
Royster, Beatrice Horn. "The Ironic Vision of Four Black Women
 Novelists: A Study of the Novels of Jessie Fauset, Nella Lar-
 sen, Zora Neale Hurston, and Ann Petry." Ph.D. Dissertation,
 Emory University, 1975.
Rush, Theressa Gunnels, Carol Fairbanks Myers and Esther Spring
 Arata. Black American Writers Past and Present. Metuchen,
 N.J.: Scarecrow, 1975.
Schraufnagel, Noel. From Apology to Protest. DeLand, Fla.:
 Everett/Edwards, 1973.
Singh, Amritjit. "The Novels of the Harlem Renaissance: A The-
 matic Study." Ph.D. Dissertation, New York University, 1973.
 _____. The Novels of the Harlem Renaissance: Twelve Black
 Writers, 1923-1933. University Park: Pennsylvania State Uni-
 versity Press, 1976.
Starkey, Marion L. "Jessie Fauset." Southern Workman 61 (May
 1932): 218-219.
Stetson, Earlene. "The Mulatto Motif in Black Fiction." Ph.D.
 Dissertation, State University of New York at Buffalo, 1976.
Young, James O. Black Writers of the Thirties. Baton Rouge:
 Louisiana State University Press, 1973.

Reviews

The Chinaberry Tree
 Becker, M. L. Saturday Review of Literature, 5 March 1932,
  p. 577.
 Booklist, 28 February 1932, p. 259.
 Boston Transcript, 23 January 1932, p. 3.
 Burgum, Edwin Berry. Opportunity 10 (March 1932): 88.
 Cleveland Open Shelf (March 1932): 8.
 Fisher, Rudolph. Books, 17 January 1932, p. 6.
 Ross, Mary. Atlantic (April 1932): 16.
 Strong, L. A. G. Spectator, 30 July 1932, p. 163.
 Sykes, Gerald. Nation, 27 July 1932, p. 88.
 Times Literary Supplement, 23 July 1932, p. 466.
 Wisconsin Library Bulletin 28 (March 1932): 90.
Comedy: American Style
 Booklist 30 (December 1938): 120.
 Boston Transcript, 13 December 1933, p. 3.
 Braithwaite, William Stanley. Opportunity 12 (January 1934):
  27-28.

Nation, 3 January 1934, p. 26.
New York Times, 19 November 1933, p. 19.
Ross, Mary. Books, 10 December 1933, p. 6.
Springfield Republican, 19 November 1933, p. 7.

Plum Bun

Bennett, Gwendolyn. Opportunity 7 (September 1929): 287.
Booklist 25 (May 1929): 321.
Books, 26 May 1929, p. 14.
Braithwaite, William Stanley. Opportunity 12 (January 1934): 27-28.
Locke, Alain. Survey, 1 June 1929, p. 325.
New Republic, 10 April 1929, p. 235.
New York Times Book Review, 3 March 1929, p. 8.
O'Sheel, Shaemas. New York World, 7 April 1929, p. 11m.
Outlook, 13 March 1929, p. 430.
St. Louis Library Bulletin 27 (August 1929): 251.
Seaver, Edwin. New York Evening Post, 23 February 1929, p. 10m.
Times Literary Supplement, 29 November 1928, p. 939.
Wisconsin Library Bulletin 25 (March 1929): 102.

There Is Confusion

Boston Transcript, 26 April 1924, p. 2.
Braithwaite, William Stanley. Opportunity 12 (January 1934): 27.
Brickell, Herschel. Literary Review, 12 April 1924, p. 661.
Cleveland Open Shelf (May 1924): 35.
Goldbeck, Eva. New York Herald and Tribune, 18 May 1924, p. 23.
Gregory, Montgomery. Opportunity 2 (June 1924): 181-182.
Literary Digest International Book Review (June 1924): 555.
New Republic, 9 July 1924, p. 192.
New York Times Book Review, 13 April 1924, p. 9.
Springfield Republican, 13 July 1924, p. 52.
Times Literary Supplement, 4 December 1924, p. 828.
Wisconsin Library Bulletin 20 (October 1924): 212.

FELTON, James A.

Novel

Fruits of Enduring Faith. New York: Exposition, 1969.

FENDERSON, Harold

Short Fiction

The Phony and Other Stories. New York: Exposition, 1959.

FERDINAND, Val see SALAAM, Kalamu ya

FERGUSON, Ira Lunan

Novels

The Biography of G. Wash Carter, White. San Francisco: Lunan-
Ferguson Library, 1969.
Ocee McRae, Texas. San Francisco: Lunan-Ferguson Library,
1962.

Short Fiction

Which One of You Is Interracial? and Other Stories. San Francisco:
Lunan-Ferguson Library, 1969.

Biography and Criticism

Rush, Theressa Gunnels, Carol Fairbanks Myers, and Esther Spring
Arata. Black American Writers Past and Present. Metuchen,
N.J.: Scarecrow Press, 1975.

FIELDS, Julia

Short Fiction

"No Great Honor." Black World 19 (June 1970): 66-70.
"Not Your Singing, Dancing Spade." Negro Digest 16 (February
1967): 54-59; also in King, Black Short Story Anthology.
"The Plot to Bring Back Dunking." Black World 22 (August 1973):
64-71.
"Ten to Seven." Negro Digest 15 (July 1966): 79-81.

FINCH, Amanda

Novel

Back Trail. New York: William-Frederick, 1951.

FIORE, Carmen Anthony

Novel

The Barrier. New York: Pageant, 1965.

FISHER, Rudolph

Novel

The Conjure-Man Dies: A Mystery Tale of Dark Harlem. New
York: Covici-Friede, 1932; New York: Arno, 1971.

The Walls of Jericho. New York: Knopf, 1928; New York: Arno, 1969. Excerpts in Calverton, An Anthology of American Negro Literature; Davis and Peplow, The New Negro Renaissance.

Short Fiction

"Across the Airshaft." (Unpublished.) Microfilm, Brown University Archives, Providence, R.I.

"The Backslider." McClure's (August 1927): 16-17, 101-104.

"Blades of Steel." Atlantic Monthly 140 (August 1927): 183-192. Also in Calverton, Anthology of American Negro Literature; Cromwell, Turner and Dykes, Readings from Negro Authors for Schools and Colleges; Huggins, Voices from the Harlem Renaissance.

"The Caucasian Storms Harlem." American Mercury 11 (August 1927): 393-399.

"City of Refuge." Atlantic Monthly 135 (February 1925): 178-187; also in Barksdale and Kinnamon, Black Writers of America; Clarke, American Negro Short Stories; O'Brien, Best American Short Stories, 1926.

"Common Meter." Part I The New York News, Illustrated Feature Section, 8 February 1930; Part II The New York News, Illustrated Feature Section, 15 February 1930.

"Dust." Opportunity 9 (February 1931): 46-47.

"Fire by Night." McClure's (December 1927): 64-67, 98-102.

"Guardian of the Law." Opportunity 11 (March 1933): 82-85, 90.

"High Yaller." Part I, Crisis 30 (October 1925): 281-286; Part II, (November 1925): 33-38; also in Davis and Redding, Cavalcade.

"John Archer's Nose." The Metropolitan, a Monthly Review (January 1935): 10-12, 47-50, 53, 67, 69-71, 73-75, 80-81.

"The Lindy Hop." (Unpublished.) Microfilm, Brown University Archives, Providence, R.I.

"The Lost Love Blues." (Unpublished.) Microfilm, Brown University Archives, Providence, R.I.

"The Man Who Passed." (Unpublished.) Microfilm, Brown University Archives, Providence, R.I.

"Miss Cynthie." Story (June 1933): 3-15; also in Burnett, Black Hands on a White Face; Clarke, Harlem; Emanuel and Gross, Dark Symphony; Hughes, The Best Short Stories by Negro Writers; Long and Collier, Afro-American Writing.

"The Promised Land." Atlantic Monthly 139 (January 1927): 37-45.

"Ringtail." Atlantic Monthly 135 (May 1925): 652-660.

"The South Lingers On." Survey Graphic, 1 March 1925, pp. 644-647.

Biography and Criticism

Bone, Robert. Down Home: A History of Afro-American Short Fiction from Its Beginnings to the End of the Harlem Renaissance. New York: G. P. Putnam's Sons, 1975.

_____. The Negro Novel in America. New Haven: Yale University Press, 1966.

Brawley, Benjamin. The Negro Genius. New York: Dodd, Mead, 1940.

Brown, Martha Hursey. "Images of Black Women: Family Roles in Harlem Renaissance Literature." D.A. Dissertation, Carnegie-Mellon University, 1976.

Davis, Arthur P. From the Dark Tower: Afro-American Writers 1900-1960. Washington, D.C.: Howard University Press, 1974.

Ford, Nick Aaron. "The Negro Author's Use of Propaganda in Imagination Literature." Ph.D. Dissertation, State University of Iowa, 1945.

Friedmann, Thomas. "The Good Guys in the Black Hats: Color Coding in Rudolf Fisher's 'Common Meter.'" Studies in Black Literature 7 (Spring 1976): 8-9.

Gayle, Addison, Jr. The Way of the New World: The Black Novel in America. Garden City, N.Y.: Anchor Press/Doubleday, 1975.

Gloster, Hugh M. Negro Voices in American Fiction. Chapel Hill: University of North Carolina Press, 1948.

Gross, Theodore L. The Heroic Ideal in American Literature. New York: Free Press, 1971.

Hemenway, Robert. The Black Novelist. Columbus, Ohio: Charles E. Merrill, 1970.

Henry, O. L. "Rudolph Fisher, An Evaluation." Crisis 78 (July 1971): 149-154.

Huggins, Nathan Irvin. Harlem Renaissance. New York: Oxford University Press, 1971.

Hughes, Langston. The Big Sea: An Autobiography. New York: Knopf, 1940.

Jackson, Blyden. "The Harlem Renaissance." In The Comic Imagination in American Literature, pp. 295-303. Edited by Louis D. Rubin, Jr. New Brunswick, N.J.: Rutgers University Press, 1973.

Perry, Margaret. Silence to the Drums: A Survey of the Literature of the Harlem Renaissance. Contributions in Afro-American and African Studies, no. 18. Westport, Conn.: Greenwood Press, 1976.

Queen, Eleanor Claudine. "A Study of Rudolph Fisher's Prose Fiction." M.A. thesis, Howard University, 1961.

Robinson, William H., Jr. Introduction to The Walls of Jericho. New York: Arno Press, 1969.

"Rudolph Fisher." Crisis 30 (July 1925): 132.

"Rudolph Fisher." McClure's (August 1927): 6.

"Rudolph Fisher." Negro History Bulletin 2 (December 1938): 19, 23.

Rush, Theressa Gunnels, Carol Fairbanks Myers, and Esther Spring Arata. Black American Writers Past and Present. Metuchen, N.J.: Scarecrow Press, 1975.

Schmuhl, R. "Treating the Harlem Human Condition." Negro History Bulletin 37 (January 1974): 196-197.

Schraufnagel, Noel. From Apology to Protest. DeLand, Fla.: Everett/Edwards, 1973.

Singh, Amritjit. "The Novels of the Harlem Renaissance: A Thematic Study." Ph.D. Dissertation, New York University, 1973.
_____. The Novels of the Harlem Renaissance: Twelve Black Writers, 1923-1933. University Park: Pennsylvania State University Press, 1976.
Turpin, Waters Edward. "Four Short Fiction Writers of the Harlem Renaissance: Their Legacy of Achievement." CLA Journal 11 (September 1967): 59-72.
Who's Who in Colored America, 1932.

Reviews

The Conjure Man Dies
    Anderson, Isaac. New York Times Book Review, 31 July 1932, p. 13.
    Booklist 29 (November 1932): 76.
    Boston Transcript, 3 August 1932, p. 3.
    Crisis 39 (September 1932): 293.
    Cuppy, Will. Books, 14 August 1932, p. 8.
    Davis, Arthur P. Opportunity 10 (October 1932): 320.
    McManis, Rumana. New York Evening Post, 30 July 1932, p. 7.
    Soskin, William. New York Evening Post, 30 July 1932, p. 7.
    Weber, W. C. Saturday Review of Literature, 13 August 1932, p. 47.
The Walls of Jericho
    Botkin, B. A. Opportunity 6 (November 1928): 346.
    Cleveland Open Shelf (December 1928): 136.
    New Statesman, 15 September 1928, p. 704.
    Saturday Review, 25 August 1928, p. 250.
    Spectator, 25 August 1928, p. 252.
    Times Literary Supplement, 6 September 1928, p. 630.
    Walrond, Eric. Books, 26 August 1928, p. 5.
    White, W. F. New York World, 5 August 1928, p. 7m.

FISHER, William

Novel

The Waiters. Cleveland: World, 1950.

Reviews

The Waiters
    Bontemps, Arna. Saturday Review of Literature, 28 March 1953, p. 16.
    Brooks, John. New York Times, 22 February 1953, p. 6.
    Kirkus, 15 December 1952, p. 770.
    Morton, Frederic. New York Herald Tribune Book Review, 22 February 1953, p. 8.
    Nation, 7 March 1953, p. 212.
    New Yorker, 7 March 1953, p. 104.

Ottley, Roi. Chicago Sunday Tribune, 22 March 1953, p. 8.
Roth, H. L. Library Journal, 15 February 1953, p. 373.
Sim, Neal. Springfield Republican, 15 March 1953, p. 7c.

FLEMISTER, John T.

Novel

Furlough from Hell: A Fantasy. New York: Exposition, 1964.

FLOYD, Silas Xavier

Short Fiction

(Collections):
Charming Stories for Young and Old. Washington, D. C.:
    Austin Jenkins, 1925 (enlarged version of Floyd's Flowers).
Floyd's Flowers; or Duty and Beauty for Colored Children.
    Atlanta: Hertel, Jenkins, 1905; New York: AMS Press,
    1970.
The New Floyd's Flowers: Short Stories for Colored People
    Old and Young. Washington, D. C.: Austin Jenkins, 1922.
Short Stories for Colored People, Both Old and Young. Wash-
    ington, D. C.: Austin Jenkins, 1920.
"The Man in Front." Voice of the Negro 3 (October 1906): 434-
    436.
"Nat Collier's Campaign Manager." Voice of the Negro 3 (June
    1906): 517-519.
"She Came at Christmas." Voice of the Negro 1 (December 1904):
    614-617.

Biography and Criticism

Barber, Max. "Our Monthly Review." Voice of the Negro 1 (Janu-
    ary 1904): 9.
Dyer, Thomas G. "An Early Black Textbook: Floyd's Flowers or
    Duty and Beauty for Colored Children." Phylon 37 (December
    1976): 359-361.

FORD, Nick Aaron

Short Fiction

"Let the Church Roll On." In Ford and Faggett, Best Short Stories
    by Afro-American Writers.
"The Majesty of the Law." In Ford and Faggett, Best Short Stories
    by Afro-American Writers.
"No Room in the Inn." In Ford and Faggett, Best Short Stories by
    Afro-American Writers.
"One Way to Victory." In Ford and Faggett, Best Short Stories by

Afro-American Writers.
"With Malice Toward None." Negro Story 1 (July-August 1944):
45-52.

Biography and Criticism

Contemporary Authors, 25/28
Rush, Theressa Gunnels, Carol Fairbanks Myers, and Esther Spring
Arata. Black American Writers Past and Present. Metuchen,
N.J.: Scarecrow Press, 1975.

FORREST, Leon

Novels

The Bloodworth Orphans. New York: Random House, 1977.
There Is a Tree More Ancient Than Eden. New York: Random
House, 1973.

Reviews

The Bloodworth Orphans
Cohen, George. Chicago Tribune Magazine, 8 May 1977, p. 7.
Phelps, Teresa Godwin. Chicago Tribune Book World, 15 May
1977, sec. 7, p. 1.
There Is a Tree More Ancient Than Eden
Baker, Houston. Black World 23 (January 1974): 67.
Book World, 15 June 1973, p. 15.
Booklist, 1 July 1973, p. 1007.
Gilbert, Zack. Black World 23 (January 1974): 70.
Kirkus, 15 March 1973, p. 336.
Library Journal, 15 May 1973, p. 1599.
Motley, Joel. Harvard Advocate 107 no. 4 (1974): 59-60.
New Leader, 19 July 1973, p. 15.
New York Times, 8 June 1973, p. 37.
New York Times Book Review, 21 October 1973, p. 48.
Publishers' Weekly, 26 March 1973, p. 68.

FORTE, Christine (Christine Forster)

Novels

A View from the Hill. New York: Vantage, 1964.
Young Tim O'Hare. New York: Vantage, 1966.

Biography and Criticism

Rush, Theressa Gunnels, Carol Fairbanks Myers, and Esther Spring
Arata. Black American Writers Past and Present. Metuchen,
N.J.: Scarecrow Press, 1975.

FRANKLIN, J. E.

Short Fiction

"The Enemy." In King, Black Short Story Anthology.

Biography and Criticism

Rush, Theressa Gunnels, Carol Fairbanks Myers, and Esther Spring
    Arata. Black American Writers Past and Present. Metuchen,
    N.J.: Scarecrow Press, 1975.

FRANKLIN, James Thomas

Novel

Crimson Altars, or A Minister's Sin. Memphis: Great South
    Press, 1895.

FULLER, Charles H., Jr.

Short Fiction

"A Love Song for Seven Little Boys Called Sam." In Adoff, Bro-
    thers and Sisters; Murray and Thomas, The Journey.
"Love Song for Willa Mae." In Alhamisi and Wangara, Black Arts.
"A Love Song for Wing." In King, Black Short Story Anthology.

Biography and Criticism

Rush, Theressa Gunnels, Carol Fairbanks Myers, and Esther Spring
    Arata. Black American Writers Past and Present. Metuchen,
    N.J.: Scarecrow Press, 1975.

FULLER, Hoyt W.

Short Fiction

"Hair Cut in Conakry." Negro Digest 12 (January 1963): 74-82.
"The Sengalese." In Clarke, American Negro Short Stories.
"Sun-Burned Soldiers." Negro Digest 11 (March 1962): 47-48.
"With Apologies to Pepito." Negro Digest 11 (February 1962):
    80-83.

Biography and Criticism

Rush, Theressa Gunnels, Carol Fairbanks Myers, and Esther Spring
    Arata. Black American Writers Past and Present. Metuchen,
    N.J.: Scarecrow Press, 1975.

FULLILOVE, Maggie Shaw

Novel

<u>Who Was Responsible.</u> Cincinnati, Ohio: Abingdon Press, 1919.

Short Fiction

"Navy Blue Velvet." <u>Half-Century</u> 2 (February 1917): 5, 17;
(March 1917): 4, 8, 17.
"Pass It On (A Christmas Story)." <u>Half-Century</u> 3 (December 1917):
6, 13.
"Sweet Peas Between." <u>Half-Century</u> 4 (April 1918): 4, 13; (May
1918): 4, 9, 13; (June 1918): 6, 11.

FULTON, David Bryant (pseud., Jack Thorne)

Novel

<u>Hanover; or, The Persecution of the Lowly.</u> n.p.: M.C.L. Hill,
1901.

Short Fiction

"The Lord of the Sky--A Pullman Porter's Story." <u>Voice of the
Negro</u> 4 (January-February 1907): 68-71.

GAINES, Ernest J.

Novels

<u>The Autobiography of Miss Jane Pittman.</u> New York: Dial, 1971;
New York: Bantam, 1972. Excerpt in <u>Negro Digest</u> (February
1971).
<u>Catherine Carmier.</u> New York: Atheneum, 1954; Chatham, N.J.:
Chatham Bookseller, 1972.
"The House and the Field: A Novel." (Unpublished.) Chapter One
in <u>Iowa Review</u> 3 (Winter 1972): 121-125.
<u>Of Love and Dust.</u> New York: Dial, 1967; New York: Bantam,
1969.

Short Fiction

(Collection): <u>Bloodline.</u> New York: Dial, 1968; New York: Bantam,
1970; New York: Norton, 1976.
"Bloodline." In Gaines, <u>Bloodline.</u>
"Boy in the Doublebreasted Suit." <u>Transfer</u> (San Francisco), 1957.
"Chippo Simon." <u>Yardbird Reader</u> 5 (1976): 229-237.
"Just Like a Tree." In Corington and William, <u>Southern Writing in
the Sixties</u>; Current-Garcia and Patrick, <u>What Is the Short Story</u>;
Davis and Redding, <u>Cavalcade</u>; Gaines, <u>Bloodline</u>; Himber,

Toward Theme in Short Fiction; King, Black Short Story Anthology.
"A Long Day in November." In Gaines, Bloodline; Hughes, The Best Short Stories by Negro Writers.
"Mary Louise." In Stegner and Scowcroft, Stanford Short Stories, 1960.
"My Grandpa and the Haint." New Mexico Quarterly (Summer 1966).
"The Sky Is Gray." Negro Digest 12 (August 1963): 73-96; also in Adoff, Brothers and Sisters; Bambara, Tales and Stories for Black Folks; Barksdale and Kinnamon, Black Writers of America; Emanuel and Gross, Dark Symphony; Ferguson, Images of Women in Literature; Gaines, Bloodline; Gasarch and Gasarch, Fiction; Long and Collier, Afro-American Writing; Matthews, Archetypal Themes in the Modern Story; Mizener, Modern Short Stories; Perrine, Story and Structure; Stein and Walters, The Southern Experience in Short Fiction.
"Three Men." In Chapman, New Black Voices; Gaines, Bloodline; Hicks, Cutting Edges; Stadler, Out of Our Lives.
"The Turtles." Transfer (San Francisco), 1956.

Biography and Criticism

Aubert, Alvin. In Contemporary Novelists. Edited by James Vinson. New York: St. Martin's Press, 1976.
Authors in the News, vol. 1. Detroit: Gale, 1976.
Beauford, Fred. "Conversation with Ernest Gaines." Black Creation 4 (Fall 1972): 16-18.
Billingsley, R. G. "Forging New Directions, The Burden of the Hero in Modern Afro-American Literature." Obsidian 1 (Winter 1975): 5-21.
"Black Writer's Views on Literary Lions and Values." Negro Digest 17 (January 1968): 27.
Bryant, Jerry H. "Ernest J. Gaines: Change, Growth, and History." Southern Review 10 (Autumn 1974): 851-864.
_____. "From Death to Life: The Fiction of Ernest J. Gaines." Iowa Review 3 (Winter 1972): 106-120.
_____. "Politics and the Black Novel." Nation, 5 April 1971, pp. 436-438.
Burke, William. "Bloodline: A Black Man's South." CLA Journal 19 (June 1976): 545-558.
Doyle, Sister Mary Ellen. "The Heroine of Black Novels." In Perspectives on Afro-American Women, pp. 112-125. Edited by Willa D. Johnson and Thomas L. Green. Washington, D.C.: ECCA Publications, 1975.
Fuller, Hoyt W. "Contemporary Negro Fiction." Southwest Review 50 (1965): 321-335.
Gayle, Addison, Jr. The Way of the New World: The Black Novel in America. Garden City, N.Y.: Anchor Press/ Doubleday, 1975.
Hicks, Walter Jackson. "An Essay on Recent American Fiction." Ph.D. Dissertation, The University of North Carolina at Chapel Hill, 1974.
Ingram, Forrest and Barbara Steinberg. "On the Verge: An Inter-

view with Ernest J. Gaines." New Orleans Review 3 no. 4 (1973): 339-344.

Jaskoski, Helen. "Power Unequal to Man: The Significance of Conjure in Works by Five Afro-American Authors." Southern Folklore Quarterly 38 (June 1974): 91-108.

Kent, George. "Struggle for the Image: Selected Books by or about Blacks during 1971." Phylon 33 (Winter 1972): 304-323.

Laney, Ruth. "A Conversation with Ernest Gaines." Southern Review 10 (January 1974): 1-14.

McDonald, Walter R. "'You Not a Bum, You a Man': Ernest Gaines's Bloodline." Negro American Literature Forum 9 (Summer 1975): 47-49.

Major, Clarence. The Dark and Feeling. New York: Third Press, 1974.

O'Brien, John. Interviews with Black Writers. New York: Liveright, 1973.

Peden, William. The American Short Story: Continuity and Change 1940-1975. Boston: Houghton Mifflin, 1975.

Rosenblatt, Roger. Black Fiction. Cambridge: Harvard University Press, 1974.

Schraufnagel, Noel. From Apology to Protest. DeLand, Fla.: Everett/Edwards, 1973.

Shelton, Frank W. "Ambiguous Manhood in Ernest J. Gaines's Bloodline." CLA Journal 19 (December 1975): 200-209.

Stoelting, Winifred L. "Human Dignity and Pride in the Novels of Ernest Gaines." CLA Journal 14 (March 1971): 340-358.

Williams, Sherley Anne. Give Birth to Brightness: A Thematic Study in Neo-Black Literature. New York: Dial, 1972.

Reviews

The Autobiography of Miss Jane Pittman
American Libraries 2 (September 1971): 897.
Best Sellers, 1 July 1972, p. 180.
Black World 20 (October 1971): 88.
Booklist, 1 April 1972, p. 664.
Bryant, J. H. Nation, 5 April 1971, p. 436.
Christian Science Monitor, 26 November 1971, p. B3.
Commonweal, 21 January 1972, p. 380.
English Journal 63 (January 1974): 65.
Kirkus, 15 February 1971, p. 190.
Library Journal, 1 March 1971, p. 860; 15 April 1971, p. 1536; 15 December 1971, p. 4161.
Life, 30 April 1971, p. 18.
Listener, 8 February 1973, p. 189.
Major, Clarence. Essence 2 (September 1971): 8; also in Major's The Dark and Feeling. New York: Third Press, 1974.
Millican, Arthenia B. CLA Journal 15 (September 1971): 95-96.
Mitchell, L. D. Best Sellers, 1 November 1971, p. 354.
New Statesman, 9 February 1973, p. 205.
New York Times Book Review, 5 December 1971, p. 82.

Observer, 4 February 1973, p. 36.
Publishers' Weekly, 8 March 1971, p. 64.
Ruffin, C. F. Christian Science Monitor, 3 June 1971, p. 9.
Saturday Review, 1 May 1971, p. 40; 27 November 1971, p. 46.
Time, 10 May 1971, p. K13.
Times Literary Supplement, 16 March 1973, p. 303.
Top of the News 28 (April 1972): 312.
Walker, Alice. New York Times Book Review, 23 May 1971, p. 6.
Wolff, Geoffrey. Newsweek, 3 May 1971, p. 102.

Bloodline

Best Sellers, 15 November 1970, p. 363.
Blackburn, Sara. Nation, 9 September 1968, p. 221.
Booklist, 1 November 1968, p. 289.
Dollen, Charles. Best Seller, 15 August 1968, p. 207.
Hicks, G. Saturday Review, 17 August 1968, p. 19.
Kirkus, 1 June 1968, p. 616.
LaFore, Laurence. New York Times Book Review, 29 September 1968, p. 57.
Library Journal 93 (July 1968): 2689.
Newsweek, 16 June 1969, p. 98.
Publishers' Weekly, 3 June 1968, p. 127.
Saturday Review of Literature, 17 August 1968, p. 19.

Catherine Carmier

Booklist, 1 March 1965, p. 649.
Fuller, Hoyt W. Negro Digest 14 (January 1965): 78.
Scannell, V. Spectator, 11 February 1966, p. 174.
Taubman, R. New Statesman, 18 February 1966, p. 232.
Times Literary Supplement, 10 February 1966, p. 97.

Of Love and Dust

Blackburn, Sara. Nation, 5 February 1968, p. 185.
Booklist, 15 December 1967, p. 490.
Burns, R. K. Library Journal, 15 January 1968, p. 208.
Elliott, Janice. New Statesman, 7 June 1968, p. 769.
Fuller, H. W. Negro Digest 17 (November 1967): 51.
Graham, K. Listener, 13 June 1968, p. 780.
Granat, Robert. New York Times Book Review, 19 November 1967, p. 83.
Howley, E. C. Best Seller, 15 November 1967, p. 334.
Kirkus, 1 September 1967, p. 1073.
Lea, James. Saturday Review, 20 January 1968, p. 29.
Price, R. G. Punch, 12 June 1968, p. 864.
Publishers' Weekly, 28 August 1967, p. 275.
Times Literary Supplement, 1 August 1968, p. 817.

GANT, Lisbeth A.

Short Fiction

"Etta's Mind." In Coombs, What We Must See.
"You've Come a Long Way, Baby." In Sanchez, We Be Word Sorcerers.

Biography and Criticism

Rush, Theressa Gunnels, Carol Fairbanks Myers, and Esther Spring
    Arata. <u>Black American Writers Past and Present</u>. Metuchen,
    N.J.: Scarecrow Press, 1975.

GARNER, Robert

Short Fiction

"A Special, Selfish Joy." <u>Yardbird Reader</u> 2 (1973): 115-119.

GAY, Henry A.

Short Fiction

"A Night in Kenitra." In Mayfield, <u>Ten Times Black</u>.

GAYLE, Addison, Jr.

Short Fiction

"The Expatriate, Story." <u>Black World</u> 19 (May 1970): 54-65.
"There Is No Other Way." <u>Negro Digest</u> 16 (May 1967): 60-70.

Biography and Criticism

Contemporary Authors, 25/28.
Rush, Theressa Gunnels, Carol Fairbanks Myers, and Esther Spring
    Arata. <u>Black American Writers Past and Present</u>. Metuchen,
    N.J.: Scarecrow Press, 1975.

GHOLSON, Rev. Edward

Fiction

<u>From Jerusalem to Jericho</u>. Boston: Chapman & Grimes, 1943.

GILBERT, Herman Cromwell

Novel

<u>That Uncertain Sound</u>. Chicago: Path, 1969.

Review

<u>That Uncertain Sound</u>
    <u>Black World</u> 19 (May 1970): 51; (August 1970): 86.

GILBERT, Mercedes

Novel

Aunt Sara's Wooden God. Boston: Christopher, 1938; Washington, D. C.: McGrath, 1969; New York: AMS Press, 1974.

Biography and Criticism

Gloster, Hugh M. Negro Voices in American Fiction. Chapel Hill: University of North Carolina Press, 1948.
New York Times, 6 March 1952, p. 31. (Obituary.)
Opportunity 9 (September 1931): 287.
Schraufnagel, Noel. From Apology to Protest: The Black American Novel. DeLand, Florida: Everett/Edwards, 1973.
Stewart, Harry T. "The Poet-Actress: A Personal Interview with Miss Mercedes Gilbert." Education: A Journal of Reputation 2 (September 1936): 7.

Review

Aunt Sara's Wooden God
Lovell, John, Jr. Journal of Negro Education 8 (January 1939): 73-74.

GILMORE, F. Grant

Novel

The Problem, a Military Novel. Rochester, N.Y.: Press of Henry Conolly Co., 1915.

GIOVANNI, Nikki

Short Fiction

"The Library." In Adoff, Brothers and Sisters.
"A Revolutionary Tale." In King, Black Short Story Anthology; Mayfield, Ten Times Black.

Biography and Criticism

Authors in the News, vol. 1. Detroit: Gale, 1976.
Bailey, P. "Nikki Giovanni: I Am Black, Female, Polite." Ebony 27 (February 1972): 49-56.
Contemporary Authors, 29/32.
Dusky, Lorraine. "Fascinating Woman." Ingenue (February 1973).
Nazer, G. "Lifestyle." Harper's Bazaar (July 1972): 50-51.
Rush, Theressa Gunnels, Carol Fairbanks Myers, Esther Spring Arata. Black American Writers Past and Present. Metuchen, N.J.: Scarecrow Press, 1975.

GIPSON, Edna

Short Fiction

"A Deep Blue Feeling." In Schulberg, From the Ashes.

GLADDEN, Frank A.

Short Fiction

"Maude." Black World 21 (June 1972): 70-74.

GOINES, Donald

Novels

Black Gangster. Los Angeles: Holloway House, 1972.
Black Girl Lost. Los Angeles: Holloway House, n.d.
Daddy Cool. Los Angeles: Holloway House, 1974.
Dopefiend, The Story of a Black Junkie. Los Angeles: Holloway
    House, 1972.
Eldorado Red. Los Angeles: Holloway House, 1974.
Inner City Hoodlum. Los Angeles: Holloway House, 1975.
Never Die Alone. Los Angeles: Holloway House, 1974.
Street Players. Los Angeles: Holloway House, 1973.
Swamp Man. Los Angeles: Holloway House, 1974.
White Man's Justice, Black Man's Grief. Los Angeles: Holloway
    House, 1973.
Whoreson, The Story of a Black Pimp. Los Angeles: Holloway
    House, 1972.

Biography and Criticism

Authors in the News, vol. 1. Detroit: Gale, 1976.

GOODWIN, Ruby Berkley

Short Fiction

With William Grant Still. Twelve Negro Spirituals (with Stories of
    Negro Life by Ruby Berkley Goodwin). New York: Handy
    Brothers Music Co., 1937.

Biography and Criticism

Rush, Theressa Gunnels, Carol Fairbanks Myers, and Esther Spring
    Arata. Black American Writers Past and Present. Metuchen,
    N.J.: Scarecrow Press, 1975.
Who's Who of American Women, 1958.

GORDON, Eugene F.

Short Fiction

"The Agenda." Opportunity 11 (December 1933): 372-374; 12 (January 1934): 18-22.
"Buzzards." Opportunity 6 (November 1928): 338-342.
"Game." Opportunity 5 (September 1927): 264-269.
"Rootbound." Opportunity 4 (September 1926): 279-283.

Biography and Criticism

Rush, Theressa Gunnels, Carol Fairbanks Myers, and Esther Spring Arata. Black American Writers Past and Present. Metuchen, N.J.: Scarecrow Press, 1975.
Who's Who in Colored America, 1927.

GRANT, John Wesley

Novel

Out of the Darkness; or, Diabolism and Destiny. Nashville: National Baptist Publishing Board, 1909.

GRAY, Wade

Novel

Her Last Performance. Omaha, Neb.: Rapid Printing & Publishing Co., 1944.

GREENE, Burkes G.

Short Fiction

"They All Go When the Wagon Comes." Black World 25 (November 1975): 54-63.

GREENFIELD, Eloise

Short Fiction

"Dream Panoply." Negro Digest 19 (January 1970): 54-58.
"Intrusion." Black World 21 (June 1972): 53-56.
"Karen's Spring." Negro Digest 15 (January 1966): 59-62.
"Noblesse Oblige." Negro Digest 15 (July 1966): 82-86.
"Not Any More." Negro Digest 18 (August 1969): 62-66; also in Murray and Thomas, The Journey.
"A Tooth for an Eye." Black World 19 (July 1970): 70-77.

GREENLEE, Sam

Novels

Baghdad Blues. New York: Bantam, 1976.
The Spook Who Sat by the Door. London: Allison & Busby, 1969;
  New York: Bantam, 1970; excerpt in Observer, March 1969.

Short Fiction

"Autumn Leaves." Negro Digest 16 (January 1967): 69-73.
"Blues for Little Prez." Black World 22 (August 1973): 54-62.
"The D. C. Blues." Negro Digest 18 (June 1969): 86-92.
"The Sign." Negro Digest 15 (February 1966): 61-66.
"Sonny's Not Blue." In King, Black Short Story Anthology.
"Sonny's Seasons." Black World 19 (October 1970): 58-63; also in
  Sanchez, We Be Word Sorcerers.
"Summer Sunday." Negro Digest 15 (September 1966): 60-61.
"Yes, We Can Sing." Negro Digest 15 (December 1965): 65-69;
  also in Mayfield, Ten Times Black.

Biography and Criticism

Burrell, W. "Rappin with Sam Greenlee." Black World 2 (July
  1971): 42-47.
Pfeiffer, John. "Black American Speculative Literature: A Check-
  list." Extrapolation 17 (December 1975): 35-43.
Rush, Theressa Gunnels, Carol Fairbanks Myers, and Esther Spring
  Arata. Black American Writers Past and Present. Metuchen,
  N. J.: Scarecrow Press, 1975.
Schraufnagel, Noel. From Apology to Protest. DeLand, Fla.:
  Everett/Edwards, 1973.
Seyerested, Per. "A Survey of Trends and Figures in Afro-Ameri-
  can Fiction." American Studies in Scandinavia 6 nos. 1-2
  (1973-74): 67-86.

Reviews

The Spook Who Sat by the Door
  Best Sellers, 15 November 1969, p. 324.
  Book World, 25 January 1970, p. 13.
  Booklist, 15 December 1969, p. 494.
  Books and Bookmen 14 (April 1969): 58.
  Library Journal, 1 January 1970, p. 83.
  Listener, 20 March 1969, p. 396.
  Negro Digest 18 (May 1969): 73.
  Newsweek, 16 June 1969, p. 98.
  Observer, 9 March 1969, p. 29.
  Publishers' Weekly, 6 October 1969, p. 50; 3 November 1969,
    p. 50.
  Punch, 30 April 1969, p. 657.
  Spectator, 4 April 1969, p. 446.
  Time, 24 October 1969, p. 108.
  Times Literary Supplement, 3 April 1969, p. 372.

GRIGGS, Sutton Elbert

Novels

The Hindered Hand; or, The Reign of the Repressionist. Nashville,
Tenn.: Orion, 1902; New York: AMS Press, 1970; Miami:
Mnemosyne, 1969; New York: AMS Press; Freeport, N.Y.:
Books for Libraries. Excerpt in Davis and Redding, Cavalcade.
Imperium in Imperio. Cincinnati: Editor, 1899; Miami: Mnemo-
syne, 1969; New York: Arno, 1969; New York: Panther House;
New York: AMS Press; Freeport, N.Y.: Books for Libraries.
Overshadowed. Nashville: Orion, 1908; New York: AMS Press,
1973; Freeport, N.Y.: Books for Libraries, 1971.
Pointing the Way. Nashville: Orion, 1902; New York: AMS Press,
1970.
Unfettered, A Novel. Nashville; Orion, 1902; New York: AMS
Press, 1970.
Wisdom's Call. Nashville: Orion, 1911; Miami: Mnemosyne,
1969; Freeport, N.Y.: Books for Libraries.

Biography and Criticism

Bell, Bernard W. "Literary Sources of the Early Afro-American
Novel." CLA Journal 18 (September 1974): 29-43.
Bone, Robert A. The Negro Novel in America. New Haven: Yale
University Press, 1966.
Davis, Arthur P. From the Dark Tower. Washington, D.C.:
Howard University Press, 1974.
Fleming, Robert E. "Sutton E. Griggs: Militant Black Novelist."
Phylon 34 (March 1973): 73-77.
Gayle, Addison, Jr. The Way of the New World: The Black Novel
in America. Garden City, N.Y.: Anchor Press/Doubleday,
1975.
Gloster, Hugh M. Negro Voices in American Fiction. Chapel Hill:
University of North Carolina Press, 1948.
_____. "Sutton E. Griggs, Novelist of the New Negro." Phylon
4 (Fourth Quarter 1943): 335-345; also in Hemenway, The
Black Novelist.
Hughes, Carl M. The Negro Novelist 1940-1950. New York: Cita-
del Press, 1953.
Pfeiffer, John. "Black American Speculative Literature: A Check-
list." Extrapolation 17 (December 1975): 35-43.
Rosenblatt, Roger. Black Fiction. Cambridge: Harvard University
Press, 1974.
Rush, Theressa Gunnels, Carol Fairbanks Myers, and Esther Spring
Arata. Black American Writers Past and Present. Metuchen,
N.J.: Scarecrow Press, 1975.
Schraufnagel, Noel. From Apology to Protest: The Black American
Novel. DeLand, Fla.: Everett/Edwards, 1973.
Seyersted, Per. "A Survey of Trends and Figures in Afro-American
Fiction." American Studies in Scandinavia 6, nos. 1-2 (1973-74):
67-86.
Stepto, Robert Burns. "From Behind the Veil: Afro-American Re-

form Literature at the Turn of the Century. " Ph. D. Dissertation, Stanford University, 1974.

Tatham, Campbell. "Reflections: Sutton Grigg's Imperium in Imperio. " Studies in Black Literature 5 (Winter 1974): 7-15.

Reviews

The Hindered Hand
    Daniels, John. Alexander's Magazine, 15 October 1905, pp. 31-32.
    Southwest Review 57 (Summer 1972): 262.

Imperium in Imperio
    Southwest Review 57 (Summer 1972): 262.

Overshadowed
    Southwest Review 57 (Summer 1972): 262.

Pointing the Way
    Southwest Review 57 (Summer 1972): 262.

Unfettered
    Southwest Review 57 (Summer 1972): 262.

GRIT, Bruce   see   Bruce, John Edward

GROSS, Werter L.

Novel

The Golden Recovery. Reno, Nev.: By the Author, 1946.

GROSVENOR, Verta Mae   see   SMART-GROSVENOR, Verta Mae

GUNN, Bill   see   GUNN, William Harrison

GUNN, William Harrison (Bill Gunn)

Novel

All the Rest Have Died. New York: Dial Press, 1964.

Biography and Criticism

"Interview with Bill Gunn. " Essence 4 (October 1973): 27, 96.

Schraufnagel, Noel. From Apology to Protest: The Black American Novel. DeLand, Florida: Everett/Edwards, 1973.

GUY, Rosa

Novel

<u>Bird at My Window</u>. Philadelphia: Lippincott, 1966.

Short Fiction

"Wade. " In Mayfield, <u>Ten Times Black</u>.

Biography and Criticism

Contemporary Authors, 17/18.
Schraufnagel, Noel. <u>From Apology to Protest: The Black American
Novel</u>. DeLand, Florida: Everett/Edwards, 1973.

Reviews

Bird at My Window
    <u>Best Sellers</u>, 15 January 1966, p. 403.
    <u>Book Week</u>, 9 January 1966, p. 16.
    <u>Booklist</u>, 1 February 1966, p. 519.
    <u>Books Today</u>, 20 February 1966, p. 6.
    <u>Kirkus</u>, 1 November 1965, p. 1131.
    <u>Library Journal</u>, 1 February 1966, p. 713.
    <u>Negro Digest</u> 15 (March 1966): 53.

HAGEDORN, Jessica Tarahata

Short Fiction

"Bump City. " <u>Yardbird Reader</u> 4 (1975): 90-93.

HAIRSTON, Loyle

Short Fiction

"Harlem on the Rocks. " In Clarke, <u>Harlem</u>.
"A Masterpiece of Satire. " <u>Freedomways</u> 6 (Second Quarter 1966):
    185-187.
"The Revolt of Brud Bascomb. " <u>Freedomways</u> 7 (Summer 1967):
    231-238.
"The Winds of Change. " <u>Freedomways</u> 3 (Winter 1963): 49-58;
    also in Clarke, <u>American Negro Short Stories</u>; Gibson and
    Anselment, <u>Black and White</u>.

HALL, Douglas

Short Fiction

"Foggy." In Ford and Faggett, Best Short Stories by Afro-American Writers.

HAMER, Martin J.

Short Fiction

"The Mountain." Negro Digest 11 (June 1962): 57-61; also in
Adoff, Brothers and Sisters.
"Sarah." In Patterson, An Introduction to Black Literature in
America; Stadler, Out of Our Lives.

HAMILTON, Bobb

Short Fiction

"Blackberry Pit." Negro Digest 14 (March 1965): 57-61.

HAMILTON, Roland T.

Short Fiction

"Symbol of Courage." In Ford and Faggett, Best Short Stories
by Afro-American Writers.

HANKINS, Paula

Short Fiction

"Testimonial." In King, Black Short Story Anthology.

HARPER, Frances Ellen Watkins

Novel

Iola Leroy; or, Shadows Uplifted. Philadelphia: Garrigues Bros.,
1893; New York: Panther House, 1968; New York: AMS Press;
Washington, D.C.: McGrath, 1969.

Biography and Criticism

Bell, Bernard W. "Literary Sources of the Early Afro-American
Novel." CLA Journal 18 (September 1974): 29-43.

Bontemps, Arna. The Harlem Renaissance Remembered. New
York: Dodd, Mead, 1972.
Brawley, Benjamin. The Negro Genius. New York: Dodd, Mead,
1940.
Burks, Mary Fair. "The First Black Literary Magazine in Ameri-
can Letters." CLA Journal 19 (March 1976): 318-320.
Dannett, Sylvia G. L. Profiles of Negro Womanhood, 2 vols.
Yonkers: Educational Heritage, 1964.
Gloster, Hugh. Negro Voices in American Literature. Chapel Hill,
N.C.: University of North Carolina Press, 1948.
Hughes, Carl M. The Negro Novelist 1940-1950. New York: Cita-
del Press, 1953.
Loggins, Vernon. The Negro Author: His Development in America
to 1900. Port Washington, N.Y.: Kennikat, 1964.
Mays, Benjamin E. The Negro's God as Reflected in His Litera-
ture. New York: Negro Universities Press, 1969.
"Negro Novelists Blazing the Way in Fiction." Negro History Bul-
letin 2 (December 1938): 17.
Oxley, Thomas L. G. "Survey of Negro Literature, 1760-1926."
Messenger 9 (February 1927): 37-39.
Riggins, Linda A. "The Works of Frances E. W. Harper."
Black World 22 (December 1972): 30-36.
Rush, Theressa Gunnels, Carol Fairbanks Myers, and Esther Spring
Arata. Black American Writers Past and Present. Metuchen,
N.J.: Scarecrow Press, 1975.
Sillen, Samuel. Women Against Slavery. New York: Masses &
Mainstream, 1955.
Williams, Sherley Anne. Give Birth to Brightness: A Thematic
Study in Neo-Black Literature. New York: Dial, 1972.

HARRIS, James Leon

Novel

Endurance. New York: Vantage, 1973.

HARRIS, Leon R.

Novel

Run Zebra, Run! A Story of American Race Conflict. New York:
Exposition, 1959.

HARRISON, Deloris

Short Fiction

"A Friend for a Season." Redbook 133 (August 1969): 74, 144-145,
148-150; also in Stadler, Out of Our Lives.

HART, Adolph W.

Short Fiction

"Madison." Black Creation 4 (Winter 1973): 4-6.

HAWKINS, Odie

Novel

Ghetto Sketches. Los Angeles: Holloway, 1972.

Short Fiction

"A Sense of Pride." Essence 7 (June 1976): 60-61, 104-106, 108.

Biography and Criticism

Rush, Theressa Gunnels, Carol Fairbanks Myers, and Esther Spring
 Arata. Black American Writers Past and Present. Metuchen,
 N.J.: Scarecrow Press, 1975.

HAYWOOD, Violet G.

Short Fiction

"The Farmer." Crisis 42 (February 1935): 40.

HEARD, Nathan C.

Novels

A Cold Fire Burning. New York: Simon & Schuster, 1974.
Howard Street. New York: Dial, 1972. Excerpt in Robinson,
 Nommo.
To Reach a Dream. New York: Dial, 1972.

Short Fiction

"Boodie the Player." In Sanchez, We Be Word Sorcerers.

Biography and Criticism

Durham, Joyce Roberta. "The City in Recent American Literature:
 Black on White: A Study of Selected Writings of Bellow, Mail-
 er, Ellison, Baldwin, and Writers of the Black Aesthetic."
 Ph.D. Dissertation, University of Maryland, 1974.
Schraufnagel, Noel. From Apology to Protest. DeLand, Fla.:
 Everett/Edwards, 1973.

Reviews

A Cold Fire Burning
    Choice 11 (September 1974): 941.
    Kirkus, 15 February 1974, p. 203.
    Library Journal, 15 May 1974, p. 1408.
    Publishers' Weekly, 18 February 1974, p. 69.
Howard Street
    Giovanni, Nikki. Negro Digest 18 (February 1969): 71-73.
    Kirkus, 1 September 1968, p. 1002.
    Lehmann-Haupt, C. New York Times, 13 December 1968, p.
        45.
    Library Journal, 15 November 1968, p. 4306; 1 April 1972,
        p. 1346.
    Publishers' Weekly, 16 September 1968, p. 70.
To Reach a Dream
    Booklist, 15 July 1972, p. 972.
    Kirkus, 1 April 1972, p. 424.
    Library Journal, 1 April 1972, p. 1346.
    Publishers' Weekly, 24 April 1972, p. 40.
    Watkins, M. New York Times, 14 July 1972, p. 28.

HENDERSON, George Wylie

Novels

Jule. New York: Creative Age, 1946.
Ollie Miss. New York: Stokes, 1935; Chatham, N.J.: Chatham
    Bookseller, 1973.

Biography and Criticism

Bone, Robert A. The Negro Novel in America. New Haven: Yale
    University Press, 1966.
Gloster, Hugh M. Negro Voices in American Fiction. Chapel Hill:
    University of North Carolina Press, 1948.
Kane, Patricia and Doris Y. Wilkinson. "Survival Strategies:
    Black Women in Ollie Miss and Cotton Comes to Harlem."
    Critique 16, no. 1 (1974): 101-109.
Schraufnagel, Noel. From Apology to Protest: The Black American
    Novel. DeLand, Florida: Everett/Edwards, 1973.
Turner, Darwin T. "The Negro Novelist and the South." Southern
    Humanities Review 1 (1967): 21-29.
Turpin, Waters. "Evaluating the Work of Contemporary Negro
    Novelists." Negro History Bulletin 11 (December 1947): 59-60,
    62-64.

Reviews

Jule
    Bixler, Paul. Book Week, 27 October 1946, p. 3.
    Cook, Fannie. Weekly Book Review, 20 October 1946, p. 10.

Creekmore, Hubert. New York Times, 13 October 1946, p. 22.
Dozier, Lois. Phylon 7 (Fourth Quarter 1946): 400-401.
Holmes, J. Welfred. Opportunity 25 (Winter 1947): 38.
Miller, Merle. Saturday Review of Literature, 12 Oct. 1946.
San Francisco Chronicle, 20 October 1946, p. 21.
Saturday Review of Literature, 12 October 1946, p. 56.
Ollie Miss
    Booklist 31 (April 1935): 267.
    Boston Evening Transcript, 10 April 1935, p. 2.
    Gannett, Lewis. New York Herald Tribune, 23 February 1935.
    Gruening, Martha. New Republic, 17 April 1935, p. 292.
    Hart, Elizabeth. New York Herald Tribune Books, 24 Feb. 1935.
    Hubert, J. H. Survey Graphic 24 (June 1935): 308.
    Perry, Edward G. Opportunity 13 (April 1935): 123.
    Quennell, Peter. New Statesman and Nation, 1 June 1935.
    Saturday Review of Literature, 9 March 1935, p. 541.
    Times Literary Supplement, 6 June 1935, p. 366.
    Walton, E. H. Forum and Century 93 (April 1935): 5.
    _____. New York Times Book Review, 24 February 1935.

HENDERSON, Stephen

Short Fiction

"The Magic Word." Negro Digest 18 (June 1969): 58-67.

HENRY, William S.

Fiction

Out of Wedlock. Boston: R. G. Badger, 1931.

HERCULES, Frank

Novels

I Want a Black Doll. New York: Simon & Schuster, 1967.
Where the Hummingbird Flies. New York: Harcourt, 1961.

Biography and Criticism

Schraufnagel, Noel. From Apology to Protest. DeLand, Fla.:
    Everett/Edwards, 1973.

Reviews

I Want a Black Doll
    Anderson, Patrick. Spectator, 7 April 1967, p. 395.

Blackburn, Sara. Nation, 5 February 1968, p. 186.
Booklist, 1 October 1967, p. 169.
Choice, 5 (October 1968): 952.
Horner, A. Books and Bookmen 12 (June 1967): 23.
Kirkus, 15 May 1967, p. 618.
Library Journal, 15 June 1967, p. 2430.
Maloff, Saul. Newsweek, 18 July 1967, p. 94.
Phillipson, J. S. Best Sellers, 1 August 1967, p. 170.
Publishers' Weekly, 8 May 1967, p. 57.
Price, R. G. Punch, 12 April 1974, p. 544.
Times Literary Supplement, 13 April 1967, p. 301.
Where the Hummingbird Flies
    Crisis 68 (October 1961): 523.
    Library Journal, 15 March 1961, p. 1158.
    Newsweek, 27 February 1961, p. 95.

HERMAN, Jerry

Short Fiction

And Death Won't Come: Three Short Stories. East St. Louis, Ill.:
    Black River Writers, 1975.

HERNTON, Calvin

Novel

Scarecrow. Garden City, N.Y.: Doubleday, 1974. Excerpt in
    Reed, 19 Necromancers from Now.

Short Fiction

"Never Alone in the World." Freedomways 3 (Spring 1963): 184-
190.

Biography and Criticism

Klotman, Phyllis Rauch. Another Man Gone: The Black Runner in
    Contemporary Afro-American Literature. Port Washington,
    N.Y.: Kennikat Press, 1977.
Rush, Theressa Gunnels, Carol Fairbanks Myers, and Esther Spring
    Arata. Black American Writers Past and Present. Metuchen,
    N.J.: Scarecrow Press, 1975.

Reviews

Scarecrow
    Black World 24 (June 1975): 91-93.
    Freedomways 14 (Second Quarter 1974): 176-177.
    Kirkus, 15 March 1974, p. 325.
    Library Journal, 15 May 1974, p. 1408.
    Publishers' Weekly, 11 March 1974, p. 43.

HERVÉ, Julia Wright

Short Fiction

"The Forget-For-Peace Program. " Black World 22 (May 1973):
56-64.

Biography and Criticism

"Black Scholar Interviews Kathleen Cleaver. " Black Scholar 3
(December 1971): 54-59.

HIGGS, E. Van.

Short Fiction

"Sketch in Blue. " Negro Digest 19 (March 1970): 53-56.

HILL, Roy

Short Fiction

Two Ways and Other Stories. State College, Pa.: Commercial
Printing, 1959; New York: Port Orange Press, 1964.

HIMES, Chester (Bomar)

Novels

All Shot Up. New York: Berkley, 1960; London: Panther, 1969;
Chatham, N.J.: Chatham Bookseller, 1973.
The Big Gold Dream. New York: Avon, 1960; New York: Berk-
ley, 1966; London: Panther, 1968.
Blind Man with a Pistol. New York: Morrow, 1969. (Also pub-
lished as Hot Day, Hot Night. New York: Dell, 1970.)
Cast the First Stone. New York: Coward-McCann, 1952; Chatham,
N.J.: Chatham Bookseller; New York: New American Libra-
ry, 1972.
Come Back, Charleston Blue see The Heat's On
Cotton Comes to Harlem. New York: Putnam, 1965; New York:
Dell, 1966. Excerpt in Murray and Thomas, Major Black
Writers.
The Crazy Kill. New York: Avon, 1959; New York: Berkley,
1959; Chatham, N.J.: Chatham Bookseller, 1959; London:
Panther, 1969.
For Love of Imabelle. Greenwich, Conn.: Fawcett, 1957; New
York: Avon, 1965; Chatham, N.J.: Chatham Bookseller, 1959.
(Also published as A Rage in Harlem. New York: Avon, 1965.)
The Heat's On. New York: Putnam, 1966; London: Muller, 1966.
(Also published as Come Back, Charleston Blue. New York:

Berkley, 1972; New York: Dell, 1967.)

Hot Day, Hot Night see Blind Man with a Pistol

If He Hollers Let Him Go. New York: Doubleday, Doran, 1945;
Chatham, N.J.: Chatham Bookseller; New York: New American Library, 1971. Excerpt in Negro Digest, January 1946.

Lonely Crusade. New York: Knopf, 1947; Chatham, N.J.: Chatham
Bookseller. Excerpt in Hill, Soon, One Morning.

Pinktoes. Paris: Olympia Press, 1961; London: Arthur Baker,
1961; New York: Putnam, 1965; New York: Dell, 1966. Excerpts in Girodais, The Olympia Reader; Kearns, The Black
Experience; Miller, Blackamerican Literature.

The Primitive. New York: New American Library, 1955; New
York: Avon, 1965. Excerpt in Margolies, A Native Sons
Reader.

A Rage in Harlem see For Love of Imabelle

The Real Cool Killers. New York: Avon, 1959; New York: Ber-
ley, 1959; Chatham, N.J.: Chatham Bookseller, 1960; London: Panther, 1969.

Run, Man, Run. New York: Putnam, 1966; New York: Dell,
1969.

The Third Generation. Cleveland: World, 1954; Chatham, N.J.:
Chatham Bookseller, 1954; New York: New American Library,
1956. Excerpt in Davis and Redding, Cavalcade.

Short Fiction

(Collection): Black on Black: Baby Sister and Selected Writings.
Garden City, N.Y.: Doubleday, 1973.

"All God's Children Got Pride." Crisis 51 (June 1944): 188-189,
204; also in Himes, Black on Black.

"All He Needs Is Feet." Crisis 50 (November 1943): 332; also in
Himes, Black on Black.

"Crazy in the Stir." Esquire 2 (August 1934): 28, 114-116.

"Every Opportunity." Esquire 7 (May 1937): 99, 129-130.

"Face in the Moon." Coronet 9 (February 1941): 59-63.

"He Seen It in the Stars." Negro Story 1 (July-August 1944): 5-9.

"Heaven Has Changed." Crisis 50 (March 1943): 78, 83; also in
Himes, Black on Black.

"In the Night." Opportunity 20 (November 1942): 334-335, 348-349;
also in Himes, Black on Black.

"Let Me at the Enemy--An' George Brown." Negro Story 1 (December-January 1944-45): 9-18.

"Lunching at the Ritzmore." Crisis 49 (October 1942): 314-315;
331; also in Himes, Black on Black.

"Make with the Shape." Negro Story 2 (August-September 1945): 3-6.

"Mama's Missionary Money." Crisis 56 (November 1949): 303,
307; also in Clarke, American Negro Short Stories; Haupt,
Man in the Fictional Mode; Himes, Black on Black.

"Marihuana and a Pistol." Esquire 13 (March 1940): 58; Himes,
Black on Black; Hughes, The Best Short Stories by Negro
Writers; Stanbury, Impact.

"Money Don't Spend in the Stir." Esquire 14 (April 1944): 75.

"A Night of New Roses." Negro Story 2 (December-January 1945):

10-14.

"The Night's for Cryin'." Esquire 7 (January 1937): 64, 146-148; also in Himes, Black on Black.

"One More Way to Die." Negro Story 2 (April-May, 1946): 10-14; also in Himes, Black on Black.

"A Penny for Your Thoughts." Negro Story 1 (March-April 1945): 14-17.

"Salute to the Passing." Opportunity 17 (March 1939): 74-79; also in Barksdale and Kinnamon, Black Writers of America.

"The Snake." Esquire 52 (October 1959): 147-149.

"So Softly Smiling." Crisis 50 (October 1943): 302, 314-316; also in Clarke, Harlem.

"The Something in a Colored Man." Esquire 25 (January 1946): 120, 158.

"The Song Says 'Keep on Smiling.'" Crisis 52 (April 1945): 103-104.

"Strictly Business." Esquire 17 (February 1942): 55, 128.

"There Ain't No Justice." Esquire 23 (April 1945): 53.

"The Things You Do." Opportunity 19 (May 1941): 141-143.

"To End All Stories." Crisis 55 (July 1948): 205, 220.

"To What Red Hell." Esquire 2 (October 1934): 100-101, 122, 127.

"Two Soldiers." Crisis 50 (January 1943): 13, 29.

"The Visiting Hour." Esquire 6 (September 1936): 76, 143-146.

Biography and Criticism

Baker, Houston, Jr. "The Quality of Hurt, the Autobiography of Chester Himes." Black World 21 (July 1972): 89-91.

Baldwin, James. "History as Nightmare." New Leader, 25 October 1947, pp. 11, 15.

Bennett, Stephen B. and William W. Nichols. "Violence in Afro-American Fiction: An Hypothesis." Modern Fiction Studies 17 (1971): 221-228.

Billingsley, Ronald G. "The Burden of the Hero in Modern Afro-American Fiction." Black World 25 (December 1975): 38-45, 66-73.

_____. "Forging New Directions: The Burden of the Hero in Modern Afro-American Literature." Obsidian 1 (Winter 1975): 5-21.

Bone, Robert A. The Negro Novel in America. New Haven: Yale University Press, 1966.

Bryant, Jerry H. "Politics and the Black Novel." Nation, 20 December 1971, p. 21.

Calder, A. "Chester Himes and the Art of Fiction." Journal of East African Research and Development (Nairobi) 1 no. 1 (1971): 3-18; no. 2 (1971): 123-140.

Chelminski, Rudolph. "Hard-bitten Old Pro Who Wrote Cotton." Life, 28 August 1970, pp. 60-61.

"Chester Himes." Encyclopedia International, 2nd ed.

"Chester Himes et le Saga de Harlem." Le Monde de Livres 13 (November 1970): 20-21.

Conrad, Earl. "Blues School of Literature." Chicago Defender, 22

December 1945, p. 11.

Contemporary Authors, 25/28.

Davis, Arthur P. From the Dark Tower. Washington, D.C.: Howard University Press, 1974.

Eisinger, Chester E. Fiction of the Forties. Chicago; Chicago University Press, 1963.

Fabre, Michel. "A Case of Rape." Black World 21 (March 1972): 39-48.

_____. "A Selected Bibliography of Chester Himes' Work." Black World 21 (March 1972): 76-78.

_____. The Unfinished Quest of Richard Wright. New York: Morrow, 1973.

Fuller, Hoyt W. "Traveler on the Long, Rough, Lonely Old Road: An Interview with Chester Himes." Black World 21 (March 1972): 4-22, 87-98.

Gayle, Addison, Jr. The Way of the New World: The Black Novel in America. Garden City, N.Y.: Anchor Press/Doubleday, 1975.

Hill, James Lee. "Bibliography of the Works of Chester Himes, Ann Petry and Frank Yerby." Black Books Bulletin 3 (Fall 1975): 60-72.

Hughes, Carl M. The Negro Novelist 1940-1950. New York: Citadel Press, 1953.

Jackson, Blyden. "The Blithe Newcomers." Phylon 16 (1955): 5-12.

Jerrett, Thomas. "Recent Fiction by Negroes." College English 16 (November 1954): 85-91.

_____. "Toward Unfettered Creativity: A Note on the Negro Novelist Coming of Age." Phylon 11 (Fourth Quarter 1950): 313-317.

Kane, Patricia and Doris Y. Wilkinson. "Survival Strategies: Black Women in Ollie Miss and Cotton Comes to Harlem." Critique 16 no. 1 (1974): 101-109.

Kent, George E. "Rhythms of Black Experience." Chicago Review 25 (1973): 76-78.

Klotman, Phyllis Rauch. Another Man Gone: The Black Runner in Contemporary Afro-American Literature. Port Washington, N.Y.: Kennikat Press, 1977.

Lash, John S. "A Long Hard Look at the Ghetto: A Critical Summary of Literature by and about Negroes in 1956." Phylon 18 (First Quarter 1957): 7-24.

Littlejohn, David. Black on White. New York: Grossman, 1966.

Lundquist, James. Chester Himes. New York: Frederick Ungar, 1976.

Margolies, Edward. "America's Dark Passimism." Saturday Review, 22 March 1969, pp. 59, 64-65.

_____. "Experiences of the Black Expatriate Writer: Chester Himes." CLA Journal 15 (June 1972): 421-427.

_____. Native Sons: A Critical Study of Twentieth-Century American Authors. New York: Lippincott, 1969.

_____. "The Thrillers of Chester Himes." Studies in Black Literature 1 (Summer 1970): 1-11.

Micha, Rene. "Les Paroissiens de Chester Himes." Les Temps

Modernes 20 (February 1965): 1507-1523.

Milliken, Stephen F. _Chester Himes: A Critical Appraisal._ Columbia: University of Missouri Press, 1976.

Mok, M. "Chester Himes." _Publishers' Weekly,_ 3 April 1972, pp. 20-21.

Nelson, Raymond. "Domestic Harlem: The Detective Fiction of Chester Himes." _Virginia Quarterly Review_ 48 (Spring 1972): 260-276.

Nichols, Charles. "The Forties: A Decade of Growth." _Phylon_ 11 (Fourth Quarter 1950): 377-380.

Peden, William. _The American Short Story: Continuity and Change_ 1940-1975. Boston: Houghton Mifflin, 1975.

"Reading Your Own." _New York Times Book Review,_ 4 June 1967, p. 7.

Reckley, Ralph. "The Castration of the Black Male: A Character Analysis of Chester Himes' Protest Novels." Ph.D. Dissertation, Rutgers University The State University of New Jersey, 1975.

Reed, Ishmael. "Chester Himes: Writer." _Black World_ 21 (March 1972): 24-38, 83-86.

Reilly, John M. In _Contemporary Novelists._ Edited by James Vinson. New York: St. Martin's Press, 1976.

Rosenblatt, Roger. _Black Fiction._ Cambridge: Harvard University Press, 1974.

Sanders, Archie D. "The Image of the Negro in Five Major Novels by Chester Himes." M.A. Thesis, Howard University, 1965.

Schraufnagel, Noel. _From Apology to Protest._ DeLand, Fla.: Everett/Edwards, 1973.

"Second Guesses for First Novelists." _Saturday Review,_ 16 February 1946, p. 13.

Simmons, Art. "Paris Scratchpad." _Jet_ (December 1970): 29.

Symons, Julian. In _Mortal Consequences: A History--From the Detective Story to the Crime Novel._ New York: Harper, 1972.

Wilkins, Roy. "Blind Revolt." _Crisis_ 52 (December 1945): 361-362.

Williams, John A. "Chester Himes Is Getting On." _New York Herald Book Review,_ 11 October 1964.

_____. "My Man Himes: An Interview with Chester Himes." In _Amistad_ 1, pp. 25-94. Edited by John A. Williams and Charles F. Harris. New York: Vintage Books, 1970.

Winslow, Henry F. "Dual Legacy." _Crisis_ 61 (April 1954): 247-248.

Reviews

The Big Gold Dream
   Publishers' Weekly, 23 June 1975, p. 78.
Black on Black: Baby Sister and Selected Writings
   Curran, T. M. _America,_ 21 July 1973, p. 44.
   Davies, R. _Times Literary Supplement,_ 25 April 1975, p. 445.
   Kent, G. E. _Chicago Review_ 25 no. 3 (1973): 73-79.
   New Statesman, 11 April 1975, p. 489.

Prairie Schooner 48 (Winter 1974-1975): 365.
Virginia Quarterly Review 49 (Summer 1973): 105.
Blind Man with a Pistol
    Black World 21 (March 1972): 51.
    Books and Bookmen 15 (October 1969): 38; 17 (October 1971): 52.
    Grant, M. K. Library Journal, 15 February 1969, p. 779.
    Lawler, D. F. Best Sellers, 15 March 1969, p. 506.
    LeJune, A. Tablet, 16 August 1969, p. 813.
    Margolies, E. Saturday Review of Literature, 22 March 1969, p. 59.
    Parley, P. Spectator, 12 July 1969, p. 48.
    Punch, 23 July 1969, p. 158.
    Rhodes, Richard. New York Times Book Review, 23 February 1969, p. 32.
    Stevens, Shane. Book World, 27 April 1969, p. 4.
    Times Literary Supplement, 7 August 1969, p. 887.
Cast the First Stone
    Burnett, W. R. Saturday Review, 17 January 1953, p. 15.
    Kirkus, 15 September 1952, p. 611.
    Millstein, Gilbert. New York Times, 18 January 1953, p. 24.
    New York Herald Tribune Book Review, 18 January 1953, p. 8.
    San Francisco Chronicle, 22 March 1953, p. 16.
    Springfield Republican, 1 March 1953, p. 18d.
Cotton Comes to Harlem
    Best Seller, 15 March 1965, p. 487.
    Boucher, Anthony. New York Times Book Review, 7 February 1965, p. 43.
    Grant, M. K. Library Journal, 1 February 1965, p. 670.
    Hentoff, Nat. Book Week, 28 March 1965, p. 11.
    Times Literary Supplement, 20 January 1966, p. 37.
The Heat's On
    Books and Bookmen 12 (October 1966): 46.
    Harris, L. Punch, 5 October 1966, p. 528.
    Johnson, B. Negro Digest 15 (March 1966): 96.
    Kirkus, 1 December 1965, p. 1198.
    Prior, M. Spectator, 23 September 1966, p. 388.
    Richardson, M. Observer, 18 September 1966, p. 27.
    Shepard, R. F. New York Times, 25 January 1966, p. 39.
Hot Day, Hot Night
    Book World, 22 February 1970, p. 13.
    Publishers' Weekly, 1 December 1969, p. 41.
If He Hollers Let Him Go
    Beach, J. W. New York Times Book Review, 2 December 1945, p. 7.
    Cayton, H. R. Book Week, 4 November 1945, p. 3.
    Clement, Rufus E. Phylon 7 (Second Quarter 1946): 210-211.
    Graves, Patsy. Opportunity 24 (Spring 1946): 98-99.
    Kirkus, 1 September 1945, p. 378.
    Lynch, W. S. Saturday Review of Literature, 17 November 1945, p. 53.
    New Yorker, 3 November 1945, p. 102.
    Rosenfeld, Isaac. New Republic, 31 December 1945, p. 909.

Searles, P. J. Weekly Book Review, 4 November 1945, p. 5.
Wilkins, Roy. Crisis 52 (December 1945): 361-362.
Wright, Marion T. Journal of Negro Education 15 (Spring 1946): 213-214.
Wright, Richard. P. M. Magazine, 25 November 1945, p. m7-m8.

Lonely Crusade
Bontemps, Arna. New York Herald Tribune Weekly Book Review, 7 September 1947, p. 8.
Brown, Lloyd L. New Masses, 9 September 1947, pp. 18-20.
Burger, N. K. New York Times, 14 September 1947, p. 20.
Butcher, Philip. Opportunity 26 (Winter 1948): 23.
Farrelly, John. New Republic, 6 October 1947, p. 30.
Kirkus, 15 July 1947, p. 372.
McKitrick, E. L. Saturday Review of Literature, 25 October 1947, p. 25.
New Yorker, 13 September 1947, p. 120.
Stoyan, Christine. Atlantic 180 (October 1947): 138.
Streater, George. Commonweal, 3 October 1947, p. 604.

Pinktoes
Best Sellers, 15 July 1965, p. 171.
Choice 2 (December 1965): 684.
Hentoff, Nat. Book Week, 8 August 1965, p. 8.
Katz, Bill. Library Journal, 1 April 1965, p. 1743.
Kirkus, 1 March 1965, p. 264.
Levin, Martin. New York Times Book Review, 15 August 1965, p. 30.
Publishers' Weekly, 16 May 1966, p. 81.
Time, 30 July 1965, p. 70.
Willis, R. Books and Bookmen 11 (February 1966): 32.
Woodford, J. Negro Digest 15 (November 1965): 49.

The Real Cool Killers
Publishers' Weekly, 16 May 1966, p. 82.

Run Man Run
Best Sellers, 1 December 1966, p. 328.
Boucher, Anthony. New York Times Book Review, 27 November 1966, p. 64.
Cuff, Sergeant. Saturday Review, 31 December 1966, p. 28.
Grant, M. K. Library Journal, 1 December 1966, p. 6004.
Harris, L. Punch, 12 July 1967, p. 73.
Kenneggy, R. Books and Bookmen 12 (September 1967): 38.
Llorens, D. Negro Digest 16 (July 1967): 78.
Prior, M. Spectator, 11 August 1967, p. 164.
Shepard, R. F. New York Times, 12 November 1966, p. 27.

Third Generation
Booklist, 15 February 1954, p. 20.
Brooks, John. New York Times Book Review, 10 January 1954, p. 29.
Byam, M. S. Library Journal, 15 January 1954, p. 145.
Fuller, Edmund. Chicago Sunday Tribune, 10 January 1954, p. 5.
Hughes, Riley. Catholic World 179 (April 1954): 72.
Kirkus, 1 November 1953, p. 716.

Levin, Martin. Saturday Review, 13 March 1954, p. 51.
Morton, Frederic. New York Herald Tribune Book Review,
10 January 1954, p. 6.
Rivers, G. B. Journal of Negro Education 24 (Winter 1955):
48-49.
San Francisco Chronicle, 7 February 1954, p. 12.

HOAGLAND, Everett

Short Fiction

"Table Talk." Black World 23 (June 1974): 76-81.

Biography and Criticism

Contemporary Authors, 33/36.
Rush, Theressa Gunnels, Carol Fairbanks Myers, and Esther Spring
Arata. Black American Writers Past and Present. Metuchen,
N.J.: Scarecrow Press, 1975.

HOLLAND, Mignon see Anderson, Mignon Holland

HOLMES, R. Ernest

Short Fiction

"Cheesy, Baby." In Coombs, What We Must See.

Biography and Criticism

Rush, Theressa Gunnels, Carol Fairbanks Myers, and Esther Spring
Arata. Black American Writers Past and Present. Metuchen,
N.J.: Scarecrow Press, 1975.

HOPKINS, Pauline Elizabeth

Novels

Contending Forces: A Romance Illustrative of Negro Life North and
South. Boston: Colored Co-operative, 1900; New York: AMS
Press, 1971; Freeport, N.Y.: Books for Libraries.
Of One Blood; or, The Hidden Self. Serialized in The Colored Maga-
zine.
Winona: A Tale of Negro Life in the South and Southwest. Serialized
in The Colored Magazine.

Biography and Criticism

Bone, Robert A. The Negro Novel in America. New Haven: Yale

University Press, 1966.

Gloster, Hugh M. Negro Voices in American Fiction. Chapel Hill: University of North Carolina Press, 1948.

Loggins, Vernon. The Negro Author: His Development in America to 1900. Port Washington, N.Y.: Kennikat, 1964.

Rush, Theressa Gunnels, Carol Fairbanks Myers, and Esther Spring Arata. Black American Writers Past and Present. Metuchen, N.J.: Scarecrow Press, 1975.

Shockley, Ann Allen. "Pauline Elizabeth Hopkins: A Biographical Excursion into Obscurity." Phylon 33 (Spring 1972): 22-26.

Reviews

Contending Forces
　　　Smith, Alberta Moore. "Comment." Colored American 3 (October 1901): 479.

HORNE, Frank M.

Short Fiction

"Concerning White People." Opportunity 12 (March 1934): 77-79.

"The Man Who Wanted to Be Red." Crisis 35 (July 1928): 225-226, 242-243.

Biography and Criticism

Primeau, Ronald. "Frank Horne and the Second Echelon Poets of the Harlem Renaissance." In The Harlem Renaissance Remembered, pp. 247-267. Edited by Arna Bontemps. New York: Dodd, Mead, 1972.

Rush, Theressa Gunnels, Carol Fairbanks Myers, and Esther Spring Arata. Black American Writers Past and Present. Metuchen, N.J.: Scarecrow Press, 1975.

Who's Who in Colored America, 3rd ed.

HORSMAN, Gallan

Novel

The Noose and the Spear: A Tale of Passion, Adventure and Violence. New York: Vantage, 1965.

HOWARD, James H. W.

Novel

Bond and Free: A True Tale of Slave Times. Harrisburg: Edwin K. Meyers, Printer & Binder, 1886; Miami: Mnemosyne, 1969; College Park, Md.: McGrath, 1969; New York: AMS Press.

Biography and Criticism

Bell, Bernard W. "Literary Sources of the Early Afro-American Novel." CLA Journal 18 (September 1974): 29-43.

HOWARD, Vanessa

Short Fiction

"Let Me Hang Loose." In Bambara, Tales and Stories for Black Folks.

HUDSON, Fred

Short Fiction

"Savage Beast and Babies." In Sanchez, Three Hundred Sixty Degrees of Blackness Comin at You.

HUDSON, William.

Short Fiction

"A Credit to the Race." Black World 26 (January 1975): 54-61.

HUGHES, Langston James

Novels

The Best of Simple. New York: Hill & Wang, 1961.
Not Without Laughter. New York: Knopf, 1930; London: Allen & Unwin, 1930; New York: Macmillan, 1969; excerpt in Fabricant and Werner, Caravan of Music Stories.
Simple Speaks His Mind. New York: Simon & Schuster, 1950.
Simple Stakes a Claim. New York: Rinehart, 1957.
Simple Takes a Wife. New York: Simon & Schuster, 1953.
Simple's Uncle Sam. New York: Hill & Wang, 1965.
Tambourines to Glory. New York: John Day, 1958; New York: Hill & Wang, 1970.

Short Fiction

(Collections):
    The Langston Hughes Reader. New York: Braziller, 1958.
    Laughing to Keep from Crying. New York: Holt, 1952.
    Something in Common and Other Stories. New York: Hill & Wang, 1963.
    The Ways of White Folks. New York: Knopf, 1934.
"African Morning." In Adoff, Brothers and Sisters; Hughes, Laugh-

ing to Keep from Crying; Hughes, Something in Common and Other Stories.

"American Dilemma." In Olsen and Swinburne, Me, Myself, and I.

"Banquet in Honor." Negro Quarterly 1 (Summer 1942): 176-178.

"Berry." Abbott's Weekly, 24 February 1934, pp. 2, 14; International Literature No. 9 (1935): 61-64; also in Hughes, The Ways of White Folks.

"Beyond Sound of Machine Gun." In Palmer, World's Best Short Stories of 1928.

"Big Meeting." Scribner's Magazine 98 (July 1935): 22-26; also in Hughes, The Langston Hughes Reader; Hughes, Laughing to Keep From Crying; Hughes, Something in Common and Other Stories.

"Blessed Assurance." In Hughes, Something in Common and Other Stories.

"The Blues I'm Playing." Scribner's Magazine 95 (May 1934): 345-351; also in Hughes, The Ways of White Folks.

"Breakfast in Virginia." In Hughes, Something in Common and Other Stories.

"Color Problems." In Olsen and Swinburne, He Who Dares; Patterson, An Introduction to Black Literature in America.

"Cora Unashamed." American Mercury 30 (September 1933): 19-24; also in Foley, Best Short Stories of 1934; Hughes, The Langston Hughes Reader; Hughes, The Ways of White Folks.

"Dear Dr. Butts." In Emanuel and Gross, Dark Symphony; Stanford, I, Too, Sing America.

"Early Autumn." In Hughes, Something in Common and Other Stories.

"Father and Son." In Hughes, Something in Common and Other Stories; Hughes, The Ways of White Folks.

"Fine Accommodations." In Hughes, Something in Common and Other Stories.

"Good Job Gone." Esquire (April 1934): 46, 142, 144; also in Hughes, Something in Common and Other Stories; Hughes, The Ways of White Folks; Shea, Strange Barriers.

"Gumption." In Hughes, Something in Common and Other Stories; Stanford, I, Too, Sing America. (Published as "Oyster's Son" in New Yorker, 12 January 1935, pp. 51-54.)

"The Gun." Hughes, Something in Common and Other Stories.

"Heaven to Hell." In Hughes, Laughing to Keep From Crying; Hughes, Something in Common and Other Stories.

"His Last Affair." In Hughes, Something in Common and Other Stories.

"Home." Esquire (May 1934): 56, 57, 93-94. Also in Gable, Many-Colored Fleece; Hughes, The Ways of White Folks.

"Little Dog." Challenge 1 (March 1934): 308; also in Gibson and Anselment, Black and White; Hughes, The Langston Hughes Reader; Hughes, The Ways of White Folks; Hughes, Something in Common and Other Stories.

"Little Old Spy." Esquire (September 1934): 47, 150, 152; also in Hughes, Laughing to Keep from Crying; Hughes, Something in Common and Other Stories.

"The Little Virgin." Messenger, November 1927, pp. 327-328.

"Luani of the Jungle." Harlem, November 1928.
"Mother and Child." In Hughes, The Ways of White Folks; North, New Masses.
"Mysterious Madame Shanghai." Afro Magazine, 15 March 1952, pp. 6-7; also in Howes and Smith, The Sea-Green Horse; Hughes, Laughing to Keep from Crying; Hughes, Something in Common and Other Stories.
"Name in the Papers." In Hughes, Laughing to Keep from Crying.
"Never Room with a Couple." In Hughes, Laughing to Keep From Crying; Hughes, Something in Common and Other Stories.
"No Place to Make Love." In Hughes, Something in Common and Other Stories.
"On the Road." Esquire (January 1935): 92, 154; also in Bowen and Van Der Beets, American Short Fiction; Gilkes, Short Story Craft; Hughes, Laughing to Keep From Crying; Hughes, Something in Common and Other Stories; Smith, Democratic Spirit; Stanford, I, Too, Sing America.
"On the Way Home." Story Magazine (May/June 1946): 70-74; also in Burnett, Black Hands on a White Face; Burnett and Burnett, Story Jubilee; Burnett and Burnett, Story: Fiction of the Forties; Hughes, The Langston Hughes Reader; Hughes, Laughing to Keep from Crying; Hughes, Something in Common and Other Stories.
"One Christmas Eve." Opportunity 11 (December 1933): 362-363; also in Gaer, Our Lives; Hughes, The Ways of White Folks; Wagenknecht, Fireside Book of Christmas Stories.
"One Friday Morning." Crisis 48 (July 1941): 216-218; also in Certner and Henry, Short Stories for Our Times; Clarke, American Negro Short Stories; Ferris, Girls, Girls, Girls; Hughes, Laughing to Keep From Crying; Hughes, The Langston Hughes Reader.
"Oyster's Son" see "Gumption"
"Passing." In Hughes, The Ways of White Folks.
"Patron of the Arts." In Hughes, The Langston Hughes Reader; Hughes, Something in Common and Other Stories.
"Poor Little Black Fellow." American Mercury 30 (November 1933): 326-335; also in Hall, The Realm of Fiction; Hughes, The Ways of White Folks.
"Powder White Faces." In Hughes, Laughing to Keep From Crying; Hughes, Something in Common and Other Stories.
"Professor." Anvil (May/June 1935): 5-8; also in Brewster, Book of Contemporary Short Stories; Hughes, Laughing to Keep From Crying; Hughes, Something in Common and Other Stories.
"Pushcart Man." In Hughes, Laughing to Keep From Crying; Hughes, Something in Common and Other Stories.
"Red Headed Baby." In Hughes, The Langston Hughes Reader; Hughes, The Ways of White Folks.
"Rejuvenation Through Joy." In Brewster, Book of Contemporary Short Stories, Hughes, The Ways of White Folks.
"Rock, Church." In Hill, Soon, One Morning; Hughes, Something in Common and Other Stories; Margolies, A Native Sons Reader.
"Rouge High." In Hughes, Laughing to Keep From Crying; Hughes,

Something in Common and Other Stories.
"The Sailor and the Steward." Anvil (July/August 1935): 28-30.
"Sailor Ashore." In Hughes, Laughing to Keep From Crying;
  Hughes, Something in Common and Other Stories.
"Saratoga Rain." Negro Story (March/April 1945): 46-47; also in
  Hughes, Laughing to Keep From Crying; Hughes, Something in
  Common and Other Stories.
"Slave on the Block." Scribner's Magazine 94 (September 1933):
  141-144; also in Dashiell, Editor's Choice; Hughes, The Lang-
  ston Hughes Reader; Hughes, The Ways of White Folks; Moon,
  Primer for White Folks.
"Slice Him Down." Esquire (May 1936): 44-45; 190; also in
  Hughes, Laughing to Keep From Crying; Hughes, Something in
  Common and Other Stories.
"Something in Common." In Hughes, The Langston Hughes Reader;
  Hughes, Laughing to Keep From Crying; Hughes, Something in
  Common and Other Stories.
"Sorrow for a Midget." Negro Digest 10 (October 1961): 68-71;
  Hughes, Something in Common and Other Stories; also on cas-
  sette: Langston Hughes. Los Angeles: Pacifica Tape Library,
  1963.
"Spanish Blood." Metropolis, 29 December 1934, pp. 21-24; Stag
  (August 1937): 9-11; also in Hughes, The Langston Hughes
  Reader; Hughes, Laughing to Keep From Crying; Hughes, Some-
  thing in Common and Other Stories.
"Tain't So." In Hughes, The Langston Hughes Reader; Hughes,
  Laughing to Keep From Crying; Hughes, Something in Common
  and Other Stories.
"Thank You M'am." In Bambara, Tales and Stories for Black Folks;
  Hughes, The Best Short Stories by Negro Writers; Hughes, The
  Langston Hughes Reader; Hughes, Something in Common and
  Other Stories; Olsen and Swinburne, Love's Blues; Stanford, I,
  Too, Sing America; also on cassette: Langston Hughes. Los
  Angeles: Pacifica Tape Library, 1963.
"Tragedy at the Baths." Esquire (October 1935): 80, 122; also in
  Hughes, The Langston Hughes Reader; Hughes, Laughing to Keep
  From Crying; Hughes, Something in Common and Other Stories.
"Trouble with the Angels." In Hughes, Laughing to Keep From
  Crying; Hughes, Something in Common and Other Stories.
"Two at the Bar." Negro Story 2 (August-September 1945): 7-8.
"Who's Passing for Who." Negro Story 2 (December-January 1945):
  35-38; also in Hughes, The Langston Hughes Reader; Hughes,
  Laughing to Keep From Crying; Hughes, Something in Common
  and Other Stories.
"Why, You Reckon?" In Hughes, Laughing to Keep From Crying;
  Hughes, Something in Common and Other Stories.
"The Young Glory of Him." Messenger (June 1927): 177-178.

Biography and Criticism

Allen, Samuel W. "Negritude and Its Relevance to the American
  Negro Writer." In The American Negro Writer and His Roots,
  pp. 8-20. New York: American Society of African Culture,
  1960.

Bell, Bernard W. The Folk Roots of Contemporary Afro-American Poetry. Detroit: Broadside Press, 1974.
Black Authors. Old Greenwich, Conn.: Listening Library, n.d. (Filmstrip.)
Bone, Robert A. Down Home: A History of Afro-American Short Fiction from Its Beginnings to the End of the Harlem Renaissance. New York: G. P. Putnam's Sons, 1975.
_____. The Negro Novel in America. New Haven, Conn.: Yale University Press, 1965.
Bontemps, Arna. "The Harlem Renaissance." Saturday Review of Literature, 22 March 1947, pp. 12-13, 44.
_____. The Harlem Renaissance Remembered. New York: Dodd, Mead, 1972.
_____. "Langston Hughes." Ebony 1 (October 1946): 19-23.
Brawley, Benjamin. The Negro Genius. New York: Dodd, Mead, 1937.
Breaux, Elwyn Ellison. "Comic Elements in Selected Prose Works by James Baldwin, Ralph Ellison, and Langston Hughes." Ed.D. Dissertation, Oklahoma State University, 1971.
Brown, Martha Hursey. "Images of Black Women: Family Roles in Harlem Renaissance Literature." D.A. Dissertation, Carnegie-Mellon University, 1976.
Bryant, James David. "Satire in the Work of Langston Hughes." Ph.D. Dissertation, Texas Christian University, 1972.
Carey, Julian C. "Jesse B. Semple Revisited and Revised." Phylon 32 (Second Quarter 1971): 158-163.
Chapman, Abraham. "The Harlem Renaissance in Literary History." CLA Journal 11 (September 1967): 38-58.
Clarke, John Henrik. "Langston Hughes and Jesse B. Semple." Freedomways 8 (Spring 1968): 167-169.
Current Biography, 1940.
Dandridge, Rita B. "The Black Woman as a Freedom Fighter in Langston Hughes' 'Simple's Uncle Sam.'" CLA Journal 18 (December 1974): 273-283.
Davis, Arthur P. From the Dark Tower: Afro-American Writers 1900-1960. Washington, D.C.: Howard University Press, 1974.
_____. "Integration and Race Literature." Phylon 17 (Second Quarter 1956): 141-146.
_____. "Jesse B. Semple: Negro American." Phylon 15 (First Quarter 1954): 21-28.
Doyle, Sister Mary Ellen. "The Heroine of Black Novels." In Perspectives on Afro-American Women, pp. 112-125. Edited by Willa D. Johnson and Thomas L. Green. Washington, D.C.: ECCA Publications, 1975.
Edwards, Sister Ann. "Three Views of Blacks: The Black Woman in American Literature." CEA Critic 37 (May 1975): 14-16.
Emanuel, James A. Langston Hughes. New York: Twayne, 1967.
_____. "Langston Hughes' First Short Story: 'Mary Minosky.'" Phylon 22 (Third Quarter 1961): 267-272.
_____. "The Literary Experiments of Langston Hughes." CLA Journal 11 (June 1968): 335-344.
_____. "The Short Fiction of Langston Hughes." Freedomways 8 (Spring 1968): 170-178.

_____. "The Short Stories of Langston Hughes." Ph. D. Dissertation, Columbia University, 1962.

_____. "'Soul' in the Works of Langston Hughes." Negro Digest 16 (September 1967): 25-30. (Excerpt.)

Evans, Mari. "I Remember Langston." Negro Digest 16 (September 1967); 36.

Fabre, Michel. The Unfinished Quest of Richard Wright. New York: Morrow, 1973.

Felgar, Robert. "Black Content, White Form." Studies in Black Literature 5 (Spring 1974): 28-31.

Fields, Julia. "The Green of Langston's Ivy." Negro Digest 16 (September 1967): 58-59.

Ford, Nick Aaron. "The Negro Author's Use of Propaganda in Imaginative Literature." Ph. D. Dissertation. State University of Iowa, 1945.

Gayle, Addison, Jr. "Langston Hughes: A Simple Commentary." Negro Digest 16 (September 1967): 53-57.

_____. The Way of the New World: The Black Novel in America. Garden City, N.Y.: Anchor Press/Doubleday, 1975.

Gloster, Hugh M. Negro Voices in American Fiction. Chapel Hill: University of North Carolina Press, 1948.

Gruening, Martha. "The Negro Renaissance." Hound and Horn 5 (1932): 504-514.

Hall, George Earlen Franklin. "Recurrent Themes in the Novels and Short Fiction of Langston Hughes." Ph. D. Dissertation, University of Utah, 1975.

Harper, Clifford Doyl. "A Study of the Disunity Theme in the Afro-American Experience: An Examination of Five Representative Novels." Ph. D. Dissertation, Saint Louis University, 1972.

Hart, Robert C. "Black-White Literary Relations in the Harlem Renaissance." American Literature 44 (January 1973): 612-628.

Huggins, Nathan Irvin. Harlem Renaissance. New York: Oxford University Press, 1971.

Jackson, Blyden. "Claude McKay and Langston Hughes: The Harlem Renaissance and More." Pembroke Magazine 6 (1975): 43-48.

_____. The Comic Imagination in American Literature. New Brunswick, N.J.: Rutgers University Press, 1973.

_____. "A Golden Mean for the Negro Novel." CLA Journal 3 (December 1959): 81-87.

_____. "The Negro's Image of the Universe as Reflected in His Fiction." CLA Journal 4 (September 1960): 22-31.

_____. "A Word About Simple." CLA Journal 11 (June 1968): 310-318; also in Jackson's The Waiting Years. Baton Rouge: Louisiana State University Press, 1976.

Joans, Ted. "The Langston I Knew." Black World 21 (September 1972): 14-19.

Kent, George. Blackness and the Adventure of Western Culture. Chicago: Third World Press, 1972.

Kinnamon, Keneth. "The Man Who Created Simple." Nation, 4 December 1967, pp. 599-601.

Klotman, Phyllis Rauch. Another Man Gone: The Black Runner

in Contemporary Afro-American Literature.   Port Washington,
N.Y.:   Kennikat Press, 1977.
_____.   "Langston Hughes's Jess B. Semple and the Blues."
Phylon 36 (March 1975):   68-77.
"Langston Hughes and the Example of 'Simple.'"   Black World 19
(June 1970):   35-38.
Love, Theressa R.   "The Black Woman in Afro-American Litera-
ture."   Paper presented at the Midwest Modern Language Asso-
ciation Meeting, Chicago, November 1975.   (Mimeographed.)
Miller, R. Baxter.   "'Done Made Us Leave Our Home':   Langston
Hughes's Not Without Laughter--Unifying Images and Three Di-
mensions."   Phylon 37 (December 1976):   362-369.
O'Daniel, Therman B., ed.   Langston Hughes: Black Genius, A
Critical Evaluation.   New York: Morrow, 1971.
Parker, John W.   "Tomorrow in the Writing of Langston Hughes."
College English 10 (May 1949):   438-441.
Peden, William.   The American Short Story: Continuity and Change
1940-1975.   Boston: Houghton Mifflin, 1975.
Perry, Margaret.   Silence to the Drums: A Survey of the Litera-
ture of the Harlem Renaissance.   Contributions in Afro-Ameri-
can and African Studies, no. 18.   Westport, Conn.:   Greenwood
Press, 1976.
Presley, James.   "The American Dream of Langston Hughes."
Southwest Review 48 (Autumn 1963):   380-386.
Ramsey, Priscilla.   "A Study of Black Identity in 'Passing' Novels
of the Nineteenth and Early Twentieth Centuries."   Studies in
Black Literature 7 (Winter 1976):   1-7.
Robinson, Anna T.   "Race Consciousness and Survival Techniques
Depicted in Harlem Renaissance Fiction."   Ph.D. Dissertation,
Pennsylvania State University, 1973.
Rosenblatt, Roger.   Black Fiction.   Cambridge: Harvard University
Press, 1974.
Schraufnagel, Noel.   From Apology to Protest.   DeLand, Fla.:
Everett/Edwards, 1973.
Seyersted, Per.   "A Survey of Trends and Figures in Afro-Ameri-
can Fiction."   American Studies in Scandinavia 6, nos. 1-2
(1973-74):   67-86.
Singh, Amritjit.   "The Novels of the Harlem Renaissance: A The-
matic Study."   Ph.D. Dissertation, New York University, 1973.
_____.   The Novels of the Harlem Renaissance: Twelve Black
Writers, 1923-1933.   University Park: Pennsylvania State Uni-
versity Press, 1976.
Starke, Catherine Juanita.   Black Portraiture in American Fiction:
Stock Characters, Archetypes, and Individuals.   New York:
Basic Books, 1971.
Turner, Darwin T.   "The Negro Novel in America: In Rebuttal."
CLA Journal 10 (December 1966):   122-134.
Turpin, Waters E.   "Four Short Fiction Writers of the Harlem
Renaissance--Their Legacy of Achievement."   CLA Journal 11
(September 1967):   59-72.
Watkins, C. A.   "Simple, Alter Ego of Langston Hughes."   Black
Scholar 2 (June 1971):   18-26.
Whitlow, Roger.   Black American Literature: A Critical History.

Chicago: Nelson Hall, 1973.

Wilkins, R. "Langston Hughes: A Tribute." Crisis 74 (June 1967): 246.

Williams, Melvin G. "Langston Hughes's Jesse B. Semple: A Black Walter Mitty." Negro American Literature Forum 10 (Summer 1976): 66-69.

_____. "Snow White." Christianity and Literature 22 (Winter 1973): 29-34.

Young, James O. Black Writers of the Thirties. Baton Rouge: Louisiana State University Press, 1973.

Reviews

Laughing to Keep from Crying

Bontemps, Arna. Saturday Review, 5 April 1952, p. 17.

Cooperman, Stanley. New Republic, 5 May 1952, p. 21.

Hedden, Wm. T. New York Herald Tribune, 30 March 1952, p. 6.

Library Journal, 15 February 1952, p. 361.

Meier, August. Crisis 59 (June-July 1952): 398-399.

Moon, Bucklin. New York Times, 23 March 1952, p. 4.

Parker, John. Phylon 13 (Fall 1952): 257-258.

Not Without Laughter

Booklist, 19 December 1930, p. 160.

Bookman (February 1930): 611.

Brown, Sterling A. Opportunity 8 (September 1930): 279-280.

Calverton, V. F. Nation, 6 August 1930, p. 157.

Carmon, W. New Masses (October 1930): 17-18.

Cleveland Open Shelf (December 1930): 148.

Crisis 37 (September 1930): 321.

New York Herald Tribune Books, 27 July 1930, p. 5.

New York Times Book Review, 3 August 1930, p. 6.

Pittsburgh Monthly Bulletin 35 (October 1930): 70.

Ross, Mary. Books, 27 July 1930, p. 5.

Saturday Review of Literature, 23 August 1930, p. 69; 6 September 1930, p. 288.

Times Literary Supplement, 2 October 1930, p. 778.

World Tomorrow 13 (December 1930): 520.

Simple Speaks His Mind

Akselrad, Rosemarie P. Phylon 22 (Winter 1961): 395.

Brown, Lloyd L. "Not So Simple." Masses & Mainstream 3 (June 1950): 81-84.

Chandler, G. Lewis. Phylon 20 (Spring 1951): 94-95.

Pfaff, William. Commonweal, 26 May 1950, p. 181.

Redding, Saunders. New York Herald Tribune, 11 June 1950, p. 13.

Smith, Hugh. Crisis 57 (June 1950): 377-378.

Smith, William. New Republic, 4 September 1950, p. 20.

Van Vechten, Carl. New York Times, 7 May 1950, p. 10.

Simple Stakes a Claim

Bonosky, Phillip. Mainstream 11 (January 1958): 53-57.

Booklist, 1 November 1957, p. 136.

Hogan, William. San Francisco Chronicle, 24 September 1957, p. 19.

Jackson, Luther. Crisis 64 (November 1957): 576-577.
Kirkus, 15 July 1957, p. 497.
Library Journal, 1 September 1957, p. 2021.
Millstein, Gilbert. New York Times Book Review, 29 September 1957, p. 41.
New Yorker, 2 November 1957, p. 195.
Parker, John. Phylon 18 (Fourth Quarter 1957): 435-436.
Simple Takes a Wife
　　Berry, Abner. Masses & Mainstream 6 (September 1953): 55-58.
　　Bontemps, Arna. New York Herald Tribune, 14 June 1953, p. 12.
　　Van Vechten, Carl. New York Times, 31 May 1953, p. 5.
Simple's Uncle Sam
　　Booklist, 15 December 1965, p. 392.
　　Choice 3 (April 1966): 122.
　　Kirkus, 1 August 1965, p. 786.
　　Library Journal, 1 November 1965, p. 4806.
　　New York Times, 11 November 1965, p. 49m.
　　Publishers' Weekly, 14 August 1967, p. 52.
　　Randall, Dudley. Negro Digest 15 (April 1966): 52.
　　Rennert, M. Book Week, 25 December 1965, p. 10.
Something in Common and Other Stories
　　Kugher, Ruben F. Library Journal, 1 February 1963, p. 574.
Tambourines to Glory
　　Best Sellers, 15 March 1970, p. 479.
　　Booklist, 1 November 1958, p. 112; 1 December 1958, p. 184.
　　Blair, Howard. San Francisco Chronicle, 4 December 1958, p. 3-3RD.
　　Bontemps, Arna. New York Herald Tribune Book Review, 7 December 1958, p. 4.
　　Coleman, John. Spectator, 25 September 1959, p. 416.
　　Guardian, 18 September 1959, p. 8.
　　Kirkus, 1 November 1958, p. 832.
　　Millstein, Gilbert. New York Times, 23 November 1958, p. 51.
　　New Yorker, 24 January 1959, p. 124.
　　Parker, John. Phylon 29 (Spring 1959): 100-101.
　　Times Literary Supplement, 25 September 1959, p. 541.
　　Waterhouse, Keith. New Statesman, 19 September 1959, p. 366.
Ways of White Folks
　　Anderson, Sherwood. Nation, 11 July 1934, p. 49.
　　Booklist 30 (July 1934): 351.
　　Boston Transcript, 30 June 1934, p. 3.
　　Brickell, Herschel. North American Review 238 (September 1934): 286.
　　Cleveland Open Shelf (July 1934): 6.
　　Gannett, Lewis. New York Herald Tribune, 27 June 1934, p. 15.
　　Gregory, Horace. Books, 1 July 1934, p. 4.
　　Gruening, Martha. New Republic, 5 September 1934, p. 108.
　　Holmes, E. C. Opportunity 12 (September 1934): 283-284.
　　Locke, Alain. Survey Graphic 23 (November 1934): 565.
　　Loggins, Vernon. Saturday Review of Literature, 14 July

1934, p. 805.
Plomer, William. Spectator, 4 January 1935, p. 25.
Streater, George. Crisis 41 (July 1934): 216.
Times Literary Supplement, 25 October 1934, p. 736.
Zugsmith, Leane. New York Times Book Review, 1 July 1934,
p. 6.

HUMPHREY, Lillie Muse

Novel

Aggie. New York: Vantage, 1955.

HUNTER, Kristin (Mrs. John I. Lattany)

Novels

God Bless the Child. New York: Scribner's, 1964; New York:
Bantam, 1970.
The Landlord. New York: Scribner's, 1966; New York: Avon,
1970.
The Survivors. New York: Scribner's, 1975.

Short Fiction

"Debut." Negro Digest 17 (June 1968): 62-69; also in Beaty, Nor-
ton Introduction to Literature: Fiction; Smart, Women & Men,
Men & Women; Stansbury, Impact; Turner, Black American
Literature: Fiction.
"Honor among Thieves." Essence 1 (April 1971): 34-35.
"How I Got in the Grocery Business." Black World 21 (June 1972):
58-64.
"An Interesting Social Study." In Cowan, et al., Three for Show;
Hughes, The Best Short Stories by Negro Writers.
"Supersonic." Mandala (Philadelphia) 1 no. 1 (1956).
"There Was a Little Girl." Rogue (New York), 1959.
"To Walk in Beauty." Sub-Deb Scoop (Philadelphia), 1953.

Biography and Criticism

Authors in the News, vol. 1. Detroit: Gale, 1976.
"Black Writer's Views on Literary Lions and Values." Negro Di-
gest 17 (January 1968): 40.
Booth, Martha F. "Black Ghetto Life Portrayed in Novels for the
Adolescent." Ph.D. Dissertation, University of Iowa, 1971.
Contemporary Authors, 13/14.
Edwards, Sister Ann. "Three Views on Blacks: The Black Woman
in American Literature." CEA Critic 37 (May 1975): 14-16.
Reilly, John M. In Contemporary Novelists. Edited by James Vin-
son. New York: St. Martin's Press, 1976.
Rush, Theressa Gunnels, Carol Fairbanks Myers, Esther Spring

Arata. Black American Writers Past and Present. Metuchen,
N.J.: Scarecrow Press, 1975.
Schraufnagel, Noel. From Apology to Protest: The Black Ameri-
can Novel. DeLand, Fla.: Everett/Edwards, 1973.
Whitlow, Roger. Black American Literature: A Critical History.
Chicago: Nelson Hall, 1973.
Williams, Gladys M. "Blind and Seeing Eyes in the Novel God
Bless the Child. " Obsidian 1 (Summer 1975): 18-26.

Reviews

God Bless the Child
> Bims, H. Negro Digest 14 (April 1965): 52.
> Bouise, O. A. Best Sellers, 15 September 1964, p. 217.
> Britton, A. Books & Bookmen 10 (July 1965): 28.
> Buckmaster, Henrietta. Christian Science Monitor, 10 Septem-
> ber 1964, p. 7.
> Critic 23 (December 1964-January 1965): 81.
> Frankel, Haskell. Book Week, 13 September 1964, p. 16.
> Kelley, M. E. Library Journal, 15 September 1964, p. 89.
> Murray, J. G. America, 12 September 1964, p. 262.
> Observer, 30 May 1965, p. 27.
> Saal, R. W. New York Times Book Review, 20 September
> 1964, p. 36.
The Landlord
> Brooks, Gwendolyn. Book Week, 8 May 1966, p. 14.
> Chapman, Abraham. Saturday Review of Literature, 14 May
> 1966, p. 45.
> Giles, Louise. Library Journal, 1 March 1966, p. 1245.
> Kirkus, 15 January 1966, p. 84.
> McAleer, J. J. Best Sellers, 1 May 1966, p. 51.
> New Yorker, 10 September 1966, p. 222.
> Randall, D. Negro Digest 16 (December 1966): 90.
> Sarris, A. New York Times Book Review, 24 April 1966,
> p. 41.
The Survivors
> Best Sellers 35 (October 1975): 197.
> Booklist, 15 May 1975, p. 941.
> Choice 12 (October 1975): 999.
> Kirkus 1 March 1975, p. 256; 15 March 1975, p. 322.
> Library Journal, 15 June 1975, p. 1240.
> Wilson Library Bulletin 50 (October 1975): 115.

HURSTON, Zora Neale

Novels

Jonah's Gourd Vine. Philadelphia: Lippincott, 1934, 1971.
Moses, Man of the Mountain. Philadelphia: Lippincott, 1939;
Chatham, N.J.: Chatham Bookseller, 1975.
Seraph on the Suwanee. New York: Scribner's, 1948; New York:
AMS Press, 1974.

Their Eyes Were Watching God. Philadelphia: Lippincott, 1937;
London: J. M. Dent, 1938; New York: Fawcett, 1969; New
York: Negro Universities Press, 1969. Excerpts in Brown,
Davis and Lee, The Negro Caravan; Hughes, The Book of Negro
Humor; Patterson, An Introduction to Black Literature in Ameri-
ca.

Short Fiction

"The Conscience of the Court." Saturday Evening Post, 18 March
1950, pp. 22-23.
"Drenched in Light." Opportunity 2 (December 1924): 371-374;
also in Cromwell, Turner and Dykes, Readings from Negro
Authors for Schools and Colleges.
"The Fire and the Cloud." Challenge 1 (September 1934): 10-12.
"The Gilded Six-Bits." Story Magazine, August 1933; also in Barks-
dale and Kinnamon, Black Writers of America; Burnett, Black
Hands on a White Face; Burnett and Foley, Story in America,
1933-1934; Clarke, American Negro Short Stories; Foley, 200
Years of Great American Short Stories; Hughes, The Best Short
Stories by Negro Writers.
"John Redding Goes to Sea." Opportunity 4 (January 1926): 16-21.
"Magnolia Flower." Spokesman, July 1925.
"Muttsy." Opportunity 4 (August 1926): 246-250, 267.
"Spunk." Opportunity 3 (June 1925): 171-173.
"Sweat." Fire! 1 (November 1926): 40-45; also in Huggins, Voices
from the Harlem Renaissance; Turner, Black American Litera-
ture: Fiction.

Biography and Criticism

Abrahams, Roger D. "Negotiating Respect: Patterns of Presenta-
tion among Black Women." Journal of American Folklore 88
(January-March 1975): 58-80.
Alsterlund, B. Biographical Sketch. Wilson Bulletin 13 (May 1939):
586.
"Anisfeld Awards to Hurston and Pierson." Publishers' Weekly, 27
February 1943, p. 1023.
Blake, Emma L. "Zora Neale Hurston: Author and Folklorist."
Negro History Bulletin 29 (April 1966): 149-150, 164.
Bone, Robert A. Down Home: A History of Afro-American Short
Fiction from Its Beginnings to the End of the Harlem Renais-
sance. New York: G. P. Putnam's Sons, 1975.
_____. The Negro Novel in America. New Haven: Yale Univer-
sity Press, 1966.
Bontemps, Arna. The Harlem Renaissance Remembered. New
York: Dodd, Mead, 1972.
Brawley, Benjamin. The Negro Genius. New York: Dodd, Mead,
1940.
Brown, Martha Hursey. "Images of Black Women: Family Roles
in Harlem Renaissance Literature." D.A. Dissertation, Carne-
gie-Mellon University, 1976.
Byrd, James W. "Zora Neale Hurston: A Novel Folklorist." Ten-

nessee Folklore Society Bulletin 21 (June 1955): 37-41.
Davidson, Colleen Tighe. "Beyond the Sentimental Heroine: The
Feminist Character in American Novels, 1899-1937." Ph.D.
Dissertation, University of Minnesota, 1975.
Davis, Arthur P. From the Dark Tower. Washington, D.C.:
Howard University Press, 1974.
Doyle, Sister Mary Ellen. "The Heroine of Black Novels." In
Perspectives on Afro-American Women, pp. 112-125. Edited
by Willa D. Johnson and Thomas L. Green. Washington, D.C.:
ECCA Publications, 1975.
Fullinwider, S. P. The Mind and Mood of Black America: Twen-
tieth Century Thought. Homewood, Ill.: Dorsey, 1969.
Gayle, Addison, Jr. Black Expression. New York: Weybright &
Talley, 1969.
_____. The Way of the New World: The Black Novel in Ameri-
ca. Garden City, N.Y.: Anchor Press/Doubleday, 1975.
Giles, James. "The Significance of Time in Zora Neale Hurston's
Their Eyes Were Watching God." Negro American Literature
Forum 6 (Spring 1972): 52.
Gloster, Hugh M. Negro Voices in American Fiction. Chapel Hill:
University of North Carolina Press, 1948.
_____. "Zora Neale Hurston, Novelist and Folklorist." Phylon
3 (Second Quarter 1943): 153-156.
Harris, Trudier. "Zora Neale Hurston, Folklorist." Paper pre-
sented at the MLA convention, San Francisco, December 1975.
Hart, Robert C. "Black-White Literary Relations in the Harlem
Renaissance." American Literature 44 (January 1973): 612-
628.
Helmick, Evelyn Thomas. "Zora Neale Hurston." The Carrell
(Journal of the Friends of the University of Miami, Florida,
Library) 2 (1970): 1-19.
Hemenway, Robert, ed. The Black Novelist. Columbus: Charles
E. Merrill, 1970.
_____. "Discoveries in the Hurston Biography." Paper pre-
sented at the MLA convention, San Francisco, December 1975.
_____. "Zora Neale Hurston." Paper presented at the MLA
convention, San Francisco, December 1975.
Howard, Lillie. "A New Look at Zora Neale Hurston's Seraph on
the Suwanee." Paper presented at the MLA meeting, New York
City, December 1976.
_____. "Zora Neale Hurston: A Non-Revolutionary Black Ar-
tist." Ph.D. Dissertation, The University of New Mexico,
1975.
Huggins, Nathan Irvin. Harlem Renaissance. New York: Oxford
University Press, 1971.
Hughes, Langston. The Big Sea. New York: Knopf, 1940.
_____. "Harlem Literati in the Twenties." Saturday Review of
Literature, 22 June 1940, pp. 13-14.
Hurst, Fannie. "Zora Hurston: A Personality Sketch." Yale Uni-
versity Library Gazette 35 (1961): 17-22.
Jackson, Blyden. "Some Negroes in the Land of Goshen." Ten-
nessee Folklore Society Bulletin 19 (December 1953): 103-107.
Kent, George. Blackness and the Adventure of Western Culture.

Chicago: Third World Press, 1972.

Kilson, Marion. "The Transformation of Eatonville's Ethnographer." Phylon 33 (Summer 1972): 112-119.

Love, Theresa R. "The Black Woman in Afro-American Literature." Paper presented at the Midwest Modern Language Association Meeting, Chicago, November 1975. (Mimeographed.)
_____. "Zora Neale Hurston's America." Papers on Language and Literature 12 (Fall 1976): 422-437.

Major, Clarence. "Tradition and Presence: Experimental Fiction by Black American Writers." American Poetry Review 5 (May/June 1976): 33-34.

Murray, Marian. Jump at the Sun: The Story of Zora Neale Hurston. New York: Third Press, 1975.

Neal, Larry. "Eatonville's Zora Neale Hurston: A Profile." In Black Review No. 2, pp. 11-24. Edited by Mel Watkins. New York: Morrow, 1972.

Perry, Margaret. Silence to the Drums: A Survey of the Literature of the Harlem Renaissance. Contributions in Afro-American and African Studies, no. 18. Westport, Conn.: Greenwood Press, 1976.

Pratt, T. "Hurston, Zora Neale: A Memoir." Negro Digest 11 (February 1962): 52-56.

Rayson, Ann L. "The Novels of Zora Neale Hurston." Studies in Black Literature 5 (Winter 1974): 1-10.

Rosenblatt, Roger. Black Fiction. Cambridge: Harvard University Press, 1974.

Royster, Beatrice Horn. "The Ironic Vision of Four Black Women Novelists: A Study of the Novels of Jessie Fauset, Nella Larsen, Zora Neale Hurston, and Ann Petry." Ph.D. Dissertation, Emory University, 1975.

Rush, Theressa Gunnels, Carol Fairbanks Myers, and Esther Spring Arata. Black American Writers Past and Present. Metuchen, N.J.: Scarecrow Press, 1975.

Sato, Hiroko. "Zora Neale Hurston Shiron." Oberon (Tokyo) 34 (1971): 30-37.

Schraufnagel, Noel. From Apology to Protest: The Black American Novel. DeLand, Fla.: Everett/Edwards, 1973.

Smith, Barbara. "The Fiction of Zora Neale Hurston." Paper presented at the MLA convention, San Francisco, December 1975.

Taylor, Clyde. "Black Folk Spirit and the Shape of Black Literature." Black World 21 (August 1972): 31-40.

Turner, Darwin T. In a Minor Chord: Three Afro-American Writers and Their Search for Identity. Carbondale & Edwardsville: Southern Illinois University Press, 1971.
_____. "The Negro Novelist and the South." Southern Humanities Review 1 (1967): 21-29.

Walker, Alice. "In Search of Zora Neale Hurston." Ms. 3 (March 1975): 74-79, 85-89.

Walker, S. Jay. "Zora Neale Hurston's Their Eyes Were Watching God: Black Novel of Sexism." Modern Fiction Studies 20 (Winter 1974-1975): 519-527.

Washington, Mary Helen. "Zora Neale Hurston: The Black Woman's Search for Identity." Black World 21 (August 1972): 68-75.

Young, James O. Black Writers of the Thirties. Baton Rouge: Louisiana State University Press, 1973.

Reviews

Jonah's Gourd Vine
> Best Sellers, 1 January 1972, p. 444.
> Booklist, 30 July 1934, p. 351.
> Brickell, Herschel. New York Post, 5 May 1934, p. 13.
> _____. North American Review 238 (July 1934): 95.
> Felton, Estelle. Opportunity 12 (August 1934): 252-253.
> Gruening, Martha. New Republic, 11 July 1934, p. 244.
> Nation 138 (June 1934): 683.
> Pinckney, Josephine. Books, 6 May 1934, p. 7.
> Plomer, William. Spectator, 4 January 1935, p. 25.
> Saturday Review, 3 November 1934, p. 344.
> Times Literary Supplement, 18 October 1934, p. 716.
> Wallace, Margaret. New York Times Book Review, 6 May 1934, p. 6.

Moses, Man of the Mountain
> Booklist, 15 December 1939, p. 150.
> Carmer, Carl. Books, 26 November 1939, p. 5.
> Hutchinson, Percy. New York Times, 19 November 1939, p. 21.
> New Yorker, 11 November 1939, p. 91.
> Slomovitz, Philip. Christian Century, 6 December 1939, p. 1504.
> Smith, M. E. Boston Transcript, 18 November 1939, p. 2.
> Untermeyer, Louis. Saturday Review of Literature, 11 November 1939, p. 11.

Seraph on the Suwanee
> Christian Science Monitor, 23 December 1948, p. 11.
> Hedden, W. T. New York Herald Tribune Weekly Book Review, 10 October 1948, p. 2.
> Kane, H. T. Chicago Sun Bookweek, 17 November 1948, p. 58.
> Kirkus, 15 August 1948, p. 415.
> Slaughter, F. G. New York Times Book Review, 31 October 1948, p. 24.

Their Eyes Were Watching God
> Booklist, 15 October 1937, p. 71.
> Brown, S. A. Nation, 16 October 1937, p. 409.
> Ferguson, Otis. New Republic, 13 October 1937, p. 276.
> Hibben, Sheila. Books, 26 September 1937, p. 2.
> Huntor, W. A. Journal of Negro Education 7 (January 1938): 71-72.
> Publishers' Weekly, 21 July 1969, p. 61.
> Stevens, George. Saturday Review of Literature, 18 September 1937, p. 3.
> Tompkins, Lucy. New York Times Book Review, 26 September 1937, p. 29.
> Time, 20 September 1937, p. 71.
> Wright, Richard. New Masses, 5 October 1937, pp. 22-25.

HYMAN, Mark

Short Fiction

"The Shepherd." In Ford and Faggett, Best Short Stories by Afro-American Writers.

ICEBERG SLIM see Beck, Robert

IMBERT, Dennis I.

Novel

The Colored Gentlemen. New Orleans: Williams Printing Service, 1931.

IMES, Nella Larsen see Larsen, Nella

JACKSON, Blyden

Novels

Operation Burning Candle. Moonachie, N.J.: Pyramid Publications, 1974.
Totem. New York: Third Press, 1974.

Biography and Criticism

Rush, Theressa Gunnels, Carol Fairbanks Myers, and Esther Spring Arata. Black American Writers Past and Present. Metuchen, N.J.: Scarecrow Press, 1975.

Reviews

Operation Burning Candle
    Best Sellers, 1 February 1975, p. 499.
    Book World, 1 December 1974, p. 4.
    Bryant, J. H. Nation, 12 November 1973, p. 501.
    Kirkus, 1 August 1973, p. 830.
    Library Journal, 1 November 1973, p. 3285.
    McKenna, Stephen. Best Sellers, 1 September 1973, p. 242.
    Publishers' Weekly, 23 July 1973, p. 64.
    Watkins, Mel. New York Times Book Review, 17 February 1974, p. 31.
Totem
    Publishers' Weekly, 4 November 1974, p. 62.

JACKSON, Franklin

Short Fiction

"Claudia." In Watkins, Black Review No. 1.

JACKSON, J. Denis (Julian Moreau)

Novel

The Black Commandos. Atlanta: Cultural Institute Press, 1967.

Biography and Criticism

Pfeiffer, John. "Black American Speculative Literature: A Checklist." Extrapolation 17 (December 1975): 35-43.

JACKSON, James Thomas

Short Fiction

"Reveille." In Schulberg, From the Ashes.
"Shade of Darkness." In Schulberg, From the Ashes.

JACKSON, Mae

Short Fiction

"Cleaning Out the Closet." Black Scholar 8 (March 1977): 31-35.
"I Remember Omar." Negro Digest 18 (June 1969): 83-85.

Biography and Criticism

Rush, Theressa Gunnels, Carol Fairbanks Myers, and Esther Spring
Arata. Black American Writers Past and Present. Metuchen,
N.J.: Scarecrow Press, 1975.

JACKSON, W. Warner

Novel

The Birth of the Martyn's Ghost: A Novel. New York: Comet,
1957.

JANSSEN, Milton W.

Novel

Divided. New York: Pageant Press, 1963.

JARRETTE, Alfred Q.

Novel

Beneath the Sky: A Novel of Love and Murder among the Poor Whites and Negroes of the Deep South. New York: Weinberg Book Supply, 1949.

Biography and Criticism

Hughes, Carl M. The Negro Novelist 1940-1950. New York: Citadel Press, 1953.
Schraufnagel, Noel. From Apology to Protest: The Black American Novel. DeLand, Florida: Everett/Edwards, 1973.

JARRY, Hawke

Novel

Black Schoolmaster. New York: Exposition, 1970.

Biography and Criticism

Rush, Theressa Gunnels, Carol Fairbanks Myers, and Esther Spring Arata. Black American Writers Past and Present. Metuchen, N.J.: Scarecrow Press, 1975.

Review

Black Schoolmaster
    Journal of Negro Education 40 (Winter 1971): 100.

JEFFERSON, Roland S.

Novel

The School on 103rd Street. New York: Vantage, 1976.

Review

The School on 103rd Street
    Black Scholar 7 (March 1976): 48-49.

JENKINS, Deaderick Franklin

Novels

It Was Not My World. Los Angeles: By the Author, 1942.
Letters to My Son. Los Angeles: By the Author, 1947.

Biography and Criticism

Rush, Theressa Gunnels, Carol Fairbanks Myers, and Esther Spring
Arata. Black American Writers Past and Present. Metuchen,
N.J.: Scarecrow Press, 1975.

Review

It Was Not My World
The Negro Yearbook, 1941-46.

JOANS, Ted

Short Fiction

"A New Fact Filled Fictions of African Reality. " In Sanchez, We
Be Word Sorcerers.

Biography and Criticism

Rush, Theressa Gunnels, Carol Fairbanks Myers, and Esther Spring
Arata. Black American Writers Past and Present. Metuchen,
N.J.: Scarecrow Press, 1975.

JOHNSON, Amelia E. (Mrs. A. E. Johnson)

Novels

Clarence and Corinne; or, God's Way. Philadelphia: American
Baptist Publication Society, 1890.
The Hazeley Family. Philadelphia: American Baptist Publication
Society, 1894.
Martina Meriden; or, What Is My Motive? Philadelphia: American
Baptist Publication Society, 1901.

Biography and Criticism

Majors, M. A. Noted Negro Women, 1893. Freeport, New York:
Books for Libraries, 1971.

JOHNSON, Charles

Novel

Faith and the Good Thing. New York: Viking, 1974.

Reviews

Faith and the Good Thing
Asrelsky, Arnold. Library Journal, 15 November 1974, p. 2982.

Black World 24 (August 1975): 92-94.
Choice 11 (February 1975): 1777.
Gottlieb, Annie. New York Times Book Review, 12 January
    1975, p. 6.
Kirkus, 1 August 1974, p. 927.
Ms. 4 (August 1975): 43.
National Observer, 9 November 1974, p. 25.
New Leader, 23 December 1974, p. 11.
New York Times Book Review, 1 June 1975, p. 26; 7 December
    1975, p. 62.
Pompea, I. N. Best Sellers, 1 January 1975, p. 436.
Publishers' Weekly, 2 September 1974, p. 62.
Sewanee Review 83 (January 1975): 212.
Time, 6 January 1975, p. 92.
Village Voice, 21 November 1974, p. 48.

JOHNSON, Clifford Vincent

Short Fiction

"Old Blues Singers Never Die." In Hughes, The Best Short Stories
    by Negro Writers; Patterson, An Introduction to Black Litera-
    ture in America.

JOHNSON, Doris

Short Fiction

"Somebody." Negro Digest 17 (November 1967): 75-77.

JOHNSON, Eugene D.

Novel

Of Human Kindness. New York: Vantage Press, n.d.

JOHNSON, Fenton

Short Fiction

(Collection): Tales of Darkest America. Chicago: The Favorite
    Magazine, 1920; Freeport, N.Y.: Books for Libraries.
"The Black Fairy." Crisis 6 (October 1913): 292-294.
"The Call of the Patriot." Crisis 13 (February 1917): 169-173.
"The Servant." Crisis 4 (August 1912): 189-190.

Biography and Criticism

Brawley, Benjamin. The Negro Genius. New York: Dodd, Mead,

1940.

Gloster, Hugh M. <u>Negro Voices in American Fiction</u>. Chapel Hill: University of North Carolina Press, 1948.

Rush, Theressa Gunnels, Carol Fairbanks Myers, and Esther Spring Arata. <u>Black American Writers Past and Present</u>. Metuchen, N.J.: Scarecrow Press, 1975.

JOHNSON, James Weldon

Novel

<u>Autobiography of an Ex-Colored Man</u>. Boston: Sherman, French, 1912; New York: Knopf, 1927; New York: Hill & Wang, 1960. Serialized in <u>Half-Century</u>, November 1919-December 1920. Excerpts in Davis and Peplow, <u>The New Negro Renaissance</u>; Davis and Redding, <u>Cavalcade</u>; Kendricks and Levitt, <u>Afro-American Voices</u>; Patterson, <u>An Introduction to Black Literature in America</u>.

Biography and Criticism

Adelman, Lynn. "A Study of James Weldon Johnson." <u>Journal of Negro History</u> 52 (January 1967): 128-145.

Amann, Clarence A. "Three Negro Classics--An Estimate." <u>Negro American Literature Forum</u> 4 (Winter 1970): 113.

Avery, William A. "James Weldon Johnson: American Negro of Distinction." <u>School and Society</u>, 3 September 1968, pp. 291-294.

Baker, H. A. "Forgotten Prototype." <u>Virginia Quarterly</u> 49 (Summer 1973): 433-449.

_____. <u>Singers of Daybreak: Studies in Black American Literature</u>. Washington, D.C.: Howard University Press, 1974.

Bell, Bernard W. <u>The Folk Roots of Contemporary Afro-American Poetry</u>. Detroit: Broadside Press, 1974.

<u>Black Authors</u>. Old Greenwich, Conn.: Listening Library, n.d. (Filmstrip.)

Bone, Robert A. <u>The Negro Novelist in America</u>. New Haven, Conn.: Yale University Press, 1965.

Bontemps, Arna. <u>The Harlem Renaissance Remembered</u>. New York: Dodd, Mead, 1972.

_____. Introduction to <u>The Autobiography of an Ex-Coloured Man</u>. New York: Hill & Wang, 1970.

Bronz, Stephen H. <u>Roots of Negro Racial Consciousness; the 1920's: Three Harlem Renaissance Authors</u>. New York: Libra, 1964.

Davis, Arthur P. <u>From the Dark Tower: Afro-American Writers 1900-1960</u>. Washington, D.C.: Howard University Press, 1974.

Ellison, Curtis William. "Black Adam: The Adamic Assertion and the Afro-American Novelist." Ph.D. Dissertation, University of Minnesota, 1970.

Fleming, Robert E. "Contemporary Themes in Johnson's Autobio-
graphy of an Ex-Colored Man." Negro American Literature
Forum 4 (1970): 120-124, 141.
Garrett, M. P. "Early Recollections of and Structural Irony in The
Autobiography of an Ex-Colored Man." Critique 13 (1971):
5-14.
Gayle, Addison, Jr. The Way of the New World: The Black Novel
in America. Garden City, N.Y.: Anchor Press/Doubleday,
1975.
Gloster, Hugh M. Negro Voices in American Fiction. Chapel Hill,
N.C.: University of North Carolina Press, 1948.
Hart, Robert C. "Black-White Literary Relations in the Harlem
Renaissance." American Literature 44 (January 1973): 612-
628.
Huggins, Nathan Irvin. Harlem Renaissance. New York: Oxford
University Press, 1971.
_____. "Irony as a Key to Johnson's The Autobiography of an
Ex-Colored Man." American Literature 43 (March 1971):
83-96.
Jackson, Miles, Jr. "James Weldon Johnson." Black World 19
(June 1970): 55-56.
_____. "Literary History: Documentary Sidelights--James Wel-
don Johnson and Claude McKay." Negro Digest 17 (June 1968):
25-29.
Kent, George. Blackness and the Adventure of Western Culture.
Chicago: Third World Press, 1972.
_____. "Patterns of the Renaissance." Black World 21 (June
1972): 13.
Killens, John O. "Another Time When Black Was Beautiful."
Black World 20 (November 1970): 20-36.
Levy, Eugene. James Weldon Johnson: Black Leader, Black
Voice. Chicago: University of Chicago Press, 1976.
Millican, Arthenia Bates. "James Weldon Johnson: In Quest of an
Afrocentric Tradition for Black American Literature." Ph.D.
Dissertation, Louisiana State University and Agricultural and
Mechanical College, 1972.
Perry, Margaret. Silence to the Drums: A Survey of the Litera-
ture of the Harlem Renaissance. Contributions in Afro-American
and African Studies, no. 18. Westport, Conn.: Greenwood
Press, 1976.
Ramsey, Priscilla. "A Study of Black Identity in 'Passing' Novels
of the Nineteenth and Early Twentieth Centuries." Studies in
Black Literature 7 (Winter 1976): 1-7.
_____. "A Study of Black Identity in 'Passing' Novels of the
Nineteenth and Early Twentieth Centuries." Ph.D. Dissertation,
The American University, 1975.
Rosenblatt, Roger. Black Fiction. Cambridge: Harvard University
Press, 1974.
Ross, Stephen M. "Audience and Irony in Johnson's The Autobio-
graphy of an Ex-Coloured Man." CLA Journal 18 (December
1974): 198-210.
Rush, Theressa Gunnels, Carol Fairbanks Myers, and Esther Spring
Arata. Black American Writers Past and Present. Metuchen,

N.J.: Scarecrow Press, 1975.

Schraufnagel, Noel. From Apology to Protest: The Black American Novel. DeLand, Fla.: Everett/Edwards, 1973.

Scruggs, Charles. "'All Dressed Up But No Place to Go': The Black Writer and His Audience During the Harlem Renaissance." American Literature 48 (January 1977): 543-563.

Skerrett, Joseph Taylor, Jr. "Take My Burden Up: Three Studies in Psychobiographical Criticism and Afro-American Fiction." Ph.D. Dissertation, Yale University, 1975.

Starke, Catherine Juanita. Black Portraiture in American Fiction: Stock Characters, Archetypes, and Individuals. New York: Basic Books, 1971.

Stepto, Robert Burns. "From Behind the Veil: Afro-American Reform Literature at the Turn of the Century." Ph.D. Dissertation, Stanford University, 1974.

Stetson, Earlene. "The Mulatto Motif in Black Fiction." Ph.D. Dissertation, State University of New York at Buffalo, 1976.

Waniek, Marilyn Nelson. "The Space Where Sex Should Be: Toward a Definition of the Black American Literary Tradition." Studies in Black Literature 6 (Fall 1975): 7-13.

Reviews

The Autobiography of an Ex-Colored Man
Booklist 24 (January 1928): 174.
Nelson, Alice Dunbar. Opportunity 5 (November 1927): 337-338.
New Republic, 1 February 1928, p. 303.
Ovington, M. W. Survey, 1 November 1927, p. 164.
Pittsburgh Monthly Bulletin 32 (December 1927): 627.
Spectator, 25 February 1928, p. 267.
Thompson, C. W. New York Times, 16 October 1927, p. 14.
Times Literary Supplement, 22 March 1928, p. 207.

JOHNSON, Joe

Short Fiction

"He Shoulda Picked Up on a Trade." Black Creation 3 (Winter 1972): 30-33.
"A Man's Best Friend." Yardbird Reader 3 (1974): 57-60.
"Yes, Jesus Loves Me." Yardbird Reader 1 (1972): 13-16.

Biography and Criticism

Rush, Theressa Gunnels, Carol Fairbanks Myers, and Esther Spring Arata. Black American Writers Past and Present. Metuchen, N.J.: Scarecrow Press, 1975.

JOHNSON, Ruth

Short Fiction

"Cross Buns for Friday." In Ford and Faggett, Best Short Stories by Afro-American Writers.

JOHNSON, William Matthews

Novel

The House on Corbet Street. New York: William-Frederick Press, 1967.

Biography and Criticism

Rush, Theressa Gunnels, Carol Fairbanks Myers, and Esther Spring Arata. Black American Writers Past and Present. Metuchen, N.J.: Scarecrow Press, 1975.

JONES, Edward P.

Short Fiction

"Harvest." Essence 7 (November 1976): 84, 108-110, 112, 114-115, 128.

JONES, Gayl

Novel

Corregidora. New York: Random House, 1975; New York: Bantam, 1976. Excerpts in Fiction 3 no. 1 (1974): 11-15.
Eva's Man. New York: Random House, 1976.

Short Fiction

"Spaces." Black Scholar 9 (June 1975): 53.
"The Welfare Check." Essence 1 (October 1970): 67, 71, 74.

Biography and Criticism

Kent, George E. "The 1975 Black Literary Scene: Significant Developments." Phylon 37 (March 1976): 100-115.
Rush, Theressa Gunnels, Carol Fairbanks Myers, and Esther Spring Arata. Black American Writers Past and Present. Metuchen, N.J.: Scarecrow Press, 1975.

Reviews

Corregidora
    Avant, J. A. New Republic, 28 June 1975, p. 27.
    Booklist, 15 May 1975, p. 941.
    Golden, Bernette. Black World 25 (February 1976): 82.
    Jefferson, Margo. Newsweek, 19 May 1975, p. 84.
    Kirkus, 15 February 1975, p. 195.
    Major, Clarence. Library Journal 100 (August 1975): 1443.
    New Outlook, 9 August 1975, p. 17.
    New York Times, 21 April 1975, p. 27.
    New York Times Book Review, 7 December 1975, p. 62.
    Publishers' Weekly, 24 March 1975, p. 40; 17 May 1976, p. 55.
    Sokolov, Raymond. New York Times Book Review, 25 May
        1975, p. 21.
    Updike, John. New Yorker, 18 August 1975, p. 79.
    Village Voice, 26 May 1975, p. 42.
    Webster, Ivan. Time, 16 June 1975, p. 79.
Eva's Man
    Booklist, 15 April 1976, p. 1164.
    Hairston, Loyle. Freedomways 16 (Second Quarter 1976):
        133-135.
    Jefferson, Margo. Newsweek, 12 April 1976, p. 102.
    Jordan, June. New York Times Book Review, 17 May 1976,
        p. 36.
    Kirkus, 1 January 1976, p. 90.
    Major, Clarence. Library Journal, 15 March 1976, p. 834.
    New Outlook, 17 April 1976, p. 19.
    New York Times, 30 April 1976, p. c17.
    Pinckney, Darryl. New Republic, 19 June 1976, p. 27.
    Publishers' Weekly, 9 February 1976, p. 92.
    Updike, John. New Yorker, 9 August 1976, p. 74.
    Virginia Quarterly Review 52 (Summer 1976): 97.

JONES, J. McHenry

Novel

Hearts of Gold: A Novel. Wheeling, W. Va.: Daily Intelligencer
    Steam Job Press, 1896; College Park, Md.: McGrath, 1969.

Biography and Criticism

Bone, Robert A. The Negro Novel in America. New Haven: Yale
    University Press, 1966.
Gloster, Hugh M. Negro Voices in American Fiction. Chapel Hill:
    University of North Carolina Press, 1948.
Rosenblatt, Roger. Black Fiction. Cambridge: Harvard University
    Press, 1974.
Rush, Theressa Gunnels, Carol Fairbanks Myers, and Esther Spring
    Arata. Black American Writers Past and Present. Metuchen,
    N.J.: Scarecrow Press, 1975.

JONES, John H.

Short Fiction

"The Harlem Rat. " Harlem Quarterly 1 (Fall-Winter 1950): 17-22.

JONES, Ralph H.

Novel

The Pepperpot Man. New York: Vantage, 1965.

Biography and Criticism

Rush, Theressa Gunnels, Carol Fairbanks Myers, and Esther Spring
Arata. Black American Writers Past and Present. Metuchen,
N.J.: Scarecrow Press, 1975.

JONES, Silas

Short Fiction

(Collection): The Price of Dirt. Dockweiller Station, Calif.: Ac-
cent of California, n.d.
"In the Dark. " In Jones, The Price of Dirt.
"The Price of Dirt. " In Jones, The Price of Dirt.
"Roman Times. " Black World 21 (January 1972): 62-65; also in
Jones, The Price of Dirt.
"Waiting for Mongo. " In Jones, The Price of Dirt.
"The Way of Shadows. " Black World 22 (March 1973): 54-62;
also in Jones, The Price of Dirt.

Biography and Criticism

Rush, Theressa Gunnels, Carol Fairbanks Myers, and Esther Spring
Arata. Black American Writers Past and Present. Metuchen,
N.J.: Scarecrow Press, 1975.

Review

Cheatwood, Kiarri. Black World 25 (February 1976): 83-85.

JONES, Yorke

Novel

The Climbers: A Story of Sun-Kissed Sweethearts. Chicago: Glad
Tidings, 1912.

JORDAN, Elsie

Novel

Strange Sinner. New York: Pageant, 1954.

KAYE, Philip B. see Adams, Alger Leroy

KELLEY, William Melvin

Novels

dem. Garden City, N.Y.: Doubleday, 1967. Excerpts in Davis
and Redding, Cavalcade; Hicks, Cutting Edges.
A Different Drummer. New York: Doubleday, 1962. Excerpts in
Margolies, A Native Sons Reader; Miller, Blackamerican Liter-
ature; Kendricks, American Voices.
A Drop of Patience. Garden City, N.Y.: Doubleday, 1965; Chatham,
N.J.: Chatham Bookseller, 1973.
Dunfords Travels Everywhere. Garden City, N.Y.: Doubleday,
1969. Excerpts in Reed, 19 Necromancers from Now.

Short Fiction

(Collection): Dancers on the Shore. Garden City, N.Y.: Double-
day, 1964; Chatham, N.J.: Chatham Bookseller, 1973.
"Brother Carlyle." In Kelley, Dancers on the Shore; Murray and
Thomas, The Scene; Stanford, I, Too, Sing America.
"Bumper's Dream." Black World 19 (October 1970): 54-57.
"Christmas with the Great Man." In Kelley, Dancers on the Shore.
"Connie." In Kelley, Dancers on the Shore; Olsen and Swinburne,
He Who Dares.
"Cry for Me." In Cahill and Cahill, Big City Stories; Kelley, Dan-
cers on the Shore; Emanuel and Gross, Dark Symphony; Long
and Collier, Afro-American Writing.
"The Dentist's Wife." In Barksdale and Kinnamon, Black Writers
of America; Smart, Women & Men, Men & Women.
"Encounter on a Rooftop." In Broer, Karl, and Weingartner, The
First Time; Cahill and Cahill, Big City Stories.
"Enemy Territory." In Ford, Black Insights, Murray and Thomas,
The Journey; Rockwitz, Life Styles.
"A Good Long Sidewalk." Negro Digest 13 (February 1964): 53-59;
also in Chapman, New Black Voices; Clarke, Harlem; Gold,
Point of Departure; Kelley, Dancers on the Shore.
"Jest Like Sam." Negro Digest 18 (October 1969): 61-64.
"The Life You Save." In Kelley, Dancers on the Shore; Margolies,
A Native Sons Reader.
"The Most Beautiful Legs in the World." In Kelley, Dancers on the
Shore.
"Not Exactly Lena Horne." In Kelley, Dancers on the Shore.
"Only Man on Liberty Street." Negro Digest 12 (March 1963):

52-59; also in Davis and Redding, Cavalcade; Kelley, Dancers
on the Shore; Turner, Black American Literature: Fiction.
"Passing." In Hicks, Cutting Edges.
"The Poker Party." In Adams, Conn and Slepian, Afro-American
Literature: Fiction; Adoff, Brothers and Sisters; Kelley, Dan-
cers on the Shore; King, Black Short Story Anthology.
"Saint Paul and the Monkeys." In James, From the Roots; Kelley,
Dancers on the Shore.
"The School." In Murray and Thomas, Major Black Writers.
"The Servant Problem." In Kelley, Dancers on the Shore.
"A Visit to Grandmother." In Ball, Designs for Reading: Short
Stories; Kelley, Dancers on the Shore.
"What Shall We Do with the Drunken Sailor?" In Kelley, Dancers
on the Shore.

Biography and Criticism

Abrahams, Willie E. Introduction to dem. New York: Collier
Books, 1969.
Anderson, Jervis. "Black Writing: The Other Side." Dissent 15
(May-June 1968): 233-242.
Beards, Richard. "Parody as Tribute: William Melvin Kelley's
A Different Drummer and Faulkner." Studies in Black Litera-
ture 5 (Winter 1974): 25-28.
Borden, William. In Contemporary Novelists. Edited by James
Vinson. New York: St. Martin's Press, 1976.
Davis, Arthur P. From the Dark Tower: Afro-American Writers
1900-1960. Washington, D.C.: Howard University Press,
1974.
Eckley, Grace. "The Awakening of Mr. Afrinnegan: Kelley's Dun-
fords Travels Everywhere and Joyce's Finnegans Wake."
Obsidian 1 (Summer 1975): 27-41.
Faulkner, Howard. "The Uses of Tradition: William Melvin Kel-
ley's A Different Drummer." Modern Fiction Studies 21 (Win-
ter 1975-1976): 535-542.
Gayle, Addison, Jr. The Way of the New World: The Black Novel
in America. Garden City, N.Y.: Anchor Press/Doubleday,
1975.
George, Felicia. "Black Woman, Black Man." Harvard Journal of
Afro-American Affairs 2 (1971): 1-17.
Ingrasci, Hugh J. "Strategic Withdrawal or Retreat: Deliverance
from Racial Oppression in Kelley's A Different Drummer and
Faulkner's Go Down, Moses." Studies in Black Literature 6
(Fall 1975): 1-6.
Jarab, Josef. "The Drop of Patience of the American Negro:
W. M. Kelley's A Different Drummer (1959), A Drop of Pa-
tience (1965)." Philologica Pragensia 12 (1969): 159-170.
Kelley, William Melvin. "Ivy League Negro." Esquire 60 (August
1963): 54-56.
Killinger, John. The Fragile Presence: Transcendence in Modern
Literature. Philadelphia: Fortress Press, 1973.
Klinkowitz, J. "Black Superfiction." North American Review 259
(Winter 1974): 69-74.

Klotman, Phyllis Rauch. Another Man Gone: The Black Runner in Contemporary Afro-American Literature. Port Washington, N.Y.: Kennikat Press, 1977.

_____. "Examination of the Black Confidence Man in Two Black Novels: The Man Who Cried I Am and dem." American Literature 44 (January 1973): 596-611.

_____. "The Passive Resistant in A Different Drummer, Day of Absence and Many Thousand Gone." Studies in Black Literature 3 (Autumn 1972): 7-12.

_____. "The White Bitch Archetype in Black Fiction." The Bulletin of the Midwest Modern Language Association 6 (Spring 1973): 96-110.

Nadeau, Robert L. "Black Jesus: A Study of Kelley's A Different Drummer." Studies in Black Literature 2 (Summer 1971): 13-15.

Pfeiffer, John. "Black American Speculative Literature: A Checklist." Extrapolation 17 (December 1975): 35-43.

Randall, Dudley. "On the Conference Beat." Negro Digest 16 (1967): 89-93.

Ro, Sigmund. "The Black Musician as Literary Hero: Baldwin's 'Sonny's Blues' and Kelley's 'Cry for Me.'" American Studies in Scandinavia 7 no. 1 (1975): 17-48.

Rosenblatt, Roger. Black Fiction. Cambridge: Harvard University Press, 1974.

Schatt, Stanley. "You Must Go Home Again: Today's Afro-American Expatriate Writers." Negro American Literature Forum 7 (Fall 1973): 80-82.

Schraufnagel, Noel. From Apology to Protest: The Black American Novel. DeLand, Fla.: Everett/Edwards, 1973.

"Talent's 'New Wave.'" Negro Digest 11 (October 1962): 43-47.

Weyant, Jill. "The Kelley Saga: Violence in America." CLA Journal 19 (December 1975): 210-220.

Weyl, Donald M. "The Vision of Man in the Novels of William Melvin Kelley." Critique 15 no. 3 (1974): 15-33.

Whitlow, Roger. Black American Literature: A Critical History. Chicago: Nelson Hall, 1973.

"William Melvin Kelley." Negro Digest 11 (October 1962): 44-46.

Williams, Gladys M. "Technique as Evaluation of Subject in A Different Drummer." CLA Journal 19 (December 1975): 221-237.

Reviews

Dancers on the Shore
    Choice 1 (June 1964): 133.
    Dolbier, M. New York Herald Tribune, 20 March 1964, p. 21.
    Harding, W. Books Today, 22 March 1964, p. 6.
    Hentoff, Nat. Reporter, 21 May 1964, p. 56.
    Katz, Bill. Library Journal, 1 April 1964, p. 1623.
    Lamott, K. Show 4 (April 1964): 48.
    Lask, T. New York Times, 20 April 1964, p. 27.
    Murray, Michele. Commonweal, 3 July 1964, p. 458.
    Rubin, Louis. New York Herald Tribune, 22 March 1964, p. 11.

Ryan, S. P. Best Sellers, 15 April 1964, p. 28.
Stevens, E. Books & Bookmen 10 (March 1965): 28.

dem

Bone, Robert. New York Times Book Review, 24 September
    1967, p. 5.
Choice 5 (September 1968): 777.
Harding, Walter. Library Journal 92 (August 1967): 2808.
Jaffe, D. Prairie Schooner 42 (Spring 1968): 83.
Kirkus, 15 July 1967, p. 828.
Publishers' Weekly, 10 July 1967, p. 177.
Resnick, H. S. Saturday Review of Literature, 28 October
    1967, p. 40.
Shapiro, F. Book World, 22 October 1967, p. 10.

A Different Drummer

Booklist, 1 July 1962, p. 751.
Byrd, James W. Phylon 24 (Spring 1963): 99.
Crisis 69 (October 1962): 502.
Galloway, D. D. Critique 6 (Winter 1963-1964): 150.
Hamilton, A. Books & Bookmen 10 (August 1965) 28.
Harding, Walter. Chicago Sunday Tribune, 10 June 1962, p. 3.
Howe, I. Harper's 239 (December 1969): 130.
Katz, Bill. Library Journal, 1 June 1962, p. 2157.
Kirkus, 1 April 1962, p. 340.
Lyell, F. H. New York Times Book Review, 17 June 1962,
    p. 24.
Morton, Robert. Show (July 1962): 93.
Pickrel, Paul. Harper's 225 (August 1962): 94.
Prescott, Orville. New York Times, 8 June 1962, p. 29.
Rogers, W. G. New York Herald Tribune Books, 17 June
    1962, p. 4.
Springfield Republican, 26 August 1962, p. 4D.
Times Literary Supplement, 24 May 1963, p. 377.
Tuchy, F. Spectator, 14 June 1963, p. 784.
White, Ellington. Kenyon Review 24 (Autumn 1962): 750.

A Drop of Patience

Balliett, W. New Yorker, 22 May 1965, p. 177.
Booklist, 1 May 1965, p. 860.
Boroff, David. New York Times Book Review, 2 May 1965,
    p. 40.
Choice 2 (1965): 387.
Craig, D. New Statesman, 11 March 1966, p. 347.
Dolbier, M. New York Herald Tribune, 9 April 1965, p. 21.
Frankel, H. National Observer, 19 April 1965, p. 21.
Hoyt, C. A. Saturday Review, 17 April 1965, p. 50.
Jennings, E. Spectator, 18 March 1966, p. 334.
Katz, Bill. Library Journal, 15 March 1965, p. 1348.
Kirkus, 1 February 1965, p. 130.
Malkin, M. A. Antiquarian Bookman, 30 August 1965, p. 732.
Murray, J. G. America, 17 April 1965, p. 584.
Newsweek, 12 April 1965, p. 113.
Prescott, O. New York Times, 9 April 1965, p. 35M.
Quinn, J. L. Best Sellers, 15 April 1965, p. 41.
Randall, Dudley. Negro Digest 14 (July 1965): 51.

Stevens, E. Books and Bookmen 11 (April 1966): 36.
Times Literary Supplement, 17 March 1966, p. 217.
Wain, J. Observer, 13 March 1966, p. 27.
Dunfords Travels Everywhere
Anderson, H. T. Best Sellers, 1 October 1971, p. 261.
Black World 20 (January 1971): 93.
Lehmann-Haupt, C. New York Times Book Review, 7 September 1970, p. 15.
Mason, Clifford. New York Times Book Review, 8 November 1970, p. 50.
Moon, Eric. Library Journal 95 (August 1970): 2717.
Wood, Michael. New York Review of Books, 11 March 1971, p. 41.

KEMP, Arnold

Novel

Eat of Me: I Am the Savior. New York: Morrow, 1972; New York: Lancer Books, 1972.

Short Fiction

"The Blue of Madness." In Coombs, What We Must See.

Reviews

Eat of Me: I Am the Savior
Black World 22 (November 1972): 90.
Book World, 10 June 1973, p. 13.
Kirkus, 15 March 1972, p. 346.
Library Journal, 1 June 1972, p. 2117.
New York Times, 29 June 1972, p. 23.
New Yorker, 22 July 1972, p. 78.
Publishers' Weekly, 13 March 1972, p. 65.
Sale, Roger. New York Review of Books, 29 June 1972, p. 30.
Williams, R. J. Best Sellers, 15 July 1972, p. 194.

KENNEDY, Mark

Novel

The Pecking Order. New York: Appleton, 1953.

Biography and Criticism

Maund, Alfred. "The Negro Novelist and the Contemporary American Scene." Chicago Jewish Forum 12 (Fall 1954): 28-34.

Reviews

The Pecking Order
Algren, Nelson. Saturday Review of Literature, 6 June 1953,
p. 16.
Booklist, 15 June 1953, p. 340.
Byam, M. S. Library Journal 78 (July 1953): 1235.
Capers, Charlotte. New York Times, 26 July 1953, p. 14.
Kirkus, 15 April 1953, p. 270.
Ottley, Roi. Chicago Sunday Tribune, 28 June 1953, p. 4.
Spencer, Joanna. New York Herald Tribune Book Review, 7
June 1953, p. 6.

KENT, George E.

Short Fiction

"Intruder." Black World 23 (January 1974): 54-62.

Biography and Criticism

Rush, Theressa Gunnels, Carol Fairbanks Myers, and Esther Spring
Arata. Black American Writers Past and Present. Metuchen,
N.J.: Scarecrow Press, 1975.

KGOSITILE, Keorapetse William

Short Fiction

"The Aboriginal Mash." Negro Digest 18 (October 1969): 54-60.
"The Favorite Grandson." Black World 22 (November 1972): 54-
58.

KILGORE, James

Short Fiction

"Cecil." Essence 3 (July 1972): 54-55.

Biography and Criticism

Rush, Theressa Gunnels, Carol Fairbanks Myers, and Esther Spring
Arata. Black American Writers Past and Present. Metuchen,
N.J.: Scarecrow Press, 1975.

KILLENS, John Oliver

Novels

And Then We Heard the Thunder. New York: Knopf, 1963.

Cotillion: Or One Good Bull Is Half the Herd. New York: Trident,
   1971; New York: Pocket Books, 1972. Excerpt in Chapman,
   New Black Voices.
'Sippi. New York: Trident, 1967. Excerpt in Patterson, An Introduction to Black Literature in America.
Youngblood. New York: Dial, 1954; Excerpt in Hughes, The Book
   of Negro Humor.

Short Fiction

"God Bless America." In Adams, Conn and Slepian, Afro-American
   Literature: Fiction; Antico and Hazelrigg, Insight Through Fic-
   tion; Clarke, American Negro Short Stories; Ford, Black In-
   sights.
"Rough Diamond." In Clarke, Harlem.
"A White Loaf of Bread." In Brown, Davis and Lee, The Negro
   Caravan.

Biography and Criticism

Berry, Abner. "Crossroads, Georgia." Masses & Mainstream 7
   (September 1954): 16-19.
Bigsby, C. W. E. "From Protest to Paradox: The Black Writer
   at Mid-Century." In In the Fifties, pp. 217-240. Edited by
   Norman Podhoretz. New York: Farrar, Straus, 1964.
Cruse, Harold. The Crisis of the Negro Intellectual. New York:
   Morrow, 1967.
Jackson, Blyden. In Contemporary Novelists. Edited by James
   Vinson. New York: St. Martin's Press, 1976.
Klotman, Phyllis Rauch. Another Man Gone: The Black Runner
   in Contemporary Afro-American Literature. Port Washington,
   N.Y.: Kennikat Press, 1977.
_____. "The White Bitch Archetype in Black Fiction." Bulletin
   of the Midwest Modern Language Association 6 (Spring 1973):
   96-110.
Schraufnagel, Noel. From Apology to Protest: The Black American
   Novel. DeLand, Fla.: Everett/Edwards, 1973.
Wiggins, William H., Jr. "The Structure and Dynamics of Folklore
   in the Novel Form: The Case of John O. Killens." Keystone
   Folklore Quarterly 17 (1972): 92-118.

Reviews

And Then We Heard the Thunder
   Algren, Nelson. New York Herald Tribune Books, 14 April
      1963, p. 8.
   Bonosky, Phillip. Mainstream 16 (March 1963): 59.
   Doyle, P. A. Best Sellers, 1 February 1963, p. 407.
   Goran, Lester. Chicago Sunday Tribune Magazine of Books,
      24 February 1963, p. 9.
   Griffin, J. H. Saturday Review of Literature, 26 January 1963,
      p. 46.
   _____. Library Journal, 1 January 1963, p. 120.

Grumbach, Doris. Critic 21 (February 1963): 82.

Levin, Martin. New York Times Book Review, 7 April 1963, p. 37.

Van Sittart, P. Spectator, 6 March 1964, p. 321.

The Cotillion: Or One Good Bull Is Half the Herd

Adams, Phoebe. Atlantic 227 (February 1971): 129.

Black World 20 (June 1971): 51; 21 (December 1971): 95.

Book Week, 9 January 1972, p. 15.

Booklist, 1 April 1971, p. 640.

Fleischer, Leonard. Saturday Review of Literature, 6 March 1971, p. 36.

Frakes, J. R. New York Times Book Review, 17 January 1971, p. 4.

Givler, M. A. Best Sellers, 15 February 1971, p. 487.

Kirkus, 1 November 1970, p. 1212.

Lask, T. New York Times, 9 February 1971, p. 41.

Library Journal, 1 December 1970, p. 4195.

New York Times Book Review, 6 June 1971, p. 3; 5 December 1971, p. 83.

New Yorker, 29 May 1971, p. 90.

Publishers' Weekly, 16 November 1970, p. 70; 22 November 1971, p. 42.

Travel 136 (December 1971): 10.

Village Voice, 17 August 1972, p. 21.

'Sippi

Goran, L. Books Today, 9 July 1967, p. 14.

Kennedy, W. National Observer, 17 July 1967, p. 19.

Kirkus, 1 April 1967, p. 438.

Publishers' Weekly, 3 April 1967, p. 49.

Williams, R. Negro Digest 17 (November 1967): 85.

Youngblood

Bernard, J. F. Best Sellers, 1 May 1966, p. 52.

Byam, M. S. Library Journal, 15 May 1954, p. 982.

Cooke, Paul. Journal of Negro Education 23 (Fall 1954): 467-469.

Hicks, Granville. New York Times, 6 June 1954, p. 24.

Kirkus, 1 February 1966, p. 145.

Nation, 21 August 1954, p. 157.

Petry, Ann. New York Herald Tribune Book Review, 11 July 1954, p. 8.

KIMBROUGH, Jess

Novel

Defender of the Angels. New York: Macmillan, 1969.

Reviews

Defender of the Angels

Hamill, P. Book World, 3 August 1969, p. 4.

Kirkus, 1 March 1969, p. 285.

Library Journal, 1 June 1969, p. 2250.
Publishers' Weekly, 3 March 1969, p. 55.

KING, Woodie, Jr.

Short Fiction

"Beautiful, Light, and Black; Our Dreams." Negro Digest 12 (June
     1963: 67-74; also in Cahill and Cahill, Big City Stories.
"Border Line." Black Creation 3 (Winter 1972): 4-5.
"Emancipation." Black Scholar 6 (June 1975): 81-83.
"The Game." In King, Black Short Story Anthology.
"Ghetto." Negro Digest 11 (August 1962): 15-18.
"Listen to the Wind." Negro Digest 17 (June 1968): 90-98; also in
     Sanchez, We Be Word Sorcerers.

Biography and Criticism

Rush, Theressa Gunnels, Carol Fairbanks Myers, and Esther Spring
     Arata. Black American Writers Past and Present. Metuchen,
     N.J.: Scarecrow Press, 1975.

KIRK, Paul

Novel

No Need to Cry. New York: Carlton, 1967.

KNIGHT, Etheridge

Short Fiction

"By Reason of the Bondage." Negro Digest 17 (February 1968):
     54-63.
"My Father, My Bottom, My Fleas." Negro Digest 15 (August
     1966): 64-71.
"On the Next Train South." Negro Digest 16 (June 1967): 87-94.
"Reaching Is His Rule." Negro Digest 15 (December 1965): 61-63.
"A Time to Mourn." In Knight, Black Voices from Prison; Chap-
     man, New Black Voices.

Biography and Criticism

Contemporary Authors, 23/24.
Whitlow, Roger. Black American Literature: A Critical History.
     Chicago: Nelson Hall, 1973.

LACY, Ed

Short Fiction

"The Right Thing." In Ford and Faggett, Best Short Stories by
Afro-American Writers.

LACY, March

Short Fiction

"Fighting Finish." In Ford and Faggett, Best Short Stories by Afro-
American Writers.
"No Fools, No Fun." In Ford and Faggett, Best Short Stories by
Afro-American Writers.

LARSEN, Nella

Novels

Passing. New York and London: Knopf, 1929; New York: Arno,
1969; New York: Negro Universities Press, 1969; New York:
Collier Books, 1971; excerpt in Davis and Peplow, The New
Negro Renaissance.
Quicksand, New York and London: Knopf, 1928; New York: Collier
Books, 1971; New York: Negro Universities Press, 1969.

Short Fiction

"Sanctuary; Story." Forum 83 (January 1930): 15-18.

Biography and Criticism

Bone, Robert A. The Negro Novel in America. New Haven: Yale
University Press, 1966.
Brawley, Benjamin. The Negro in Literature and Art. New York:
Duffield, 1930.
Brown, Martha Hursey. "Images of Black Women: Family Roles
in Harlem Renaissance Literature." D.A. Dissertation, Carne-
gie-Mellon University, 1976.
Davidson, Colleen Tighe. "Beyond the Sentimental Heroine: The
Feminist Character in American Novels, 1899-1937." Ph.D.
Dissertation, University of Minnesota, 1975.
Davis, Arthur P. From the Dark Tower. Washington, D.C.:
Howard University Press, 1974.
Doyle, Sister Mary Ellen. "The Heroine of Black Novels." In
Perspectives on Afro-American Women, pp. 112-125. Edited
by Willa D. Johnson and Thomas L. Green. Washington, D.C.:
ECCA Publications, 1975.
Ford, Nick Aaron. "The Negro Author's Use of Propaganda in Ima-
ginative Literature." Ph.D. Dissertation, State University of

Iowa, 1945.

Gayle, Addison, Jr. The Way of the New World: The Black Novel in America. Garden City, N.Y.: Anchor Press/Doubleday, 1975.

Gloster, Hugh M. Negro Voices in American Fiction. Chapel Hill: University of North Carolina Press, 1948.

Hemenway, Robert. The Black Novelist. Columbus, Ohio: Charles E. Merrill, 1970.

Huggins, Nathan Irvin. Harlem Renaissance. New York: Oxford University Press, 1971.

Klotman, Phyllis Rauch. Another Man Gone: The Black Runner in Contemporary Afro-American Literature. Port Washington, N.Y.: Kennikat Press, 1977.

"Letter Explaining the Circumstances Under Which 'Sanctuary' Was Written." Forum 83, supplement 41 (April 1930).

Mays, Benjamin E. The Negro's God as Reflected in His Literature. New York: Negro Universities Press, 1969.

Mootry, Maria Katella. "Studies in Black Pastoral: Five Afro-American Writers." Ph.D. Dissertation, Northwestern University, 1974.

Perry, Margaret. Silence to the Drums: A Survey of the Literature of the Harlem Renaissance. Contributions in Afro-American and African Studies, no. 18. Westport, Conn.: Greenwood Press, 1976.

Ramsey, Priscilla Barbara Ann. "A Study of Black Identity in 'Passing' Novels of the Nineteenth and Early Twentieth Centuries." Ph.D. Dissertation, The American University, 1975.

_____. "A Study of Black Identity in 'Passing' Novels of the Nineteenth and Early Twentieth Centuries." Studies in Black Literature 7 (Winter 1976): 1-7.

Robinson, Anna T. "Race Consciousness and Survival Techniques Depicted in Harlem Renaissance Fiction." Ph.D. Dissertation, Pennsylvania State University, 1973.

Royster, Beatrice Horn. "The Ironic Vision of Four Black Women Novelists: A Study of the Novels of Jessie Fauset, Nella Larsen, Zora Neale Hurston, and Ann Petry." Ph.D. Dissertation, Emory University, 1975.

Sato, Hiroko. "Under the Harlem Shadow: A Study of Jessie Fauset and Nella Larsen." In The Harlem Renaissance Remembered, pp. 217-240. New York: Dodd, Mead, 1972.

Singh, Amritjit. "The Novels of the Harlem Renaissance: A Thematic Study." Ph.D. Dissertation, New York University, 1973.

_____. The Novels of the Harlem Renaissance: Twelve Black Writers, 1923-1933. University Park: Pennsylvania State University Press, 1976.

Stetson, Earlene. "The Mulatto Motif in Black Fiction." Ph.D. Dissertation, State University of New York at Buffalo, 1976.

Thornton, Hortense E. "Sexism as Quagmire: Nella Larsen's Quicksand." CLA Journal 16 (March 1973): 285-301.

Youman, Mary Mabel. "Nella Larsen's Passing: A Study in Irony." CLA Journal 18 (December 1974): 235-241.

Reviews

Passing
Cleveland Open Shelf (July 1929): 110.
Dawson, M. C. Books, 28 April 1929, p. 6.
Du Bois, W. E. B. Crisis 36 (July 1929): 234.
Hyman, Esther. Bookman 69 (June 1929): 427.
Labaree, Mary Fleming. Opportunity 7 (August 1929): 255.
New York Times, 28 April 1929, p. 14.
Seabrook, W. B. Saturday Review of Literature, 18 May 1929,
p. 1017.
Times Literary Supplement, 12 December 1929, p. 1060.
Quicksand
Boston Transcript, 20 June 1928, p. 2.
Bradford, Roark. Books, 13 May 1928, p. 22.
Cleveland Open Shelf (July 1928): 91.
Hayden, K. S. American Academy of Political and Social
Science Annals 140 (November 1928): 345.
Matthews, T. S. New Republic, 30 May 1928, p. 50.
New Statesman, 2 June 1928, p. 260.
New York Times, 8 April 1928, p. 16.
Opportunity 7 (January 1929): 25.
Parsons, A. B. Nation, 9 May 1928, p. 540.
Pittsburgh Monthly Bulletin 33 (June 1928): 321.
Times Literary Supplement, 26 July 1928, p. 553.
World Tomorrow 11 (November 1928): 474.

LATIMORE, Jewel C. see Amini, Johari

LAWSON, Edward

Short Fiction

"The Ebony Elephant." In Ford and Faggett, Best Short Stories by
Afro-American Writers.

LAWSON, J. M.

Short Fiction

"Roll Call." Essence 7 (June 1976): 8, 12.

LAWSON, Jennifer

Short Fiction

"Early Morning Calls." Essence 7 (August 1976): 54-55, 90.

LEAKS, Sylvester

Short Fiction

"The Blues Begins. " In Hughes, The Best Short Stories by Negro
    Writers.

Biography and Criticism

Rush, Theressa Gunnels, Carol Fairbanks Myers, and Esther Spring
    Arata. Black American Writers Past and Present. Metuchen,
    N.J.: Scarecrow Press, 1975.

LEE, Audrey

Novels

The Clarion People. New York: McGraw, 1968.
The Workers. New York: McGraw, 1969.

Short Fiction

"Alienation. " Black World 21 (November 1971): 64-66.
"Antonio Is a Man. " Essence 2 (January 1972): 44-45.
"The Block. " Black World 19 (October 1970): 65-72.
"Eulogy for a Public Servant. " Black World 25 (January 1976):
    54-57.
"I'm Going to Move Out of This Emotional Ghetto. " Negro Digest
    19 (December 1969): 63-68.
"A Man Is a Man." Essence 1 (February 1971): 40-41, 68, 70.
"Moma; Story." Negro Digest 18 (February 1969): 53-65.
"The Ride. " Essence 1 (June 1970): 60-61.

Biography and Criticism

Contemporary Authors, 25/28.

Reviews

The Clarion People
    Casey, G. Best Sellers, 15 May 1968, p. 89.
    Giovanni, N. Negro Digest 17 (September/October 1968): 14.
    Kirkus, 15 March 1968, p. 357.
    Levin, M. New York Times Book Review, 19 May 1968, p. 37.
    Library Journal, 15 June 1968, p. 2521.
    Morse, J. M. Hudson Review 21 (Autumn 1968): 522.
    Publishers' Weekly, 12 February 1968, p. 71.
The Workers
    Kirkus, 1 July 1969, p. 694.
    Library Journal 94 (July 1969): 2640.
    Publishers' Weekly, 30 June 1969, p. 62.

LEE, George Washington

Novel

River George. New York: Macauley, 1937; New York: AMS Press,
1975.

Short Fiction

Beale Street Sundown. New York: Field, 1942.

Biography and Criticism

Gloster, Hugh M. Negro Voices in American Fiction. Chapel Hill:
University of North Carolina Press, 1948.

Reviews

River George
Beckwith, E. C. New York Times Book Review, 20 June
1937, p. 16.
Bell, Lisle. Books, 18 April 1937, p. 18.
Beale Street Sundown
Carter, Elmer Anderson. Opportunity 12 (October 1934): 314.

LEE, James F.

Novel

The Victims. New York: Vantage, 1959.

LEE, John M.

Novel

Counter Clockwise. New York: Malliet, 1940.

Reviews

Counter Clockwise
Harrison, William. Crisis 47 (September 1940): 299.
Lawson, Edward. Opportunity 18 (March 1940): 93.

LESTER, Julius

Short Fiction

(Collection): Long Journey Home: Stories from Black History.
New York: Dial, 1972. Includes:
"Ben."

"Long Journey Home. "
"Louis. "
"The Man Who Was a Horse. "
"Satan on My Track. "
"When Freedom Came. "
"Jack and the Devil's Daughter. " In Murray and Thomas, The
    Scene.
"The Valley of the Shadow of Death. " In Watkins, Black Review
    No. 2.

Biography and Criticism

Bell, Bernard W. "Literary Sources of the Early Afro-American
    Novel. " CLA Journal 18 (September 1974): 29-43.
Contemporary Authors, 17/18.
"Interview. " Arts in Society 5 (1968): 228-230.
Meras, Phyllis. "An Interview with Julius Lester. " Nation, 22
    June 1970, pp. 762-763.

LEWIS, Ronald

Novel

The Last Junkie. New York: Amuru, 1973.

LINCOLN, C. Eric

Short Fiction

"Dangerous Day in Mississippi. " Negro Digest 11 (November 1961):
    86-96.

Biography and Criticism

Contemporary Authors, 2R.

LIPSCOMB, Ken

Novel

Duke Casanova. New York: Exposition, 1958.

LOFTY, Paul.

Short Fiction

"Chapter X from an Untitled Novel. " In Reed, 19 Necromancers
    from Now.

LOMAX, Almena

Short Fiction

"In the Faraway Country of Montgomery, Alabama. " Harper's 237
(September 1968): 51-52.

Biography and Criticism

Stein, M. L. Blacks in Communication. New York: Julian Messner, 1972.

LUBIN, Gilbert

Novel

The Promised Land. Boston: Christopher, 1930.

LUCAS, Curtis

Novels

Angel. New York: Lion, 1953.
Flour Is Dusty. Philadelphia: Dorrance, 1943.
Forbidden Fruit. New York: Universal, 1953.
Lila. New York: Lion, 1955.
So Low, So Lonely. New York: n. p., 1952.
Third Ward Newark. Chicago: Ziff Davis, 1946.

Biography and Criticism

Bone, Robert A. The Negro Novel in America. New Haven: Yale
University Press, 1966.
Hughes, Carl M. The Negro Novelist 1940-1950. New York: Cita-
del Press, 1953.
Schraufnagel, Noel. From Apology to Protest: The Black American
Novel. DeLand, Fla.: Everett/Edwards, 1973.

Reviews

Flour Is Dusty
Burke, Arthur E. Crisis 51 (November 1944): 363.
Christian Century, 2 February 1944, p. 147.
Springfield Republican, 6 February 1944, p. 7e.

LYMAN, James C.

Short Fiction

"The Two Worlds. " In James, From These Roots.

McCALL, Valaida Potter (pseud., W. J. McCall)

Novel

Sunrise Over Alabama. New York: Comet, 1959.

McCALL, W. J. see McCall, Valaida Potter

McCLELLAN, George Marion (McLellan)

Short Fiction

Old Greenbottom Inn, and Other Stories. Louisville, Ky.: By the
Author, 1906; New York: AMS Press, 1975.

Biography and Criticism

Culp, Daniel Wallace. American Negro: His History and Literature.
New York: Arno Press, 1969.
Gloster, Hugh M. Negro Voices in American Fiction. Chapel Hill:
University of North Carolina Press, 1948.
Jaskoski, Helen. "Power Unequal to Man: The Significance of
Conjure in Works by Five Afro-American Authors." Southern
Folklore Quarterly 38 (June 1974): 91-108.
Rush, Theressa Gunnels, Carol Fairbanks Myers, and Esther Spring
Arata. Black American Writers Past and Present. Metuchen,
N.J.: Scarecrow Press, 1975.

McCLUSKEY, John

Novel

Look What They Done to My Song. New York: Random, 1974.

Short Fiction

"The Pilgrims." In Coombs, What We Must See.

Reviews

Look What They Done to My Song
    Black World 24 (July 1975): 51-52.
    Choice 12 (April 1975): 221.
    El-Kati, Mahmoud. Black Scholar 7 (March 1976): 49-50.
    Kent, George E. Phylon 36 (June 1975): 182-203.
    Kirkus, 1 September 1974, p. 962.
    Levin, Martin. New York Times Book Review, 17 November
        1974, p. 52.
    New Yorker, 25 November 1974, p. 194.
    Publishers' Weekly, 16 September 1974, p. 53.

Thompson, J. A. Library Journal, 15 April 1975, p. 782.
Village Voice, 31 October 1974, p. 49.

McGIRT, James

Short Fiction

The Triumphs of Ephraim. Philadelphia: McGirt, 1907.

Biography and Criticism

Isani, Mukhtar Ali. "The Exotic and Protest in Earlier Black Literature: The Use of Alien Setting and Character." Studies in Black Literature 5 (Summer 1974): 9-14.

McKAY, Claude (pseud., Eli Edwards)

Novels

Banana Bottom. New York and London: Harper, 1933; Chatham, N.J.: Chatham Bookseller, 1970; New York: Harcourt Brace Jovanovich, 1970.
Banjo: A Story without a Plot. New York: Harper, 1929; New York: Harcourt Brace Jovanovich, 1970; excerpt in Huggins, Voices from the Harlem Renaissance.
Home to Harlem. New York: Harper, 1928; Chatham, N.J.: Chatham Bookseller, 1973; excerpts in Brown, Davis and Lee, The Negro Caravan; Calverton, Anthology of American Negro Literature; Clarke, Harlem; Cooper, The Passion of Claude McKay; Davis and Peplow, The New Negro Renaissance; Davis and Redding, Cavalcade; James, From the Roots.

Short Fiction

(Collections):
Gingertown. New York: Harper, 1932.
The Passion of Claude McKay: Selected Prose and Poetry, 1912-1948. Edited by Wayne Cooper. New York: Schocken Books, 1973.
"Agricultural Show." In McKay, Gingertown.
"Brownskin Blues." In McKay, Gingertown.
"Crazy Mary." In McKay, Gingertown.
"Highball." In McKay, Gingertown.
"A Little Lamb to Lead Them." African (May/June 1938).
"Little Lincoln." Liberator (February 1922).
"Little Sheik." In McKay, Gingertown.
"Mattie and Her Sweetman." In Cooper, The Passion of Claude McKay; McKay, Gingertown.
"Near-White." In McKay, Gingertown.
"Nigger Lover." In McKay, Gingertown.
"Prince of Porto Rico." In McKay, Gingertown.

"The Strange Burial of Sue." In Cooper, The Passion of Claude
McKay; McKay, Gingertown.
"Truant." In Gasarch and Gasarch, Fiction; McKay, Gingertown;
Smart, Women & Men, Men & Women.
"When I Pounded the Pavement." In McKay, Gingertown.
"Yeoman Abdul's Funeral." (From unpublished novel, "Harlem
Glory.") In Cooper, The Passion of Claude McKay.

Biography and Criticism

Arden, Eugene. "The Early Harlem Novel." Phylon 20 (Spring
1950): 25-31.
Barksdale, Richard K. "Symbolism and Irony in McKay's Home to
Harlem." CLA Journal 15 (March 1972): 338-344.
Bone, Robert. Down Home: A History of Afro-American Short
Fiction from Its Beginnings to the End of the Harlem Renais-
sance. New York: G. P. Putnam's Sons, 1975.
_____. The Negro Novel in America. New Haven: Yale Uni-
versity Press, 1966.
Bontemps, Arna. The Harlem Renaissance Remembered. New
York: Dodd, Mead, 1972.
Brawley, Benjamin. The Negro Genius. New York: Dodd, Mead,
1940.
Brown, Lloyd W. "The Expatriate Consciousness in Black Ameri-
can Literature." Studies in Black Literature 3 (Summer 1972):
9-11.
Brown, Martha Hursey. "Images of Black Women: Family Roles
in Harlem Renaissance Literature." D. A. Dissertation, Car-
negie-Mellon University, 1976.
Cameron, May. "Claude McKay Declares Negro Writers Can Ad-
vance Only by Losing Self-Consciousness: An Open Letter to
Claude McKay." New York Post, 22 May 1937.
Collier, Eugenia W. "The Four-Way Dilemma of Claude McKay."
CLA Journal 15 (March 1972): 345-353.
_____. "Heritage from Harlem." Black World 20 (November
1970): 52-59.
Conroy, Sr. Mary James. "Claude McKay: Negro Poet and Nove-
list." Ph.D. Dissertation, University of Notre Dame, 1968.
_____. "The Vagabond Motif in the Writings of Claude McKay."
Negro American Literature Forum 5 (Spring 1971): 15-23.
Cooper, Wayne. "Claude McKay and the New Negro of the 1920's."
Phylon 25 (Fall 1964): 297-306; also in The Black American
Writer, pp. 53-65. Edited by C. W. E. Bigsby. DeLand, Flo-
rida: Everett/Edwards, 1969.
_____. Introduction to The Passion of Claude McKay. New York:
Schocken, 1973.
Davis, Arthur P. From the Dark Tower: Afro-American Writers
1900-1960. Washington, D. C.: Howard University Press,
1974.
Du Bois, W. E. B. "The Browsing Reader." Crisis 35 (June
1928): 202.
Felgar, Robert. "Black Content, White Form." Studies in Black
Literature 5 (Spring 1974): 28-31.

Ford, Nick Aaron. "The Negro Author's Use of Propaganda in Imaginative Literature." Ph. D. Dissertation, State University of Iowa, 1945.

Gayle, Addison, Jr. The Way of the New World: The Black Novel in America. Garden City, N. Y.: Anchor Press/Doubleday, 1975.

Giles, James R. Claude McKay. New York: Twayne, 1976.

Gloster, Hugh M. Negro Voices in American Fiction. Chapel Hill: University of North Carolina Press, 1948.

Gruening, Martha. "The Negro Renaissance." Hound and Horn 5 (1932): 504-514.

Hart, Robert C. "Black-White Literary Relations in the Harlem Renaissance." American Literature 44 (January 1973): 612-628.

Helbling, Mark Irving. "Primitivism and the Harlem Renaissance." Ph. D. Dissertation, University of Minnesota, 1972.

Hoehn, Matthew Anthony, ed. Catholic Authors: Contemporary Biographical Sketches 1930-1952. Newark: St. Mary's Abbey, 1948-1952.

Huggins, Nathan Irvin. Harlem Renaissance. New York: Oxford University Press, 1971.

Isaacs, Harold R. "Five Writers and Their African Ancestors." Phylon 21 (Fall 1960): 243-265.

Jackson, Blyden. "Claude McKay and Langston Hughes: The Harlem Renaissance and More." Pembroke Magazine 6 (1975): 43-48.

_____. "The Harlem Renaissance." In The Comic Imagination in American Literature, pp. 295-303. Edited by Louis D. Rubin, Jr. New Brunswick, N. J.: Rutgers University Press, 1973.

Jackson, Miles M. "Literary History: Documentary Sidelights-- James Weldon Johnson and Claude McKay." Negro Digest 17 (June 1968): 25-29.

Kaye, Jacquelin. "Claude McKay's Banjo." Présence Africaine no. 73 (1970): 165-169.

Kent, George. Blackness and the Adventure of Western Culture. Chicago: Third World Press, 1972.

_____. "Claude McKay's Banana Bottom Reappraised." CLA Journal 18 (December 1974): 222-234.

_____. "Patterns of the Renaissance." Black World 21 (June 1972): 13.

_____. "The Soulful Way of Claude McKay." Black World 20 (November 1970): 37-51.

Lang, Phyllis Martin. "Claude McKay: Evidence of a Magic Pilgrimage." CLA Journal 16 (June 1973): 475-484.

_____. "Claude McKay: The Later Years, 1934-1948." Ph. D. Dissertation, University of Illinois at Urbana-Champaign, 1972.

Larson, Charles R. "Three Harlem Novels of the Jazz Age." Critique 11 no. 3 (1969): 66-78.

Major, Clarence. "Dear Jake and Ray." American Poetry Review 4 (1975): 40-42.

Mootry, Maria Katella. "Studies in Black Pastoral: Five Afro-American Writers." Ph. D. Dissertation, Northwestern University, 1974.

Perry, Margaret. Silence to the Drums: A Survey of the Litera-
ture of the Harlem Renaissance. Contributions in Afro-Ameri-
can and African Studies, no. 18. Westport, Conn.: Greenwood
Press, 1976.
Priebe, Richard. "The Search for Community in the Novels of
Claude McKay." Studies in Black Literature 3 (Summer 1972):
22-30.
Pyne-Timothy, Helen. "Perceptions of the Black Woman in the
Work of Claude McKay." CLA Journal 19 (December 1975):
152-164.
Ramchand, Kenneth. "Claude McKay and Banana Bottom." South-
ern Review (Australia 4 (1970): 53-66.
Robinson, Anna T. "Race Consciousness and Survival Techniques
Depicted in Harlem Renaissance Fiction." Ph.D. Dissertation,
Pennsylvania State University, 1973.
Rosenblatt, Roger. Black Fiction. Cambridge: Harvard University
Press, 1974.
Rush, Theressa Gunnels, Carol Fairbanks Myers, and Esther Spring
Arata. Black American Writers Past and Present. Metuchen,
N.J.: Scarecrow Press, 1975.
Scruggs, Charles. "'All Dressed Up But No Place to Go': The
Black Writer and His Audience During the Harlem Renaissance."
American Literature 48 (January 1977): 543-563.
Singh, Amritjit. "The Novels of the Harlem Renaissance: A The-
matic Study." Ph.D. Dissertation, New York University, 1973.
_____. The Novels of the Harlem Renaissance: Twelve Black
Writers, 1923-1933. University Park: Pennsylvania State Uni-
versity Press, 1976.
Smith, Robert A. "Claude McKay: An Essay in Criticism." Phy-
lon 9 (Third Quarter 1948): 270-273.
Starke, Catherine Juanita. Black Portraiture in American Fiction:
Stock Characters, Archetypes, and Individuals. New York:
Basic Books, 1971.
Stoff, Michael B. "Claude McKay and the Cult of Primitivism."
In The Harlem Renaissance Remembered, pp. 126-145. Edited
by Arna Bontemps. New York: Dodd, Mead, 1972.
Sutton, Thomas. "Threefold Vision in the Works of Claude McKay."
Ph.D. Dissertation, University of Miami, 1975.
Turpin, Waters E. "Four Short Fiction Writers of the Harlem
Renaissance--Their Legacy of Achievement." CLA Journal 11
(September 1967): 59-72.
Van Mol, Kay R. "Primitivism and Intellect in Toomer's Cane and
McKay's Banana Bottom: The Need for an Integrated Black
Consciousness." Negro American Literature Forum 10 (Summer
1976): 48-52.
Wall, Cheryl A. "Paris and Harlem: Two Cultural Capitals."
Phylon 35 (March 1974): 64-73.
Whitlow, Roger. Black American Literature: A Critical History.
Chicago: Nelson Hall, 1973.
Young, James O. Black Writers of the Thirties. Baton Rouge:
Louisiana State University Press, 1973.

Reviews

Banana Bottom
  Book World, 24 March 1974, p. 4.
  Boston Transcript, 5 April 1933, p. 2.
  Nation, 17 May 1933, p. 564.
  New York Times Book Review, 2 April 1933, p. 16; 14 July
    1974, p. 30.
  Ross, Mary. Books, 2 April 1933, p. 5.
  Saturday Review of Literature, 8 April 1933, p. 529.
Banjo: A Story Without a Plot
  Bailey, R. S. Bookman 69 (May 1929): 311.
  Bennett, Gwendolyn B. Opportunity 7 (August 1929): 254-255.
  Brooks, W. R. Outlook and Independent, 19 June 1929, p. 311.
  Kirchwey, Freda. Nation, 22 May 1929, p. 614.
  McGuiness, Clifford. Books, 12 May 1929, p. 7.
  New York Times Book Review, 12 May 1929, p. 8.
  Odum, H. W. Saturday Review of Literature, 27 July 1929,
    p. 2.
  Times Literary Supplement, 27 June 1929, p. 512.
  White, Walter. New York World, 9 June 1929, p. 7m.
Gingertown
  Bookman 75 (May 1932): 5.
  Boston Transcript, 30 March 1932, p. 2.
  Fisher, Rudolph. Books, 27 March 1932, p. 3.
  Nation, 10 August 1932, p. 130.
  New York Times, 3 April 1932, p. 7.
  Times Literary Supplement, 12 May 1932, p. 352.
Home to Harlem
  Abbott, R. S. Chicago Daily Tribune, 9 June 1928, p. 14.
  Bennett, G. B. Books, 11 March 1928, p. 5.
  Best Sellers, 1 August 1965, p. 194.
  Boston Transcript, 24 March 1928, p. 3.
  Brickell, Herschell. Opportunity 6 (May 1928): 151-152.
  Chamberlain, J. R. New York Times Book Review, 11 March
    1928, p. 5; 24 June 1928, p. 2.
  Hartley, L. P. Saturday Review, 18 August 1928, p. 218.
  Holliday, R. C. New York Evening Post, 21 April 1928, p. 12.
  Hunt, D. L. American Academy of Political and Social Science
    Annals 140 (November 1928): 339.
  Matthews, T. S. New Republic, 30 May 1928, p. 50.
  Mortimer, Raymond. Nation and Athenaeum, 23 June 1928, p.
    397.
  New Statesman, 18 August 1928, p. 591.
  Niles, Abbe. New York World, 11 March 1928, p. 11m.
  Outlook and Independent, 18 April 1928, p. 636.
  Roscoe, Burton. Bookman 67 (April 1928): 183.
  Springfield Republican, 25 March 1928, p. 7f.
  Times Literary Supplement, 12 July 1928, p. 518.
  Van Doren, Mark. Nation, 28 March 1928, p. 351.
  Whipple, Leon. Survey, 1 May 1928, p. 178.

McLELLAN, George Marion see McClellan, George Marion

McPHERSON, James Alan

Short Fiction

(Collection): Hue and Cry: Short Stories by James Alan McPherson.
Greenwich, Conn.: Fawcett, 1968 (1970).
"An Act of Prostitution." In McPherson, Hue and Cry.
"All the Lonely People." In McPherson, Hue and Cry.
"The Faithful." Atlantic 231 (April 1973): 38-39; also in Abrahams,
Prize Stories 1974; The O. Henry Awards.
"Gold Coast." Atlantic 222 (November 1968): 74-81; also in Foley
and Burnett, The Best American Short Stories of 1969; Ford,
Black Insights; McPherson, Hue and Cry; New and Rosengarten,
Modern Stories in English.
"Hue and Cry." In McPherson, Hue and Cry; Timko, 29 Short
Stories.
"A Matter of Vocabulary." Atlantic 223 (February 1969): 55-63;
also in McPherson, Hue and Cry.
"A New Place." In McPherson, Hue and Cry.
"Of Cabbages and Kings." Atlantic 223 (April 1969): 57-63; also
in McPherson, Hue and Cry; Oates, Scenes from American Life.
"On Trains." In McPherson, Hue and Cry.
"Private Domain." In McPherson, Hue and Cry.
"Problems of Art." Iowa Review 6 (Spring 1975): 53-67.
"The Silver Bullet." In Abrahams, Prize Stories 1973: The O.
Henry Awards; Foley, Best American Short Stories 1973.
"A Solo Song: for Doc." In Chapman, New Black Voices; McPher-
son, Hue and Cry.
"Story of a Scar." Atlantic 232 (December 1973): 77-83; also in
Abrahams, Prize Stories 1975: The O. Henry Awards.

Biography and Criticism

Laughlin, Rosemary M. "Attention, American Folklore: Doc Craft
Comes Marching In." Studies in American Fiction 1 (Autumn
1973): 220-227.
Rosenblatt, Roger. Black Fiction. Cambridge: Harvard University
Press, 1974.

Reviews

Hue and Cry
Booklist, 15 September 1969, p. 107.
Cassill, R. V. Book World, 25 May 1969, p. 4.
Christ, Ronald. Commonweal, 19 September 1969, p. 570.
Cosgrave, M. S. Horn Book 45 (October 1969): 553.
Gropman, Donald. Christian Science Monitor, 31 July 1969,
p. 11.
Hicks, Granville. Saturday Review, 24 May 1969, p. 47.
Howe, Irving. Harper's 239 (December 1969): 137.

Jordan, Clive J. New Statesman, 21 November 1969, p. 739.
Kirkus 37 (March 1969): 269.
Lafore, Laurence. New York Times Book Review, 1 June
    1969, p. 26.
Library Journal, 15 May 1969, p. 2002.
Loprete, N. J. Best Sellers, 1 July 1969, p. 141.
Negro Digest 19 (November 1969): 86.
Observer, 7 December 1969, p. 30.
Publishers' Weekly, 10 March 1969, p. 70; 16 March 1970,
    p. 57.
Spectator, 22 November 1969, p. 716.
Sullivan, W. Sewanee Review 78 (July 1970): 531.
Times Literary Supplement, 25 December 1969, p. 1465.

McRAE, John C17X

Short Fiction

"Revelations 23:1--oo. " In Sanchez, We Be Word Sorcerers.

MADDEN, Will Anthony

Short Fiction

Five More. New York: Exposition, 1963.
Sextette. New York: Exposition, 1972.
Two and One: Two Short Stories and a Play. New York: Exposi-
    tion, 1961.

MAHONEY, William

Novel

Black Jacob. New York: Macmillan, 1969.

Biography and Criticism

Schraufnagel, Noel. From Apology to Protest: The Black Ameri-
    can Novel. DeLand, Fla.: Everett/Edwards, 1973.

Reviews

Black Jacob
    Blackburn, Sara. Nation, 14 April 1969, p. 475.
    Corodinas, Peter. Best Sellers, 15 May 1969, p. 475.
    Cunningham, Frank. Saturday Review of Literature, 5 April
        1969, p. 39.
    Elrod, J. M. Library Journal, 15 March 1969, p. 462.
    Karp, David. New York Times Book Review, 9 March 1969,
        p. 38.

Kirkus, 1 January 1969, p. 27.

MAJOR, Clarence.

Novels

All-Night Visitors. New York: Olympia, 1969; New York: Univer-
 sity Place Book Shop, 1973. Excerpt in Reed, 19 Necroman-
 cers from Now.
No. New York: Emerson Hall, 1973.
Reflex and Bone Structure. Brooklyn: Fiction Collective, 1975;
 New York: Braziller, 1975.

Short Fiction

"An Area in the Cerebral Hemisphere." In Statements.
"Dossy O." Black Creation 3 (Summer 1972): 4-5.
"Early Grave." Fiction 1 no. 3 (1972): [8].
"Excerpts from Inlet: A Novel in Progress." Black Scholar 8
 (March 1977): 20-26.
"The Future." In Mayfield, Ten Times Black.
"A Life Story." Essence 2 (February 1972): 53, 65.
"Social Work." Black Scholar 6 (June 1975): 35-39.
"Ten Pecan Pies." Essence 4 (December 1973): 64-65, 86, 88.

Biography and Criticism

Contemporary Authors, 13/16R.
Klinkowitz, Jerome. "Clarence Major's Superfiction." Yardbird
 Reader 4 (1975): 1-12.
_____. Literary Disruptions: The Making of a Post-Contempo-
 rary American Fiction. Urbana: University of Illinois Press,
 1975.
_____. "Reclaiming a (New) Black Experience: The Fiction of
 Clarence Major." Oyez Review 8 (Winter 1973): 86-90.
O'Brien, John. Interviews with Black Writers. New York: Live-
 right, 1973; also in Major's The Dark and Feeling. New York:
 Third Press, 1974.
"Work with the Universe: An Interview with Clarence Major and
 Victor Hernández Cruz." Nickel Review (1969); also in Major's
 The Dark and Feeling, pp. 115-123. New York: Third Press,
 1974.

Reviews

All-Night Visitors
 Lehmann-Haupt, C. New York Times, 7 April 1969, p. 45.
 Negro Digest 19 (December 1969): 85.
 New York Times, 7 April 1969, p. 41.
 Publishers' Weekly, 25 March 1969, p. 52.
No
 Best Sellers 33 (June 1973): 105.

New York Times Book Review, 1 July 1973, p. 22.
Publishers' Weekly, 19 March 1973, p. 62.
Reflex and Bone Structure
    Booklist, 15 January 1976, p. 667.
    Carolina Quarterly 28 (Spring 1976): 115.
    Choice 13 (March 1976): 71.
    Kirkus, 15 September 1975, p. 1084.
    Library Journal, 15 January 1976, p. 360.
    New York Times Book Review, 30 November 1975, p. 61.
    Publishers' Weekly, 13 October 1975, p. 104.

MARCUS, Lorraine

Short Fiction

"Bridal Shower." Essence 7 (August 1976): 68-69, 92-94.

MARSHALL, Lila

Short Fiction

"I Had a Colored Maid." Negro Story 1 (May-June 1944): 5-8.
"Viney Taylor." Negro Story 1 (July-August 1944): 23-27.

MARSHALL, Paule

Novels

Brown Girl, Brownstones. New York: Random, 1959; Chatham
    N.J.: Chatham Bookseller, 1972; New York: Avon, 1970.
The Chosen Place, The Timeless People. New York: Harcourt
    Brace Jovanovich, 1969; New York: Avon, 1976.

Short Fiction

(Collection): Soul Clap Hands and Sing. New York: Atheneum,
    1961; Chatham, N.J.: Chatham Bookseller, 1971.
"Barbados." In Barksdale and Kinnamon, Black Writers of America;
    Ford, Black Insights; Marshall, Soul Clap Hands and Sing; Pat-
    terson, An Introduction to Black Literature in America.
"Brazil." In Emanuel and Gross, Dark Symphony; Gasarch and Ga-
    sarch, Fiction; Marshall, Soul Clap Hands and Sing.
"British Guiana." In Marshall, Soul Clap Hands and Sing.
"Brooklyn." In Davis and Redding, Cavalcade; Ford, Black Insights;
    Marshall, Soul Clap Hands and Sing.
"Reena." Harper's 225 (October 1962): 154-163; also in Washing-
    ton, Black-Eyed Susans.
"Return of the Native: Chapter from a Novel Being Written." Free-
    domways 4 (Summer 1964): 358-366.
"Some Get Wasted." In Clarke, Harlem.

"To Da-duh, In Memoriam." In Chapman, Black Voices; Long and Collier, Afro-American Writing.

Biography and Criticism

Benston, Kimberly. "Architectural Imagery and Unity in Paule Marshall's Brown Girl, Brownstones." Negro American Literature Forum 9 (Fall 1975): 67-76.

Braithwaite, Edward. "Rehabilitation." Critical Quarterly 13 (Summer 1971): 175-183.

_____. "West Indian History and Society in the Art of Paule Marshall's Novel." Journal of Black Studies 1 (December 1970): 225-238.

Brown, Lloyd W. "Beneath the North Star: The Canadian Image in Black Literature." Dalhousie Review 50 (Autumn 1970): 317-329.

_____. "The Rhythms of Power in Paule Marshall's Fiction." Novel: A Forum on Fiction 7 (Winter 1974): 159-167.

Kapai, Leela. "Dominant Themes and Technique in Paule Marshall's Fiction." CLA Journal 16 (September 1972): 49-59.

Keizs, Marcia. "Themes and Style in the Works of Paule Marshall." Negro American Literature Forum 9 (Fall 1975): 67.

Love, Theresa R. "The Black Woman in Afro-American Literature." Paper presented at the Midwest Modern Language Association Meeting, Chicago, November 1975. (Mimeographed.)

Nazareth, Peter. "Paule Marshall's Timeless People." New Letters 40 (Autumn 1973): 113-131.

Reilly, John M. In Contemporary Novelists. Edited by James Vinson. New York: St. Martin's Press, 1976.

Rosenblatt, Roger. Black Fiction. Cambridge: Harvard University Press, 1974.

Schraufnagel, Noel. From Apology to Protest: The Black American Novel. DeLand, Fla.: Everett/Edwards, 1973.

Stoelting, Winifred L. "Time Past and Time Present: The Search for Viable Links in The Chosen Place, The Timeless People by Paule Marshall." CLA Journal 16 (September 1972): 60-71.

Washington, Mary Helen. "Black Women Image Makers." Black World 23 (August 1974): 10-18.

Whitlow, Roger. Black American Literature: A Critical History. Chicago: Nelson Hall, 1973.

Reviews

Brown Girl, Brownstones
Best Sellers, 15 August 1970, p. 195.
Booklist, 15 October 1959, p. 119.
Buckmaster, Henrietta. Saturday Review of Literature, 29 August 1959, p. 14.
Cinqimani, F. L. Library Journal, 1 September 1959, p. 2522.
Kirkus, 1 July 1959, p. 461.
New York Herald Tribune Book Review, 16 August 1959, p. 5.
New Yorker, 19 September 1959, p. 191.
Shrapnel, Norman. Manchester Guardian and Evening News,

19 August 1960, p. 5.
Times Literary Supplement, 19 August 1960, p. 533.

The Chosen Place, The Timeless People
Bone, Robert. New York Times Book Review, 30 November
1969, p. 4.
Book Week, 28 December 1969, p. 10.
Booklist, 15 December 1969, p. 495.
Buckmaster, Henrietta. Christian Science Monitor, 22 January
1970, p. 9.
Burroway, Janet. New Statesman, 2 October 1970, p. 426.
Kirkus, 15 August 1969, p. 885.
Lask, F. New York Times Book Review, 8 November 1969,
p. 35.
Negro Digest 19 (January 1970): 52.
New York Times, 8 November 1969, p. 31.
Publishers' Weekly, 11 August 1969, p. 41.
Purcell, Donald. Library Journal, 15 September 1969, p. 3084.
Rhodes, Richard. Book World, 28 December 1969, p. 10.
Spectator, 19 December 1970, p. 810; 26 December 1970, p.
848; 2 January 1971, p. 23.
Village Voice, 8 October 1970, p. 6.

Soul Clap Hands and Sing
Ascherson, Neal. New Statesman, 13 April 1962, p. 535.
Benet, Rosemary. Book of the Month Club News, 9 December
1961, n.p.
Buckmaster, Henrietta. New York Times, 1 October 1961,
p. 37.
Chicago Sunday Tribune Magazine of Books, 1 October 1961,
p. 3.
Fasick, A. Library Journal 86 (August 1961): 2682.
Hassan, I. Saturday Review of Literature, 16 September 1961,
p. 30.
Hutchens, John K. New York Herald Tribune, 12 December
1961, p. 19.
New York Herald Tribune, 17 September 1961, p. 6.
New Yorker, 23 September 1961, p. 180.
San Francisco Sunday Chronicle, 28 January 1962, p. 32.

MARTINEZ, Joe

Short Fiction

"Rehabilitation and Treatment." In Chapman, New Black Voices;
Knight, Black Voices from Prison.

MARVIN X (El Muhajir; Marvin Jackman)

Short Fiction

"The Parable of the Sleeping Lion." Black Scholar 6 (June 1975):
17.

"Three Parables." Black World 19 (June 1970): 84-87.

MASON, B. J.

Novel

The Jerusalem Freedom Manufacturing Co. New York: Paperback
    Library, 1971.

MATHEUS, John

Short Fiction

"Citadel." Crisis 38 (November 1931): 378-379.
"Clay." Opportunity 4 (October 1926): 311-313, 330-331.
"Fog." Opportunity 3 (May 1925): 143-147.
"General Drums." In Johnson, Ebony and Topaz.
"Mr. Bradford Teaches Sunday School: A Story for Easter."
    Opportunity 4 (April 1926): 122-125, 135.
"Nomah." Opportunity 9 (July 1931): 214-217.
"Sallico." Opportunity 15 (August 1937): 236-239.
"Sand." Opportunity 4 (July 1926): 215-216.
"Swamp Moccasin." Crisis 33 (December 1926): 67-69.

Biography and Criticism

Perry, Margaret. Silence to the Drums: A Survey of the Litera-
    ture of the Harlem Renaissance. Contributions in Afro-Ameri-
    can and African Studies, no. 18. Westport, Conn.: Greenwood
    Press, 1976.
Rush, Theressa Gunnels, Carol Fairbanks Myers, and Esther Spring
    Arata. Black American Writers Past and Present. Metuchen,
    N.J.: Scarecrow Press, 1975.

MATHIS, Sharon Bell

Short Fiction

"Arthur." Essence 2 (March 1972): 50-51.
"Ernie Father." Black World 22 (June 1973): 57-59.

Biography and Criticism

Rush, Theressa Gunnels, Carol Fairbanks Myers, and Esther Spring
    Arata. Black American Writers Past and Present. Metuchen,
    N.J.: Scarecrow Press, 1975.

MATTHEWS, Ralph

Short Fiction

"Fisherman's Luck." In Ford and Faggett, Best Short Stories by Afro-American Writers.

MAYFIELD, Julian

Novels

The Grand Parade. New York: Vanguard, 1961. (Published as Nowhere Street. New York: Warner Paperback Library, 1968.)
The Hit. New York: Vanguard, 1957; London: M. Joseph, 1957; New York: Belmont-Tower, 1970.
The Long Night. New York: Vanguard, 1958; London: M. Joseph, 1960.
Nowhere Street see The Grand Parade

Short Fiction

"Black on Black: A Political Love Story." Black World 21 (February 1972): 54-71; also in Mayfield, Ten Times Black.

Biography and Criticism

Contemporary Authors, 13/16R.
Cruse, Harold. The Crisis of the Negro Intellectual. New York: Morrow, 1967.
Davis, Arthur P. From the Dark Tower: Afro-American Writers 1900-1960. Washington, D.C.: Howard University Press, 1974.
Emanuel, James A. In Contemporary Novelists. Edited by James Vinson. New York: St. Martin's Press, 1976.
O'Brien, John. Interviews with Black Writers. New York: Liveright, 1973.
Schraufnagel, Noel. From Apology to Protest: The Black American Novel. DeLand, Fla.: Everett/Edwards, 1973.

Reviews

The Grand Parade
    Blotner, Joseph. New York Times Book Review, 18 June 1961, p. 26.
    Bonosky, Phillip. Mainstream 14 (July 1962): 59-61.
    Brown, F. L. Chicago Sunday Tribune, 18 June 1961, p. 4.
    Cruttwell, Patrick. Guardian, 9 February 1962, p. 7.
    Griffin, L. W. Library Journal, 1 May 1961, p. 1796.
    Interracial Review 35 (May 1962): 127.
    Moore, H. T. Saturday Review of Literature, 3 June 1961, p. 23.

Punch, 14 February 1962, p. 297.
Redding, Saunders. New York Herald Tribune Books, 9 July
    1961, p. 9.
Times Literary Supplement, 9 February 1962, p. 85.
Times Weekly Review, 15 February 1962, p. 10.
The Hit
    Barnett, Abraham. Library Journal, 15 October 1957, p. 2543.
    Bonosky, Phillip. Mainstream 11 (January 1958): 53-57.
    Hughes, Langston. New York Herald Tribune Book Review, 20
        October 1957, p. 12.
    Kirkus, 15 August 1957, p. 598.
    Millstein, Gilbert. New York Times, 29 December 1957, p. 4.
    Redding, Saunders. Saturday Review of Literature, 19 October
        1957, p. 21.
    Watkins, Charlotte Crawford. Journal of Negro Education 27
        (Spring 1958): 163-164.
The Long Night
    Booklist, 15 November 1958, p. 156.
    Byam, M. S. Library Journal, 1 October 1958, p. 2766.
    Jacobson, Dan. Spectator, 15 January 1960, p. 83.
    Kirkus, 15 August 1958, p. 623.
    Naipaul, V. S. New Statesman, 9 January 1960, p. 50.
    New York Herald Tribune Book Review, 26 October 1958, p. 16.
    Perrott, Roy. Guardian, 8 January 1960, p. 6.
    Time, 20 October 1958, p. 108.
    Times Literary Supplement, 22 January 1960, p. 54.

MAYS, James A.

Fiction

Mercy Is King. Los Angeles: Crescent Publications, 1975.

MEADDOUGH, R. J., III

Short Fiction

"The Death of Tommy Grimes." In Gibson and Anselment, Black
    and White; Hughes, Best Short Stories by Negro Writers.
"The Other Side of Christmas." Freedomways 7 (Fall 1967): 316-
    324; also in Clarke, Harlem.
"Poppa's Story." Liberator 9 (March 1969): 14-16. Also in Stad-
    ler, Out of Our Lives.

MELFORD, Larry

Short Fiction

"Pay Day." Black Creation 2 (Summer 1971): 28-29.
"An Unfavored Star." Black Creation 3 (Fall 1971): 44-45.

Biography and Criticism

Rush, Theressa Gunnels, Carol Fairbanks Myers, and Esther Spring
Arata. Black American Writers Past and Present. Metuchen,
N.J.: Scarecrow Press, 1975.

MERIWETHER, Louise M.

Novel

Daddy Was a Number Runner. Englewood Cliffs, N.J.: Prentice-
Hall, 1970; New York: Pyramid, 1971.

Short Fiction

"Daddy Was a Number Runner." Antioch Review 27 (Fall 1967):
325-337; also in Clarke, Harlem; Stadler, Out of Our Lives.
"A Happening in Barbados." Essence 2 (June 1971): 58-59; also
in King, Black Short Story Anthology; Washington, Black-Eyed
Susans.
"That Girl from Creektown." In Watkins, Black Review No. 2.

Biography and Criticism

"Daddy Was a Number Runner." Ebony 25 (July 1970): 98-103.
Harper, Clifford Doyl. "A Study of the Disunity Theme in the Afro-
American Experience: An Examination of Five Representative
Novels." Ph.D. Dissertation, Saint Louis University, 1974.
Schraufnagel, Noel. From Apology to Protest: The Black American
Novel. DeLand, Fla.: Everett/Edwards, 1973.
Schulberg, Budd. "Black Phoenix: An Introduction." Antioch Re-
view 27 (Fall 1967): 277-284.

Reviews

Daddy Was a Number Runner
    American Libraries 1 (December 1970): 1088.
    Baurle, Ruth. Saturday Review of Literature, 23 May 1970,
        p. 51.
    Black World 19 (May 1970): 51; 19 (July 1970): 85.
    Book World, 20 June 1971, p. 11.
    Booklist, 1 April 1971, p. 654.
    English Journal 60 (May 1971): 657.
    Guiney, E. M. Library Journal, 15 February 1970, p. 685.
    Kirkus, 1 January 1970, p. 22; 1 February 1970, p. 119.
    Library Journal, 15 September 1970, p. 3080; 15 December
        1970, p. 4328.
    Marshall, Paule. New York Times Book Review, 28 June
        1970, p. 31.
    New Statesman, 7 January 1972, p. 23.
    New York Times Book Review, 6 December 1970, p. 100.
    Observer, 9 January 1972, p. 31.

Publishers' Weekly, 19 January 1970, p. 78; 3 May 1971, p. 58.
Saturday Review, 24 July 1971, p. 42.
Sissman, L. E. New Yorker, 11 July 1970, p. 77.
Times Literary Supplement, 21 January 1972, p. 57.
Top of the News 27 (April 1971): 309.

MESCHI, Howard

Short Fiction

"If We Could See. " In Ford and Faggett, Best Short Stories by
   Afro-American Writers.

MICHEAUX, Oscar

Novels

The Case of Mrs. Wingate. New York: Book Supply Co. , 1945;
   New York: AMS Press, 1975.
The Conquest; The Story of a Negro Pioneer, by the Pioneer. Lin-
   coln, Nebr. : Woodruff, 1913; Washington, D. C. : McGrath,
   1968; also available in microfiche: The Microbook Library of
   American Civilization. Chicago: Library Resources, 1971
   (LAC 15812).
The Forged Note; a Romance of the Darker Races. Lincoln, Nebr. :
   Western Book Supply, 1915.
The Homesteader. Sioux City, Ia. : Western Book Supply, 1917;
   Washington, D. C. : McGrath, 1969.
The Masquerade, an Historical Novel. New York: Book Supply Co. ,
   1947; New York: AMS Press, 1976.
The Wind from Nowhere: A Novel. New York: Book Supply Co. ,
   1943.

Biography and Criticism

Bone, Robert A. The Negro Novel in America. New Haven: Yale
   University Press, 1966.
Gloster, Hugh M. Negro Voices in American Fiction. Chapel Hill:
   University of North Carolina Press, 1948.
Half Century 6 (May 1919): 13-14.
Hughes, Carl M. The Negro Novelist 1940-1950. New York: Cita-
   del Press, 1953.

Review

The Wind from Nowhere
   Crisis 51 (June 1944): 202.

MIDDLETON, Henry Davies

Short Fiction

"Jane Joins the Tolliers." Half Century 4 (March 1918): 4, 13;
   (April 1918): 5.
"The Ragtime Regiment." Crisis 14 (September 1917): 252-255.
"The Sacrificial Turkeys." Half Century 3 (November 1917): 5, 13.

MILLER, Ezekiel Harry

Novel

The Protestant. Boston: Christopher, 1933.

MILLER, Kelly

Short Fiction

"An Oblique Prayer." Voice of the Negro 2 (November 1905): 766-770.

Biography and Criticism

Rush, Theressa Gunnels, Carol Fairbanks Myers, and Esther Spring
   Arata. Black American Writers Past and Present. Metuchen,
   N.J.: Scarecrow Press, 1975.

MILLER, May (Mrs. John Sullivan)

Short Fiction

"One Blue Star." Opportunity 23 (Summer 1945): 142-143.

Biography and Criticism

Rush, Theressa Gunnels, Carol Fairbanks Myers, and Esther Spring
   Arata. Black American Writers Past and Present. Metuchen,
   N.J.: Scarecrow Press, 1975.

MILLICAN, Arthenia Bates   see   Bates, Arthenia

MILLS, Alison

Novel

Francisco. Berkeley, Calif.: Reed, Cannon & Johnson, n.d.
   Excerpt in Yardbird Reader 2 (1973): 207-218.

Reviews

Francisco
>   Clipman, W. H.   "Everything to Everybody."   Obsidian 1 (Summer 1975):   93-98.

MILNER, Ron

Short Fiction

"Junkie-Joe Had Some Money."   In Gibson and Anselment, Black and White; Hughes, The Best Short Stories by Negro Writers.

MIMS, Harley

Short Fiction

"Memoirs of a Shoeshine Boy."   In Schulberg, From the Ashes.

MINUS, Marian

Short Fiction

"The Fine Line."   Opportunity 17 (November 1939):   333-337, 351.
"Half-Bright."   Opportunity 18 (September 1940):   271-274.

MITCHELL, Leroy E., Jr.

Short Fiction

"A New Image."   Negro History Bulletin 26 (October 1962):   69, 71.

MITCHELL, Loften

Novel

The Stubborn Old Lady Who Resisted Change.   New York: Emerson Hall, 1973.

Biography and Criticism

Rush, Theressa Gunnels, Carol Fairbanks Myers, and Esther Spring Arata.   Black American Writers Past and Present.   Metuchen, N.J.:   Scarecrow Press, 1975.

MONTAGUE, W. Reginald

Novel

Ole Man Mose: A Novel of the Tennessee Valley. New York: Exposition, 1957.

MOODY, Anne

Short Fiction

Mr. Death: Four Stories. New York: Harper, 1975. Includes:
      "All Burnt Up."
      "Bobo."
      "The Cow."
      "Mr. Death."

Reviews

Mr. Death: Four Stories
    Best Sellers 35 (February 1976): 362.
    Kirkus, 15 September 1975, p. 1074.
    New York Times Book Review, 16 November 1975, p. 32.
    Publishers' Weekly, 29 September 1975, p. 5.
    School Library Journal 22 (December 1975): 60.
    Virginia Quarterly Review 52 (Summer 1976): 97.

MOODY, David Reese

Short Fiction

"Consequence." In Schulberg, From the Ashes.

MOON, Albert

Short Fiction

"The Award." In Ford and Faggett, Best Short Stories by Afro-
American Writers.

MOORE, Birdell Chew

Short Fiction

"The Promise of Strangers." In Schulberg, From the Ashes.

MOREAU, Junius see Jackson, J. Denis

MORELAND, Charles King, Jr.

Short Fiction

"The Top Hat Motel." Negro Digest 18 (June 1969): 72-82.

MORRIS, Earl J.

Novel

The Cop. New York: Exposition, 1951.

MORRISON, C. T.

Novel

The Flame in the Icebox: An Episode of the Vietnam War. New
York: Exposition, 1968.

MORRISON, Toni

Novels

The Bluest Eye. New York: Holt, Rinehart & Winston, 1970; New
York: Pocket Books, 1972; excerpt in Washington, Black-Eyed
Susans.
Sula. New York: Knopf, 1974; also in Redbook, January 1974.

Biography and Criticism

Bischoff, Joan. "The Novels of Toni Morrison: Studies in Thwarted
Sensitivity." Studies in Black Literature 6 (Fall 1975): 21-23.
Contemporary Authors, 29/32.
"Conversation with Alice Childress and Toni Morrison." Black
Creation 6 (Annual 1974-1975): 90-92.
Harris, Jessica. "Toni Morrison." Essence 7 (December 1976):
54, 56-57.

Reviews

The Bluest Eye
    Black World 20 (May 1971): 51.
    Booklist, 1 May 1971, p. 729.
    Choice 8 (October 1971): 1018.
    Frankel, Haskel. New York Times Book Review, 1 November
        1970, p. 46.
    Kirkus, 15 August 1970, p. 902; 15 September 1970, p. 1058.
    Marvin, P. H. Library Journal, 1 November 1970, p. 3806.
    New York Times, 13 November 1970, p. 35.
    Newsweek, 30 November 1970, p. 95c.

Publishers' Weekly, 24 August 1970, p. 45.
Sissman, L. E. New Yorker, 23 January 1971, p. 92.

Sula

Black World 23 (June 1974): 51.
Blackburn, Sara. New York Times Book Review, 30 December
1973, p. 3.
Book World, 3 February 1974, p. 3; 8 December 1974, p. 8.
Booklist, 15 March 1974, p. 774.
Bryant, J. H. Nation, 6 July 1974, p. 23.
Choice 11 (March 1974): 92.
Davis, Faith. Harvard Advocate 107 no. 4 (1974): 61-62.
Francis, W. A. C. Best Sellers, 15 January 1974, p. 469.
Hudson Review 27 (Summer 1974): 283.
Kirkus, 1 November 1973, p. 1225.
Marvin, P. H. Library Journal 98 (August 1973): 2336.
Ms. 3 (December 1974): 34.
New Republic, 9 March 1974, p. 31.
New York Times, 7 January 1974, p. 29.
New York Times Book Review, 2 June 1974, p. 6; 1 December
1974, p. 70.
Newsweek, 30 December 1974, p. 62.
Playboy 21 (March 1974): 22.
Prescott, P. S. Newsweek, 7 January 1974, p. 63.
Publishers' Weekly, 5 November 1973, p. 56; 4 August 1975,
p. 59.
Smith, Barbara. Freedomways 14 (First Quarter 1974): 69-72.
Times Literary Supplement, 4 October 1974, p. 1062.
Village Voice, 7 March 1974, p. 21.

MOTLEY, Willard

Novels

Knock on Any Door. New York: Appleton-Century, 1947; New York:
New American Library, 1950.
Let No Man Write My Epitaph. New York: Random House, 1958.
Let Noon Be Fair. New York: Putnam, 1966.
Tourist Town. New York: Putnam, 1965.
We Fished All Night. New York: Appleton-Century-Crofts, 1951;
New York: AMS Press, 1974.

Short Fiction

"The Almost White Boy." In Hill, Soon, One Morning; Hughes,
The Best Short Stories by Negro Writers; Kissin, Stories in
Black and White; Patterson, An Introduction to Black Literature
in America; Stanford, I, Too, Sing America.

Biography and Criticism

Baylis, John F. "Nick Romano: Father and Son." Negro American Literature Forum 3 (Spring 1969): 18-21.

Bigsby, C. W. E. "From Protest to Paradox: The Black Writer at Mid-Century." In In the Fifties, pp. 217-240. Edited by Norman Podhoretz. New York: Farrar, Straus, 1964.

Bone, Robert A. The Negro Novel in America. New Haven: Yale University Press, 1966.

Davis, Arthur P. From the Dark Tower: Afro-American Writers 1900-1960. Washington, D. C.: Howard University Press, 1974.

Fleming, Robert E. "Willard Motley's Urban Novels." Umija: Southwestern Afro-American Journal 1 (Summer 1973): 15-19.

Ford, Nick Aaron. "Four Popular Negro Novelists." Phylon 15 (First Quarter 1954): 29-39.

Gelfant, Blanche Housman. The American City Novel. Norman: University of Oklahoma Press, 1954.

Giles, James R. "Willard Motley's Concept of 'Style' and 'Material.'" Studies in Black Literature 4 (Spring 1973): 4-6.

_____ and Jerome Klinkowitz. "The Emergence of Willard Motley in Black American Literature." Negro American Literature Forum 6 (Summer 1972): 31-34.

_____ and Karen Magee Myers. "Naturalism as Principle and Trap: Theory and Execution in Willard Motley's We Fished All Night." Studies in Black Literature 7 (Winter 1976): 19-22.

_____ and N. Jill Weyant. "The Short Fiction of Willard Motley." Negro American Literature Forum 9 (Spring 1975): 3-16.

Hughes, Carl M. The Negro Novelist 1940-1950. New York: Citadel Press, 1953.

Klinkowitz, Jerome and Karen Wood. "The Making and Unmaking of Knock on Any Door." Proof 3 (1973): 121-137.

"Knock on Any Door." Look, 30 September 1947, pp. 21-31.

Major, Clarence. "Willard Motley: A Vague Ghost After the Father." Nickel Review, 3 October 1969; also in Major's Dark and Feeling. New York: Third Press, 1974.

Maund, Alfred. "The Negro Novelist and the Contemporary American Scene." Chicago Jewish Forum 12 (Fall 1954): 28-34.

New York Times, 5 March 1965, p. 30. (Obituary.)

Rayson, Ann L. "Prototypes for Nick Romano of Knock on Any Door: From the Diaries in the Collected Manuscripts of the Willard Motley Estate." Negro American Literature Forum 8 (1974): 248-251.

Rideout, Walter Bates. The Radical Novel in the United States, 1900-1954. Cambridge: Harvard University Press, 1956.

Schraufnagel, Noel. From Apology to Protest: The Black American Novel. DeLand, Fla.: Everett/Edwards, 1973.

Weyant, Nancy Jill. "The Craft of Willard Motley's Fiction." Ph. D. Dissertation, Northern Illinois University, 1975.

"Willard Motley." Ebony 2 (September 1947): 47-50.

Wood, Charles. "The Adventure Manuscript: New Light on Willard Motley's Naturalism." Negro American Literature Forum 6 (Summer 1972): 35-39.

Reviews

Knock on Any Door
        Adams, P. L. Atlantic 180 (July 1947): 126.

Bontemps, Arna. New York Herald Tribune Weekly Book Review, 18 May 1947, p. 8.

Booklist, 15 June 1947, p. 331.

Butcher, Philip. Opportunity 25 (Fall 1947): 221-222.

Catholic World 166 (December 1947): 286.

Cayton, H. R. New Republic, 12 May 1947, p. 30.

Cross, J. E. Library Journal, 1 May 1947, p. 734.

Hanson, Harry. Survey Graphic 36 (August 1947): 450.

Hexter, M. B. Saturday Review of Literature, 24 May 1947, p. 13.

Jackson, J. H. San Francisco Chronicle, 10 June 1947, p. 18.

Kirkus, 1 February 1947, p. 79.

Kogan, Herman. Chicago Sun Book Week, 11 May 1947, p. 2.

Lee, Charles. New York Times, 4 May 1947, p. 3.

Light, James. New Masses, 17 June 1947, p. 17.

New Yorker, 24 May 1947, p. 101.

Prescott, Orville. Yale Review 36 (Summer 1947): 765.

Rago, Henry. Commonweal, 25 June 1947, p. 359.

Wheeler, Charles Enoch. Crisis 55 (January 1948): 26-27.

Wisconsin Library Bulletin 43 (July 1947): 119.

Wright, Marion T. Journal of Negro Education 17 (Winter 1948): 73-74.

Let No Man Write My Epitaph

Algren, Nelson. Nation, 16 August 1958, p. 78.

_____. Chicago Sunday Tribune, 17 August 1958, p. 1.

Booklist, 1 September 1958, p. 23.

Bryant, J. W. Library Journal, 15 September 1958, p. 2442.

Dempsey, David. New York Times, 10 August 1958, p. 18.

Geismar, Maxwell. New York Herald Tribune Book Review, 17 August, 1958, p. 4.

Hicks, Granville. Saturday Review of Literature, 9 August 1958, p. 11.

Hogan, William. San Francisco Chronicle, 4 August 1958, p. 29.

Kirkus, 1 June 1958, p. 390.

New Yorker, 23 August 1958, p. 92.

Time, 11 August 1958, p. 74.

Let Noon Be Fair

Algren, Nelson. Book Week, 6 March 1966, p. 5.

Books Today, 12 February 1967, p. 13.

Coleman, Alexander. New York Times Book Review, 27 February 1966, p. 42.

Cook, B. National Observer, 14 March 1966, p. 21.

Donahugh, R. H. Library Journal, 1 February 1966, p. 715.

Donoso, J. Saturday Review, 12 March 1955, p. 152.

Galloway, D. Spectator, 15 July 1966, p. 87.

Goran, L. Books Today, 27 February 1966, p. 1.

Horner, A. Books and Bookmen 12 (October 1966): 40.

Kirkus, 15 December 1965, p. 1242.

Kitching, J. Publishers' Weekly, 17 January 1966, p. 129.

Newsweek, 28 February 1966, p. 94.

Poore, C. New York Times, 24 February 1966, p. 39m.

Randall, D. Negro Digest 15 (May 1966): 90.

We Fished All Night
  Alman, David. Masses & Mainstream 5 (February 1952): 61-
    64.
  Cain, J. M. New York Times, 18 November 1951, p. 4.
  Cromie, Robert. Chicago Sunday Tribune, 25 November 1951,
    p. 3.
  Gray, James. Saturday Review of Literature, 8 December
    1951, p. 20.
  Jackson, J. H. San Francisco Chronicle, 29 November 1951,
    p. 20.
  Kingery, R. E. Library Journal, 1 December 1951, p. 2006.
  Kirkus, 1 October 1951, p. 586.
  New Yorker, 24 November 1951, p. 165.
  Redding, J. S. New York Herald Tribune Book Review, 25
    November 1951, p. 8.
  Swados, Harvey. Nation, 29 December 1951, p. 572.
  Time, 26 November 1951, p. 120.

MUHAJIR, El see Marvin X

MULLER-THYM, Thomas

Short Fiction

"A Word About Justice." In Coombs, What We Must See.

MURRAY, Albert

Novel

Trainwhistle Guitar. New York: McGraw-Hill, 1974.

Short Fiction

"Stonewall Jackson's Waterloo." In Margolies, A Native Sons Read-
    er; Stadler, Out of Our Lives.
"Train Whistle Guitar." In Bambara, Tales and Stories for Black
    Folks; Beaty, The Norton Introduction to Literature; Clarke,
    American Negro Short Stories; Emanuel and Gross, Dark Sym-
    phony; Taylor, The Short Story.

Biography and Criticism

Beauford, Fred. "Conversation with Al Murray." Black Creation
    3 (Summer 1972): 26-27.
Berry, J. "Musical Literature: Work of A. Murray." Nation,
    15 January 1977, pp. 55-57.
Contemporary Authors, 49/52.
Lindberg, J. "Black Aesthetic: Minority or Mainstream? North
    American Review 260 (Winter 1975): 48-52.

Rush, Theressa Gunnels, Carol Fairbanks Myers, and Esther Spring
    Arata. Black American Writers Past and Present. Metuchen,
    N.J.: Scarecrow Press, 1975.
Sheppard, R. Z. "Soul: Straight Up, No Ice." Time, 10 January
    1972, p. 65.

Reviews

Trainwhistle Guitar
    Atlantic Monthly 234 (December 1974): 120.
    Avant, J. A. Library Journal 99 (August 1974): 1986.
    Book World, 8 December 1974, p. 8.
    Booklist, 15 July 1974, p. 1225.
    Carolina Quarterly 26 (Fall 1974): 100.
    Choice 11 (July/August 1974): 762.
    Edwards, T. R. New York Review of Books, 18 June 1974,
        p. 38.
    Hudson, Theodore R. Black Scholar 7 (September 1975): 51-
        52.
    Kirkus, 1 February 1974, p. 143.
    Lindsay, L. W. Christian Science Monitor, 10 April 1974,
        p. F5.
    McDavid, Douglas. Library Journal, 15 October 1974, p. 2751.
    Mercier, Vivian. Saturday Review/World, 4 May 1974, p. 51.
    New Leader, 2 May 1974, p. 5.
    New York Times Book Review, 1 December 1974, p. 72.
    Publishers' Weekly, 4 February 1974, p. 65; 13 October 1975,
        p. 113.
    Wideman, John. New York Times Book Review, 12 May 1974,
        p. 7.

MURRAY, Samuel M., Jr.

Short Fiction

"Brooklyn." In Sanchez, Three Hundred and Sixty Degrees of
    Blackness Comin at You; Sanchez, We Be Word Sorcerers.

MYERS, Walter D.

Short Fiction

"Bubba." Essence 3 (November 1972): 56-57.
"Dark Side of the Moon." Black Creation 3 (Fall 1971): 26-29.
"The Fare to Drown Point." In Coombs, What We Must See.
"The Going On." Black World 2 (March 1971): 61-67.
"Gums." In Sanchez, We Be Word Sorcerers.
"How Long Is Forever?" Negro Digest 18 (June 1969): 52-57.

Biography and Criticism

Contemporary Authors, 33/36.
Rush, Theressa Gunnels, Carol Fairbanks Myers, and Esther Spring
Arata. Black American Writers Past and Present. Metuchen,
N.J.: Scarecrow Press, 1975.

NAZEL, Joseph Jr.

Novels

The Black Exorcist. Los Angeles: Holloway House, 1974.
Black Fury. Los Angeles: Holloway House, 1976.
The Black Gestapo. Los Angeles: Holloway House, 1975.
Black Is Back. Black Series, No. 2. New York: Pinnacle Books,
1974.
Black Prophet. Los Angeles: Holloway House, 1976.
Canadian Kill. Los Angeles: Holloway House, 1974.
Death for Hire. Los Angeles: Holloway House, 1975.
Iceman, No. 1: Billion Dollar Death. Los Angeles: Holloway
House, 1974.
Iceman, No. 2: The Golden Shaft. Los Angeles: Holloway House,
1974.
Iceman, No. 3: Slick Revenge. Los Angeles: Holloway House,
1974.
Iceman, No. 4: Sunday Fix. Los Angeles: Holloway House, 1974.
Iceman, No. 5: Spinning Target. Los Angeles: Holloway House,
1974.
Iceman, No. 7: The Shakedown. Los Angeles: Holloway House,
1975.
My Name Is Black. Black Series, No. 1. New York: Pinnacle
Books, 1973.

Reviews

The Name Is Black
Publishers' Weekly, 17 September 1973, p. 59.

NEAL, Larry

Short Fiction

"Sinner Man Where You Gonna Run To?" In Jones and Neal, Black
Fire.

Biography and Criticism

Rush, Theressa Gunnels, Carol Fairbanks Myers, and Esther Spring
Arata. Black American Writers Past and Present. Metuchen,
N.J.: Scarecrow Press, 1975.

NELSON, Annie Greene

Novels

After the Storm. Columbia, S.C.: Hampton, 1942.
The Dawn Appears. Columbia, S.C.: Hampton, 1944.

NEWSOME, Mary Effie Lee

Short Fiction

"He Will Come Back Easter." Opportunity 4 (April 1926): 126-127.
"House of Hark Back." Crisis 35 (1928): 33.
"Little Cornish, The 'Blue Boy.'" Opportunity 5 (April 1927): 117.
"The Morning of Life." Opportunity 4 (April 1926): 126-127.

Biography and Criticism

Rush, Theressa Gunnels, Carol Fairbanks Myers, and Esther Spring
    Arata. Black American Writers Past and Present. Metuchen,
    N.J.: Scarecrow Press, 1975.
Who's Who in Colored America, 5th ed.

NOEL, Abe see Caldwell, Lewis A. H.

NUGENT, Richard Bruce

Short Fiction

"Beyond Where the Star Stood Still." Crisis 77 (December 1970):
    405-408.
"Sahdji." In Locke, The New Negro.

OCCOMY, Marita Bonner see Bonner, Marita

OFFORD, Carl

Novels

The Naked Fear. New York: Ace, 1954.
The White Face. New York: McBride, 1943.

Short Fiction

"Gentle Native." Masses & Mainstream 1 (September 1948): 8-16.
"The Green Green Grass and a Gun." Masses & Mainstream 2
    (February 1949): 39-43.
"Low Sky." In Seaver, Cross-Section, 1944.

"So Peaceful in the Country. " In Burnett, Black Hands on a White Face; Clarke, American Negro Short Stories.

Biography and Criticism

Hughes, Carl M. The Negro Novelist 1940-1950. New York: Citadel Press, 1953.
Schraufnagel, Noel. From Apology to Protest: The Black American Novel. DeLand, Fla.: Everett/Edwards, 1973.

Reviews

The White Face
    Bell, Lisle. Weekly Book Review, 16 May 1943, p. 12.
    Feld, Rose. New York Times Book Review, 23 May 1943, p. 12.
    Herbst, Josephine. Book Week, 9 May 1943, p. 4.
    Holmes, J. Welfred. Opportunity 22 (Winter 1944): 35-36.
    Moon, H. L. New Republic, 21 May 1943, p. 741.
    Rose, Ernestine. Library Journal, 1 May 1943, p. 363.
    Springfield Republican, 6 June 1943, p. 7e.
    Trilling, Diana. Nation, 5 June 1943, p. 816.

OJI, Abayome

Short Fiction

"Cookie Crumbs. " In Sanchez, Three Hundred and Sixty Degrees of Blackness Comin at You.

OKORE, Ode

Short Fiction

"The Mermaid. " Essence 7 (September 1976): 82-83, 98, 100-103.

OKPAKU, Joseph O. O.

Short Fiction

"Under the Iroko Tree. " Literary Review 2 (Summer 1968): 481-554.

Biography and Criticism

Contemporary Authors, 29/32.
Rush, Theressa Gunnels, Carol Fairbanks Myers, and Esther Spring Arata. Black American Writers Past and Present. Metuchen, N.J. Scarecrow Press, 1975.
Who's Who in America, 1972-1973.

OLIVER, Diane A.

Short Fiction

"The Closet on the Top Floor." In Corrington and Williams, South-
ern Writing in the Sixties.
"Health Service." Negro Digest 15 (November 1965): 72-79.
"Mint Juleps Not Served Here." Negro Digest 16 (March 1967):
58-66.
"Neighbors." Sewanee Review 74 (Spring 1966): 470-488.
Also in Abrahams, Prize Stories, 1967; Adoff, Brothers and
Sisters; Casmier and Souder, Coming Together; Margolies, A
Native Sons Reader; Mizener, Modern Short Stories, 3rd. ed;
Stein and Walters, The Southern Experience in Short Fiction.
"Traffic Jam." Negro Digest 15 (July 1966): 69-78.

Biography and Criticism

Llorens, David. "Remembering a Young Talent." Negro Digest 15
(September 1966): 88-89.

OLIVER, James B.

Short Fiction

"A 'For God and Country' Thing, Circa 1940." Black World 21
(March 1972): 53-64.

OLIVER, Kitty

Short Fiction

"Mama." Essence 7 (October 1976): 80-81, 98, 100-101.

PARKS, Gordon

Novels

The Learning Tree. New York: Harper & Row, 1963; Greenwich,
Conn.: Fawcett, 1970; excerpts in Austin, Fenderson and Nelson, The Black Man and the Promise of America; "The Learning Tree." Old Greenwich, Conn.: Listening Library, n.d.
(LP recording).

Biography and Criticism

Authors in the News, vol. 2. Detroit: Gale Research Co., 1976.
Contemporary Authors, 41/44.
Harnan, Terry. Gordon Parks: Black Photographer and Film
Maker. Champaign, Ill.: Garrard, 1972.

Rush, Theressa Gunnels, Carol Fairbanks Myers, and Esther Spring
Arata. Black American Writers Past and Present. Metuchen,
N.J.: Scarecrow Press, 1975.
Schraufnagel, Noel. From Apology to Protest: The Black Ameri-
can Novel. DeLand, Fla.: Everett/Edwards, 1973.
Turk, Midge. Gordon Parks. New York: Crowell, 1971.

Reviews

The Learning Tree
    Balliett, Whitney. New Yorker, 2 November 1973, p. 209.
    Cosmopolitan 138 (September 1963): 25.
    Crisis 70 (December 1963): 634.
    De Bellis, Jack. Sewanee Review 72 (Summer 1974): 531.
    Dempsey, David. New York Times Book Review, 15 September
        1963, p. 4.
    Grumbach, Doris. Critic 22 (October 1963): 84.
    Hass, Victor P. Chicago Sunday Tribune Magazine of Books,
        8 September 1963, p. 3.
    Hentoff, Nat. New York Herald-Tribune Books, 25 August
        1963, p. 6.
    Library Journal, 1 October 1963, p. 3646.
    Moynahan, Julian. New York Review of Books, 26 September
        1963, p. 16.
    Prescott, Orville. New York Times Book Review, 26 August
        1963, p. 25.
    Saturday Review of Literature, 3 October 1964, p. 58.
    Time, 6 September 1963, p. 86.
    Times Literary Supplement, 4 June 1964, p. 471.
    Vonckx, Anne. Book-of-the-Month Club News, 13 October 1963.

PARRISH, Clarence R.

Novel

Images of Democracy (I Can't Go Home). New York: Carlton,
    1967.

PATTERSON, Lindsay

Short Fiction

"Miss Nora." Essence 1 (July 1970): 32, 72; also in Coombs,
    What We Must See.
"Red Bonnet." In Gibson and Anselment, Black and White; Hughes,
    The Best Short Stories by Negro Writers; Patterson, An Intro-
    duction to Black Literature in America.
"T-Baby." Essence 3 (May 1972): 70, 86, 90, 94.

Biography and Criticism

Rush, Theressa Gunnels, Carol Fairbanks Myers, and Esther Spring

Arata. Black American Writers Past and Present. Metuchen,
N.J.: Scarecrow Press, 1975.

PATTERSON, Orlando

Novels

An Absence of Ruins. London: Hutchinson, 1967.
The Children of Sisyphus. London: Hutchinson, 1964; Boston:
Houghton Mifflin, 1965. (Also published as Dinah. Elmhurst,
N.Y.: Pyramid Books, 1968.)
Die the Long Day. New York: Morrow, 1972; Philadelphia: Cur-
tis, 1973.
Dinah see The Children of Sisyphus

Short Fiction

"One for a Penny." In Salkey, Island Voices.
"The Very Funny Man: A Tale in Two Moods." In Salkey, Island
Voices.

Biography and Criticism

New, W. H. In Contemporary Novelists. Edited by James Vinson.
New York: St. Martin's Press, 1976.
Rush, Theressa Gunnels, Carol Fairbanks Myers, and Esther Spring
Arata. Black American Writers Past and Present. Metuchen,
N.J.: Scarecrow Press, 1975.

Reviews

The Absence of Ruins
    Rhodes, Eric. New Statesman, 7 April 1967, p. 477.
    Times Literary Supplement, 13 April 1967, p. 301.
The Children of Sisyphus
    Cruttwell, Patrick. Hudson Review 18 (Autumn 1965): 499.
    Newsweek, 12 April 1965, p. 113A.
    Times Literary Supplement, 2 April 1964, p. 269.
Die the Long Day
    Black World 22 (February 1973): 78.
    Booklist, 1 September 1972, p. 29.
    Choice 9 (January 1973): 1448.
    Kirkus, 15 April 1972, p. 496.
    Library Journal 97 (July 1972): 2434.
    New Leader, 24 July 1972, p. 16.
    New York Times Book Review, 10 September 1972, p. 46.
    Publishers' Weekly, 1 May 1972, p. 48.

PATTERSON, Thomas C.

Short Fiction

"Special Assignment. " In Ford and Faggett, Best Short Stories by
     Afro-American Writers.

PAULDING, James E.

Novel

Sometime Tomorrow. New York: Carlton, 1965.

PERKINS, Charles

Novel

Portrait of a Young Man Drowning. New York: Simon & Schuster,
     1962.

PERRY, Richard

Novel

Changes. Indianapolis: Bobbs-Merrill, 1974.

Short Fiction

"For You, There Is Only the Dancing. " Black World 23 (June 1974):
     61.

Reviews

Changes
     Kirkus, 1 April 1974, p. 388.
     Library Journal, 1 June 1974, p. 1567.
     New York Times Book Review, 15 September 1974, p. 37.
     Publishers' Weekly, 27 May 1974, p. 57.

PETRY, Ann Lane

Novels

Country Place. Boston: Houghton Mifflin, 1947; London: M. Jo-
     seph, 1948; Chatham, N.J.: Chatham Bookseller, 1971.
The Narrows. Boston: Houghton Mifflin, 1953; Chatham, N.J.:
     Chatham Bookseller, 1973; New York: Pyramid, 1971.
The Street. Boston: Houghton Mifflin, 1946; New York: Pyramid,
     1969; excerpts in Adams, Conn and Slepian, Afro-American Lit-

erature: Fiction; Davis and Redding, Cavalcade; Somerville,
   Intimate Relationships.

Short Fiction

(Collection): Miss Muriel and Other Stories. Boston: Houghton
   Mifflin, 1971.
"The Bones of Louella Brown. " Opportunity 25 (Fall 1947): 189-
   192, 226-230; also in Petry, Miss Muriel.
"Doby's Gone. " Phylon 5 (Fourth Quarter 1944): 361-366; also in
   Petry, Miss Muriel.
"Has Anyone Seen Miss Dora Dean?" New Yorker, 25 October 1958,
   pp. 41-48; also in Petry, Miss Muriel.
"In Darkness and Confusion. " In Clarke, Harlem; Klotz and Abca-
   rian, The Experience of Fiction; Petry, Miss Muriel; Seaver,
   Cross Section, 1947.
"Like a Winding Sheet. " Crisis 52 (November 1945): 317-318, 331-
   332; also in Barksdale and Kinnamon, Black Writers of America;
   Cahill, Women and Fiction; Foley, Best American Short Stories,
   1946; James, From the Roots; Petry, Miss Muriel.
"The Migraine Workers. " Redbook 129 (May 1967): 66-67, 125-
   127; also in Petry, Miss Muriel.
"Miss Muriel. " In Hill, Soon, One Morning; Kissin, Stories in
   Black and White; Petry, Miss Muriel.
"Mother Africa. " In Petry, Miss Muriel.
"The Necessary Knocking at the Door. " '47 Magazine of the Year
   1 (August 1947): 39-44; also in Petry, Miss Muriel.
"The New Mirror. " New Yorker 61 (May 1965): 28-55; also in
   Petry, Miss Muriel; Stadler, Out of Our Lives.
"Olaf and His Girl Friend. " Crisis 52 (May 1945): 135-137, 147;
   also in Petry, Miss Muriel.
"On Saturday the Siren Sounds at Noon. " Crisis 50 (December
   1943): 368-369.
"Solo on the Drums. " '47 Magazine of the Year 1 (October 1947):
   105-110; also in Murray and Thomas, Major Black Writers;
   Petry, Miss Muriel.
"The Witness. " Redbook 136 (February 1971): 80-81; 126-134;
   also in Petry, Miss Muriel.

Biography and Criticism

Bone, Robert A. The Negro Novel in America. New Haven: Yale
   University Press, 1966.
Contemporary Authors, 7/8.
Current Biography, 1946.
Davis, Arthur P. From the Dark Tower: Afro-American Writers
   1900-1960. Washington, D.C.: Howard University Press,
   1974.
Dempsey, David. "Uncle Tom's Ghost and the Literary Abolition-
   ist. " Antioch Review 6 (September 1946): 442-448.
Doyle, Sister Mary Ellen. "The Heroine of Black Novels. " In
   Perspectives on Afro-American Women, pp. 112-125. Edited
   by Willa D. Johnson and Thomas L. Green. Washington, D.C.:

ECCA Publications, 1975.

Eisinger, Chester E. Fiction of the Forties. Chicago: Chicago University Press, 1963.

Emanuel, James A. In Contemporary Novelists. Edited by James Vinson. New York: St. Martin's Press, 1976.

"First Novel." Ebony 1 (April 1946): 35-39.

Gayle, Addison, Jr. The Way of the New World: The Black Novel in America. Garden City, N.Y.: Anchor Press/Doubleday, 1975.

Gloster, Hugh M. Negro Voices in American Fiction. Chapel Hill: University of North Carolina Press, 1948.

Green, Marjorie. "Ann Petry Planned to Write." Opportunity 24 (April-June 1946): 78-79.

Hill, James Lee. "Bibliography of the Works of Chester Himes, Ann Petry and Frank Yerby." Black Books Bulletin 3 (Fall 1975): 60-72.

Hughes, Carl M. The Negro Novelist 1940-1950. New York: Citadel Press, 1953.

Ivy, James W. "Ann Petry Talks About First Novel." Crisis 53 (February 1946): 48-49.

_____. "Mrs. Petry's Harlem." Crisis 53 (May 1946): 154-155.

Jaskoski, Helen. "Power Unequal to Man: The Significance of Conjure in Works by Five Afro-American Authors." Southern Folklore Quarterly 38 (June 1974): 91-108.

Lattin, Vernon. "Ann Petry's Fiction: The Rebellion of a Black Intellectual." Paper presented at the MLA meeting, New York City, December 1976.

Littlejohn, David. Black on White: A Critical Survey of Writing by American Negroes. New York: Grossman, 1966.

Madden, David. "Ann Petry: 'The Witness.'" Studies in Black Literature 6 (Fall 1975): 24-26.

Maund, Alfred. "The Negro Novelist and the Contemporary American Scene." Chicago Jewish Forum 12 (1954): 28-34.

O'Brien, John. Interviews with Black Writers. New York: Liveright, 1973.

"On an Author." New York Herald Tribune, 16 August 1953, p. 3.

Peden, William. The American Short Story: Continuity and Change 1940-1975. Boston: Houghton Mifflin, 1975.

_____. "The Black Explosion." Studies in Short Fiction 12 (Summer 1975): 231-242.

Rosenblatt, Roger. Black Fiction. Cambridge: Harvard University Press, 1974.

Royster, Beatrice Horn. "The Ironic Vision of Four Black Women Novelists: A Study of the Novels of Jessie Fauset, Nella Larsen, Zora Neale Hurston, and Ann Petry." Ph.D. Dissertation, Emory University, 1975.

Schraufnagel, Noel. From Apology to Protest: The Black American Novel. DeLand, Fla.: Everett/Edwards, 1973.

Shinn, Thelma J. "Women in the Novels of Ann Petry." Critique 16 no. 1 (1974): 110-120.

Reviews

Country Place
    Butcher, Margaret J. W. Journal of Negro Education 17 (Spring 1948): 169.
    Butcher, Philip. Opportunity 26 (Summer 1948): 113-115.
    Downing, Francis. Commonweal, 2 January 1948, p. 306.
    Feld, Rose. New York Herald Tribune Weekly Book Review, 5 October 1947, p. 6.
    Kirkus, 1 July 1947, p. 346.
    Library Journal, 1 September 1947, p. 1196.
    New Yorker, 4 October 1947, p. 122.
    San Francisco Chronicle, 19 December 1947, p. 20.
    Smith, Bradford. Saturday Review of Literature, 18 October 1947, p. 17.
    Smith, J. C. Atlantic 180 (November 1947): 178.
    Sullivan, Richard. New York Times, 28 September 1947, p. 12.
    Thompson, E. B. Chicago Sun Book Week, 19 October 1947, p. 8.
    Wisconsin Library Bulletin 43 (November 1947): 154.
    Yglesias, Jose. New Masses, 9 December 1947, p. 18.
Miss Muriel and Other Stories
    Booklist, 15 September 1971, p. 83.
    Griffin, L. W. Library Journal 96 (July 1971): 2348.
    Harpole, J. Marinda. Renaissance 2, Issue One (1971): 45-46.
    Kazin, Alfred. Saturday Review, 2 October 1971, p. 33.
    Kirkus, 1 June 1971, p. 608.
    Library Journal, 15 November 1971, p. 3915.
    Publishers' Weekly, 12 July 1971, p. 66.
    Ruffin, C. F. Christian Science Monitor, 19 August 1971, p. 10.
    Saturday Review, 2 October 1971, p. 33.
The Narrows
    Bontemps, Arna. Saturday Review of Literature, 22 August 1953, p. 11.
    Booklist, 1 September 1953, p. 14.
    Chicago Sunday Tribune, 23 August 1953, p. 5.
    Hughes, Riley. Catholic World 178 (December 1953): 235.
    Kirkus, 1 June 1953, p. 342.
    Morris, Wright. New York Times, 16 August 1953, p. 4.
    Munn, L. S. Springfield Republican, 13 September 1953, p. 8c.
    Nation, 29 August 1953, p. 177.
    New Yorker, 29 August 1953, p. 78.
    Ross, Mary. New York Herald Tribune Book Review, 16 August 1953, p. 3.
    Smith, E. T. Library Journal 78 (July 1953): 1232.
    Taylor, Ivan E. Journal of Negro Education 23 (Winter 1954): 60-61.
    Time, 17 August 1953, p. 94.
    Voiles, Jane. San Francisco Chronicle, 26 August 1953, p. 17.
    Wisconsin Library Bulletin 49 (October 1953): 212.
The Street
    Bixler, Paul. Book Week, 10 February 1946, p. 4.

Bontemps, Arna. Weekly Book Review, 10 February 1946, p.
    4.
Booklist, 1 March 1946, p. 213.
Butterfield, Alfred. New York Times, 10 February 1946, p. 6.
Catholic World 163 (May 1946): 187.
Christian Science Monitor, 8 February 1946, p. 14.
Clemmons, Lucy Lee. Phylon 7 (First Quarter 1946): 98-99.
Cleveland Open Shelf (May 1946): 12.
Davis, Arthur P. Journal of Negro Education 15 (Fall 1946):
    648-649.
Ivy, J. W. Crisis 53 (May 1946): 154-155.
Kingery, R. E. Library Journal, 1 January,1946, p. 54.
Kirkus, 1 December 1945, p. 528.
Moody, J. N. Commonweal, 22 February 1946, p. 486.
Moon, Bucklin. New Republic, 11 February 1946, p. 193.
New Yorker, 9 February 1946, p. 98.
Prescott, Orville. Yale Review 35 (Spring 1946): 574.
Riis, Roger William. Opportunity 24 (Summer 1946): 157.
Saturday Review of Literature, 2 March 1946, p. 30.
Smith, J. C. Atlantic 177 (April 1946): 172.
Springer, Gertrude. Survey Graphic 35 (June 1946): 230.
Trilling, Diana. Nation, 9 March 1946, p. 290.
Wisconsin Library Bulletin 42 (April 1946): 60.

PHARR, Robert Deane

Novels

The Book of Numbers. Garden City, N.Y.: Doubleday, 1969; New
    York: Avon, 1970.
S. R. O. Garden City, N.Y.: Doubleday, 1971.
The Soul Murder Case: A Confession of the Victim. New York:
    Avon, 1972.

Short Fiction

"The Numbers Writer." New York Magazine, 22 September 1969;
    also in Chapman, New Black Voices.

Biography and Criticism

Contemporary Authors, 49/52.
O'Brien, John and Raman K. Singh. "Interview with Robert Deane
    Pharr." Negro American Literature Forum 8 (1974): 244-246.
Schraufnagel, Noel. From Apology to Protest: The Black Ameri-
    can Novel. DeLand, Fla.: Everett/Edwards, 1973.
Whitlow, Roger. Black American Literature: A Critical History.
    Chicago: Nelson Hall, 1973.

Reviews

The Book of Numbers
    Archer, W. H. Best Sellers, 1 May 1969, p. 59.

Booklist, 1 July 1969, p. 1210.
Donahugh, Robert. Library Journal, 15 April 1969, p. 1650.
Gross, R. A. Newsweek, 16 June 1969, p. 98.
Kirkus, 1 February 1969, p. 136.
Kuehl, Linda. Commonweal, 26 December 1969, p. 386.
Levin, Martin. New York Times Book Review, 27 April 1967,
      p. 36.
Life, 4 April 1969, p. 10.
New York Times, 4 April 1969, p. 31.
Publishers' Weekly, 3 February 1969, p. 58; 27 April 1970.
Spectator, 29 August 1970, p. 217.
Time, 6 June 1969, p. 113.
Times Literary Supplement, 30 October 1971, p. 1241.

S. R. O.
Booklist, 1 December 1971, p. 319.
Bryant, Jerry. Nation, 13 November 1971, p. 536.
Carew, Jan. New York Times Book Review, 31 October 1971,
      p. 7.
Donahugh, R. H. Library Journal, 15 September 1971, p.
      2793.
Kirkus, 1 August 1971, p. 832.
National Observer, 13 November 1971, p. 23.
New York Times Book Review, 5 December 1971, p. 84.
Phillipson, J. S. Best Sellers, 1 November 1971, p. 358.
Publishers' Weekly, 26 July 1971, p. 45.

The Soul Murder Case
Levin, M. New York Times, 28 September 1975, p. 37.

PHILLIPS, Jane

Novel

Mojo Hand. New York: Trident Press, 1969; New York: Pocket
      Books, 1969.

Biography and Criticism

Murray, Albert. The Omni-Americans: New Perspectives on Black
      Experience and American Culture. New York: Outerbridge,
      1970.

Reviews

Mojo Hand
Choice 4 (June 1967): 423.
Fuller, H. W. Negro Digest 16 (September 1967): 95.
Keehan, A. Best Sellers, 15 November 1966, p. 312.
Library Journal, 15 October 1966, p. 4175.
Weber, Nancy. New Leader, 19 December 1966, p. 22.

PICKENS, William

Short Fiction

The Vengeance of the Gods and Three Other Stories of Real Ameri-
can Life. Introduction by John Bishop Hurst. Philadelphia:
The A.M.E. Book Concern, 1922; Freeport, N.Y.: Books for
Libraries; New York: AMS Press, 1975.

PICKNEY, Darryl

Short Fiction

"Waking Up in Samoa." Harvard Advocate 107 no. 4 (1974): 41-42.

PITTS, Gertrude

Novel

Tragedies of Life. Newark: By the Author, 1939.

POLITE, Carlene Hatcher

Novels

The Flagellants. New York: Farrar, Straus & Giroux, 1967; excerpts in Robinson, Nommo; Watkins and David, To Be a Black
Woman.
Sister X and the Victims of Foul Play. Farrar, Straus & Giroux,
1975; excerpt in Yardbird Reader 4 (1975): 140-151.

Biography and Criticism

Contemporary Authors, 23/24R.
Lottman, H. R. "Authors and Editors." Publishers' Weekly, 12
June 1967, pp. 20-21.
Schraufnagel, Noel. From Apology to Protest: The Black American
Novel. DeLand, Fla.: Everett/Edwards, 1973.

Reviews

The Flagellants
Ebert, Roger. American Scholar 36 (Autumn 1967): 682.
Freedman, Richard. Book Week, 16 July 1967, p. 11.
Giovanni, N. Negro Digest 17 (January 1968): 97.
Gross, R. A. Newsweek, 16 June 1969, p. 96.
Hill, W. B. Best Sellers, 1 July 1967, p. 139.
Howe, Irving. Harper's 239 (December 1969): 130.
Kauffman, Stanley. New Republic, 24 June 1967, p. 18.
Kirkus, 15 April 1967, p. 525.

Observer, 3 March 1968, p. 23.
Publishers' Weekly, 17 April 1967, p. 53; 6 May 1968, p. 47.
Raphael, Frederic. New York Times Book Review, 11 June
    1967, p. 40.
Sayre, Nora. Nation, 9 October 1967, p. 344.
Young, B. A. Punch, 13 March 1968, p. 402.
Sister and the Victims of Foul Play
    Harris, Jessica. Essence 74 (May 1976): 44.
New York Times, 23 November 1975, p. 24.
New Yorker, 8 December 1975, p. 194.

POLLARD, Freeman

Novel

Seeds of Turmoil: A Novel of American PW's Brainwashed in
    Korea. New York: Exposition, 1959.

POSTON, Ted

Short Fiction

"Rat Joiner Routs the Klan." In Gibson and Anselment, Black and
    White; Hill, Soon, One Morning.
"Revolt of the Evil Fairies." In Hughes, The Best Short Stories
    by Negro Writers; Moon, Primer for White Folks; Olsen and
    Swinburne, Dreamers of Dreams; Patterson, An Introduction to
    Black Literature in America.

Biography and Criticism

Billingsley, Ronald G. "The Burden of the Hero in Modern Afro-
    American Fiction." Black World 25 (December 1975): 38-45,
    66-73.
_____. "Forging New Directions: The Burden of the Hero in
    Modern Afro-American Literature." Obsidian 1 (Winter 1975):
    5-21. (Same as above.)
Rush, Theressa Gunnels, Carol Fairbanks Myers, and Esther Spring
    Arata. Black American Writers Past and Present. Metuchen,
    N.J.: Scarecrow Press, 1975.
Stein, M. L. Blacks in Communications. New York: Messner,
    1972.

POTTER, Valaida (pseud., W. J. McCall)

Novel

Sunrise Over Alabama. New York: Comet, 1959.

POWE, Blossom

Short Fiction

"Christmas in the Ghetto." Schulberg, From the Ashes.

POWELL, Adam Clayton, Sr.

Novel

Picketing Hell; A Fictitious Narrative. New York: W. Malliet, 1942.

Biography and Criticism

Richardson, Ben A. Great American Negroes. New York: T. Y. Crowell, 1945.

Rush, Theressa Gunnels, Carol Fairbanks Myers, and Esther Spring Arata. Black American Writers Past and Present. Metuchen, N.J.: Scarecrow Press, 1975.

Schraufnagel, Noel. From Apology to Protest: The Black American Novel. DeLand, Fla.: Everett/Edwards, 1973.

Who's Who in Colored America, vols. 1 and 2.

PRETTO, Clarita C.

Novel

The Life of Autumn Holliday. New York: Exposition, 1958.

PRIESTLEY, Eric John

Short Fiction

"The Seed of a Slum's Eternity." In Coombs, What We Must See.

Biography and Criticism

Rush, Theressa Gunnels, Carol Fairbanks Myers, and Esther Spring Arata. Black American Writers Past and Present. Metuchen, N.J.: Scarecrow Press, 1975.

PRITCHARD, Norman Henry II

Short Fiction

"Hoom." In Reed, 19 Necromancers from Now.

Biography and Criticism

Rush, Theressa Gunnels, Carol Fairbanks Myers, and Esther Spring
Arata. Black American Writers Past and Present. Metuchen,
N.J.: Scarecrow Press, 1975.

PROPES, Arthur

Short Fiction

"All That Glitters." In Ford and Faggett, Best Short Stories by
Afro-American Writers.

PRYOR, George Langhorne

Novel

Neither Bond Nor Free. New York: J. S. Ogilvie, 1902.

PUCKETT, G. Henderson

Fiction

One More Tomorrow. New York: Vantage, 1959.

RAMSEY, Leroy L.

Fiction

The Trial and the Fire. New York: Exposition, 1967. (Includes
three stories.)

RANDALL, Dudley

Short Fiction

"A Cup for the Loser." Negro History Bulletin 26 (October 1962):
76.
"The Cut Throat." Negro Digest 13 (July 1964): 53-55.
"Incident on a Bus." Negro Digest 14 (August 1965): 70-71; also
in Sanchez, We Be Word Sorcerers.

Biography and Criticism

Contemporary Authors, 25/28.
Rush, Theressa Gunnels, Carol Fairbanks Myers, and Esther Spring
Arata. Black American Writers Past and Present. Metuchen,
N.J.: Scarecrow Press, 1975.
Who's Who in the Midwest, 1973-74.

RAPHAEL, Lennox

Short Fiction

"Afrogun. " Yardbird Reader 1 (1972): 67-72.

RASMUSSEN, Emil Michael

Novel

The First Night. New York: Wendell Malliet, 1947.

Biography and Criticism

Hughes, Carl M. The Negro Novelist 1940-1950. New York: Citadel Press, 1953.

REDDING, Saunders (Jay Saunders Redding)

Novel

Stranger and Alone. New York: Harcourt, Brace, 1950; excerpt
in Ford, Black Insights.

Short Fiction

"Rosalie. " Negro Quarterly 1 (Fall 1942): 255-274.

Biography and Criticism

Arts in Society 5 (Summer-Fall 1968): 273-274. (Interview.)
Bone, Robert A. The Negro Novel in America. New Haven: Yale
University Press, 1966.
Contemporary Authors, 4.
Current Biography, 1969.
Hughes, Carl M. The Negro Novelist 1940-1950. New York: Cita-
del Press, 1953.
Rush, Theressa Gunnels, Carol Fairbanks Myers, and Esther Spring
Arata. Black American Writers Past and Present. Metuchen,
N.J.: Scarecrow Press, 1975.
Schraufnagel, Noel. From Apology to Protest: The Black American
Novel. DeLand, Fla.: Everett/Edwards, 1973.

Reviews

Stranger and Alone
Brown, Lloyd L. Masses & Mainstream 3 (April 1950): 88-90.
Christian Century, 12 April 1950, p. 465.
Conroy, Jack. Chicago Sun-Times, 23 March 1958, p. 6.
Ellison, Ralph. New York Times Book Review, 19 February
1950, p. 4.

Hanson, Harry. Survey 86 (March 1950): 156.
Harrison, W. K. Library Journal, 1 February 1950, p. 172.
Heath, Priscilla. Christian Science Monitor, 17 February
     1950, p. 14.
Lovell, John, Jr. Journal of Negro Education 20 (Winter 1951):
     67-69.
New Yorker, 18 February 1950, p. 97.
Petry, Ann. Saturday Review of Literature, 25 February 1950,
     p. 18.
Pickrel, Paul. Yale Review 39 (Spring 1950): 575.
Rosenberger, Coleman. New York Herald Tribune Book Review,
     19 February 1950, p. 7.
San Francisco Chronicle, 19 February 1950, p. 14.
Saturday Review of Literature, 17 February 1951, p. 9.
Watkins, S. C. Chicago Sunday Tribune, 19 February 1950,
     p. 13.

REED, Ishmael

Novels

Flight to Canada. New York: Random House, 1976; excerpts in
     Fiction 3 nos. 2 and 3 (1975): 7-8; Iowa Review 6 (Spring
     1975): 74-82; Statements: New Fiction from the Fiction Col-
     lection.
The Free-Lance Pallbearers. Garden City, N.Y.: Doubleday,
     1967; Chatham, N.J.: Chatham Bookseller, 1975; excerpts in
     Ford, Black Insights; Robinson, Nommo.
The Last Days of Louisiana Red. New York: Random House, 1974.
Mumbo Jumbo. Garden City, N.Y.: Doubleday, 1972; New York:
     Bantam, 1973; excerpt in Reed, 19 Necromancers from Now.
Yellow Back Radio Broke-Down. Garden City, N.Y.: Doubleday
     1969; New York: Bantam, 1972; Chatham, N.J.: Chatham
     Bookseller, 1975; excerpt in Hicks, Cutting Edges.

Biography and Criticism

Abel, Robert H. "Reed's 'I Am a Cowboy in the Boat of Ra.'"
     Explicator 30: Item 81.
Ambler, Madge. "Ishmael Reed: Whose Radio Broke Down?"
     Negro American Literature Forum 6 (Winter 1972): 125-131.
Beauford, Fred. "Conversation with Ishmael Reed." Black Creation
     4 (1973): 12-15.
Bellamy, Joe David. The New Fiction: Interview with Innovative
     American Writers. Urbana: University of Illinois Press, 1974.
Bush, Roland. "Werewolf of the Wild West." Black World 23
     (January 1974): 51-52, 64-66.
Contemporary Authors, 23/24R.
Cooper, A. "Call Him Ishmael." Newsweek, 2 June 1975, p. 70.
Duff, Gerald. "Reed's The Free-Lance Pallbearers." Explication
     32 (1974): Item 69.
Durham, Joyce Roberta. "The City in Recent American Literature:

Black on White: A Study of Selected Writings of Bellow, Mailer, Ellison, Baldwin and Writers of the Black Aesthetic." Ph. D. Dissertation, University of Maryland, 1974.

Emerson, O. B. "Cultural Nationalism in Afro-American Literature. In The Cry of Home, pp. 211-244. Edited by H. Ernest Lewald. Knoxville: University of Tennessee Press, 1972.

Ford, Nick Aaron. "A Note on Ishmael Reed: Revolutionary Novelist." Studies in the Novel 3 (Summer 1971): 180-189.

Fox, Robert Elliot. "The Mirrors of Caliban: A Study of the Fiction of LeRoi Jones (Imamu Amiri Baraka), Ishmael Reed and Samuel R. Delany." Ph. D. Dissertation, State University of New York at Buffalo, 1976.

Gayle, Addison, Jr. In Contemporary Novelists. Edited by James Vinson. New York: St. Martin's Press, 1976.

_____. The Way of the New World: The Black Novel in America. Garden City, N.Y.: Anchor Press/Doubleday, 1975.

Hassan, Ihab. Contemporary American Literature 1945-1972: An Introduction. New York: Frederick Ungar, 1973.

"An Interview with Ishmael Reed." Journal of Black Poetry 1 (Summer-Fall 1969): 72-75.

Kent, George E. "Notes on the 1974 Black Literary Scene." Phylon 36 (June 1975): 182-203.

Klinkowitz, J. "Black Superfiction." North American Review 259 (Winter 1974): 69-74.

_____. Literary Disruptions: The Making of a Post-Contemporary American Fiction. Urbana: University of Illinois Press, 1975.

Lipton, Lawrence. "Robin the Cock & Doopeyduk Doing the Boogaloo in Harry San with Rusty Jethroe and Letterhead America..." Cavalier No. 70 (1967).

Major, Clarence. "Tradition and Presence: Experimental Fiction by Black American Writers." American Poetry Review 5 (May/June 1976): 33-34.

Moss, Robert F. "Four Portraits: Novelist--Ishmael Reed, Actor/Director--Douglas Turner Ward." Saturday Review, 15 November 1975, p. 17.

O'Brien, John. Interviews with Black Writers. New York: Liveright, 1973.

Pfeiffer, John. "Black American Speculative Literature: A Checklist." Extrapolation 17 (December 1975): 35-43.

Reed, Ishmael. "Ishmael Reed on Ishmael Reed." Black World 23 (June 1974): 20-35.

Schmitz, Neil. "Neo-HooDoo: The Experimental Fiction of Ishmael Reed." Twentieth Century Literature 20 (April 1974): 126-140.

Test, George A. "The Cliché as Archetype." Satire Newsletter 7 (Fall 1969): 79.

Whitlow, Roger. Black American Literature: A Critical History. Chicago: Nelson Hall, 1973.

Reviews

Flight to Canada
    Bellamy, J. D. Saturday Review, 2 October 1976, p. 35.

Best Sellers 36 (January 1977): 320.
Book World, 14 November 1976, p. L4.
Booklist, 15 September 1976, p. 122.
Charyn, Jerome. New York Times Book Review, 19 September 1976, p. 5.
Choice 13 (January 1977): 1439.
Firestone, B. M. Library Journal 101 (August 1976): 1659.
Fleming, Robert. Freedomways 16 (Fourth Quarter 1976): 257-258.
Harper's 253 (October 1976): 100.
Kirkus, 15 July 1976, p. 810.
National Observer, 9 October 1976, p. 25.
New Yorker, 22 November 1976, p. 210.
Newsweek, 20 December 1976, p. 96.
Nordell, Roderick. Christian Science Monitor, 20 October 1976, p. 25.
Publishers' Weekly, 9 August 1976, p. 67.
White, Edmund. Nation, 18 September 1976, p. 247.

The Free-Lance Pallbearers

Alder, D. Book World, 3 March 1968, p. 20.
Blackburn, Sara. Nation, 5 February 1968, p. 186.
Howe, I. Harper's 239 (December 1969): 130.
Joye, B. Phylon 29 (Winter 1968): 410.
Kirkus, 15 September 1967, p. 1163.
Listener, 9 January 1969, p. 56.
Negro Digest 18 (February 1969): 68.
Newsweek, 16 June 1969, p. 96.
Publishers' Weekly, 11 September 1967, p. 66; 23 June 1969, p. 57.
Punch, 29 January 1969, p. 179.
Times Literary Supplement, 9 January 1969, p. 31.
Tucker, M. Commonweal, 26 January 1968, p. 508.

The Last Days of Louisiana Red

Black World 24 (June 1975): 51.
Booklist, 1 December 1974, p. 367.
Choice 12 (March 1975): 77.
Kirkus, 15 August 1974, p. 899.
Library Journal, 1 December 1974, p. 3147.
National Observer, 30 November 1974, p. 23.
New Leader, 23 December 1974, p. 10.
New York Times, 21 October 1974, p. 31.
New Yorker, 4 November 1974, p. 208.
Newsweek, 2 June 1975, p. 70.
Nordell, Roderick. Christian Science Monitor, 18 December 1974, p. 9.
Partisan Review 42 (Spring 1975): 311.
Publishers' Weekly, 16 September 1974, p. 52.
Sale, Roger. New York Review of Books, 12 December 1974, p. 18.
Scholes, Robert. New York Times Book Review, 10 November 1974, p. 2.
Sheppard, R. Z. Time, 21 October 1974, p. 119.

Smith, Barbara. New Republic, 23 November 1974, p. 53.
Village Voice, 7 November 1974, p. 41.
Mumbo Jumbo
Avant, J. A. Library Journal, 1 October 1972, p. 3182.
Black World 22 (December 1972): 63.
Book World, 16 September 1973, p. 13.
Booklist, 15 September 1972, p. 69.
Bryant, J. H. Nation, 25 September 1972, p. 245.
Cash, E. A. Best Sellers, 1 October 1972, p. 299.
Choice 10 (March 1973): 97.
Christian Science Monitor, 1 September 1972, p. 13.
Edwards, T. R. New York Review of Books, 5 October 1972,
p. 23.
Gordon, Andrew. Saturday Review, 14 October 1972, p. 76.
Kirkus, 1 June 1972, p. 641.
Nation, 25 September 1972, p. 245.
New Republic, 16 September 1972, p. 31.
New York Times, 9 August 1972, p. 35.
New York Times Book Review, 6 August 1972, p. 1; 3 Decem-
ber 1972, p. 78.
Nordell, Roderick. Christian Science Monitor, 6 September
1972, p. 13.
Publishers' Weekly, 19 June 1972, p. 57.
Sheppard, R. Z. Time, 14 August 1972, p. 67.
Village Voice, 15 March 1973, p. 19.
Yellow Back Radio Broke-Down
Black World 23 (January 1974): 51.
Childs, James. Library Journal 94 (July 1969):
2643.
Fleischer, Leonore. Book World, 10 August 1969,
p. 3.
Guardian Weekly, 22 May 1971, p. 19.
Howe, Irving. Harper's 239 (December 1969): 141.
Kirkus, 1 June 1969, p. 611.
Life, 15 August 1969, p. 12.
National Observer, 25 August 1969, p. 17.
Negro Digest 19 (December 1969): 95.
New York Times, 1 August 1969, p. 31.
Newsweek, 16 June 1969, p. 96.
Publishers' Weekly, 26 May 1969, p. 49.
Sissman, L. E. New Yorker, 11 October 1969, p. 200.
Times Literary Supplement, 25 June 1971, p. 726.

REID, Alice

Short Fiction

"And Shed a Murderous Tear." Negro Digest 13 (December 1963):
54-63.
"Corina." Negro Digest 11 (August 1962): 53-58.
"Give Us This Day." Black World 23 (June 1974): 72-75.

"JoJo Banks and the Treble Clef." <u>Essence</u> 5 (October 1974): 88-89.

"Night of the Senior Ball." <u>Negro Digest</u> 12 (November 1962): 58-61.

"Yes We Are Afraid." <u>Negro Digest</u> 11 (October 1962): 11-14.

RHODES, Hari

Novel

<u>The Hollow and the Human</u>. New York: Vantage, 1976.

Biography and Criticism

<u>Contemporary Authors</u>, 19/20.

Schraufnagel, Noel. <u>From Apology to Protest: The Black American Novel</u>. DeLand, Fla.: Everett/Edwards, 1973.

RICHARDSON, Alice I.

Short Fiction

"A Right Proper Burial." In Coombs, <u>What We Must See</u>.

RICHARDSON, Nola

Fiction

<u>Even in a Maze</u>. Los Angeles: Crescent Publications, 1975.

Biography and Criticism

Rush, Theressa Gunnels, Carol Fairbanks Myers, and Esther Spring Arata. <u>Black American Writers Past and Present</u>. Metuchen, N.J.: Scarecrow Press, 1975.

RICHARDSON, Willis

Short Fiction

"He Holds His Head Too High. A Washington Boyhood." <u>Crisis</u> 74 (July 1967): 292-300.

Biography and Criticism

Rush, Theressa Gunnels, Carol Fairbanks Myers, and Esther Spring Arata. <u>Black American Writers Past and Present</u>. Metuchen, N.J.: Scarecrow Press, 1975.

RILEY, Clayton

Short Fiction

"Now That Henry Is Gone." In Clarke, Harlem.

RIVERS, Conrad Kent.

Short Fiction

"Chinese Food, A Short Story." Negro Digest 12 (October 1966): 53-56.
"Goodby, Baby Boy." Negro Digest 13 (April 1964): 55-58.
"Mother to Son." In Hughes, The Best Short Stories by Negro Writers.

Biography and Criticism

Rush, Theressa Gunnels, Carol Fairbanks Myers, and Esther Spring Arata. Black American Writers Past and Present. Metuchen, N.J.: Scarecrow Press, 1975.

ROBERSON, Sadie L.

Short Fiction

Killer of the Dream: Short Stories. New York: Comet, 1963.

ROBERTS, Walter Adolphe

Novel

Mayor Harding of New York: A Novel. New York: Mohawk Press, 1931.

ROBINSON, Billy "Hands"

Short Fiction

"Love, a Hard-Legged Triangle." Black Scholar 3 (September 1971): 29-48.

ROBINSON, Rose

Novel

Eagle in the Air. New York: Crown, 1969; New York: Bantam, 1971.

Short Fiction

"Esther." Essence 2 (August 1971): 62-63, 79.

Reviews

Eagle in the Air
Benedict, Estelle. Library Journal, 15 May 1969, p. 2002.
Best Sellers, 1 March 1971, p. 531.
Blackburn, Sara. Nation, 28 July 1969, p. 90.
Booklist, 1 October 1969, p. 177.
Contemporary Review 217 (October 1970): 213.
Hankenson, Albert. Library Journal, 15 September 1969, p. 3233.
Kirkus, 15 March 1969, p. 335.
New Statesman, 14 August 1970, p. 185.
New Yorker, 2 August 1969, p. 75.
Observer, 20 September 1970, p. 28.
Park, C. C. Book World, 21 September 1969, p. 16.
Publishers' Weekly, 24 March 1969, p. 53.
Weir, M. R. Best Sellers, 1 June 1969, p. 95.

RODGERS, Carolyn

Short Fiction

"Blackbird in a Cage." Negro Digest 16 (August 1967): 66-71;
also in Adoff, Brothers and Sisters.
"A Statistic Trying to Make It Home." Negro Digest 18 (June 1969):
68-71.
"Walk Wid Jesus." Essence 2 (April 1972): 39.

ROGERS, Joel Augustus

Novels

Blood Money. n.p., n.p., 1923.
The Golden Door. n.p., n.p., 1927.
She Walks in Beauty. Los Angeles: Western, 1963.

Reviews

She Walks in Beauty
Crisis 70 (December 1973): 636.
Library Journal, 15 October 1963, p. 3863.

ROLLINS, Bryant

Novel

Danger Song. Garden City, N.Y.: Doubleday, 1967; New York:

Macmillan, 1971.

Biography and Criticism

Contemporary Authors, 49/52.

Reviews

Danger Song
>Booklist, 1 September 1969, p. 49.
Carroll, J. M.   Library Journal, 15 March 1967, p. 1178.
Kirkus, 1 February 1967, p. 160.
Levin, Martin.   New York Times Book Review, 14 May 1967, p. 48.
McDonnell, T. P.   Critic 26 (August 1967):   72.
Publishers' Weekly, 30 January 1967, p. 108.
Siggins, C. M.   Best Sellers, 15 May 1967, p. 76.

ROLLINS, Lamen

Novel

The Human Race a Gang.   New York: Carlton, 1965.

ROSEBROUGH, Sadie Mae

Novel

Wasted Travail.   New York: Vantage, 1951.

ROSS, Fran

Fiction

Oreo.   New York: Grey Falcon Press, 1975.

Reviews

Oreo
>Booklist, 15 January 1975, p. 485.
Essence 5 (April 1975): 15.
Library Journal, 15 January 1975, p. 146.
Publishers' Weekly, 28 October 1974, p. 42.

ROSS, G. H.

Novel

Beyond the River.   Boston: Meador, 1938.

ROYAL, A. Bertrand

Novel

Which Way to Heaven? New York: Vantage, 1970.

Biography and Criticism

Rush, Theressa Gunnels, Carol Fairbanks Myers, and Esther Spring
    Arata. Black American Writers Past and Present. Metuchen,
    N.J.: Scarecrow Press, 1975.

RUSS, George B.

Novel

Over Edom, I Lost My Shoe. New York: Carlton, 1970.

Biography and Criticism

Rush, Theressa Gunnels, Carol Fairbanks Myers, and Esther Spring
    Arata. Black American Writers Past and Present. Metuchen,
    N.J.: Scarecrow Press, 1975.

RUSSELL, Charlie

Short Fiction

"Klactoveedsedstene." In Adams, Conn and Slepian, Afro-American
    Literature: Fiction.
"Quietus." In Hughes, The Best Short Stories by Negro Writers.

SALAAM, Kalamu ya (Val Ferdinand)

Short Fiction

"Second Line/Cutting the Body Loose." In Coombs, What We Must
    See.
"Sister Bibi." In Sanchez, We Be Word Sorcerers.

Biography and Criticism

Rush, Theressa Gunnels, Carol Fairbanks Myers, and Esther Spring
    Arata. Black American Writers Past and Present. Metuchen,
    N.J.: Scarecrow Press, 1975.

SANCHEZ, Sonia

Short Fiction

"After Saturday Night Comes Sunday. " Black World 2 (March 1971):
   53-59; also in Coombs, What We Must See; Sanchez, We Be
   Word Sorcerers.

Biography and Criticism

Contemporary Authors, 33/36.

SANDA   see   Stowers, Walter H.

SANDERS, Tom

Novel

Her Golden Hour.   Houston: By the Author, 1929.

SAVOY, Willard

Novel

Alien Land.   New York: E. P. Dutton, 1949; New York: New
   American Library, 1950.

Biography and Criticism

Schraufnagel, Noel.   From Apology to Protest: The Black American Novel. DeLand, Fla. : Everett/Edwards, 1973.

Reviews

Alien Land
   Algren, Nelson.   Chicago Sun, 20 April 1949.
   Bontemps, Arna.   New York Herald-Tribune Weekly Book Re-
      view, 17 April 1949, p. 6.
   Booklist, 1 April 1949, p. 254; 15 April 1949, p. 281.
   Catholic World, 169 (July 1949):   319.
   Kirkus, 1 February 1949, p. 67.
   Manchester, W. R.   Springfield Republican, 20 May 1949, p.
      4D.
   Petry, Ann.   Saturday Review of Literature, 30 April 1949,
      p. 16.
   Reynolds, Horace.   Christian Science Monitor, 21 April 1949,
      p. 16.
   San Francisco Chronicle, 8 May 1949, p. 21.
   Terry, C. V.   New York Times Book Review, 3 April 1949,
      p. 20.

White, Peter. Commonweal, 29 April 1949, p. 75.
Wisconsin Library Bulletin 45 (May 1949): 89.

SCHUYLER, George Samuel

Novels

Black No More: Being an Account of the Strange and Wonderful
    Workings of Science in the Land of the Free A.D. 1933-1940.
    New York: Macauley, 1931; College Park, Md.: McGrath,
    1969; New York: Macmillan, 1970; excerpts in Brown, Davis
    and Lee, Negro Caravan; Long and Collier, Afro-American
    Writing; Miller, Blackamerican Literature.
Slaves Today, A Story of Liberia. New York: Brewer, Warren &
    Putnam, 1931; College Park, Md.: McGrath, 1969; New York:
    AMS Press, 1969.

Biography and Criticism

Bone, Robert A. The Negro Novel in America. New Haven: Yale
    University Press, 1966.
Davis, Allison. "Our Negro Intellectuals." Crisis 35 (August
    1928): 268.
Davis, Arthur P. From the Dark Tower: Afro-American Writers
    1900-1960. Washington, D.C.: Howard University Press, 1974.
Gayle, Addison, Jr. The Way of the New World: The Black Novel
    in America. Garden City, N.Y.: Anchor Press/Doubleday,
    1975.
"George S. Schuyler: Iconoclast." Crisis 72 (October 1965):
    484-485.
"George S. Schuyler Interview: Ishmael Reed and Steve Cannon."
    Yardbird Reader 2 (1973): 83-104.
Gloster, Hugh M. Negro Voices in American Fiction. Chapel Hill:
    University of North Carolina Press, 1948.
Isani, Mukhtar Ali. "The Exotic and Protest in Earlier Black Lit-
    erature; The Use of Alien Setting and Character." Studies in
    Black Literature 5 (Summer 1974): 9-14.
Jackson, Blyden. "The Harlem Renaissance." In The Comic Ima-
    gination in American Literature, pp. 295-303. Edited by Louis
    D. Rubin, Jr. New Brunswick, N.J.: Rutgers University
    Press, 1973.
Klotman, Phyllis Rauch. Another Man Gone: The Black Runner in
    Contemporary Afro-American Literature. Port Washington,
    N.Y.: Kennikat Press, 1977.
Peplow, Michael W. "George Schuyler, Satirist: Rhetorical De-
    vices in Black No More." CLA Journal 18 (December 1974):
    242-257.
Perry, Margaret. Silence to the Drums: A Survey of the Litera-
    ture of the Harlem Renaissance. Contributions in Afro-Ameri-
    can and African Studies, no. 18. Westport, Conn.: Greenwood
    Press, 1976.
Ramsey, Priscilla. "A Study of Black Identity in 'Passing' Novels

of the Nineteenth and Early Twentieth Centuries." Studies in Black Literature 7 (Winter 1976): 1-7.
Robinson, Anna T. "Race Consciousness and Survival Techniques Depicted in Harlem Renaissance Fiction." Ph.D. Dissertation, Pennsylvania State University, 1973.
Rosenblatt, Roger. Black Fiction. Cambridge: Harvard University Press, 1974.
Schraufnagel, Noel. From Apology to Protest: The Black American Novel. DeLand, Fla.: Everett/Edwards, 1973.
Singh, Amritjit. "The Novels of the Harlem Renaissance: A Thematic Study." Ph.D. Dissertation, New York University, 1973.
_____. The Novels of the Harlem Renaissance: Twelve Black Writers, 1923-1933. University Park: Pennsylvania State University Press, 1976.
Whitlow, Roger. Black American Literature: A Critical History Chicago: Nelson Hall, 1973.
Williams, Sherley Ann. Give Birth to Brightness: A Thematic Study in Neo-Black Literature. New York: Dial, 1972.
Winslow, H. F. "George S. Schuyler: Fainting Traveler." Midwest Journal 5 (Summer 1953): 24-45.
Young, James O. Black Writers of the Thirties. Baton Rouge: Louisiana State University Press, 1973.

Reviews

Black No More
  Bookman 72 (February 1931): vii.
  Boston Transcript, 21 February 1931, p. 2.
  Davis, Arthur P. Opportunity 9 (March 1931): 89-90.
  Ehrlich, Leonard. Saturday Review of Literature, 2 May 1931, p. 799.
  Fisher, Rudolph. Books, 1 February 1931, p. 5.
  Hanson, Harry. New York World, 16 January 1931, p. 14.
  New York Times, 1 February 1931, p. 9.
  Survey, 1 June 1931, p. 290.
  VanDoren, Dorothy. Nation, 25 February 1931, p. 218.

SCOTT-HERON, Gil

Novels

The Nigger Factory. New York: Dial, 1972.
The Vulture. Derby, Conn.: Belmont Tower, 1971.

Biography and Criticism

Rush, Theressa Gunnels, Carol Fairbanks Myers, and Esther Spring Arata. Black American Writers Past and Present. Metuchen, N.J.: Scarecrow Press, 1975.

Reviews

The Nigger Factory
    Choice 9 (September 1972): 817.
    Davis, L. J. Book World, 12 March 1972, p. 11.
    Fessler, A. L. Library Journal, 1 February 1972, p. 517.
    Kirkus, 15 January 1972, p. 95.
    New Yorker, 20 May 1972, p. 139.
    Publishers' Weekly, 17 January 1972, p. 57.
The Vulture
    Gant, Liz. Black World 20 (July 1971): 96.
    Kirkus, 1 May 1970, p. 528.
    Library Journal 95 (July 1970): 2520.
    Publishers' Weekly, 11 May 1970, p. 40.
    Welburn, Ron. Essence 1 (February 1971): 73.

SCREEN, Robert Martin

Novel

We Can't Run Away from Here. New York: Vantage, 1958.

SELF, Charles

Short Fiction

"Ndugu from Tougaloo." In Watkins, Black Review No. 2.

SENNA, Carl

Short Fiction

In Shuman, A Galaxy of Black Writing.

Biography and Criticism

Rush, Theressa Gunnels, Carol Fairbanks Myers, and Esther Spring
    Arata. Black American Writers Past and Present. Metuchen,
    N.J.: Scarecrow Press, 1975.

SHACKLEFORD, Otis M.

Fiction

Lillian Simmons; or, The Conflict of Sections. Kansas City, Mo.:
    Burton, 1915.

Biography and Criticism

Bone, Robert A. The Negro Novel in America. New Haven: Yale

University Press, 1966.
Gloster, Hugh M. Negro Voices in American Fiction. Chapel Hill:
  University of North Carolina Press, 1948.

SHANGE, ntozake

Fiction

"sassafrass cypress & indigo. " Yardbird Reader 4 (1975): 55-63;
  excerpt in Ms. 5 (August 1976): 82-85.

SHAW, Letty M.

Novel

Angel Mink. New York: Comet, 1957.

SHAW, O'Wendell

Novel

Greater Need Below. Columbus: Bi-Monthly Negro Book Club,
  1936; New York: AMS Press, 1972.

Short Fiction

"Chief Mourner. " Negro Story 1 (May-June 1944): 44-48. (Originally published in the Pittsburgh Courier.)

Biography and Criticism

Gloster, Hugh M. Negro Voices in American Fiction. Chapel Hill:
  University of North Carolina Press, 1948.
Schraufnagel, Noel. From Apology to Protest: The Black American
  Novel. DeLand, Fla.: Everett/Edwards, 1973.

Review

Greater Need Below
  Lee, Ulysses. Opportunity 15 (August 1937): 246-247.

SHOCKLEY, Ann Allen

Novel

Loving Her. Indianapolis: Bobbs-Merrill, 1974.

Short Fiction

"Abraham and the Spirit. " Negro Digest 8 (July 1950): 85-91.

"Ah, The Young Black Poet. " New Letters 41 (December 1974): 45-60.
"Ain't No Use in Crying. " Negro Digest 17 (December 1967): 69- 78.
"The Faculty Party. " Black World 21 (November 1971): 54-63.
"The Funeral. " In Stadler, Out of Our Lives.
"Is She Relevant. " Black World 2 (January 1971): 58-65.
"Monday Will Be Better. " Negro Digest 13 (May 1964): 54-65.
"Picture Prize. " Negro Digest 11 (October 1962): 53-60.
"The Saga of Private Julius Cole. " Black World 23 (March 1974): 54-70.
"To Be a Man. " Negro Digest 18 (July 1969): 54-65.

Biography and Criticism

Contemporary Authors, 49/52.
Shockley, Ann A. and Sue Chandler. Living Black American Authors: A Biographical Dictionary. New York: Bowker, 1973.

Reviews

Loving Her
    Black World 24 (September 1975): 89-90.
    Kirkus, 15 May 1974, p. 552.
    Library Journal 99 (August 1974): 1986.
    Ms. 3 (April 1975): 120.
    Publishers' Weekly, 20 May 1974, p. 59.

SHORE, Herbert L.

Short Fiction

"The Resurrection and the Life. " Phylon 22 (Fourth Quarter 1961): 368-390.

SHORES, Minnie T.

Novels

Americans in America. Boston: Christopher, 1966.
Publicans and Sinners. New York: Comet, 1960.

SIMMONS, Bernadette

Short Fiction

"Dialogue Between Two Brothers. " In Sanchez, Three Hundred and Sixty Degrees of Blackness Comin at You.

SIMMONS, Herbert Alfred

Novels

Corner Boy. Boston: Houghton Mifflin, 1957.
Man Walking on Egg Shells. Boston: Houghton Mifflin, 1962; except in Negro Digest, January 1962.

Biography and Criticism

Contemporary Authors, 3.
Schraufnagel, Noel. From Apology to Protest: The Black American Novel. DeLand, Fla.: Everett/Edwards, 1973.

Reviews

Corner Boy
    Jet, 25 February 1960, pp. 4-5.
Man Walking on Egg Shells
    Griffin, Richard G. Library Journal, 1 January 1962, p. 114.
    Manville, Bill. New York Herald Tribune, 25 March 1962,
        p. 4.
    Millstein, Gilbert. New York Times, 22 April 1962, p. 22.
    Times Literary Supplement, 21 September 1962, p. 706.
    Times Weekly Review, 19 October 1962, p. 94.

SKEETER, Sharyn Jeanne

Short Fiction

"So What Would You Do If You Saw the Virgin." Fiction 4 no. 1
    (1975): 23-24.

Biography and Criticism

Rush, Theressa Gunnels, Carol Fairbanks Myers, and Esther Spring
    Arata. Black American Writers Past and Present. Metuchen,
    N.J.: Scarecrow Press, 1975.

SKINNER, Theodosia B.

Short Fiction

Ice Cream from Heaven. New York: Vantage, 1962.

Review

Ice Cream from Heaven
    Heidkamp, Mary Jean. Community 23 (December 1963): 12.

SLIM, Iceberg see BECK, Robert

SMART-GROSVENOR, Verta Mae (pseud., Verta Mae)

Short Fiction

"For Once in My Life (A Short Statement)." In Sanchez, We Be
    Word Sorcerers.
"Send for You Yesterday, Now Here You Come Today." Essence
    5 (November 1974): 77, 91-92, 94, 98.

Biography and Criticism

Garland, P. "Vibes from Verta Mae." Ebony 26 (March 1971):
    86-88.

SMITH, Daniel

Novel

A Walk in the City. Cleveland: World, 1972.

Reviews

A Walk in the City
    Kirkus, 1 January 1971, p. 25.
    Library Journal, 15 May 1971, p. 1730.
    New York Times Book Review, 23 May 1971, p. 46.
    Publishers' Weekly, 1 February 1971, p. 65; 12 November
        1973, p. 41.

SMITH, Jean W.

Short Fiction

"Frankie Mae." Negro Digest 17 (June 1968): 84-89; also in King,
    Black Short Story Anthology; Washington, Black-Eyed Susans.
"The Machine." Negro Digest 7 (November 1967): 60-74.
"Somethin-to-Eat." Black World 2 (June 1971): 70-76.
"That She Would Dance No More." Negro Digest 16 (January 1967):
    59-68; also in Jones and Neal, Black Fire.

SMITH, Joe (pseud.)

Novel

Dagmar of Green Hills. New York: Pageant, 1957.

SMITH, John Caswell, Jr.

Short Fiction

"Fighter." Atlantic 177 (May 1946): 107-112; also in Brickel,
Prize Stories; Clarke, American Negro Short Stories.

Biography and Criticism

Opportunity 15 (September 1937): 283; 25 (Summer 1947): 157.

SMITH, Rubardia K.

Short Fiction

"Needin'." Essence 74 (May 1976): 64-65, 105-106, 108.

SMITH, Vern E.

Novel

The Jones Men. Chicago: Regnery, 1974; New York: Warner,
1976.

Reviews

The Jones Men
    Best Sellers, 15 October 1974, p. 362.
    Booklist, 1 December 1974, p. 367.
    Critic 33 (January 1975): 75.
    Ellman, Richard. New York Times Book Review, 29 September
        1974, p. 4.
    Kirkus, 15 July 1974, p. 763.
    New Yorker, 7 October 1974, p. 177.
    Oberbeck, S. K. Newsweek, 14 October 1974, p. 118.
    Publishers' Weekly, 12 August 1974, p. 50.
    Smyser, Craig. Houston Chronicle, 26 January 1975; Newsbank--
        Literature (January-February 1975): Card 14: D7.
    Times Literary Supplement, 30 May 1975, p. 585.
    Yamamoto, Mitsu. Library Journal 99 (August 1974): 1987.

SMITH, William Gardner

Novels

Anger at Innocence. New York: Farrar, Straus, 1950; Chatham
    N.J.: Chatham Bookseller, 1973.
The Last of the Conquerors. New York: Farrar, Straus, 1948;
    Chatham, N.J.: Chatham Bookseller, 1973; excerpt in Negro
    Digest, November 1948.

South Street. New York: Farrar, 1954; Chatham, N.J.: Chatham
    Bookseller, 1973.
The Stone Face. New York: Farrar, Straus, 1963; Chatham, N.J.:
    Chatham Bookseller, 1975.

Biography and Criticism

Bigsby, C. W. E. "From Protest to Paradox: The Black Writer
    at Mid-Century." In In the Fifties, pp. 217-240. Edited by
    Norman Podhoretz. New York: Farrar, Straus, 1964.
Black World 26 (February 1975): 97.
Bone, Robert A. The Negro Novel in America. New Haven: Yale
    University Press, 1966.
Bryant, Jerry H. "Individuality and Fraternity: The Novels of
    William Gardner Smith." Studies in Black Literature 3 (Summer
    1972): 1-8.
Gayle, Addison, Jr. The Way of the New World: The Black Novel
    in America. Garden City, N.Y.: Anchor Press/Doubleday,
    1975.
Schatt, Stanley. "You Must Go Home Again: Today's Afro-Ameri-
    can Expatriate Writers." Negro American Literature Forum 7
    (Fall 1973): 80-82.
Schraufnagel, Noel. From Apology to Protest: The Black Ameri-
    can Novel. DeLand, Fla.: Everett/Edwards, 1973.

Reviews

Last of the Conquerors
    Atlantic 182 (October 1948): 110.
    Clement, Rufus E. Phylon 10 (First Quarter 1949): 96.
    Conroy, Jack. Chicago Sun, 17 August 1948.
    Cowley, Malcolm. New Republic, 27 September 1948, p. 33.
    Crisis 55 (November 1948): 346-347.
    Dempsey, David. New York Times, 5 September 1948, p. 6.
    Ellis, Harry. Christian Science Monitor, 16 September 1948,
        p. 11.
    Foley, Martha. Survey Graphic 37 (December 1948): 500.
    Kirkus, 1 June 1948, p. 269.
    Roddan, Samuel. Canadian Forum 28 (December 1948): 212.
    Spencer, Joanna. New York Herald-Tribune Weekly Book Re-
        view, 22 August 1948, p. 3.
The Stone Face
    Library Journal, 1 January 1964, p. 136.

SMYTHWICK, Charles A., Jr.

Novel

False Measure: A Satirical Novel of the Lives of Objectives of
    Upper Middle-Class Negroes. New York: William-Frederick,
    1954.

SPENCE, Raymond

Novel

Nothing Black But a Cadillac. New York: Putnam, 1969.

Reviews

Nothing Black But a Cadillac
    Best Sellers, 15 March 1969, p. 509.
    Hall, W. F. Canadian Literature (Autumn 1969): 101.
    Levin, M. New York Times Book Review, 16 February 1969,
        p. 52.
    Library Journal, 1 March 1969, p. 1020.
    Publishers' Weekly, 22 September 1969, p. 86.

SPENCE, Tomas

Novel

[With Eric Heath.] Martin Larwin. New York: Pageant, 1954.

SPENCER, Gilmore

Short Fiction

"Mulatto Flair." In Ford and Faggett, Best Short Stories by Afro-
    American Writers.

SPENCER, Mary Etta

Novel

The Resentment. Philadelphia: A. M. E. Book Concern, 1921.

Short Fiction

"Beyond the Years." Opportunity 7 (October 1929): 311.

Biography and Criticism

Bone, Robert A. The Negro Novel in America. New Haven: Yale
    University Press, 1966.

STEELE, Shelby

Short Fiction

"Survivor's Row." Black World 25 (March 1976): 54-67.

STERN, Harold

Novel

Blackland. Garden City, N.Y.: Doubleday, 1970; New York: Belmont-Tower, 1971.

Reviews

Blackland
Best Sellers, 15 January 1970, p. 399.
Kirkus, 1 November 1969, p. 1172.
Library Journal 94 (1969): 4541; 95 (1970): 1971.
Publishers' Weekly, 27 October 1969, p. 55.

STEVENSON, C. Leigh

Short Fiction

"Over the Line." In Ford and Faggett, Best Short Stories by Afro-
American Writers.

STEWART, John

Short Fiction

(Collection): Curving Road Stories. Urbana, Ill.: University of
Illinois Press, 1975.
"The Americanization of Rhythm." Black Scholar 6 (June 1975):
73-77.

Reviews

Curving Road Stories
Choice 12 (November 1975): 1170.
Major, Clarence. Library Journal, 1 September 1975, p. 1571.
Miller, A. D. Black Scholar 7 (May 1976): 53-54.
O'Hara, J. D. New York Times Book Review, 26 October
1975, p. 50.
Publishers' Weekly, 31 March 1975, p. 52.
Purdie, Carelese. Black Books Bulletin 3 (Winter 1975): 36.
Virginia Quarterly Review 52 (Spring 1976): 60.

STEWART, Ollie

Short Fiction

"Soft Boiled." In Ford and Faggett, Best Short Stories by Afro-
American Writers.

STILES, Thelma Jackson

Short Fiction

"Juanita." Essence 5 (July 1974): 36-37, 76.

Biography and Criticism

Rush, Theressa Gunnels, Carol Fairbanks Myers, and Esther Spring
   Arata. Black American Writers Past and Present. Metuchen,
   N.J.: Scarecrow Press, 1975.

STOKES, Tony

Short Fiction

Short Stories by Tony Stokes. New York: Rannick Amuru, 1973.

STONE, Chuck (Charles Sumner Stone)

Novel

King Strut. Indianapolis: Bobbs-Merrill, 1970.

Reviews

King Strut
   Best Sellers, 15 November 1970, p. 340.
   Black World 20 (January 1971): 91.
   Blackwell, Angela. Black Scholar 3 (February 1972): 58-59. °
   Kirkus, 15 July 1970, p. 768.
   Library Journal, 1 October 1970, p. 3306.
   Publishers' Weekly, 27 July 1970, p. 66.

STOWERS, Walter H. (pseud., Sanda)

Novel

[With W. H. Anderson.] Appointed. Detroit: Detroit Law Printing, 1894.

Biography and Criticism

Bone, Robert A. The Negro Novel in America. New Haven: Yale
   University Press, 1966.

SUBLETTE, Walter (pseud., S. W. Edwards)

Novel

Go Now in Darkness. Chicago: Baker, 1964.

Biography and Criticism

Rush, Theressa Gunnels, Carol Fairbanks Myers, and Esther Spring
Arata. Black American Writers Past and Present. Metuchen,
N.J.: Scarecrow Press, 1975.

SUTTON, Charyn D.

Short Fiction

"Sukkie's Song." Black World 24 (June 1975): 67-69.

SYDNOR, W. Leon

Novel

Veronica. New York: Exposition, 1956.

TARTER, Charles L.

Novel

Family of Destiny. New York: Pageant, 1954.

TAYLOR, Geraldine

Short Fiction

"Strength." Essence 5 (February 1975): 58-59, 85.

TAYLOR, Jeanne A.

Short Fiction

"A House Divided." Antioch Review 27 (Fall 1967): 298-305; also
in Chapman, New Black Voices.
"The House on Mettler Street." In Schulberg, From the Ashes.
"Only Clowns Passing Through." Essence 5 (May 1974): 60-61,
89-90.
"Where De A Rain Go?" In Sanchez, Three Hundred and Sixty Degrees of Blackness Comin at You.

THELWELL, Mike

Short Fiction

"Bright an' Mownin' Star." Massachusetts Review 7 (Autumn 1966): 655-670; also in Chapman, New Black Voices; Gibson and Anselment, Black and White; Stadler, Out of Our Lives.
"Community of Victims." Negro Digest 13 (January 1964): 53-60; also in Burnett and Burnett, The Stone Soldier.
"Direct Action." In Burnett and Burnett, Prize College Stories, 1963; Kissin, Stories in Black and White; Patterson, An Introduction to Black Literature in America.
"The Organizer." In Angus, The Trouble Is; Burnett, Black Hands on a White Face; Burnett and Burnett, Story: The Yearbook of Discovery, 1968; Carpenter and Neumeyer, Elements of Fiction; Gulassa, The Fact of Fiction.

THOMAS, Will

Novel

God Is for White Folks. New York: Creative Age, 1947. (Published under the title, Love Knows No Barriers. New York: New American Library, 1951.)

Short Fiction

"Hill to Climb." Crisis 53 (June 1946): 173-174.

Biography and Criticism

Bone, Robert A. The Negro Novel in America. New Haven: Yale University Press, 1966.
Hughes, Carl M. The Negro Novelist 1940-1950. New York: Citadel Press, 1953.
Schraufnagel, Noel. From Apology to Protest: The Black American Novel. DeLand, Fla.: Everett/Edwards, 1973.

Reviews

God Is for White Folks
    Bolman, H. P. Library Journal 72 (August 1947): 1110.
    Borland, Hal. New York Times Book Review, 5 October 1947, p. 32.
    Butcher, Philip. Opportunity 26 (Summer 1948): 114.
    Feld, Rose. New York Herald Tribune Weekly Book Review, 19 October 1947, p. 24.
    New Yorker, 27 September 1947, p. 112.
    Reeves, Elizabeth W. Journal of Negro Education 17 (Spring 1948): 167-168.
    Rothland, N. L. Saturday Review of Literature, 4 October 1947, p. 20.
    San Francisco Chronicle, 11 June 1948, p. 16.

THOMPSON, Eloise Bibb   see   BIBB, Eloise

THOMPSON, James W.

Short Fiction

"See What Tomorrow Brings. " In King, Black Short Story Anthology.

Biography and Criticism

Negro History Bulletin 26 (October 1962): 67-68.

THOMPSON, Jim

Novels

Nothing But a Man. New York: Popular Library, 1970.
The Undefeated. New York: Popular Library, 1969.

Review

Nothing But a Man
        Publishers' Weekly, 12 January 1970, p. 66.

THOMPSON, Samuel

Short Fiction

"Bruzz. " Freedomways 2 (Spring 1962): 191-196.

THORNE, Jack   see   FULTON, David Bryant

THORNHILL, Lionel L.

Short Fiction

The Huge Steel Bolt and Other Stories and Poems. New York:
        Vantage, 1966. (Published under the title, The Love Thief.
        New York: Graphicopy, 1973.)

Biography and Criticism

Rush, Theressa Gunnels, Carol Fairbanks Myers, and Esther Spring
        Arata. Black American Writers Past and Present. Metuchen,
        N.J.: Scarecrow Press, 1975.

THORUP, Lester W.

Novel

Came the Harvest. New York: Carlton, 1966.

THURMAN, Wallace

Novels

The Blacker the Berry: A Novel of Negro Life. New York:
　　Macaulay, 1929; New York: Arno Press, 1969; New York:
　　AMS Press, 1969; New York: Collier Books, 1969.
Infants of the Spring. New York: Macaulay, 1932; Freeport, N.Y.:
　　Books for Libraries; New York: AMS Press, 1975; excerpts in
　　Davis and Peplow, The New Negro Renaissance.
[With Abraham L. Furman.] The Interne. New York: Macaulay,
　　1932.

Short Fiction

"Cordelia the Crude, a Harlem Sketch." Fire! (1929): 5; also in
　　Turner, Black American Literature: Fiction.
"Grist in the Mill." Messenger, 1926; also in Barksdale and Kinna-
　　mon, Black Writers of America.

Biography and Criticism

Arden, Eugene. "The Early Harlem Novel." Phylon 20 (Spring
　　1959): 25-31.
Bone, Robert A. The Negro Novel in America. New Haven: Yale
　　University Press, 1966.
Brawley, Benjamin. The Negro Genius. New York: Dodd, Mead,
　　1940.
Brown, Martha Hursey. "Images of Black Women: Family Roles
　　in Harlem Renaissance Literature." D.A. Dissertation, Carne-
　　gie-Mellon University, 1976.
Davis, Arthur P. From the Dark Tower: Afro-American Writers
　　1900-1960. Washington, D.C.: Howard University Press,
　　1974.
Doyle, Sister Mary Ellen. "The Heroine of Black Novels." In
　　Perspectives on Afro-American Women, pp. 112-125. Edited
　　by Willa D. Johnson and Thomas L. Green. Washington, D.C.:
　　ECCA Publications, 1975.
Ford, Nick Aaron. "The Negro Author's Use of Propaganda in
　　Imaginative Literature." Ph.D. Dissertation, State University
　　of Iowa, 1945.
Gayle, Addison, Jr. The Way of the New World: The Black Novel
　　in America. Garden City, N.Y.: Anchor Press/Doubleday,
　　1975.
Gloster, Hugh M. Negro Voices in American Fiction. Chapel Hill:
　　University of North Carolina Press, 1948.

Haslam, Gerald. "Wallace Thurman: A Western Renaissance Man."
Western American Literature 6 (Spring 1971): 53-59.
Henderson, Mae Gwendolyn. "Portrait of Wallace Thurman." In
The Harlem Renaissance Remembered, pp. 147-170. Edited by
Arna Bontemps. New York: Dodd, Mead, 1972.
Hughes, Langston. The Big Sea. New York: Knopf, 1940.
_____. "Harlem Literati in the Twenties." Saturday Review of
Literature, 22 July 1940, pp. 13-14.
Jackson, Blyden. "The Harlem Renaissance." In The Comic Ima-
gination in American Literature, pp. 295-303. Edited by Louis
D. Rubin. New Brunswick, N.J.: Rutgers University Press,
1973.
Kent, George. Blackness and the Adventure of Western Culture.
Chicago: Third World Press, 1972.
O'Daniel, Therman B. Introduction to The Blacker the Berry.
New York: Macmillan, 1970.
Perkins, Huel D. "Renaissance 'Renegade'?: Wallace Thurman."
Black World 25 (February 1976): 29-35.
Perry, Margaret. Silence to the Drums: A Survey of the Litera-
ture of the Harlem Renaissance. Contributions in Afro-Ameri-
can and African Studies, no. 18. Westport, Conn.: Greenwood
Press, 1976.
Ramsey, Priscilla. "A Study of Black Identity in 'Passing' Novels
of the Nineteenth and Early Twentieth Centuries." Studies in
Black Literature 7 (Winter 1976): 1-7.
Robinson, William H. Introduction to The Blacker the Berry. New
York: Arno, 1969.
Rosenblatt, Roger. Black Fiction. Cambridge: Harvard University
Press, 1974.
Scruggs, Charles. "'All Dressed Up But No Place to Go': The
Black Writer and His Audience During the Harlem Renaissance."
American Literature 48 (January 1977): 543-563.
Singh, Amritjit. "The Novels of the Harlem Renaissance: A The-
matic Study." Ph.D. Dissertation, New York University, 1973.
_____. The Novels of the Harlem Renaissance: Twelve Black
Writers, 1923-1933. University Park: Pennsylvania State Uni-
versity Press, 1976.
Wall, Cheryl A. "Paris and Harlem: Two Cultural Capitals."
Phylon 35 (March 1974): 64-73.
Young, James O. Black Writers of the Thirties. Baton Rouge:
Louisiana State University Press, 1973.

Reviews

The Blacker the Berry
    Bookman 69 (April 1929): 24.
    Boston Transcript, 23 March 1929, p. 6.
    Calverton, V. F. Books, 26 May 1929, p. 14.
    Carter, Eunice Hunton. Opportunity 7 (May 1929): 162-163.
    Du Bois, W. E. B. Crisis 36 (July 1929): 234.
    Locke, Alain. Survey, 1 June 1929, p. 329.
    McHugh, Vincent. New York Evening Post, 8 March 1929,
        p. 11m.

New York Times Book Review, 17 March 1929, p. 6.
O'Sheel, Shaemas. New York World, 7 April 1929, p. 11m.
Springfield Republican, 1 September 1929, p. 7e.
Infants of the Spring
    Books, 21 February 1932, p. 16.
    Gruening, Martha. Saturday Review of Literature, 12 March
        1932, p. 585.
    Nation, 10 February 1932, p. 176.
    New York Times, 28 February 1932, p. 22.
    Taylor, Lois. Opportunity 10 (March 1932): 89.
The Interne
    Books, 15 May 1932, p. 8.
    New York Times, 5 June 1932, p. 17.
    Springfield Republican, 15 May 1932, p. 7e.

TILLMAN, Carolyn

Fiction

Life on Wheels. Los Angeles: Crescent Publications, 1975.

TOOMER, Jean

Fiction

(Collection): Cane.[1] New York: Boni & Liveright, 1923, 1975;
    New York: University Place Press, 1967; New York: Harper
    & Row, 1968.
"Avey. " In Antico and Hazelrigg, Insight Through Fiction; Emanuel
    and Gross, Dark Symphony; Long and Collier, Afro-American
    Writing; Toomer, Cane.
"Becky. " Liberator 5 (October 1922): 22; also in Hayman and
    Rabkin, An Introduction to the Analysis of Narrative Prose;
    Larson, Prejudice; Schneider, The Range of Literature; Fiction,
    3rd ed.; Toomer, Cane.
"Blood Burning Moon. " Prairie (March-April 1923): 18; also in
    Current-Garcia and Patrick, What Is the Short Story?, rev. ed.;
    Davis and Peplow, The New Negro Renaissance; James, From
    the Roots; Mellard, Four Modes; Best Short Stories of 1923;
    Nagel, Vision and Value; Toomer, Cane.
"Bona and Paul. " In Huggins, Voices from the Harlem Renais-
    sance; Toomer, Cane.
"Calling Jesus" see "Nora"
"Carma. " Liberator 5 (September 1922): 5; also in Toomer,
    Cane.

---

[1]Although Cane is classified as poetry by Jean Wagner in Black
Poets of the United States (Urbana: University of Illinois, 1973,
p. 260), much criticism focuses on Cane as short fiction or as
a novel.

"A Certain November." Dubuque Dial, 1 November 1935, pp. 107-112.

"Easter." Little Review 11 (Spring 1925): 3-7.

"Esther." Modern Review 1 (January 1923): 50; also in Davis and Redding, Cavalcade; Emanuel and Gross, Dark Symphony; Patterson, An Introduction to Black Literature in America; Toomer, Cane.

"Fern." Little Review 9 (Autumn 1932): 25; also in Burnett, Seas of God; Calverton, Anthology of American Negro Literature; Ferguson, Images of Women in Literature; Hughes, The Best Short Stories by Negro Writers; Toomer, Cane; Turner, Black American Literature; Fiction.

"Mr. Costyve Duditch." Dial 85 (December 1928): 460-476.

"Nora." Double Dealer 4 (September 1922): 132; published as "Calling Jesus" in Toomer's Cane.

"Rhobert." In Davis and Peplow, The New Negro Renaissance; Toomer, Cane.

"Seventh Street." Broom 4 (December 1922): 3; also in Toomer, Cane.

"Theater." In Klotz and Abcarian, The Experience of Fiction; Toomer, Cane.

"Winter on Earth." In Kreymborg, The Second American Caravan.

"York Beach." In Kreymborg, Mumford, and Rosenfeld, New American Caravan.

Biography and Criticism

(Collection): Durham, Frank. The Merrill Studies in "Cane." Columbus: Charles E. Merrill, 1971.

Ackley, Donald G. "Theme and Vision in Jean Toomer's Cane." Studies in Black Literature 1 (Spring 1970): 45-65.

Antonides, Chris. "Jean Toomer: The Burden of Impotent Pain." Ph.D. Dissertation, Michigan State University, 1975.

Armstrong, John. "The Real Negro." New York Tribune, 14 October 1923, p. 26; also in Durham, Studies in Cane.

Baker, Houston A., Jr. Singers of Daybreak: Studies in Black American Literature. Washington, D.C.: Howard University Press, 1974.

Bell, Bernard W. "The Afroamerican Novel and Its Tradition." Ph.D. Dissertation, University of Massachusetts, 1970.

Blake, Susan L. "The Spectatorial Artist and the Structure of Cane." CLA Journal 17 (June 1974): 516-534.

Bone, Robert A. Down Home: A History of Afro-American Short Fiction from Its Beginnings to the End of the Harlem Renaissance. New York: G. P. Putnam's Sons, 1975.

_____. The Negro Novel in America. New Haven: Yale University Press, 1966.

Bontemps, Arna. Foreword to Cane. New York: Harper, 1969.

_____. "The Harlem Renaissance." Saturday Review, 22 March 1947, pp. 12-13, 44.

_____. The Harlem Renaissance Remembered. New York: Dodd, Mead, 1972.

_____. "The Negro Renaissance: Jean Toomer and the Harlem

Writers of the 1920's. " In Durham, Studies in Cane.
_____. "Remembering Cane." BANC! 2 (May/June 1972):
9-10.
Braithwaite, William Stanley. "The Negro in American Literature."
Crisis 28 (September 1924): 204-210; also in The New Negro,
pp. 19-44. Edited by Alain Locke. New York: Albert &
Charles Boni, 1925.
Brawley, Benjamin. The Negro in Literature and Art in the United
States. New York: Duffield, 1929.
Brown, Martha Hursey. "Images of Black Women: Family Roles
in Harlem Renaissance Literature." D.A. Dissertation, Car-
negie-Mellon University, 1976.
Cancel, Rafael A. "Male and Female Inter-Relationship in Toomer's
Cane." Negro American Literature Forum 5 (Spring 1971):
25-31.
Chandler, Sue P. "Books by Jean Toomer in the Fisk University
Library Special Collections." BANC! 2 (May/June 1972): 17.
Chase, Patricia. "The Women in Cane." CLA Journal 14 (March
1971): 259-273.
Christ, Jack M. "Jean Toomer's 'Bona and Paul': The Innocence
and Artifice of Words." Negro American Literature Forum 9
(Summer 1975): 44-46.
Christian, Barbara. "Spirit Bloom in Harlem. The Search for a
Black Aesthetic During the Harlem Renaissance: The Poetry of
Claude McKay, Countee Cullen, and Jean Toomer." Ph.D.
Dissertation, Columbia University, 1970.
Cooke, Michael G. "The Descent into the Underworld and Modern
Black Fiction." Iowa Review 5 (Fall 1974): 72-90.
Davenport, Franklin. "Mill House." BANC! 2 (May/June 1972):
6-7.
Davis, Arthur P. From the Dark Tower: Afro-American Writers
1900-1960. Washington, D.C.: Howard University Press,
1974.
Davis, Charles T. "Jean Toomer and the South: Region and Race
as Elements within a Literary Imagination." Studies in the
Literary Imagination 7 (Fall 1974): 23-37.
Dickerson, Mary Jane. "Sherwood Anderson and Jean Toomer:
A Literary Relationship." Studies in American Fiction 1 (Au-
tumn 1973): 163-175.
Dillard, Mabel. "Behind the Veil of Jean Toomer's Esthetic." In
Durham, Studies in Cane.
_____. "Jean Toomer: Herald of the Negro Renaissance."
Ph.D. Dissertation, Ohio University, 1967.
Duncan, Bowie. "Jean Toomer's Cane: A Modern Black Oracle."
CLA Journal 15 (March 1972): 323-333.
Durham, Frank. "The Poetry Society of South Carolina's Turbulent
Year: Self-Interest, Atheism, and Jean Toomer." Southern
Humanities Review 5 (Winter 1971): 76-80.
Edwards, Sister Ann. "Three Views on Blacks: The Black Woman
in American Literature." CEA Critic 37 (May 1975): 14-16.
Ellison, Curtis William. "Black Adam: The Adamic Assertion and
the Afro-American Novelist." Ph.D. Dissertation, University
of Minnesota, 1970.

Emerson, O. B. "Cultural Nationalism in Afro-American Litera-
ture." In The Cry of Home, pp. 211-244. Edited by H. Er-
nest Lewald. Knoxville: University of Tennessee Press, 1972.
Farrison, W. Edward. "Jean Toomer's Cane Again." CLA Jour-
nal 15 (March 1972): 295-302.
Faulkner, Howard. "The Buried Life: Jean Toomer's Cane."
Studies in Black Literature 7 (Winter 1976): 1-5.
Felgar, Robert. "Black Content, White Form." Studies in Black
Literature 5 (Spring 1974): 28-31.
Frank, Waldo. Foreword to Cane. New York: Boni & Liveright,
1923.
Fullinwider, S. P. "Jean Toomer: Lost Generation, or Negro
Renaissance?" Phylon 27 (Fourth Quarter 1956): 396-403;
also in Durham, Studies in Cane.
Gayle, Addison, Jr. The Way of the New World: The Black Novel
in America. Garden City, N.Y.: Anchor Press/Doubleday,
1975.
Gloster, Hugh M. Negro Voices in American Fiction. Chapel Hill:
University of North Carolina Press, 1948; also in Durham,
Studies in Cane.
Grant, Sister Mary Kathryn. "Images of Celebration in Cane."
Negro American Literature Forum 5 (Spring 1971): 32-34, 36.
Griffin, John C. "A Chat with Marjory Content Toomer." Pem-
broke Magazine 5 (January 1974): 15-27.
_____. "Jean Toomer: A Bibliography." South Carolina Review
7 (April 1975): 61-64.
Gross, Theodore L. The Heroic Ideal in American Literature.
New York: Free Press, 1971.
Gysin, Fritz. The Grotesque in American Negro Fiction. The
Cooper Monographs on English and American Literature no. 22.
Basel, Switzerland: Francke Verlag Bern, 1975.
Hart, Robert C. "Black-White Literary Relations in the Harlem
Renaissance." American Literature 44 (January 1973): 612-
628.
Hayashi, Susanna. "Dark Odyssey: Descent into the Underworld in
Black American Fiction." Ph.D. Dissertation, Indiana Univer-
sity, 1971.
Helbing, Mark. "Primitivism and the Harlem Renaissance." Ph.D.
Dissertation, University of Minnesota, 1972.
_____. "Sherwood Anderson and Jean Toomer." Negro Ameri-
can Literature Forum 9 (Summer 1975): 35-39.
Huggins, Nathan Irvin. Harlem Renaissance. New York: Oxford
University Press, 1971.
Hughes, Langston. The Big Sea. New York: Knopf, 1940.
Innes, Catherine L. "The Unity of Jean Toomer's Cane." CLA
Journal 15 (March 1972): 306-322.
Jackson, Blyden. "The Harlem Renaissance." In The Comic Ima-
gination in American Literature, pp. 295-303. Edited by Louis
D. Rubin, Jr. New Brunswick, N.J.: Rutgers University
Press, 1973.
_____. The Waiting Years. Baton Rouge: Louisiana State Uni-
versity Press, 1976.
"Just Americans." Time, 28 March 1932, p. 19; also in Durham,
Studies in Cane.

Kopf, George. "The Tensions in Jean Toomer's 'Theater.'" CLA Journal 17 (June 1974): 498-503.

Kousaleos, Peter G. "A Study of the Language, Structure, and Symbolism in Jean Toomer's Cane and N. Scott Momaday's House Made of Dawn. Ph. D. Dissertation, Ohio University, 1973.

Kraft, James. "Jean Toomer's Cane." Markham Review 2 (October 1970): 61-63.

Krasny, Michael J. "Jean Toomer and the Quest for Consciousness." Ph. D. Dissertation, University of Wisconsin, 1972.

_____. "Jean Toomer's Life Prior to Cane: A Brief Sketch of the Emergence of a Black Writer." Negro American Literature Forum 9 (Summer 1975): 40-41.

Larson, Charles. The Novel in the Third World. Washington, D. C.: Inscape, 1976.

Leiber, Todd. "Design and Movement in Cane." CLA Journal 13 (September 1969): 35-50.

Littlejohn, David. Black on White. New York: Grossman, 1966.

Locke, Alain. Four Negro Poets. New York: Simon & Schuster, 1927.

_____. "From Native Son to Invisible Man: A Review of the Literature of the Negro for 1952." Phylon 14 (First Quarter 1953): 34-44; also in Durham, Studies in Cane.

Ludington, C. J., Jr. "Four Authors View the South." Southern Humanities Review 6 (Winter 1972): 1-4.

McConnell, Frank D. "Black Words and Black Becoming." Yale Review 63 (Winter 1974): 193-210.

McKeever, Benjamin F. "Cane as Blues." Negro American Literature Forum 4 (July 1970): 61-63.

Major, Clarence. "Tradition and Presence: Experimental Fiction by Black American Writers." American Poetry Review 5 (May/June 1976): 33-34.

Margolies, Edward. Native Sons. Philadelphia: Lippincott, 1968.

Martin, Odette C. "Cane: Method and Myth." Obsidian 2 (Spring 1976): 5-20.

Mason, Clifford. "Jean Toomer's Black Authenticity." Black World 20 (January 1970): 70-76.

Matthews, George C. "Toomer's Cane: The Artist and His World." CLA Journal 17 (June 1974): 543-559.

Mellard, James M. "Symbolism and Demonism: The Lyrical Mode in Fiction." Southern Humanities Review 7 (Winter 1973): 37-51.

Mintz, Steven. "Jean Toomer: A Biographical Sketch." BANC! 2 (May/June 1972): 1-3.

Mootry, Maria Katella. "Studies in Black Pastoral: Five Afro-American Writers." Ph. D. Dissertation, Northwestern University, 1974.

Munson, Gorham B. "The Significance of Jean Toomer." Opportunity 3 (September 1925): 262-263; also in Durham, Studies in Cane.

Nower, Joyce. "Foolin' Master." Satire Newsletter 7 (Fall 1969): 5-10.

Otto, George Edward. "Religious Society of Friends." BANC! 2 (May/June 1972): 9-10.

Perry, Margaret. Silence to the Drums: A Survey of the Literature of the Harlem Renaissance. Contributions in Afro-American and African Studies, no. 18. Westport, Conn.: Greenwood Press, 1976.

Ramsey, Priscilla Barbara Ann. "A Study of Black Identity in 'Passing' Novels of the Nineteenth and Early Twentieth Centuries." Ph.D. Dissertation, The American University, 1975.

Redding, J. Saunders. "American Negro Literature." American Scholar 18 (Spring 1949): 137-148.

Reilly, John M. "Jean Toomer: An Annotated Checklist of Criticism." Resources for American Literary Study 4 (1974): 27-56.

_____. "The Search for Black Redemption: Jean Toomer's Cane." Studies in the Novel 2 (Fall 1970): 312-324.

Robinson, Anna T. "Race Consciousness and Survival Techniques Depicted in Harlem Renaissance Fiction." Ph.D. Dissertation, Pennsylvania State University, 1973.

Rosenfeld, Paul. "Jean Toomer." Men Seen: Twenty-Four Modern Authors. New York: Dial Press, 1925; also in Durham, Studies in Cane.

Rosenblatt, Roger. Black Fiction. Cambridge: Harvard University Press, 1974.

Scruggs, Charles. "'All Dressed Up But No Place to Go.' The Black Writer and His Audience During the Harlem Renaissance." American Literature 48 (January 1977): 543-563.

_____. "Mark of Cain and the Redemption of Art: A Study in Theme and Structure of Jean Toomer's Cane." American Literature 44 (May 1972): 276-291.

Seyersted, Per. "A Survey of Trends and Figures in Afro-American Fiction." American Studies in Scandinavia 6 nos. 1-2 (1973-74): 67-86.

Shaw, Brenda Joyce Robinson. "Jean Toomer's Life Search for Identity as Realized in Cane." D.A., Middle Tennessee State University, 1975.

Shockley, Ann Ellen [sic.]. "Dedicated to Jean Toomer." BANC! 2 (May/June 1972): i-ii.

Singh, Amritjit. "The Novels of the Harlem Renaissance: A Thematic Study." Ph.D. Dissertation, New York University, 1973.

_____. The Novels of the Harlem Renaissance: Twelve Black Writers, 1923-1933. University Park: Pennsylvania State University Press, 1976.

Singh, Raman K. "The Black Novel and Its Tradition." Colorado Quarterly 20 (Summer 1971): 23-29.

Smith, Cynthia Janis. "Escape and Quest in the Literature of Black Americans." Ph.D. Dissertation, Yale University, 1974.

Smith, James Frederick, Jr. "From Symbol to Character: The Negro in American Fiction of the Twenties." Ph.D. Dissertation, Pennsylvania State University, 1972.

Spiller, Hortense. "Towards a 'Separate Peace': Notes on the Life of Jean Toomer." Harvard Advocate 107 no. 4 (1974): 47-48, 66-71.

Spofford, William K. "The Unity of Part One of Jean Toomer's Cane." Markham Review 3 (May 1972): 58-60.

Stein, Marian L. "The Poet-Observer and 'Fern' in Jean Toomer's Cane." Markham Review 2 (October 1970): 64-65.

Taylor, Clyde. "The Second Coming of Jean Toomer." Obsidian 1 (Winter 1975): 37-57.

Thompson, Larry E. "Jean Toomer: As Modern Man." Renaissance 2, Issue One (1971): 7-10; also in The Harlem Renaissance Remembered, pp. 51-62. Edited by Arna Bontemps. New York: Dodd, Mead, 1972.

Turner, Darwin T. "And Another Passing." Negro American Literature Forum (Fall 1967): 3-4.

_____. "Cane (Jean Toomer)." The Twentieth Century American Novel Series. DeLand, Fla.: Everett/Edwards, n.d. (Cassette.)

_____. In a Minor Chord: Three Afro-American Writers and Their Search for Identity. Urbana: Southern Illinois University Press, 1971.

_____. "Jean Toomer's Cane; Critical Analysis." Negro Digest 18 (January 1969): 54-61.

Turpin, Waters E. "Four Short Fiction Writers of the Harlem Renaissance--Their Legacy of Achievement." CLA Journal 11 (September 1967): 59-72.

Van Mol, Kay R. "Primitivism and Intellect in Toomer's Cane and McKay's Banana Bottom: The Need for an Integrated Black Consciousness." Negro American Literature Forum 10 (Summer 1976): 48-52.

Waldron, Edward E. "The Search for Identity in Jean Toomer's 'Esther.'" CLA Journal 14 (March 1971): 277-280.

Watkins, Patricia. "Is There a Unifying Theme in Cane?" CLA Journal 15 (March 1972): 303-305.

Welch, William. "The Gurdjieff Period." BANC! 2 (May/June 1972): 6-7.

Westerfield, Hargis. "Jean Toomer's 'Fern': A Mythical Dimension." CLA Journal 14 (March 1971): 274-276.

Whitlow, Roger. Black American Literature: A Critical History. Chicago: Nelson Hall, 1973.

Who's Who in America 17 (1932-33).

Reviews

Cane

Armstrong, John. New York Tribune, 14 October 1923, p. 26.

Bone, Robert A. New York Times Book Review, 19 January 1969, p. 3.

Brickell, Herschell. Literary Review of the New York Evening Post, 8 December 1923, p. 33.

Brooklyn Life, 10 November 1923, p. 3.

Choice 5 (December 1968): 1312.

Dial 76 (January 1924): 92.

Du Bois, W. E. B. Crisis 27 (February 1924): 162.

Gregory, Montgomery. Opportunity 12 (December 1923): 374-375.

Jellinek, Roger. New York Times, 21 January 1969, p. 45.

Josephson, Matthew. Broom 5 (October 1923): 179-180.

Lasker, Bruno. Survey, 1 November 1923, pp. 190-191.
Littell, Robert. New Republic, 26 December 1923, p. 126.
Parsons, Alice Beals. World Tomorrow 7 (March 1924): 96.
Sergeant, Elizabeth Shepley. New Republic, 12 May 1926,
    pp. 371-372.
Royster, Philip. BANC! 2 (May/June 1972): 11-14.
Springfield Republican, 23 December 1923, p. 9a.

TORRES, Brenda

Short Fiction

"Convergence. " Black World 26 (February 1975): 54-59.

TOURE, Askia Muhammad

Short Fiction

"Of Fathers and Sons. " In Sanchez, We Be Word Sorcerers.

TURPIN, Waters Edward

Novels

O Canaan! New York: Doubleday, Doran, 1939; New York: AMS
    Press, 1975.
The Rootless. New York: Vantage Press, 1957.
These Low Grounds. New York: Harper, 1937; excerpt in Ford,
    Black Insights; Brown, Davis, and Lee, Negro Caravan.

Biography and Criticism

Fleming, Robert E. "Overshadowed by Richard Wright: Three
    Black Chicago Novelists. " Negro American Literature Forum
    7 (Fall 1973): 75-79.
Ford, Nick Aaron. "In Memoriam: Tribute to Waters E. Turpin
    (1910-1968). " CLA Journal 12 (March 1969): 281-282.
Gloster, Hugh M. Negro Voices in American Fiction. Chapel Hill:
    University of North Carolina Press, 1948.
Rush, Theressa Gunnels, Carol Fairbanks Myers, and Esther Spring
    Arata. Black American Writers Past and Present. Metuchen,
    N.J.: Scarecrow Press, 1975.

Reviews

O Canaan!
    Booklist 36 (September 1939): 10.
    Chase, R. A. Boston Transcript, 19 August 1939, p. 3.
    Kazin, Alfred. New York Herald Tribune Books, 23 July 1939,
        p. 4.

Lee, Ulysses. Opportunity 17 (October 1939): 312-313.
Marsh, F. T. New York Times Book Review, 16 July 1939,
     p. 4.
New Republic, 4 October 1939, p. 252.
New Yorker, 15 July 1939, p. 64.
Pratt Institute Quarterly (Autumn 1939): 29.
Saturday Review of Literature, 22 July 1939, p. 20.
These Low Grounds
Lee, Ulysses. Opportunity 15 (November 1937): 347.
Saturday Review of Literature, 25 September 1937, p. 28.
Suskin, William. New York Herald Tribune Books, 19 Septem-
     ber 1937, p. 14.
Time, 20 September 1937, p. 71.
Tucker, Augusta. New York Times Book Review, 26 September
     1937, p. 6.
Wright, Richard. New Masses, 5 October 1937, p. 22-25.

VAN DYKE, Henry

Novels

Blood of Strawberries. New York: Farrar, Straus & Giroux, 1965.
Dead Piano. New York: Farrar, Straus & Giroux, 1971.
Ladies of the Rachmaninoff Eyes. New York: Farrar, Straus &
     Giroux, 1965; New York: Manor Books, 1973; Chatham, N.J.:
     Chatham Bookseller, 1975.

Short Fiction

"Ruth's Story." In Patterson, An Introduction to Black Literature
     in America.

Biography and Criticism

Contemporary Authors, 49/52.

Reviews

Blood of Strawberries
     Freedman, Richard. Book World, 19 January 1969, p. 12.
     Griffin, L. W. Library Journal, 15 December 1968, p. 4665.
     Hicks, Granville, Saturday Review, 4 January 1969, p. 93.
     Kirkus, 1 November 1968, p. 1248.
     Levin, Martin. New York Times Book Review, 5 January 1969,
          p. 33.
     New Outlook, 24 February 1969, p. 21.
     New York Times, 4 January 1969, p. 25.
     Publishers' Weekly, 4 November 1968, p. 47.
     Sharpe, D. F. Best Sellers, 15 February 1969, p. 470.
     Virginia Quarterly Review 45 (Spring 1969): xlix.
Dead Piano
     Best Sellers, 15 October 1971, p. 336.

Black World 21 (June 1972): 86.
Callendar, Newgate. New York Times Book Review, 31 Octo-
ber 1971, p. 30.
Griffin, L. W. Library Journal 96 (August 1971): 2548.
Kirkus, 1 July 1971, p. 699.
Loftin, Eloise. Black Creation 3 (Winter 1972): 54-55.
New Outlook, 4 December 1971, p. 24.
Publishers' Weekly, 28 June 1971, p. 61.
Thompson, J. Harper's 243 (October 1971): 120.
Ladies of the Rachmaninoff Eyes
Best Sellers, 15 June 1965, p. 134.
Booklist, 15 April 1965, p. 787.
Fleischer, L. Publishers' Weekly, 12 December 1966, p. 58.
Fremont-Smith, E. New York Times, 15 May 1965, p. 29.
Hicks, Granville. Saturday Review, 12 June 1965, p. 35.
Kirkus, 1 April 1965, p. 395.
Levin, Martin. New York Times Book Review, 23 May 1965,
p. 46.
Observer, 24 October 1965, p. 28.
MacManus, Patricia. Book Week, 16 May 1965, p. 18.
Raines, C. A. Library Journal, 1 June 1965, p. 2586.
Randall, D. Negro Digest 14 (August 1965): 88.
Times Literary Supplement, 4 November 1965, p. 986.
Wall Street Journal, 9 July 1965, p. 6.

VAN PEEBLES, Melvin

Novels

Un américain en enfer. Translated by Paule-Eugénie Truffert.
Paris: Éditions Denoël, 1965.
A Bear for the FBI. New York: Trident, 1968; excerpt in Adoff,
Brothers and Sisters.
La Fête à Harlem. Paris: J. Martineau, 1967.
Just an Old Sweet Song. New York: Ballantine, 1976.
Le Permission. Paris: J. Martineau, 1967.
The True American: A Folk Fable. Garden City, N.Y.: Double-
day, 1976.

Short Fiction

"The True American." Playboy 23 (February 1976): 64-66, 78,
136, 138, 140, 142-143.

Biography and Criticism

Bauerle, R. F. "The Theme of Absurdity in Melvin Van Peebles'
A Bear for the FBI." Notes on Contemporary Literature 1
(September 1971): 11-12.
Coleman, Horace W. "Melvin Van Peebles." Journal of Popular
Culture 5 (Fall 1972): 368-384.
"Interview." Black Creation (Fall 1971).

Klinkowitz, J. "Black Superfiction." North American Review 259 (Winter 1974): 69-74.

Scobie, W. I. "Supernigger Strikes." London Magazine 12 (April-May 1972): 111-116.

Schraufnagel, Noel. From Apology to Protest: The Black American Novel. DeLand, Fla.: Everett/Edwards, 1973.

Reviews

A Bear for the FBI

    Hill, W. B. Best Sellers, 15 October 1968, p. 286.

    Kirkus, 1 July 1968, p. 716.

    Levin, M. New York Times Book Review, 6 October 1968, p. 40.

    Library Journal, 1 November 1968, p. 4168.

    Negro Digest 18 (April 1969): 90.

    Publishers' Weekly, 15 July 1968, p. 55; 15 September 1969, p. 62.

The True American: A Folk Fable

    Booklist, 1 March 1976, p. 960.

    Choice 13 (July 1976): 668.

    Jaffee, D. Best Sellers 36 (June 1976): 73-74.

    New Yorker, 1 March 1976, p. 100.

VERNE, Berta (pseud.)

Novel

Elastic Fingers. New York: Vantage, 1969.

VERTA MAE see Smart-Grosvenor, Verta Mae

VOGLIN, Peter

Novel

Now You Lay Me Down to Sleep. Dallas: n.p., 1962.

VROMAN, Mary Elizabeth

Short Fiction

"See How They Run." Negro Digest 10 (November 1951): 52-68; also in Ferguson, Images of Women in Literature; Schneiderman, By and About Women.

Biography and Criticism

Rush, Theressa Gunnels, Carol Fairbanks Myers, and Esther Spring

Arata. Black American Writers Past and Present. Metuchen,
N.J.: Scarecrow Press, 1975.

WALKER, Alice

Novels

Meridian. New York: Harcourt Brace Jovanovich, 1976; excerpts
    in Ms. 4 (May 1976): 67-70; Essence 7 (July 1976): 35-40,
    73-78.
The Third Life of Grange Copeland. New York: Harcourt Brace
    Jovanovich, 1970; New York: Avon, 1971; condensed in Red-
    book, May 1971.

Short Fiction

(Collection): In Love and Trouble: Stories of Black Women. New
    York: Harcourt Brace Jovanovich, 1973.
"The Child Who Favored Daughter Walker." Denver Quarterly 2
    (Summer 1967): 99-108; also in Walker, In Love and Trouble.
"The Diary of an African Nun: a Short Story." Freedomways 8
    (Summer 1968): 226-229.
"Entertaining God." In Walker, In Love and Trouble.
"Everyday Use." Harper's 246 (April 1973): 74-81; also in Cahill,
    Women and Fiction; Walker, In Love and Trouble; Washington,
    Black-Eyed Susans.
"The First Day." Freedomways 4 (Fourth Quarter 1974): 314-316.
"The Flowers." In Walker, In Love and Trouble.
"Her Sweet Jerome." In Ferguson, Images of Women in Literature:
    Sanchez, We Be Word Sorcerers; Walker, In Love and Trouble.
"'Really, Doesn't Crime Pay?'" In Walker, In Love and Trouble.
"The Revenge of Hannah Kemhuff." Ms. 2 (July 1973): 70-72;
    90-93; also in Foley, Best American Short Stories: 1974;
    Walker, In Love and Trouble.
"Roselily." Ms. 1 (August 1972): 44-47; also in Walker, In Love
    and Trouble.
"Strong Horse Tea." Negro Digest 17 (June 1968): 53-60; also in
    King, Black Short Story Anthology; Walker, In Love and Trouble.
"A Sudden Trip Home." Essence 2 (September 1971): 58-59.
"To Hell with Dying." In Bambara, Tales and Stories for Black
    Folks; Gibson and Anselment, Black and White; Schneider, The
    Range of Literature: Fiction, 3rd ed.; Sherrill and Robertson-
    Rose, Four Elements; Stadler, Out of Our Lives; Walker, In
    Love and Trouble.
"We Drink the Wine in France." In Walker, In Love and Trouble.
"The Welcome Table." In Exum, Keeping the Faith; Walker, In
    Love and Trouble.

Biography and Criticism

Anderson, Jo Ann. "Beyond the Stereotypes." Freedomways 16
    (Third Quarter 1976): 192-194.

Callahan, John. "Reconsideration: The Higher Ground of Alice
  Walker." New Republic, 14 September 1974, pp. 21-22.
Contemporary Authors, 37/40.
Doyle, Sister Mary Ellen. "The Heroine of Black Novels." In
  Perspectives on Afro-American Women, pp. 112-125. Edited
  by Willa D. Johnson and Thomas L. Green. Washington, D. C.:
  ECCA Publications, 1975.
Emanuel, James A. In Contemporary Novelists. Edited by James
  Vinson. New York: St. Martin's Press, 1976.
Harris, Jessica. "An Interview with Alice Walker." Essence 7
  (July 1976): 33.
Harris, Trudier. "Violence in The Third Life of Grange Copeland."
  CLA Journal 19 (December 1975): 238-247.
Hoffman, Nancy. "Understanding Alice Walker's 'Sammy Lou':
  Must You Be What You Teach?" Paper presented at the MLA
  meeting, New York City, December 1976.
O'Brien, John, ed. Interviews with Black Writers. New York:
  Liveright, 1973.
O'Leary, Donald J. Freedomways 9 (Winter 1969): 70-73.
Peden, William. The American Short Story: Continuity and Change
  1940-1975. Boston: Houghton Mifflin, 1975.
————. "The Black Explosion." Studies in Short Fiction 12
  (Summer 1975): 231-242.
Rush, Theressa Gunnels, Carol Fairbanks Myers, and Esther Spring
  Arata. Black American Writers Past and Present. Metuchen,
  N.J.: Scarecrow Press, 1975.
Smith, Barbara. "The Souls of Black Women." Ms. 2 (February
  1974): 42-43, 78.
Washington, Mary Helen. "Black Women Image Makers." Black
  World 23 (August 1974): 10-18.
"Women on Women." American Scholar 41 (Fall 1972): 599-622.

Reviews

In Love and Trouble: Stories of Black Women
  Black World 23 (October 1974): 51.
  Book World, 18 November 1973, p. 1; 5 May 1974, p. 4.
  Booklist, 1 January 1974, p. 473; 15 January 1974, p. 538.
  Bouise, O. A. Best Sellers, 15 October 1973, p. 335.
  Bryant, J. H. Nation, 12 November 1973, p. 501.
  Choice 10 (January 1974): 1723.
  Freedomways 14 (First Quarter 1974): 59-62.
  Goodwin, June. Christian Science Monitor, 19 September
    1973, p. 11.
  Library Journal, 15 December 1973, p. 3692.
  Maginnis, Ruth. Library Journal, 15 November 1973, p. 3476.
  Ms. 2 (February 1974): 42.
  New Republic, 14 September 1974, p. 21.
  Pfeffer, S. B. Library Journal 98 (August 1973): 2338.
  Watkins, M. New York Times Book Review, 17 March 1974,
    p. 40.
Meridian
  Best Sellers 36 (Summer 1976): 187.

Choice 13 (Summer 1976): 829-830.
Cooke, M. G. Yale Review 66 (October 1976): 146-155.
Jefferson, M. Newsweek, 31 May 1976, pp. 71-72.
Marcus, G. New Yorker, 7 June 1976, pp. 133-136.
National Observer, 17 July 1976, p. 17.
Piercy, M. New York Times Book Review, 23 May 1976, p. 5.
Rogers, Norma. Freedomways 16 (Second Quarter 1976): 120-122.
The Third Life of Grange Copeland
Coles, Robert. New Yorker, 27 February 1971, p. 104.
Hendin, Josephine. Saturday Review of Literature, 22 August 1970, p. 55.
Kirkus, 1 July 1970, p. 711.
Kramer, V. A. Library Journal 95 (July 1970): 2522.
New Leader, 25 January 1971, p. 19.
Publishers' Weekly, 25 May 1970, p. 55.
Schorer, Mark. American Scholar 40 (Winter 1970-1971): 168.
Theroux, Paul. Book World, 13 September 1970, p. 2.

WALKER, Drake

Novel

Buck and the Preacher. New York: Popular Library, 1971.

Biography and Criticism

Rush, Theressa Gunnels, Carol Fairbanks Myers, and Esther Spring Arata. Black American Writers Past and Present. Metuchen, N.J.: Scarecrow Press, 1975.

WALKER, Evan K.

Short Fiction

"Harlem Transfer: Story." Black World 19 (May 1970): 66-76; also in Coombs, What We Must See; King, Black Short Story Anthology; Mayfield, Ten Times Black.
"Legacy." Black World 21 (December 1971): 64-76; also in Sanchez, We Be Word Sorcerers.

WALKER, Margaret (Mrs. F. J. Alexander)

Novel

Jubilee. Boston: Houghton Mifflin, 1966; New York: Bantam, 1975; excerpts in Chambers and Moon, Right On!; Stanford, I, Too, Sing America.

Biography and Criticism

Current Biography, 1943.
Davis, Arthur P. From the Dark Tower: Afro-American Writers 1900-1960. Washington, D.C.: Howard University Press, 1974.
Gayle, Addison, Jr., ed. Black Expression: Essays by and about Black Americans in the Creative Arts. New York: Weybright & Talley, 1969.
Littlejohn, David. Black on White: A Critical Survey of Writing by American Negroes. New York: Grossman, 1966.
Love, Theresa R. "The Black Woman in Afro-American Literature." Paper presented at the Midwest Modern Language Association meeting, Chicago, November 1975. (Mimeographed.)
Malkoff, Karl. Crowell's Handbook of Contemporary American Poetry. New York: T. Y. Crowell, 1973.
Rowell, Charles H. "An Interview with Margaret Walker." Black World 25 (December 1975): 4-17.
Rush, Theressa Gunnels, Carol Fairbanks Myers, and Esther Spring Arata. Black American Writers Past and Present. Metuchen, N.J.: Scarecrow Press, 1975.
Schraufnagel, Noel. From Apology to Protest: The Black American Novel. DeLand, Fla.: Everett/Edwards, 1973.
Vinson, James, ed. Contemporary Novelists. New York: St. Martin's Press, 1972.
Walker, Margaret. How I Wrote Jubilee. Chicago: Third World Press, 1972.
_____ and Nikki Giovanni. A Poetic Equation: Conversations Between Nikki Giovanni and Margaret Walker. Washington, D.C.: Howard University Press, 1974.
Whitlow, Roger. Black American Literature: A Critical History. Chicago: Nelson Hall, 1973.
Young, James O. Black Writers of the Thirties. Baton Rouge: Louisiana State University Press, 1973.

Reviews

Jubilee
Barrow, William. Negro Digest 16 (February 1967): 93-95.
Booklist, 1 September 1966, p. 35.
Carvlin, Eugene. Community 26 (February 1967): 13.
Chapman, Abraham. Saturday Review of Literature, 24 September 1966, p. 43.
Christian Science Monitor, 29 September 1966, p. 11.
Davenport, Guy. National Review, 4 October 1966, p. 1001.
Davis, Lester. Freedomways 7 (Summer 1967): 258-260.
Dykeman, Wilma. New York Times Book Review, 25 September 1966, p. 52.
Giles, L. Library Journal, 15 October 1966, p. 4978.
Hass, V. P. Books Today, 25 September 1966, p. 5.
Kirkus, 15 July 1966, p. 711.
Kitching, J. Publishers' Weekly, 15 August 1966, p. 61.
Maroney, Sheila. Crisis 73 (November 1966): 493.

Marriett, V. Books and Bookmen 12 (September 1967): 46.
Oppenheim, J. E. Best Sellers, 1 October 1966, p. 229.
Publishers' Weekly, 21 August 1967, p. 76.
Renek, Morris. Book Week, 2 October 1966, p. 8.
Times Literary Supplement, 29 June 1967, p. 583.

WALKER, Thomas Hamilton Beb

Novel

Bebbly; or, The Victorious Preacher. Gainesville, Fla.: Pepper,
1910.

WALKER, Victor Steven

Short Fiction

"The Long Sell." In Chapman, New Black Voices.

WALLACE, Elisabeth West

Novel

Scandal at Daybreak. New York: Pageant, 1954.

WALROND, Eric

Short Fiction

(Collection): Tropic Death. New York: Boni & Liveright, 1926;
New York: Macmillan, 1954, 1972.
"The Adventures of Kit Skyhead and Mistah Beauty." Vanity Fair
(March 1925).
"Black Pin." In Walrond, Tropic Death.
"By the River Avon." Crisis 54 (January 1947): 16-17.
"A Cholo Romance." Opportunity 2 (June 1924): 177-181.
"City Love." In Kreymborg, et al., American Caravan; Huggins,
Voices from the Harlem Renaissance.
"Cynthia Goes to the Prom." Opportunity 1 (November 1923):
342-343.
"Drought." In New and Rosengarten, Modern Stories in English;
Walrond, Tropic Death.
"On Being a Domestic." Opportunity 1 (August 1923): 234.
"Palm Porch." In Walrond, Tropic Death.
"Panama Gold." In Walrond, Tropic Death.
"The Stone Rebounds." Opportunity 1 (September 1923): 277-278.
"Subjection." In Barksdale and Kinnamon, Black Writers of Ameri-
ca; Walrond, Tropic Death.
"Vignettes of the Dusk." Opportunity 2 (January 1924): 19-20.

"Tropic Death." In Walrond, Tropic Death.
"Vampire Bat." In Walrond, Tropic Death.
"The Voodoo's Revenge." Opportunity 3 (July 1925): 209-213.
"The Wharf Rats. In Copy, 1927; Walrond, Tropic Death.
"White Snake." In Walrond, Tropic Death.
"The Yellow One." In Calverton, Anthology of American Negro
    Literature; Emanuel and Gross, Dark Symphony; Walrond,
    Tropic Death.

Biography and Criticism

Bone, Robert A. Down Home: A History of Afro-American Short
    Fiction from Its Beginnings to the End of the Harlem Renais-
    sance. New York: G. P. Putnam's Sons, 1975.
Brawley, Benjamin. The Negro Genius. New York: Dodd, Mead,
    1940.
Gloster, Hugh M. Negro Voices in American Fiction. Chapel Hill:
    University of North Carolina Press, 1948.
Rush, Theressa Gunnels, Carol Fairbanks Myers, and Esther Spring
    Arata. Black American Writers Past and Present. Metuchen,
    N.J.: Scarecrow Press, 1975.

Reviews

Tropic Death
    Boston Transcript, 6 November 1926, p. 4.
    Calverton, V. F. Survey, 1 November 1926, p. 159.
    Du Bois, W. E. B. Crisis 33 (1927): 152.
    Frank, Waldo. Opportunity 4 (November 1926): 352.
    Herrick, Robert. New Republic, 10 November 1926, p. 332.
    Hughes, Langston. New York Herald Tribune, 5 December
        1926, p. 9.
    New York Times, 17 October 1926, p. 6.
    New York World, 21 November 1926, p. 10m.
    Springfield Republican, 31 October 1926, p. 7f.

WAMBLE, Thelma

Novels

All in the Family. New York: New Voices, 1953.
Look Over My Shoulder. New York: Vantage, 1969.

WARD, Matthew

Novel

The Indignant Heart. New York: New Books, 1952.

WARD, Thomas Playfair

Novels

The Clutches of Circumstances. New York: Pageant, 1954.
The Right to Live. New York: Pageant, 1953.
The Truth That Makes Men Free. New York: Pageant, 1955.

WARDLOW, Xavier X Lowtricia

Short Fiction

"The Gift of Mercilessness." In Sanchez, We Be Word Sorcerers.

WARING, Robert L.

Novel

As We See It. Washington, D. C.: C. F. Sudworth, 1910.

Biography and Criticism

Gloster, Hugh M. Negro Voices in American Fiction. Chapel Hill:
University of North Carolina Press, 1948.

WARNER, Samuel Jonathan

Novel

Madam President-Elect: A Novel. New York: Exposition, 1956.

WARNTZ, Chris

Short Fiction

"Courtney Go Huntin'." Black World 24 (December 1974): 55-59.

WASHINGTON, Doris V.

Novel

Yulan. New York: Carlton, 1954.

WATKINS, Richard T.

Short Fiction

"My Man Quick-Sand." Black Creation 5 (Fall 1973): 4-8.

WATSON, Roberta Bruce

Novel

Closed Doors. New York: Exposition, 1967.

Biography and Criticism

Rush, Theressa Gunnels, Carol Fairbanks Myers, and Esther Spring
Arata. Black American Writers Past and Present. Metuchen,
N.J.: Scarecrow Press, 1975.

WEBB, Charles Lewis

Novel

Sasebo Diary. New York: Vantage, 1964.

Biography and Criticism

Rush, Theressa Gunnels, Carol Fairbanks Myers, and Esther Spring
Arata. Black American Writers Past and Present. Metuchen,
N.J.: Scarecrow Press, 1975.

WEBB, Frank J.

Novel

The Garies and Their Friends. London: Routledge, 1857; New
York: Arno, 1969.

Biography and Criticism

Bogardus, R. F. "Frank J. Webb's The Garies and Their Friends:
An Early Black Novelist's Venture into Realism." Studies in
Black Literature 5 (Summer 1974): 15-20.
Bone, Robert A. The Negro Novel in America. New Haven: Yale
University Press, 1966.
DeVries, James H. "The Tradition of the Sentimental Novel in The
Garies and Their Friends." CLA Journal 17 (December 1973):
241-249.
Fleming, Robert E. "Humor in the Early Black Novel." CLA
Journal 17 (December 1973): 256-257, 259-260.
Gayle, Addison, Jr. The Way of the New World: The Black Novel

in America. Garden City, N.Y.: Anchor Press/Doubleday, 1975.

Gloster, Hugh M. Negro Voices in American Fiction. Chapel Hill: University of North Carolina Press, 1948.

Loggins, Vernon. The Negro Author: His Development in America to 1900. Port Washington, N.Y.: Kennikat, 1964.

Ramsey, Priscilla. "A Study of Black Identity in 'Passing' Novels of the Nineteenth and Early Twentieth Centuries." Studies in Black Literature 7 (Winter 1976): 1-7.

Rush, Theressa Gunnels, Carol Fairbanks Myers, and Esther Spring Arata. Black American Writers Past and Present. Metuchen, N.J.: Scarecrow Press, 1975.

Schraufnagel, Noel. From Apology to Protest: The Black American Novel. DeLand, Fla.: Everett/Edwards, 1973.

WEBSTER, Bill

Novel

One by One. Garden City, N.Y.: Doubleday, 1972.

Biography and Criticism

Rush, Theressa Gunnels, Carol Fairbanks Myers, and Esther Spring Arata. Black American Writers Past and Present. Metuchen, N.J.: Scarecrow Press, 1975.

Reviews

One by One
　　Booklist, 15 December 1972, p. 381.
　　Library Journal, 1 May 1972, p. 1744.
　　New York Times Book Review, 29 October 1972, p. 59.
　　Publishers' Weekly, 26 June 1972, p. 56.
　　Virginia Quarterly Review 48 (Spring 1973): 57.

WELBURN, Ron

Short Fiction

"Moon Woman, Sunday's Child." Essence 2 (October 1971): 62-63.
"The Nightsong of Dashiki Henry." In Cassill, Intro # 3.

Biography and Criticism

Rush, Theressa Gunnels, Carol Fairbanks Myers, and Esther Spring Arata. Black American Writers Past and Present. Metuchen, N.J.: Scarecrow Press, 1975.

WELLS, Jack Calvert

Novel

Out of the Deep. Boston: Christopher, 1958.

WELLS, Moses Peter

Short Fiction

Three Adventurous Men. New York: Carlton, 1963.

WEST, Dorothy

Novel

The Living Is Easy. Boston: Houghton Mifflin, 1948; New York: Arno, 1970; excerpt in Hill, Soon, One Morning.

Short Fiction

"The Black Dress." Opportunity 12 (May 1934): 140-158.
"Jack in the Pot." In Clarke, Harlem.
"Mammy." Opportunity 18 (October 1940): 298-302.
"The Typewriter." Opportunity 4 (July 1926): 220-223, 233-234.

Biography and Criticism

Bone, Robert A. The Negro Novel in America. New Haven: Yale University Press, 1966.
Hughes, Carl M. The Negro Novelist 1940-1950. New York: Citadel Press, 1953.
Perry, Margaret. Silence to the Drums: A Survey of the Harlem Renaissance. Contributions in Afro-American and African Studies, no. 18. Westport, Conn.: Greenwood Press, 1976.
Schraufnagel, Noel. From Apology to Protest: The Black American Novel. DeLand, Fla.: Everett/Edwards, 1973.
Whitlow, Roger. Black American Literature: A Critical History. Chicago: Nelson Hall, 1973.

Reviews

The Living Is Easy
    Bontemps, Arna. New York Herald Tribune Weekly Book Review, 13 June 1948, p. 16.
    Booklist, 1 June 1948, p. 337.
    Boyle, F. A. Library Journal, 1 May 1948, p. 709.
    Butcher, Philip. Opportunity 26 (Summer 1948): 114.
    Cadman, Florence. Commonweal, 25 June 1948, p. 264.
    Kirkus, 15 March 1948, p. 149.
    Krim, Seymour. New York Times, 16 May 1948, p. 5.

Moon, Henry Lee. Crisis 55 (October 1948): 308.
New Yorker, 15 May 1948, p. 122.
Thompson, E. B. Chicago Sun Book Week, 20 June 1948, p.
    8x.

WEST, John B.

Novels

Bullets Are My Business. New York: New American Library,
    1960.
Cobra Venom. New York: New American Library, 1960.
Death on the Rocks. New York: New American Library, 1961.
An Eye for an Eye. New York: New American Library, 1959.
Never Kill a Cop. New York: New American Library, 1961.
A Taste for Blood. New York: New American Library, 1960.

WHITE, Edgar

Short Fiction

"Loimos." In King, Black Short Story Anthology.
"Novel." Yardbird Reader 1 (1972): 75-76.
"Sursum Corda (Lift Up Your Hearts)." In Coombs, What We Must
    See.

WHITE, Thomas J.

Novel

To Hell and Back at Sixteen. New York: Carlton, 1970.

WHITE, Wallace

Short Fiction

"Kiss the Girls for Me." In Coombs, What We Must See.

WHITE, Walter Francis

Novels

The Fire in the Flint. New York: Knopf, 1924; New York: Negro
    Universities Press, 1969.
Flight. New York: Knopf, 1926; New York: Negro Universities
    Press, 1969.

Biography and Criticism

Bardolph, Richard. The Negro Vanguard. New York: Rinehart, 1959.

Bone, Robert A. The Negro Novel in America. New Haven: Yale University Press, 1966.

Bontemps, Arna. The Harlem Renaissance Remembered. New York: Dodd, Mead, 1972.

Brawley, Benjamin. The Negro Genius. New York: Dodd, Mead, 1940.

_____. The Negro in Literature and Art. New York: Duffield, 1930.

Brown, Martha Hursey. "Images of Black Women: Family Roles in Harlem Renaissance Literature." D.A. Dissertation, Carnegie-Mellon University, 1976.

Cannon, Poppy. A Gentle Knight, My Husband Walter White. New York: Rinehart, 1956.

Davis, Arthur P. From the Dark Tower: Afro-American Writers 1900-1960. Washington, D.C.: Howard University Press, 1974.

Hart, Robert C. "Black-White Literary Relations in the Harlem Renaissance." American Literature 44 (January 1973): 612-628.

Hughes, Carl M. The Negro Novelist 1940-1950. New York: Citadel Press, 1953.

"Life Story of Walter White." Our World 10 (January 1957): 48-52.

Lomax, Michael A. "Fantasies of Affirmation: The 1920 Novel of Negro Life." CLA Journal 16 (December 1972): 232-246.

Mays, Benjamin E. The Negro's God as Reflected in His Literature. New York: Negro Universities Press, 1969.

Perry, Margaret. Silence to the Drums: A Survey of the Literature of the Harlem Renaissance. Contributions in Afro-American and African Studies, no. 18. Westport, Conn.: Greenwood Press, 1976.

Ramsey, Priscilla. "A Study of Black Identity in 'Passing' Novels of the Nineteenth and Early Twentieth Centuries." Studies in Black Literature 7 (Winter 1976): 1-7.

Richardson, Ben A. Great American Negroes. New York: T. Y. Crowell, 1945.

Robinson, Anna T. "Race Consciousness and Survival Techniques Depicted in Harlem Renaissance Fiction." Ph.D. Dissertation, Pennsylvania State University, 1973.

Rosenblatt, Roger. Black Fiction. Cambridge: Harvard University Press, 1974.

Rush, Theressa Gunnels, Carol Fairbanks Myers, and Esther Spring Arata. Black American Writers Past and Present. Metuchen, N.J.: Scarecrow Press, 1975.

Schraufnagel, Noel. From Apology to Protest: The Black American Novel. DeLand, Fla.: Everett/Edwards, 1973.

Scruggs, Charles. "'All Dressed Up But No Place to Go': The Black Writer and His Audience During the Harlem Renaissance." American Literature 48 (January 1977): 543-563.

Singh, Amritjit. "The Novels of the Harlem Renaissance: A Thematic Study." Ph.D. Dissertation, New York University, 1973.

_____ . The Novels of the Harlem Renaissance: Twelve Black
Writers, 1923-1933. University Park: Pennsylvania State Uni-
versity Press, 1976.
Waldron, Edward Elvis. "Walter White and the Harlem Renais-
sance." Ph.D. Dissertation, Arizona State University, 1975.
"Walter White." Crisis 62 (April 1955): 227-229.
"Walter White." Opportunity 3 (February 1925): 58; 15 (July
1937): 219.
"Walter White Funeral." Crisis 62 (April 1955): 229-232.
Youman, Mary Mabel. "The Other Side of Harlem: The Middle-
Class Novel and the New Negro Renaissance." Ph.D. Disserta-
tion, University of Kentucky, 1976.
Young, James O. Black Writers of the Thirties. Baton Rouge:
Louisiana State University Press, 1973.

Reviews

Fire in the Flint
Bercovici, Konrad. Nation, 8 October 1924, p. 386.
Bookman 60 (November 1924): 342.
Boston Transcript, 17 December 1924, p. 5.
Brickell, Herschel. Literary Review, 1 November 1924, p. 14.
Du Bois, W. E. B. Crisis 29 (1924): 25.
Independent, 27 September 1924, p. 202.
Johnson, Charles S. Opportunity 2 (November 1924): 344-345.
Kirchwey, Freda. New York Tribune, 28 September 1924, p. 5.
New York Times Book Review, 14 September 1924, p. 9.
Pangborn, H. L. Literary Digest International Book Review
(November 1924): 850.
Saturday Review of Literature (1924): 91.
Survey, 1 November 1924, p. 160.
Flight
Bell, Lisle. Nation, 28 July 1926, p. 89.
Booklist 23 (November 1926): 85.
Boston Transcript, 29 May 1926, p. 4.
Cleveland Open Shelf (November 1926): 123.
Crawford, J. W. Literary Digest International Book Review
(July 1926): 519.
Gruening, Ernest. Saturday Review of Literature, 10 July 1926,
p. 918.
Horne, Frank. Opportunity 4 (July 1926): 227. See also Nella
Larsen Imes' letter on Horne review, 4 (September 1926):
295; Horne reply 4 (October 1926): 326; W. White letter on
Horne review 4 (October 1926): 326.
Independent, 8 May 1926, p. 555.
New Republic, 1 September 1926, p. 53.
New York Times Book Review, 11 April 1926, p. 9.
Outlook, 4 August 1926, p. 479.
Survey, 1 September 1926, p. 695.
Times Literary Supplement, 9 December 1926, p. 908.
Van Vechten, Carl. Books, 11 April 1926, p. 3.
World Tomorrow 9 (April 1926): 133.
Yust, Walter. Literary Review, 24 April 1926, p. 4.

WIDEMAN, John E.

Novels

A Glance Away. New York: Harcourt, Brace, World, 1967;
    Chatham, N.J.: Chatham Bookseller, 1975.
Hurry Home. New York: Harcourt, Brace, World, 1970.
The Lynchers. New York: Harcourt, Brace, World, 1973; New
    York: Dell, 1974.

Biography and Criticism

Frazier, Kermit. "The Novels of John Wideman: An Analysis."
    Black World 24 (June 1975): 18-38.
Journal of Negro History 48 (January 1963): 66.
Klinkowitz, Jerome. Literary Disruptions: The Making of a Post-
    Contemporary American Fiction. Urbana: University of Illinois
    Press, 1975.
Knight, H. "Rhodes Scholar Family." Negro Digest 12 (May 1963):
    11-16.
O'Brien, John. Interviews with Black Writers. New York: Live-
    right, 1973.
Rush, Theressa Gunnels, Carol Fairbanks Myers, and Esther Spring
    Arata. Black American Writers Past and Present. Metuchen,
    N.J.: Scarecrow Press, 1975.

Reviews

A Glance Away
    Booklist, 1 January 1968, p. 533.
    Bouise, O. A. Best Sellers, 15 September 1967, p. 231.
    Caldwell, S. R. Saturday Review of Literature, 21 October
        1967, p. 36.
    Ebert, Roger. American Scholar 36 (Autumn 1967): 682.
    Griffin, L. W. Library Journal 92 (July 1967): 2608.
    Kirkus, 15 June 1967, p. 713.
    Publishers' Weekly, 19 June 1967, p. 80.
    Roskolenko, Harry. New York Times Book Review, 10 Septem-
        ber 1967, p. 56.
    Time, 8 September 1967, p. D12.
Hurry Home
    Goodman, J. New York Times Book Review, 19 April 1970,
        p. 41.
    Leonard, J. New York Times Book Review, 2 April 1970, p.
        37.
    Library Journal, 15 March 1970, p. 1050.
    Saturday Review of Literature, 2 May 1970, p. 40.
The Lynchers
    Best Sellers, 1 July 1974, p. 178.
    Book World, 22 April 1973, p. 15.
    Brickner, R. P. New York Times Book Review, 29 April
        1973, p. 25.
    Broyard, A. New York Times, 15 May 1973, p. 43.

Contemporary Review 15 (Autumn 1974): 539.
Fessler, P. L. Library Journal, 15 March 1973, p. 888.
Flora, J. M. Michigan Quarterly Review 14 (Winter 1975):
101.
Levin, M. New York Times Book Review, 17 March 1974,
p. 38.
New York Times Book Review, 10 June 1973, p. 40; 2 Decem-
ber 1973, p. 76.
Prescott, P. S. Newsweek, 7 May 1973, p. 99.
Ryan, F. L. Best Sellers, 1 June 1973, p. 106.
Walker, Jim. Black Creation 5 (Fall 1973): 42-43.

WIGGINS, Walter, Jr.

Novel

Dreams in Reality of the Undersea Craft. New York: Pageant,
1954.

WILKINSON, Brenda Scott

Short Fiction

"Rosa Lee Loves Bennie." In Sanchez, We Be Word Sorcerers.

Biography and Criticism

Rush, Theressa Gunnels, Carol Fairbanks Myers, and Esther Spring
Arata. Black American Writers Past and Present. Metuchen,
N.J.: Scarecrow Press, 1975.

WILLIAMS, Chancellor

Novels

Have You Been to the River? New York: Exposition, 1952.
The Raven. Philadelphia: Dorrance, 1943.

Reviews

The Raven
Christian Century, 5 January 1944, p. 20.
Wallace, Margaret. New York Times Book Review, 9 January
1944, p. 26.

WILLIAMS, Dennis A.

Novel

[With Spero Pines.] Them That's Not. New York: Emerson Hall, 1973

Short Fiction

"Sunset Boogie." Black Scholar 8 (March 1977): 208.

WILLIAMS, Edward G.

Novel

Not Like Niggers. New York: St. Martin's Press, 1969.

WILLIAMS, John Alfred

Novels

The Angry Ones. New York: Ace, 1960; New York: Pocket Books, 1970. (See also One for New York.)

Captain Blackman: A Novel. Garden City, N.Y.: Doubleday, 1972.

The Junior Bachelor Society. Garden City, N.Y.: Doubleday, 1976; excerpt in Yardbird Reader 5 (1976): 49-63.

The Man Who Cried I Am. Boston: Little, Brown, 1967; New York: New American Library, 1972; excerpts in Davis and Redding, Cavalcade; Reed, 19 Necromancers from Now.

Mothersill and the Foxes. Garden City, N.Y.: Doubleday, 1975.

Night Song. New York: Farrar, Straus & Cudahy, 1961; New York: Pocket Books, 1970; Chatham, N.J.: Chatham Bookseller, 1975; excerpts in Ford, Black Insights.

One for New York: Chatham, N.J.: Chatham Bookseller, 1975. (Originally published as The Angry Ones, 1960.)

Sissie. New York: Farrar, Straus & Cudahy, 1963; Chatham, N.J.: Chatham Bookseller, 1975.

Sons of Darkness, Sons of Light: A Novel of Some Probability. Boston: Little, Brown, 1969; New York: Pocket Books, 1970.

Short Fiction

"Father and Son." Negro Digest 12 (January 1963): 59-60.

"The Figure Eight." In Adoff, Brothers and Sisters; Haupt, Man in the Fictional Mode.

"A Good Season." In King, Black Short Story Anthology.

"Joey's Sled." Negro Digest 12 (January 1963): 58-59.

"Navy Black (A Novel in Progress)." In Williams, Beyond the Angry Black; Mellard, Four Modes.

"Son in the A⸍ ᵗʲ ᵒon." In Casty, The Shape of Fiction; Cowan, et al., Three for Show; Emanuel and Gross, Dark Symphony; Gulassa, The Fact of Fiction; Hills and Hills, How We Live; Howard and Tracz, The Age of Anxiety; Margolies, A Native Sons Reader; Morse, The Choices of Fiction; Patterson, An Introduction to Black Literature in America.

Biography and Criticism

Beauford, Fred. "John Williams: Agent Provocateur." Black

Creation 2 (Summer 1971): 4-6.
Bryant, Jerry H. "John A. Williams: The Political Use of the Novel." Critique 16 no. 3 (1975): 81-100.
Burke, William Martin. "Modern Black Fiction and the Literature of Oppression." Ph. D. Dissertation, University of Oregon, 1971.
_____. "The Resistance of John A. Williams: The Man Who Cried I Am." Critique 15 no. 3 (1974): 5-14.
Cash, Earl A. "The Evolution of a Black Writer: John A. Williams." Ph. D. Dissertation, University of New Mexico, 1972.
_____. John A. Williams: The Evolution of a Black Writer. New York: Third Press, 1975.
Collier, Eugenia. "A Journey into Our Tragic Past or Our Hopeful Future?" Third Press Review 1 (September/October 1975): 50-51. (Review of Cash's John A. Williams: The Evolution of a Black Writer.)
Contemporary Authors, 53/56.
Emerson, O. B. "Cultural Nationalism in Afro-American Literature." In The Cry of Home. Edited by H. Ernest Lewald. Knoxville: University of Tennessee Press, 1972, pp. 211-244.
Fleming, Robert E. "The Nightmare Level of The Man Who Cried I Am." Contemporary Literature 14 (Spring 1973): 186-196.
Gayle, Addison, Jr. In Contemporary Novelists. Edited by James Vinson. New York: St. Martin's Press, 1976.
_____. The Way of the New World: The Black Novel in America. Garden City, N.Y.: Anchor Press/Doubleday, 1975.
Henderson, David. "The Man Who Cried I Am: A Critique." In Black Expression, pp. 365-371. Edited by Addison Gayle, Jr. New York: Weybright & Talley, 1969.
Klotman, Phyllis Rauch. Another Man Gone: The Black Runner in Contemporary Afro-American Literature. Port Washington, N.Y.: Kennikat Press, 1977.
_____. "Examination of the Black Confidence Man in Two Black Novels: The Man Who Cried I Am and dem." American Literature 44 (January 1973): 596-611.
Major, Clarence. The Dark and Feeling. New York: Third Press, 1974.
O'Brien, John. "Art of John A. Williams." American Scholar 42 (Summer 1973): 489-494.
_____. Interviews with Black Writers. New York: Liveright, 1973.
_____. "Seeking a Humanist Level: Interview with John A. Williams." Arts in Society 10 (Spring-Summer 1973): 94-99.
Peavy, Charles D. "Four Revolutionary Novels, 1899-1969." Journal of Black Studies 1 (December 1970): 219-223.
Pfeiffer, John. "Black American Speculative Literature: A Checklist." Extrapolation 17 (December 1975): 35-43.
Rosenblatt, Roger. Black Fiction. Cambridge: Harvard University Press, 1974.
Schraufnagel, Noel. From Apology to Protest: The Black American Novel. DeLand, Fla.: Everett/Edwards, 1973.
Seyersted, Per. "A Survey of Trends and Figures in Afro-Ameri-

can Fiction. " American Studies in Scandinavia 6, nos. 1-2 (1973-1974): 67-86.
Skerrett, Joseph T. , Jr.   "Interview with John A. Williams." Black World 25 (January 1976): 58-67, 93-97.
Smith, Anneliese H.   "A Pain in the Ass: Metaphor in John A. Williams' The Man Who Cried I Am." Studies in Black Literature 3 (Autumn 1972): 25-27.
Walcott, Ronald.   "The Early Fiction of John A. Williams." CLA Journal 16 (December 1972): 198-213.
_____.   "The Man Who Cried I Am: Crying in the Dark." Studies in Black Literature 3 (Spring 1972): 24-32.
Whitlow, Roger. Black American Literature: A Critical History. Chicago: Nelson Hall, 1973.

Reviews

Captain Blackman: A Novel
Booklist, 1 September 1972, p. 31.
Choice 9 (December 1972): 1295.
Davis, George. New York Times Book Review, 21 May 1972, p. 4.
Fleischer, Leonard. Saturday Review-Science, 13 May 1972, p. 85.
Kiniery, Paul. Best Sellers, 15 July 1972, p. 198.
Kirkus, 15 March 1972, p. 352.
Mano, D. K. National Review, 1 September 1972, p. 961.
Moon, Eric. Library Journal, 1 May 1972, p. 1742.
Negro History Bulletin 35 (November 1972): 167.
New York Times Book Review, 4 June 1972, p. 22; 3 December 1972, p. 74.
O'Connell, S. Massachusetts Review 14 (Winter 1973): 190.
Publishers' Weekly, 28 February 1972, p. 71.
Sale, Roger. New York Review of Books, 5 October 1972, p. 34.
The Junior Bachelor Society
Ebony 31 (July 1976): 29.
Gold, Ivan. New York Times Book Review, 11 July 1976, p. 32.
Harris, Jessica. Essence 7 (August 1976): 39.
Kirkus, 15 March 1976, p. 348.
Marr, V. W. Library Journal, 15 June 1976, p. 1450.
Muller, Gil. Nation, 18 September 1976, p. 249.
New Yorker, 16 August 1976, p. 90.
Publishers' Weekly, 22 March 1976, p. 44.
The Man Who Cried I Am: A Novel
Booklist, 15 December 1967, p. 491.
Byatt, A. S. New Statesman, 29 March 1968, p. 421.
Choice 5 (September 1968): 780.
Coleman, J. Observer, 31 March 1968, p. 29.
Corodimas, Peter. Best Sellers, 1 November 1967, p. 310.
Fleming, R. E. Contemporary Literature 14 (Spring 1973): 186.

Fleming, T. J. New York Times Book Review, 29 October 1967, p. 66.

Fremont-Smith, E. New York Times, 13 November 1967, p. 45.

Hamilton, I. Listener, 4 April 1968, p. 448.

Joyce, B. Phylon 29 (Winter 1968): 410.

Kersch, Gerald. Saturday Review of Literature, 28 October 1967, p. 34.

Kirkus, 15 August 1967, p. 992.

Lee, D. L. Negro Digest 17 (March 1968): 51.

Leonard, J. New York Times Book Review, 29 October 1967, p. 66.

Maloff, Saul. Newsweek, 27 November 1967, p. 100.

Moon, Eric. Library Journal, 15 September 1967, p. 3058.

Observer, 25 April 1971, p. 27.

O'Connell, S. Nation, 29 January 1968, p. 154.

Publishers' Weekly, 4 September 1967, p. 50.

Richards, C. Books and Bookmen 13 (June 1968): 31.

Szanto, G. H. Catholic World 207 (April 1968): 44.

Times Literary Supplement, 11 April 1968, p. 365.

Mothersill and the Foxes

Bode, Carl. Baltimore Sun, 2 March 1975; Newsbank--Literature (March-April 1975): Card 30: G12.

Kirkus, 1 November 1975, p. 1175.

Lampley, James T. Black Scholar 7 (January-February 1976): 43-44.

Mason, B. J. Chicago Sun-Times, 2 February 1975; Newsbank--Literature (January-February 1975): Card 16: A9-10.

New Outlook, 17 August 1976, p. 17.

Perkins, Huel D. Black World 24 (June 1975): 89-91.

Prairie Schooner 50 (Spring 1976): 87.

Publishers' Weekly, 11 November 1974, p. 87.

Night Song

Barrett, William. Atlantic 209 (January 1962): 98.

Gehman, Richard. Chicago Sunday Tribune, 12 November 1961, p. 8.

Goodhart, Eugene. Critique 5 (Winter 1962-1963): 126.

Healy, G. M. Springfield Republican, 24 December 1961, p. 4D.

Hentoff, Nat. Commonweal, 3 November 1961, p. 155.

Kirkus, 15 August 1961, p. 748.

Moon, Eric. Library Journal, 1 November 1961, p. 3807.

Redding, Saunders. New York Herald Tribune Books, 26 November 1961, p. 14.

Rogers, W. G. Saturday Review, 16 December 1961, p. 21.

San Francisco Chronicle, 5 November 1961, p. 29.

Southern, Terry. Nation, 17 November 1962, p. 332.

Spectator, 20 April 1962, p. 518.

Trubman, Robert. New Statesman, 10 August 1962, p. 178.

West, Richard. Guardian, 4 May 1962, p. 9.

Sissie

Barrett, William. Atlantic 211 (February 1963): 133.

Best Sellers, 1 February 1963, p. 410.

Boroff, David. Saturday Review, 30 March 1963, p. 49.

Buckler, Ernest. New York Times Book Review, 2 June 1963, p. 21.

Galloway, D. D. Critique 6 (Winter 1963-1964): 150.

Goram, Lester. Chicago Sunday Tribune Magazine of Books, 31 March 1963, p. 3.

Grumbach, Doris. Critic 21 (April 1963): 83.

Hentoff, Nat. New York Herald Tribune Books, 14 April 1963, p. 8.

Moon, Eric. Library Journal, 1 February 1963, p. 578.

Pickrel, Paul. Harper 226 (April 1963): 94.

Thompson, John. New York Review of Books 1 (1963): 32.

Winslow, H. F. Crisis 70 (May 1963): 313.

Sons of Darkness, Sons of Light; a Novel of Some Probability

Buckmaster, Henrietta. Christian Science Monitor, 7 August 1969, p. 7.

Choice 7 (March 1970): 84.

Fleming, T. J. New York Times Book Review, 29 June 1969, p. 4.

Hood, S. Listener, 16 April 1970, p. 519.

Howe, Irving. Harper's Magazine 239 (December 1969): 135.

Kuehl, L. Commonweal, 13 February 1970, p. 536.

Leonard, J. New York Times Book Review, 1 July 1969, p. 43.

Long, R. E. Saturday Review of Literature, 4 October 1969, p. 48.

Moon, Eric. Library Journal, 15 June 1969, p. 2455.

O'Hara, T. Best Sellers, 1 July 1969, p. 146.

Sheed, Wilfred. Book World, 29 June 1969, p. 5.

Time, 11 July 1969, p. 80.

Times Literary Supplement, 7 May 1970, p. 499.

WILLIAMS, Lorna V.

Short Fiction

"A Little Learning." Studies in Black Literature 6 (Summer 1975): 11-13.

WILLIAMS, M.

Short Fiction

"The Lies." Essence 7 (November 1976): 51.

WILLIAMS, S. A.

Short Fiction

"Tell Martha Not to Moan." Massachusetts Review 9 (Summer 1968): 443-458; also in Exum, Keeping the Faith.

WILLIAMS-FORDE, Billy

Fiction

Requiem for a Black American Capitalist. New York: Troisieme
   Canadian, 1975.

WILLIAMSON, Harvey M.

Short Fiction

"The Old Woman." Crisis 41 (November 1934): 324-325.

Biography and Criticism

Rush, Theressa Gunnels, Carol Fairbanks Myers, and Esther Spring
   Arata. Black American Writers Past and Present. Metuchen,
   N.J.: Scarecrow Press, 1975.

WILSON, Carl Thomas David

Novel

The Half Caste. Ilfracombe, England: A. H. Stockwell, 1964.

WILSON, Mrs. H. E.

Fiction

Our Nig; or, Sketches from the Life of a Free Black, in a Two-
   Story White House, North. Showing that Slavery's Shadows
   Fall Even There. Boston: G. C. Rand & Avery, 1859.

WILSON, Pat

Novel

The Sign of Keola. New York: Carlton, 1961.

WILSON, Welford

Short Fiction

"Poh' Inch Worm." Opportunity 20 (January 1942): 274-276.
"Solidarity Forever." Opportunity 20 (July 1942): 208-210; (August
   1942): 242-244.

WINSTON, Harry

Short Fiction

"Greater Love." In Ford and Faggett, Best Short Stories by Afro-American Writers.
"Life Begins at Forty." In Ford and Faggett, Best Short Stories by Afro-American Writers.

WOLF, Shirley

Short Fiction

"Terror." Essence 7 (August 1976): 14.

WOOBY, Philip

Novel

Nude to the Meaning of Tomorrow: A Novel of a Lonely Search. New York: Exposition, 1959.

WOOD, Debbie

Short Fiction

"Sunday School." Essence 7 (November 1976): 54, 150, 152.

WOOD, Lillian E.

Novel

Let My People Go. Philadelphia: A. M. E. Book Concern, 1922.

WOOD, Odella Phelps

Novel

High Ground. New York: Exposition, 1945.

Biography and Criticism

Hughes, Carl M. The Negro Novelist 1940-1950. New York: Citadel Press, 1953.

Review

High Ground
    Crisis 53 (November 1946): 345-346.

WOODS, Barbara

Short Fiction

"The Final Supper." In Mayfield, Ten Times Black.

WOODS, William B.

Novel

Lancaster Triple Thousand: A Novel of Suspense. New York: Ex-
    position, 1956.

WRIGHT, Charles Stevenson

Novels

The Messenger. New York: Farrar, Straus, 1963; New York:
    Manor Books, 1974.
The Wig: A Mirror Image. New York: Farrar, Straus & Giroux,
    1966; excerpt in Reed, 19 Necromancers from Now.

Short Fiction

"The Act of Surrender." Yardbird Reader 2 (1973): 173-177.
"A New Day." In Hughes, The Best Short Stories by Negro Writers;
    Patterson, An Introduction to Black Literature in America.
"Sonny and the Sailor." Negro Digest 17 (August 1968): 63-67.

Biography and Criticism

Campenni, Frank. In Contemporary Novelists. Edited by James
    Vinson. New York: St. Martin's Press, 1976.
Contemporary Authors, 11/12R.
Foster, F. S. "Charles Wright: Black, Black Humorist." CLA
    Journal 15 (September 1973): 44-53.
Klinkowitz, Jerome. "The New Black Writer and the Old Black
    Art." Fiction International 1 (1973): 123-127.
Major, Clarence. "Traditional and Presence: Experimental Fiction
    by Black American Writers." American Poetry Review 5 (May/
    June 1976): 33-34.
O'Brien, John. Interviews with Black Writers. New York: Live-
    right, 1973.
Rush, Theressa Gunnels, Carol Fairbanks Myers, and Esther Spring
    Arata. Black American Writers Past and Present. Metuchen,
    N.J.: Scarecrow Press, 1975.
Schraufnagel, Noel. From Apology to Protest: The Black Ameri-
    can Novel. DeLand, Fla.: Everett/Edwards, 1973.
Schultz, Max F. Black Humor Fiction of the Sixties: A Pluralistic
    Definition of Man and His World. Athens: Ohio University
    Press, 1973.

Sedlack, Robert P. "Jousting with Rats: Charles Wright's The
   Wig." Satire Newsletter 7 (Fall 1969): 37-39.

Reviews

The Messenger
   Adams, Robert. Esquire 60 (October 1963): 26.
   Balliett, Whitney. New Yorker, 2 November 1963, p. 206.
   Barrett, William. Atlantic 212 (August 1963): 121.
   Brooke-Rose, C. Spectator, 20 March 1964, p. 394.
   Byam, Milton. Library Journal 88 (July 1963): 2730.
   Curley, Thomas. Commonweal, 20 September 1963, p. 566.
   Grumbach, Doris. Critic 22 (August 1963): 83.
   Hamilton, A. Books and Bookmen 10 (July 1965): 48.
   Hentoff, Nat. Reporter, 4 July 1963, p. 40.
   Jackson, K. G. Harper 227 (September 1963) p. 115.
   Kiely, Robert. Nation, 29 June 1963, p. 549.
   Kluger, Richard. New York Herald Tribune Books, 9 June
      1963, p. 7.
   Meixner, J. A. Kenyon Review 25 (Autumn 1963): 729.
   Rich, Alan. New York Times, 2 July 1963, p. 27.
   Schikel, Richard. Show 3 (August 1963): 38.
   Taubman, R. New Statesman, 24 April 1964, p. 647.
The Wig: A Mirror Image
   Baker, R. Books and Bookmen 12 (May 1967): 34.
   Byam, Milton. Library Journal, 15 February 1966, p. 968.
   Commonweal, 29 April 1966, p. 182.
   Davis, D. M. National Observer, 4 April 1966, p. 19.
   Galloway, D. Southern Review 4 (Summer 1968): 850.
   Kirkus, 15 December 1965, p. 1241.
   Knickerbocker, C. New York Times, 5 March 1966, p. 25.
   Morgan, E. New Statesman, 3 February 1967, p. 156.
   Mudrick, Marion. Hudson Review 19 (Summer 1966): 305.
   Navasky, V. S. Books Today, 27 February 1966, p. 7.
   _____. New York Times Book Review, 27 February 1966,
      p. 4.
   Negro Digest 15 (August 1966): 81.
   Shuttleworth, M. Punch, 15 February 1967, p. 246.
   Teachout, P. R. Nation, 18 April 1966, p. 467.
   Times Literary Supplement, 9 March 1967, p. 199.
   Wolff, G. A. Book Week, 27 March 1966, p. 3.

WRIGHT, Richard

Novels

"Islands of Hallucinations." Unpublished. Excerpt in Hill, Soon,
   One Morning.
Lawd Today. New York: Walker, 1963; New York: Hearst Corp.,
   1963.
The Long Dream. Garden City, N.Y.: Doubleday, 1958; London:
   Angus & Robertson, 1960; Chatham, N.J.: Chatham Bookseller,

1969; New York: Ace Books, n.d.
Native Son. New York: Harper, 1940, 1957, 1966, 1969; New York: Modern Library, 1942; New York: New American Library, 1961, 1964.
The Outsider. New York: Harper, 1953; New York: Harper & Row, 1969.
Savage Holiday. New York: Avon, 1954; Universal, 1965; Chatham, N.J.: Chatham Bookseller, 1975.

Short Fiction

(Collections):
> Eight Men. Cleveland: World, 1961; New York: Avon, 1961; New York: Pyramid.
> Uncle Tom's Children: Four Novellas. New York: Harper, 1938; New York: Harper & Row, 1965, 1969; New York: New American Library, 1963. (Also published as Uncle Tom's Children: Five Long Stories. New York: Harper, 1940.)

"Almos' a Man." Harper's Bazaar 74 (January 1940): 40-41; also in Best American Short Stories, 1941; Cerf, Modern American Short Stories; Grayson, Half-a-Hundred; Kielty, Treasury of Short Stories; O. Henry Memorial Prize Stories of 1940; Wright, Eight Men as "The Man Who Was Almost a Man."
"Big, Black Good Man." In Wright, Eight Men; Foley and Burnett, Best American Short Stories, 1958.
"Big Boy Leaves Home." In Kreymborg, et al., The New Caravan; Wright, Uncle Tom's Children. Margolies, A Native Sons Reader; Weimer, Modern American Classics.
"Bright and Morning Star." New Masses, 10 May 1938, pp. 97-99, 116-124; also in Best Short Stories of 1939; Foley and Rothberg, U.S. Stories; Wright, Uncle Tom's Children, 1940 ed.
"Down by the Riverside." In Kern and Griggs, This America; Wright, Uncle Tom's Children.
"Fire and Cloud." Story Magazine No. 12 (March 1938): 9-41; also in O. Henry Memorial Prize Stories of 1938; Wright, Uncle Tom's Children.
"Long Black Song." In Wright, Uncle Tom's Children.
"Man, God Ain't Like That." In Wright, Eight Men.
"Man of All Works." In Wright, Eight Men.
"The Man Who Killed a Shadow." Zero (Paris) 1 (Spring 1949): 45-53; also in Wright, Eight Men.
"The Man Who Lived Underground." Accent 2 (Spring 1942): 170-176.
"The Man Who Lived Underground." In Seaver, Cross Section. (Different version from story published in Accent.) Also in Wright, Eight Men.
"The Man Who Saw the Flood." In Gibson and Anselment, Black and White; Wright, Eight Men. (See also "Silt.")
"The Man Who Was Almost a Man." See "Almos' a Man."
"The Man Who Went to Chicago." In Wright, Eight Men.
"Silt." New Masses, 24 August 1937, pp. 19-20; also in Wright, Eight Men as "The Man Who Saw the Flood."

"Superstition." Abbot's Monthly Magazine No. 2 (April 1931): 45-
47, 64-66, 72-73.
"What You Don't Know Won't Hurt You." In Strode, Social Insight
Through Short Stories.

Biography and Criticism

(Collections):
 Abcarian, Richard, ed. Richard Wright's Native Son: A
  Critical Handbook. Belmont, Calif.: Wadsworth, 1970.
 Baker, Houston A., Jr., ed. Twentieth Century Interpretations
  of Native Son. Englewood Cliffs, N.J.: Prentice-Hall,
  1973.
 Gibson, Donald B., ed. Five Black Writers: Essays on Wright,
  Ellison, Baldwin, Hughes and Leroi Jones. New York:
  York University Press, 1970.
 Hemenway, Robert, ed. The Black Novelist. Columbus:
  Charles E. Merrill, 1970.
 Singh, Raman K. and Peter Fellowes, eds. Black Literature
  in America. New York: T. Y. Crowell, 1970.
Algren, Nelson. "Remembering Richard Wright." Nation 28
January 1961, p. 85.
Amis, Lola J. "Richard Wright's Native Son: Notes." Negro
American Literature Forum 8 (1974): 240-243.
Ashour, Radwa M. "The Search for a Black Poetics: A Study of
Afro-American Critical Writings." Ph.D. Dissertation, Univer-
sity of Massachusetts, 1975.
Avery, Evelyn Gross. "Rebels and Victims: The Fiction of Richard
Wright and Bernard Malamud." Ph.D. Dissertation, University
of Oregon, 1976.
Bakish, David. Richard Wright. New York: Ungar, 1973.
Baldwin, James. "Everybody's Protest Novel." Partisan Review
16 (June 1949): 578-585; also in Baldwin's Notes of a Native
Son. Boston: Beacon Press, 1955; Hemenway, The Black
Novelist.
_____. "Many Thousand Gone." Partisan Review 18 (November-
December 1951): 665-680; also in Baldwin's Notes of a Native
Son. Boston: Beacon Press, 1955; Abcarian, Richard Wright's
"Native Son"; Gibson, Five Black Writers.
_____. "Princes and Powers." Encounter 8 (January 1957):
52-60; also in Baldwin's Nobody Knows My Name. New York:
Dial, 1961.
_____. "Richard Wright." Encounter 16 (April 1961): 58-60;
also in Baldwin's Nobody Knows My Name. New York: Dial,
1961 (entitled "The Exile").
_____. "The Survival of Richard Wright." Reporter, 16 May
1961, pp. 52-55; also in Baldwin's Nobody Knows My Name.
New York: Dial, 1961 (entitled "Eight Men").
Baldwin, Richard E. "The Creative Vision of Native Son." Massa-
chusetts Review 14 (Spring 1973): 378-390.
Baron, Dennis E. "The Syntax of Perception in Richard Wright's
Native Son." Language and Style 9 (Winter 1976): 17-18.

Bayliss, John F. "Native Son: Protest or Psychological Study?" Negro American Literature Forum 1 (Fall 1967): 5-6.

Beach, Joseph Warren. "The Dilemma of the Black Man in a White World." New York Times, 2 December 1945, p. 7.

de Beauvoir, Simone. "Impressions of Richard Wright: An Interview with Simone de Beauvoir." Studies in Black Literature 1 (Autumn 1970): 3-5.

Beja, Morris. "It Must Be Important: Negroes in Contemporary American Fiction." Antioch Review 24 (Fall 1964): 323-336.

Bell, Bernard W. The Folk Roots of Contemporary Afro-American Poetry. Detroit: Broadside Press, 1974.

Benson, Brian Joseph. "The Short Fiction of Richard Wright." Ph.D. Dissertation, University of South Carolina, 1972.

Berry, Faith. "On Richard Wright in Exile: Portrait of a Man as Outsider." Negro Digest 18 (December 1968): 27-37.

Billingsley, Ronald G. "The Burden of the Hero in Modern Afro-American Fiction." Black World 25 (December 1975): 38-45; 66-73.

_____. "Forging New Directions: The Burden of the Hero in Modern Afro-American Literature." Obsidian 1 (Winter 1975): 5-21. (Same as above.)

Black Authors. Old Greenwich, Conn.: Listening Library, n.d. (Filmstrip.)

"Black Boy." Life, 4 June 1945, pp. 87-93.

Blake, Nelson Manfred. Novelists' America: Fiction as History, 1910-1940. Syracuse: Syracuse University Press, 1969.

Bland, Edward. "Social Forces Shaping the Negro Novel." Negro Quarterly 1 (Fall 1942): 241-248.

Bolton, H. Philip. "The Role of Paranoia in Richard Wright's Native Son." Kansas Quarterly 7 (Summer 1975): 111-124.

Bone, Robert A. The Negro Novel in America. New Haven: Yale University Press, 1966; also in Abcarian, Richard Wright's "Native Son."

_____. Richard Wright. Minneapolis: University of Minnesota Press, 1969.

Brignano, Russell Carl. Richard Wright: An Introduction to the Man and His Works. Pittsburgh: University of Pittsburgh Press, 1970.

Britt, David. "Native Son: Watershed of Negro Protest Literature." Negro American Literature Forum 1 (Fall 1967): 4-5.

Brivic, Sheldon. "Conflict of Values: Richard Wright's Native Son." Novel 7 (Spring 1974): 231-245.

Brown, Cecil M. "Richard Wright: Complexes and Black Writing Today." Negro Digest 18 (December 1968): 78-82; also in Abcarian, Richard Wright's "Native Son."

Brown, Deming Bronson. Soviet Attitudes Toward American Writing. Princeton: Princeton University Press, 1962.

Brown, Lloyd W. "Black Entitles: Names as Symbols in Afro-American Literature." Studies in Black Literature 1 (Spring 1970): 16-44.

_____. "Stereotypes in Black and White: The Nature of Perception in Wright's Native Son." Black Academy Review 1 (Fall 1970): 35-44.

Brown, Sterling A. "The Literary Scene, Chronicle and Comment."
  Opportunity 16 (April 1938): 120-121.
Bryant, Jerry H. "Wright, Ellison, Baldwin--Exorcising the De-
  mon." Phylon 37 (June 1976): 174-188.
Burgum, Edwin Berry. "The Art of Richard Wright's Short Sto-
  ries." Quarterly Review of Literature 1 (Spring 1944): 198-
  211; also in Gibson, Five Black Writers.
_____. "The Promise of Democracy in the Fiction of Richard
  Wright." Science and Society 7 (Fall 1943): 338-352; also in
  Abcarian, Richard Wright's "Native Son."
Burke, William Martin. "Modern Black Fiction and the Literature
  of Oppression." Ph.D. Dissertation, University of Oregon,
  1971.
Burns, Ben. "Return of the Native Son." Ebony 7 (December
  1951): 100.
Bush, Joseph Bevans. "The Alienation of Richard Wright: A Native
  Son Remembered." In A Galaxy of Black Writing, pp. 63-66.
  Edited by R. Baird Shuman. Durham, N.C.: Moore Publishing,
  1970.
Cauley, Anne O. "A Definition of Freedom in the Fiction of Richard
  Wright." CLA Journal 19 (March 1976): 327-346.
Cayton, Horace R. "The Curtain." Negro Digest 18 (December
  1968): 11-15.
_____. Long Old Road. New York: Trident Press, 1965.
Charney, Maurice. "James Baldwin's Quarrel with Richard Wright."
  American Quarterly 15 (Spring 1963): 65-75.
Cleaver, Eldridge. Soul on Ice. New York: McGraw-Hill, 1967;
  also in Abcarian, Richard Wright's "Native Son"; Hemenway,
  The Black Novelist.
Cohn, David L. "The Negro Novel: Richard Wright." Atlantic
  Monthly 165 (May 1940): 659-661; also in Abcarian, Richard
  Wright's "Native Son."
Conrad, Earl. "Blues School of Literature." Chicago Defender, 22
  December 1945, p. 11.
Cosgrove, William. "Strategies of Survival: The Gimmick Motif
  in Black Literature." Studies in the Twentieth Century 15
  (Spring 1975): 109-127.
Cowan, Cathryn Osburn. "Black/White Stereotypes in the Fiction of
  Richard Wright, James Baldwin, and Ralph Ellison." Ph.D.
  Dissertation, St. Louis University, 1972.
Creekmore, Hubert. "Social Factors in Native Son." University of
  Kansas City Review 8 (Winter 1941): 136-143.
Cruse, Harold. The Crisis of the Negro Intellectual. New York:
  William Morrow, 1967.
Current Biography, 1940.
Davis, Arthur P. From the Dark Tower: Afro-American Writers
  1900-1960. Washington, D.C.: Howard University Press,
  1974.
_____. "The Outsider as a Novel of Race." Midwest Journal 7
  (Winter 1955-1956): 320-326.
Delpech, Jeanine. "An Interview with Native Son." Crisis 57
  (November 1950): 625-626, 678.
Demarest, David R., Jr. "Richard Wright: The Meaning of Vio-

lence." Negro American Literature Forum 8 (1974): 236-239.
"Discussion of R. Wright's Novel Native Son." Phylon 23 (Fourth
Quarter 1962): 364-368.
Donlan, D. "Cleaver on Baldwin on Wright." Clearing House 48
(April 1974): 508-509.
Eden, Walter Anthony. "A Critical Approach to Autobiography:
Techniques and Themes in Sherwood Anderson, Benedetto Croce,
Jean-Paul Sartre, and Richard Wright." Ph. D. Dissertation,
New York University, 1975.
Eisinger, Chester E. Fiction of the Forties. Chicago: University
of Chicago Press, 1963.
Ellison, Curtis William. "Black Adam: The Adamic Assertion and
the Afro-American Novelist." Ph. D. Dissertation, University
of Minnesota, 1970.
Ellison, Ralph. "A Rejoinder." New Leader, 3 February 1964,
pp. 15-22; reprinted as Part II of "The World and the Jug"
in Ellison's Shadow and Act; also in Gibson, Five Black Writers.
_____. "Richard Wright's Blues." Antioch Review 5 (Summer
1947): 198-211; also in Ellison's Shadow and Act; Addison
Gayle, Jr., Black Expression. New York: Weybright & Talley,
1969.
_____. "The World and the Jug." New Leader, 9 December
1963): 22-26; reprinted as Part I of "The World and the Jug"
in Ellison's Shadow and Act; also in Abcarian, Richard Wright's
"Native Son"; Gibson, Five Black Writers.
Emanuel, James A. "Fever and Feeling: Notes on the Imagery in
Native Son." Negro Digest 18 (December 1968): 16-26; also in
Abcarian, Richard Wright's "Native Son."
Embree, Edwin. 13 Against the Odds. Port Washington, N. Y.:
Kennikat, 1967.
Emerson, O. B. "Cultural Nationalism in Afro-American Litera-
ture." In The Cry of Home, pp. 211-244. Edited by H. Er-
nest Lewald. Knoxville: University of Tennessee Press, 1972.
Evans, Oliver. The Ballad of Carson McCullers: A Biography.
New York: Coward-McCann, 1966.
Fabre, Michel. The Unfinished Quest of Richard Wright. Trans.
Isabel Barzun. New York: William Morrow, 1973.
Fisher, Dorothy Canfield. Introduction to Native Son. New York:
Harper, 1940; also in Abcarian, Richard Wright's "Native Son."
Fontaine, William T. "Toward a Philosophy of the American Negro
Literature." Présence Africaine Nos. 24-25 (February-May
1969): 164-176.
Ford, James W. "The Case of Richard Wright: A Disservice to
the Negro People." Daily Worker, 5 September 1944, p. 6.
Ford, Nick A. "Four Popular Negro Novelists." Phylon 15 (First
Quarter 1954): 29-39.
_____. "The Ordeal of Richard Wright." College English 15
(October 1953): 87-94; also in Gibson, Five Black Writers.
_____. "Richard Wright, a Profile." Chicago Jewish Forum 21
(Fall 1962): 26-30.
French, Warren. "The Lost Potential of Richard Wright." In The
Black American Writer, vol. 1, pp. 125-142. Edited by

C. W. E. Bigsby. Deland, Fla.: Everett/Edwards, 1969.
_____. The Social Novel at the End of an Era. Carbondale: Southern Illinois University Press, 1966.
Fuller, Hoyt W. "Contemporary Negro Fiction." Southwest Review 50 (Autumn 1965): 321-335.
_____. "On the Death of Richard Wright." Southwest Review 46 (Autumn 1961): 334-337.
Fullinwider, S. P. The Mind and Mood of Black America. Homewood, Ill.: Dorsey Press, 1969.
Gayle, Addison, Jr. "Cultural Nationalism: The Black Novel and the City." Liberator 9 (July 1969): 14-17.
_____. "A Defense of James Baldwin." CLA Journal 10 (March 1967): 201-208.
_____. "Richard Wright: Beyond Nihilism." Negro Digest 18 (December 1968): 5-10; also in Abcarian, Richard Wright's "Native Son."
_____. The Way of the New World: The Black Novel in America. Garden City, N.Y.: Anchor Press/Doubleday, 1975.
Gerard, Albert. "Humanism and Negritude: Notes on the Contemporary Afro-American Novel." Diogenes 37 (Spring 1962): 115-133.
Gibson, Donald B. "Richard Wright and the Tyranny of Convention." CLA Journal 12 (June 1969): 344-357.
_____. "Richard Wright: A Bibliographical Essay." CLA Journal 12 (June 1969): 360-365.
Giles, James E. "Richard Wright's Successful Failure: A New Look at Uncle Tom's Children." Phylon 4 (September 1973): 256-266.
Glicksberg, Charles I. "The Alienation of Negro Literature." Phylon 11 (First Quarter 1950): 49-58; also in Singh and Fellowes, Black Literature in America.
_____. "Existentialism in The Outsider." Four Quarters 7 (January 1958): 17-26.
_____. "The Furies in Negro Fiction." Western Review 13 (Winter 1949): 107-114.
_____. "Negro Fiction in America." South Atlantic Quarterly 45 (October 1946): 477-488; also in Abcarian, Richard Wright's "Native Son."
Gloster, Hugh M. Negro Voices in American Fiction. Chapel Hill: University of North Carolina Press, 1948.
_____. "Richard Wright: Interpreter of Racial and Economic Maladjustments." Opportunity 19 (December 1941): 361-365, 383.
Gounard, Jean-Francois. "Richard Wright as a Black Writer in Exile." CLA Journal 17 (March 1974): 307-317.
Graham, Don B. "Lawd Today and the Example of The Wasteland." CLA Journal 17 (March 1974): 327-332.
Green, Gerald. "Back to Bigger." Kenyon Review 28 (September 1966): 521-539.
Gross, Seymour L. "'Dalton' and Color-Blindness in Native Son." Mississippi Quarterly 27 (1973-1974): 75-77.
_____. "Native Son and 'The Murders in the Rue Morgue': An Addendum." Poe Studies 8 (June 1975): 23.

Gross, Theodore L. "The Idealism of Negro Literature in America." Phylon 30 (Spring 1969): 5-10.

Gysin, Gritz. The Grotesque in American Negro Fiction. The Cooper Monographs on English and American Literature no. 22. Basel, Switzerland: Francke Verlag Bern, 1975.

Hand, Clifford. "The Struggle to Create Life in the Fiction of Richard Wright." In The Thirties: Fiction, Poetry, Drama, pp. 81-87. Edited by Warren French. DeLand, Fla.: Everett/ Edwards, 1967.

Harrington, Ollie. "The Last Days of Richard Wright." Ebony 16 (February 1961): 83-94.

Hayashi, Susanna. "Dark Odyssey: Descent into the Underworld in Black American Fiction." Ph.D. Dissertation, Indiana University, 1971.

Haymon, Theresa Lenora Drew. "Alienation in the Life and Works of Richard Wright." Ph.D. Dissertation, Loyola University of Chicago, 1976.

Hill, Herbert, Horace Cayton, Arna Bontemps, and Saunders Redding. "Reflections on Richard Wright: A Symposium on an Exiled Native Son." In Anger, and Beyond: The Negro Writer in the United States, pp. 196-212. Edited by Herbert Hill. New York: Perennial Library/Harper & Row, 1968; also in Gibson, Five Black Writers.

Howe, Irving. "Black Boys and Native Sons." Dissent 10 (Autumn 1963): 353-368; also in Abcarian, Richard Wright's "Native Son."; Gibson, Five Black Writers.

_____. "A Reply to Ralph Ellison." New Leader, 3 February 1964, pp. 12-14.

_____. "Richard Wright: A Word of Farewell." New Republic, 13 February 1961, pp. 17-18.

Hughes, Carl Milton. The Negro Novelist 1940-1950. New York: Citadel Press, 1953.

Hughes, Langston. "Richard Wright's Last Guest at Home." Ebony 16 (February 1961): 94.

Hyman, Stanley Edgar. The Promised End: Essays and Reviews. Cleveland: World, 1963; also in Singh and Fellowes, Black Literature in America.

_____. "Richard Wright Reappraised." Atlantic 225 (March 1970): 127-132.

Isaacs, Harold R. "Five Writers and Their African Ancestors." Phylon 21 (Third Quarter 1960): 243-265; (Fourth Quarter 1960) 317-336; also in Singh and Fellowes, Black Literature in America.

Jackson, Blyden. "The Negro's Negro in Negro Literature." Michigan Quarterly Review 4 (Fall 1965): 290-295; also in Singh and Fellowes, Black Literature in America.

_____. "Richard Wright: Black Boy from America's Black Belt and Urban Ghettos." CLA Journal 12 (June 1969): 287-309; also in Jackson's The Waiting Years: Essays on American Negro Literature. Baton Rouge: Louisiana State University Press 1976.

_____. "Richard Wright in a Moment of Truth." Southern Literary Journal 1971; also in Jackson's The Waiting Years:

Essays on American Negro Literature. Baton Rouge: Louisiana State University Press, 1976.

Jackson, Esther M. "The American Negro and the Image of the Absurd." _Phylon_ 23 (Winter 1962): 359-371.

Jarrett, Thomas D. "Recent Fiction by Negroes." _College English_ 16 (November 1954): 85-91.

Jaskoski, Helen. "Power Unequal to Man: The Significance of Conjure in Works by Five Afro-American Authors." _Southern Folklore Quarterly_ 38 (June 1974): 91-108.

Jeffers, Lance. "Afro-American Literature, the Conscience of Man." _Black Scholar_ 2 (January 1971): 47-53.

Jones, Howard M. "Up From Slavery: Richard Wright's Story." _Saturday Review_, 3 March 1945, pp. 9-10.

Jordan, June. "On Richard Wright and Zora Neale Hurston: Notes Toward a Balancing of Love and Hatred." _Black World_ 23 (August 1974): 4-8.

Kennedy, James G. "The Content and Form of _Native Son._" _College English_ 34 (November 1972): 269-286.

Kent, George. _Blackness and the Adventure of Western Culture._ Chicago: Third World Press, 1972.

_____. "On the Future Study of Richard Wright." _CLA Journal_ 12 (June 1969): 366-370.

_____. "Richard Wright: Blackness and the Adventure of Western Culture." _CLA Journal_ 12 (June 1969): 322-343.

Killinger, John. _The Fragile Presence: Transcendence in Modern Literature._ Philadelphia: Fortress Press, 1973.

Kim, Kichung. "Wright, The Protest Novel, and Baldwin's Faith." _CLA Journal_ 17 (March 1974): 387-396.

Kinnamon, Keneth. _The Emergence of Richard Wright: A Study in Literature of Society._ Urbana: University of Illinois Press, 1972.

_____. "_Native Son:_ The Personal, Social and Political Background." _Phylon_ 30 (Spring 1969): 66-72; also in Abcarian, _Richard Wright's "Native Son."_

_____. "The Pastoral Impulse in Richard Wright." _Mid-Continent American Studies Journal_ 10 (Spring 1969): 41-47.

_____. "Richard Wright's Use of 'Othello' in _Native Son._" _CLA Journal_ 12 (June 1969): 358-359.

Klotman, Phyllis Rauch. _Another Man Gone: The Black Runner in Contemporary Afro-American Literature._ Port Washington, N.Y.: Kennikat Press, 1977.

_____ and Melville Yancey. "The Gift of Double Vision, Possible Political Implications of Richard Wright's 'Self-Consciousness' Thesis." _CLA Journal_ 16 (September 1972): 106-116.

Knox, George. "The Negro Novelist's Sensibility and the Outsider Theme." _Western Humanities Review_ 11 (Spring 1957): 137-148.

Kostelanetz, Richard. "The Politics of Unresolved Quests in the Novels of Richard Wright." _Xavier University Studies_ 8 (1969): 31-64.

Lawson, L. A. "Cross Damon, Kierkegaardian Man of Dread." _CLA Journal_ 14 (March 1971): 298-316.

LeClair, Thomas. "The Blind Leading the Blind: Wright's _Native_

Son and a Brief Reference to Ellison's Invisible Man." CLA Journal 13 (March 1970): 315-320.

Lehan, Richard. "Existentialism in Recent American Fiction." Texas Studies in Literature and Language 1 (Summer 1959): 181-202.

Lewis, Theophilus. "The Saga of Bigger Thomas." Catholic World 153 (May 1941): 201-206.

Littlejohn, David. Black on White: A Critical Survey of Writing by American Negroes. New York: Grossman, 1966.

Locke, Alain. "Of Native Sons: Real and Otherwise." Opportunity 19 (January 1941): 4-9.

McBride, Rebecca Susan. "Richard Wright's Use of His Reading of Fiction: 1927-1940." Ph.D. Dissertation, University of Pennsylvania, 1975.

McCall, Dan. The Example of Richard Wright. New York: Harcourt, Brace & World, 1969.

McConnell, Frank D. "Black Words and Black Becoming." Yale Review 63 (Winter 1974): 193-210.

Madden, David. Proletarian Writers of the Thirties. Carbondale and Edwardsville: Southern Illinois University Press, 1968.

Maduka, Chukwadi Thomas. "Politics and the Intellectual Hero: Achebe, Abrahams, Flaubert, and Wright." Ph.D. Dissertation, University of Iowa, 1976.

Major, Clarence. The Dark and Feeling. New York: Third Press, 1974.

Marcus, Steven. "The American Negro in Search of Identity." Commentary 16 (November 1953): 456-463.

Margolies, Edward L. The Art of Richard Wright. Carbondale: Southern Illinois University Press, 1969.

_____, ed. Native Sons; A Critical Study of Twentieth Century Negro American Authors. Philadelphia: Lippincott, 1968.

Mason, Clifford. "Native Son Strikes Home: Black Fiction: A Second Look." Life, 8 May 1970, p. 18.

Maxwell, Joan Lovell Bauerly. "Themes of Redemption in Two Major American Writers, Ralph Ellison and Richard Wright." Ph.D. Dissertation, University of Oregon, 1976.

Mebane, Mary Elizabeth. "The Family in the Works of Charles W. Chesnutt and Selected Works of Richard Wright." Ph.D. Dissertation, University of North Carolina at Chapel Hill, 1973.

Miller, Eugene E. "Voodoo Parallels in Native Son." CLA Journal 16 (September 1972): 81-95.

Miller, James Arthur. "The Struggle for Identity in the Major Works of Richard Wright." Ph.D. Dissertation, State University of New York at Buffalo, 1976.

Mills, Moylan Chew. "The Literary Reputation of Richard Wright." Ph.D. Dissertation, University of Pennsylvania, 1974.

Mitchell, L. D. "Richard Wright's Artistry." Crisis 82 (February 1975): 62-66.

Mootry, Maria Katella. "Studies in Black Pastoral: Five Afro-American Writers." Ph.D. Dissertation, Northwestern University, 1974.

Murray, Albert. The Omni-Americans: New Perspectives on Black Experience and American Culture. New York: Outerbridge, 1970.

_____. "Something Different, Something More." In Anger and Beyond, pp. 112-137. Edited by Herbert Hill. New York: Harper & Row, 1966.

Nagel, James. "Images of 'Vision' in Native Son." University Review 36 (December 1969): 109-115.

O'Daniel, Therman B. "James Baldwin: An Interpretive Study." CLA Journal 7 (September 1963): 37-47.

Owens, William A. Introduction to Native Son. New York: Harper, 1957.

Padmore, Dorothy. "A Letter from Dorothy Padmore." Studies in Black Literature 1 (Autumn 1970): 5-9.

Peden, William. The American Short Story: Continuity and Change 1940-1975. Boston: Houghton Mifflin, 1975.

Pyros, John. "Richard Wright: A Black Novelist's Experience in Film." Negro American Literature Forum 9 (Summer 1975): 53-54.

Rascoe, Burton. "Negro Novel and White Reviewers." American Mercury 50 (May 1940): 113-117; also in Abcarian, Richard Wright's "Native Son."

Ray, David and Robert M. Farnsworth, eds. Richard Wright: Impressions and Perspectives. Ann Arbor: University of Michigan Press, 1973.

Redding, J. Saunders. "The Alien Land of Richard Wright." In Soon, One Morning: New Writing by American Negroes, 1940-1962, pp. 50-59. Edited by Herbert Hill. New York: Knopf, 1963; also in Gibson, Five Black Writers.

Reed, Kenneth. "Native Son: An American Crime and Punishment." Studies in Black Literature 1 (Summer 1970): 33-34.

Reilly, John. Afterword to Native Son. New York: Harper & Row, 1966.

_____. In Contemporary Novelists. Edited by James Vinson. New York: St. Martin's Press, 1976.

"Richard Wright, Writer, 52, Dies." New York Times, 30 November 1960, p. 37.

Rickels, Milton and Patricia. Richard Wright. Austin, Tex.: Steck-Vaughn, 1970.

Ridenour, Ronald. "'The Man Who Lived Underground': A Critique." Phylon 31 (Spring 1970): 54-57.

Rideout, Walter B. The Radical Novel in the United States 1900-1954: Some Interrelations of Literature and Society. Cambridge: Harvard University Press, 1956.

Rosenblatt, Roger. Black Fiction. Cambridge: Harvard University Press, 1974.

Sanders, Ronald. "Richard Wright and the Sixties." Midstream 14 (August-September 1968): 28-40; reprinted as "Richard Wright Then and Now: Relevance for the Sixties" in Negro Digest 18 (December 1968): 83-98.

Sartre, Jean-Paul. What Is Literature? Trans. Bernard Frechtman. New York: Philosophical Library, 1949.

Savory, Jerold J. "Bigger Thomas and the Book of Job: The Epigraph to Native Son." Negro American Literature Forum 9 (Summer 1975): 55-56.

Schraufnagel, Noel. From Apology to Protest: The Black American

Novel. DeLand, Fla.: Everett/Edwards, 1973.
Scott, Nathan A. "The Dark and Haunted Tower of Richard Wright." Graduate Comment 7 (July 1964): 92-99; also in Gibson, Five Black Writers; Hemenway, The Black Novelist.
_____. "Judgment Marked by a Cellar: The American Negro Writer and the Dialectic of Despair." University of Denver Quarterly 2 (Summer 1967): 5-35.
_____. "Search for Beliefs: Fiction of Richard Wright." University of Kansas City Review 23 (Autumn 1956): 19-24.
_____. "Search for Beliefs: Richard Wright." University of Kansas City Review 23 (Winter 1956): 131-138.
Seyersted, Per. "A Survey of Trends and Figures in Afro-American Fiction." American Studies in Scandinavia 6, nos. 1-2 (1973-1974): 67-86.
Sherr, P. C. "Richard Wright, The Expatriate Pattern." Black Academy Review 2 (Spring-Summer 1971): 81-89.
Shreve, Darrell Rhea, Jr. "The Fact of Blackness: Black Existentialism in Richard Wright's Major Fiction." Ph.D. Dissertation, University of Minnesota, 1976.
Siegel, Paul N. "The Conclusion of Richard Wright's Native Son." PMLA 89 (May 1974): 517-523.
Silberman, Charles E. Crisis in Black and White. New York: Random House, 1964.
Sillen, Samuel. "The Meaning of Bigger Thomas." New Masses, 30 April 1940, pp. 26-28.
_____. "'Native Son': Pros and Con." New Masses, 21 May 1940, pp. 23-26.
_____. "The Response to 'Native Son.'" New Masses, 23 April 1940, pp. 25-27.
Singh, Amritjit. "Misdirected Responses to Bigger Thomas." Studies in Black Literature 5 (Summer 1974): 5-8.
Singh, Raman K. "The Black Novel and Its Tradition." Colorado Quarterly 20 (Summer 1971): 1.
_____. "Some Basic Ideas and Ideals in Richard Wright's Fiction." CLA Journal 13 (September 1969): 78-84.
_____. "Wright's Tragic Vision in The Outsider." Studies in Black Literature 1 (Autumn 1970): 23-27.
Skerrett, Joseph Taylor, Jr. "Take My Burden Up: Three Studies in Psychobiographical Criticism and Afro-American Fiction." Ph.D. Dissertation, Yale University, 1975.
Slochower, Harry. No Voice Is Wholly Lost...: Writers and Thinkers in War and Peace. New York: Creative Age Press, 1945.
Smith, Barbara. "Sexual Politics in the Fiction of Richard Wright." Paper presented at the MLA meeting, New York City, December 1976.
Smith, Cynthia Janis. "Escape and Quest in the Literature of Black Americans." Ph.D. Dissertation, Yale University, 1974.
Smith, William Gardner. "Black Boy in France." Ebony 8 (July 1953): 32-36, 39-42.
_____. "Richard Wright (1908-1960): The Compensation for the Wound." Two Cities no. 6 (Summer 1961): 67-69.
Sprandel, Katherine Richards. "Richard Wright's Hero: From

Initiate and Victim to Rebel and Isolate (An Achronological Study). " Ph. D. Dissertation, Michigan State University, 1973.

Starr, Alvin. "The Concept of Fear in the Works of Stephen Crane and Richard Wright. " Studies in Black Literature 6 (Summer 1975): 6-10.

Sullivan, Richard. Afterword to Native Son. New York: New American Library, 1961.

Tischler, Nancy M. Black Masks: Negro Characters in Modern Southern Fiction. University Park: Pennsylvania State University Press, 1969.

Traylor, Eleanor E. Williams. "Wright's Mythic and Grotesque Settings: Some Critical Approaches to the Fiction of Richard Wright. " Ph. D. Dissertation, The Catholic University of America, 1976.

Turner, Darwin T. "Native Son and The Outsider (Richard Wright). " The Twentieth Century American Novel Series. DeLand, Fla. : Everett/Edwards, n. d. (Cassette.)

_____. "The Negro Novelist and the South. " Southern Humanities Review 1 (1967): 21-29.

_____. "The Outsider: Revision of an Idea. " CLA Journal 12 (June 1969): 310-321.

Vogel, Albert W. "The Education of the Negro in Richard Wright's Black Boy. " Journal of Negro History 35 (Spring 1966): 195-198.

Walton, Martha R. "Major Concerns of the Black Novel in America in Relation to the American Mainstream. " Ph. D. Dissertation, University of Denver, 1973.

Waniek, Marilyn Nelson. "The Space Where Sex Should Be: Toward a Definition of the Black American Literary Tradition. " Studies in Black Literature 6 (Fall 1975): 7-13.

Wasserman, Jerry. "Embracing the Negative: Native Son and Invisible Man. " Studies in American Fiction 4 (Spring 1976): 83-104.

Webb, Constance. Richard Wright, A Biography. New York: Putnam, 1968.

Weiss, Adrian. "What Next for Richard Wright?" Phylon 10 (Second Quarter 1949): 161-167.

_____. "A Portrait of the Artist as a Black Boy. " Bulletin of the Rocky Mountain Modern Language Association 28 (1974): 93-101.

Weitz, Morris. Philosophy of the Arts. Cambridge: Harvard University Press, 1950.

Wertham, Frederic. "An Unconscious Determinant in Native Son. " In Psychoanalysis and Literature, pp. 321-325. Edited by Hendrik M. Runenbeck. New York: E. P. Dutton, 1964.

White, Ralph K. "Black Boy: A Value-Analysis. " Journal of Abnormal and Social Psychology 42 (October 1947): 440-461.

Whitman, Alden. "Richard Wright: The Final, Perplexing Chapters of Black Boy. " Book World, 22 May 1977, pp. 1, 8-9.

Widmer, Kingsley. "The Existential Darkness: Richard Wright's The Outsider. " Wisconsin Studies in Contemporary Literature 1 (Fall 1960): 13-21; also in Gibson, Five Black Writers.

Williams, John A. Introduction to White Man, Listen! Garden City,

N.Y.: Doubleday/Anchor, 1964.

_____. The Most Native of Sons: A Biography of Richard
Wright. Garden City, N.Y.: Doubleday, 1970.

_____. "On Wright, Wrong, and Black Reality." Negro Digest
18 (December 1968): 25.

Winslow, Henry F. "Richard Nathaniel Wright: Destroyer and
Preserver (1908-1960)." Crisis 69 (March 1962): 149-163,
187.

Reviews

Eight Men

Baldwin, James. Reporter, 16 March 1961, p. 52.

Benet, Rosemary. Book-of-the-Month-Club News (March 1961):
10.

Booklist, 15 January 1961, p. 294.

Bookmark 20 (April 1961): 169.

Bromwell, Gloria. Midstream 7 (Spring 1961): 110.

Bryant, J. A., Jr. Sewanee Review 71 (Winter 1963): 115.

Byam, M. S. Library Journal, 1 December 1960, p. 4394.

Dvorak, Jarmila. Books Abroad 36 (Spring 1962): 208.

Gilman, Richard. Commonweal, 28 April 1961, p. 130.

Howe, Irving. New Republic, 13 February 1961, p. 17.

Kirkus, 15 November 1960, p. 973.

La Farge, John. America, 28 January 1961, p. 573.

Lee, Laurence. Chicago Sunday Tribune, 22 January 1961, p.
4.

Newsweek, 9 January 1961, p. 82.

Redding, Saunders. New York Herald Tribune Lively Arts, 22
January 1961, p. 33.

Rogers, W. G. Saturday Review of Literature, 21 January
1961, p. 65.

Scott, Nathan A. Kenyon Review 23 (Spring 1961): 337.

Sullivan, Richard. New York Times Book Review, 22 January
1961, p. 5.

Wisconsin Library Bulletin 57 (September 1961): 309.

Lawd Today

Bannon, B. A. Publishers' Weekly, 5 September 1966, p. 71.

Bradbury, M. Punch, 5 May 1965, p. 676.

Brophy, B. New Statesman, 4 June 1965, p. 886.

Fuller, Edmund. Chicago Sunday Tribune Magazine of Books,
14 April 1963, p. 8.

Gannett, Lewis. New York Herald Tribune Books, 5 May 1963,
p. 10.

Giles, Louise. Library Journal, 1 April 1963, p. 1549.

Hicks, Granville. Saturday Review of Literature, 30 March
1963, p. 37.

Lynd, Staughton. Commentary 36 (September 1963): 255.

Saturday Review of Literature, 25 October 1969, p. 42.

Stevens, E. Books and Bookmen 10 (June 1965): 35.

Time, 5 April 1963, p. 106.

Times Literary Supplement, 29 April 1965, p. 324.

Vansittart, P. Spectator, 23 April 1965, p. 540.

Wardle, I. Observer, 18 April 1965, p. 27.
Wordsworth, C. Manchester Guardian, 29 April 1965, p. 11.
The Long Dream
    Barnett, A. N. Library Journal, 15 October 1958, p. 2843.
    Bonosky, Phillip. Mainstream 12 (February 1959): 49-51.
    Dunlea, William. Commonweal, 31 October 1958, p. 131.
    Geismer, Maxwell. New York Herald Tribune Book Review,
      16 November 1958, p. 10.
    Hatch, Robert. Nation, 25 October 1958, p. 297.
    Hicks, Granville. Saturday Review of Literature, 18 October
      1958, p. 13.
    New Yorker, 8 November 1958, p. 210.
    Ottley, Roi. Chicago Sunday Tribune, 26 October 1958, p. 3.
    Redding, Saunders. New York Times, 26 October 1958, p. 4.
    Saturday Review of Literature, 15 October 1969, p. 42.
    Shapiro, Charles. New Republic, 24 November 1958, p. 17.
    Time, 27 October 1958, p. 94.
    Times Literary Supplement, 27 October 1961, p. 765.
Native Son
    Atlantic 225 (March 1970): 127.
    Booklist, 1 April 1940, p. 307.
    Books and Bookmen 18 (April 1973): 141.
    Brown, Sterling. Opportunity 18 (June 1940): 185-186.
    Catholic World 151 (May 1940): 243.
    Christian Century, 24 April 1940, p. 546.
    Cleveland Open Shelf (May 1940): 12.
    Cowley, Malcolm. New Republic, 18 March 1940, p. 382.
    Daniels, J. Saturday Review of Literature, 2 March 1940, p.
      5.
    Fadiman, Clifton. New Yorker, 2 March 1940, p. 60.
    Jenkins, Joseph H., Jr. Phylon 1 (Second Quarter 1940):
      195-196.
    Jones, H. M. Boston Transcript, 2 March 1940, p. 1.
    Lehmann, Rosamond. Spectator, 19 April 1940, p. 574.
    Marriot, Charles. Manchester Guardian, 16 April 1940, p. 3.
    Marshall, Margaret. Nation, 16 March 1940, p. 367.
    New Statesman, 28 August 1970, p. 242.
    New York Times Book Review, 3 March 1940, p. 2.
    Pratt Institute Quarterly (Autumn 1940): 24.
    Rugoff, Milton. Books, 3 March 1940, p. 5.
    Saturday Review of Literature, 23 March 1940, p. 8; 2 Septem-
      ber 1944, p. 6.
    Skillin, Edward. Commonweal, 8 March 1940, p. 438.
    Springfield Republican, 10 March 1940, p. 7e.
    Time, 4 March 1940, p. 72.
    Times Literary Supplement, 27 April 1940, p. 205.
    West, Anthony. New Statesman and Nation, 20 April 1940, p. 542.
    Wisconsin Library Bulletin 36 (May 1940): 101.
    Wyke, Marguerite. Canadian Forum 20 (May 1940): 60.
    Yale Review 29 (Summer 1940): 10.
The Outsider
    Adams, Phoebe. Atlantic 191 (May 1953): 77.
    Bontemps, A. Saturday Review of Literature, 28 March 1953, p.
      15.

Booklist, 1 March 1953, p. 213; 15 March 1953, p. 238.
Brown, Lloyd L. Masses & Mainstream 6 (May 1953): 62-64.
Byam, M. S. Library Journal, 15 April 1953, p. 732.
Hicks, Granville. New York Times Book Review, 22 March
    1953, p. 1.
Hughes, M. C. Commonweal, 10 April 1952, p. 29.
Hughes, Riley. Catholic World 177 (May 1953): 154.
Kirkus, 15 January 1953, p. 54.
Munn, L. S. Springfield Republican, 14 June 1953, p. 9c.
Nation, 18 April 1953, p. 331.
New Yorker, 28 March 1953, p. 127.
Ottley, Roi. Chicago Sunday Tribune, 22 March 1953, p. 3.
Pickrel, Paul. Yale Review 42 (Summer 1953): 10.
Raleigh, J. H. New Republic, 4 May 1953, p. 19.
Rugoff, Milton. New York Herald Tribune Book Review, 22
    March 1953, p. 4.
Sawyer, Roland. Christian Science Monitor, 30 April 1953,
    p. 11.
Time, 30 March 1953, p. 90.
U. S. Quarterly Book Review 9 (June 1953): 166.
Vogler, Lewis. San Francisco Chronicle, 5 April 1953, p. 19.
Watkins, Charlotte Crawford. Journal of Negro Education 23
    (Spring 1954): 153-154.
Uncle Tom's Children
    Booklist, 1 May 1938, p. 318.
    Brown, S. A. Nation, 16 April 1938, p. 448.
    _____. Opportunity 16 (April 1938): 120-121.
    Cowley, Malcolm. New Republic, 6 April 1938, p. 280.
    Hurston, Z. N. Saturday Review of Literature, 2 April 1938,
        p. 32.
    Lovell, John, Jr. Journal of Negro Education 8 (January 1939):
        71-73.
    Marsh, F. T. Books, 8 May 1938, p. 3.
    Time, 28 March 1938, p. 63.
    Tourtellot, A. B. Boston Transcript, 9 April 1938, p. 1.
    Van Gelder, Robert. New York Times Book Review, 3 April
        1938, p. 7.

WRIGHT, Sarah

Novel

This Child's Gonna Live. New York: Delacorte, 1969; New York:
    Dell, 1971.

Biography and Criticism

Rush, Theressa Gunnels, Carol Fairbanks Myers, and Esther Spring
    Arata. Black American Writers Past and Present. Metuchen,
    N.J.: Scarecrow Press, 1975.
Schraufnagel, Noel. From Apology to Protest: The Black American
    Novel. DeLand, Fla.: Everett/Edwards, 1973.

Reviews

This Child's Gonna Live
    Adams, P. Atlantic 224 (July 1969): 110.
    Best Sellers, 1 August 1969, p. 168.
    Howe, I. Harper's 239 (December 1969): 130.
    Kirkus, 15 April 1969, p. 474.
    Library Journal 94 (1969): 2004.
    Negro Digest 18 (August 1969): 51.
    New York Times Book Review, 29 June 1969, p. 4.
    Publishers' Weekly, 21 April 1969, p. 63; 7 September 1970,
        p. 62.
    Times Literary Supplement, 16 October 1969, p. 1177.

WYNBUSH, Octavia B.

Short Fiction

"The Black Streak." Crisis 52 (October 1945): 286-287, 301.
"Conjure Man." Crisis 45 (March 1938): 71-73, 82, 89-90.
"The Conversion of Harvey." Crisis 43 (March 1936): 76-78.
"The Noose." Opportunity 9 (December 1931): 369-371.
"Ticket Home: A Christmas Story." Crisis 46 (January 1939):
    7-8, 29.

YERBY, Frank

Novels

Benton's Row. New York: Dial, 1954; New York: Dell, 1969.
Captain Rebel. New York: Dial, 1956; New York: Dell, 1972.
The Dahomean: An Historical Novel. New York: Dial, 1971; New
    York: Dell, 1972.
The Devil's Laughter. New York: Dial, 1953; New York: Dell,
    1972.
Fairoaks: A Novel. New York: Dial, 1957; New York: Dell,
    1969.
Floodtide. New York: Dial, 1950; New York: Dell, 1967.
The Foxes of Harrow. New York: Dial, 1946; New York: Dell,
    1972; excerpt in Negro Digest, June 1946.
The Garfield Honor. New York: Dial, 1961; New York: Dell,
    1973.
Gillian. New York: Dial, 1960; New York: Dell, 1972.
The Girl from Storyville. New York: Dial, 1972.
Goat Song: A Novel of Ancient Greece. New York: Dial, 1967;
    New York: Dell, 1974.
The Golden Hawk. New York: Dial, 1948; New York: Dell,
    1972.
Griffin's Way. New York: Dial, 1962; New York: Dell,
    1972.

Jarrett's Jade: A Novel. New York: Dial, 1959; New York: Dell, 1976.
Judas, My Brother: The Story of the Thirteenth Disciple. New York: Dial, 1968; New York: Dell, 1970.
An Odor of Sanctity: A Novel of Medieval Moorish Spain. New York: Dial, 1965; New York: Dell, 1972.
The Old Gods Laugh: A Modern Romance. New York: Dial, 1964; New York: Dell, 1973.
Pride's Castle. New York: Dial, 1949; New York: Dell, 1968.
A Rose for Ana Maria. New York: Dial, 1975; New York: Dell, 1977.
The Saracen Blade. New York: Dial, 1952; New York: Pocket Books, 1965; New York: Dell, 1973.
The Serpent and the Staff. New York: Dial, 1958; New York: Dell, 1972.
Speak Now: A Modern Novel. New York: Dial, 1969; New York: Dell, 1970.
Tobias and the Angel. New York: Dial, 1975; New York: Dell, 1976.
The Treasure of Pleasant Valley. New York: Dial, 1955; New York: Dell, 1973; London: Heinemann, 1976.
The Vixens. New York: Dial, 1947; New York: Dell, 1972; excerpt in Negro Digest, March 1948.
The Voyage Unplanned. New York: Dial, 1974.
A Woman Called Fancy. New York: Dial, 1951; New York: Dell, 1971.

Short Fiction

"Health Card." Harper's 188 (May 1944): 548-553; also in Carey, Quest for Meaning; Fenton, Best Short Stories of World War II; Hughes; The Best Stories by Negro Writers; Patterson, An Introduction to Black Literature in America.
"The Homecoming." Common Ground 6 (Spring 1946): 41-47; also in Clarke, American Negro Short Stories; James, From the Roots.
"My Brother Went to College." Tomorrow 5 (January 1946): 9-12; also in Turner, Black American Literature: Fiction.
"Roads Going Down." Common Ground 5 (Summer 1945): 67-72.
"The Thunder of God." New Anvil (April-May 1939): 508.
"White Magnolias." Phylon 5 (Fourth Quarter 1944): 319-326.

Biography and Criticism

Bone, Robert A. The Negro Novel in America. New Haven: Yale University Press, 1966.
Breit, Harvey. The Writer Observed. Cleveland: World, 1956.
Campenni, Frank. In Contemporary Novelists. Edited by James Vinson. New York: St. Martin's Press, 1976.
Contemporary Authors, 11/12R.
Ford, Nick Aaron. "Four Popular Negro Novelists." Phylon 15 (First Quarter 1954): 29-39.
Fuller, Hoyt W. "Famous Writer Faces a Challenge." Ebony 21

(June 1966): 188-190, 192-194.

Gloster, Hugh. "Race and the Negro Writer. " Phylon 11 (Fourth Quarter 1950): 369-371.

_____ . "The Significance of Frank Yerby. " Crisis 55 (January 1948): 12-13.

"The Golden Corn: He Writes to Please. " Time, 29 November 1954, p. 97.

Graham, Maryemma. "Frank Yerby, King of the Costume Novel. " Essence 6 (October 1975): 70-71, 88-89, 91-92.

Hemenway, Robert, ed. The Black Novelist. Columbus, Ohio: Charles E. Merrill, 1970.

Hill, James Lee. "Bibliography of the Works of Chester Himes, Ann Petry, and Frank Yerby. " Black Books Bulletin 3 (Fall 1975): 60-72.

Hughes, Carl M. The Negro Novelist 1940-1950. New York: Citadel Press, 1953.

Jackson, Blyden. "Full Circle. " Phylon 9 (First Quarter 1948): 30-35.

Jarrett, Thomas. "Recent Fiction by Negroes. " College English 16 (November 1954): 85-91.

Jet, 16 June 1960, pp. 4-5. (Interview.)

Lash, John S. "Dimension in Racial Experience: A Critical Survey of Literature by and about Negroes in 1958. " Phylon 20 (Second Quarter 1959): 115-131.

_____ . "A Long Hard Look at the Ghetto: A Critical Summary of Literature by and about Negroes in 1956. " Phylon 18 (First Quarter 1957): 7-24.

Locke, Alain. "Dawn Patrol: A Review of the Literature of the Negro for 1948. " Phylon 10 (First Quarter 1949): 5-13; Part II, 167-172.

_____ . "The High Price of Integration: A Review of the Literature of the Negro for 1951. " Phylon 13 (First Quarter 1952): 7-18.

"Mystery Man of Letters. " Ebony 10 (February 1955): 31-32, 35-38.

Nye, Russel B. The Unembarrassed Muse. New York: Dial Press, 1970.

Schraufnagel, Noel. From Apology to Protest: The Black American Novel. DeLand, Fla.: Everett/Edwards, 1973.

"The Task of the Negro Writer. " Negro Digest 14 (April 1965): 54-83. (Symposium.)

Turner, Darwin T. "Frank Yerby as Debunker. " Massachusetts Review 9 (Summer 1968): 569-577; also in Hemenway, The Black Novelist.

_____ . "Frank Yerby: Golden Debunker. " Black Books Bulletin 1 (1973): 4-9, 30-33.

_____ . "The Negro Novelist and the South. " Southern Humanities Review 1 (1967): 21-29.

_____ . "The Tragedy of Goat Song. " Negro Digest 17 (July 1968): 51-52, 81-82.

Yerby, Frank. "How and Why I Write the Costume Novel. " Harper 219 (October 1959): 145-150.

Reviews

Benton's Row
  Match, Richard. New York Times, 5 December 1954, p. 52.
  New York Herald Tribune Book Review, 19 December 1954,
    p. 8.
  Time, 29 November 1954, p. 97.
  Yates, William. Chicago Sunday Tribune, 28 November 1954,
    p. 4.
Bride of Liberty
  Chicago Sunday Tribune, 14 November 1954, p. 47.
  Kirkus, 15 July 1954, p. 440.
  New York Herald Tribune Book Review, Part II, 14 November
    1954, p. 34.
Captain Rebel
  Lee, Charles. New York Times Book Review, 23 September
    1956, p. 31.
  Manston, S. P. Saturday Review of Literature, 27 October
    1956, p. 26.
  Poteate, Robert. New York Herald Tribune Book Review, 14
    October 1956, p. 8.
  Springfield Republican, 16 September 1956, p. 10c.
  Yates, William. Chicago Sunday Tribune, 16 September 1956,
    p. 2.
The Dahomean
  Best Sellers, 1 September 1971, p. 255.
  Black World 21 (February 1972): 51.
  Booklist, 1 October 1971, p. 133.
  Books and Bookmen 17 (February 1972): 67.
  Contemporary Review 220 (January 1972): 46.
  Kirkus, 15 May 1971, p. 574.
  Library Journal, 15 June 1971, p. 2105.
  New York Times Book Review, 17 October 1971, p. 34.
  Publishers' Weekly, 10 May 1971, p. 38.
  Spectator, 14 July 1973, p. 52.
The Devil's Laughter
  Lee, Charles. New York Times Book Review, 15 November
    1953, p. 39.
  New York Herald Tribune Book Review, 4 October 1953, p. 18.
  San Francisco Chronicle, 1 November 1953, p. 27.
  Time, 23 November 1953, p. 122.
  Yates, William. Chicago Sunday Tribune, 1 November 1953,
    p. 5.
Fairoaks: A Novel
  Mansten, S. P. Saturday Review of Literature, 24 August
    1957, p. 17.
  Match, Richard. New York Times Book Review, 8 September
    1957, p. 32.
  New York Herald Tribune Book Review, 22 September 1957,
    p. 13.
  Yates, William. Chicago Sunday Tribune, 25 August 1957, p. 5.
Floodtide
  Chicago Sun-Times, 5 September 1950, p. 6.

Christian Science Monitor, 14 October 1950, p. 15.
Grant, J. M. Saturday Review of Literature, 30 September
      1950, p. 33.
Kirkus, 15 August 1950, p. 479.
New York Herald Tribune Book Review, 22 October 1950, p. 25.
New York Times Book Review, 10 September 1950, p. 33.
Time, 4 September 1950, p. 84.
Yates, William. Chicago Sunday Tribune, 27 August 1950,
      p. 5.
The Foxes of Harrow
      Bontemps, Arna. Book Week, 10 February 1946, p. 1.
      Booklist, 1 March 1946, p. 214.
      Christian Science Monitor, 16 February 1946, p. 14.
      Jackson, Blyden. Journal of Negro Education 15 (Fall 1946):
            649-652.
      Kane, H. T. Weekly Book Review, 24 February 1946, p. 8.
      Kirkus, 15 January 1946, p. 19.
      Locke, Alain. Phylon 7 (First Quarter 1947): 20.
      McElfresh, M. H. Library Journal, 15 February 1946, p. 281.
      Match, Richard. New York Times, 10 February 1946, p. 8.
      New Yorker, 9 February 1946, p. 96.
      Rothman, N. L. Saturday Review of Literature, 23 February
            1946, p. 38.
      Saturday Review of Literature, 23 February 1949, p. 12.
The Garfield Honor
      Levin, Martin. New York Times, 17 December 1961, p. 22.
The Girl from Storyville
      Best Sellers, 15 October 1972, p. 337.
      Book World, 10 September 1972, p. 15.
      Kirkus, 1 July 1972, p. 749.
      Library Journal 97 (August 1972): 2650.
      New York Times Book Review, 17 September 1972, p. 49.
      Publishers' Weekly, 3 July 1972, p. 36.
Goat Song: A Novel of Ancient Greece
      Conlin, R. Best Sellers, 15 February 1968, p. 445.
      Kirkus, 1 November 1967, p. 1343.
      Lazenby, F. D. Library Journal, 15 December 1967, p. 4527.
      Publishers' Weekly, 23 October 1967, p. 48; 2 June 1969, p.
            138.
      Turner, D. T. Negro Digest 17 (July 1968): 51.
The Golden Hawk
      Best Sellers, 1 May 1972, p. 72.
      Kirkus, 15 April 1948, p. 198.
      New York Herald Tribune Weekly Book Review, 30 May 1948,
            p. 10.
      New Yorker, 24 April 1948, p. 105.
      Pick, Robert. Saturday Review of Literature, 8 May 1948, p.
            25.
      Textor, Clinton. Chicago Sun Bookweek, 25 April 1948, p. 8x.
      Watson, Wilbur. New York Times, 2 May 1948, p. 22.
Griffin's Way
      Burcky, Claire. Chicago Sunday Tribune Magazine of Books,
            16 September 1962, p. 5.

Extension (December 1962): 10.

Levin, Martin. New York Times, 9 December 1962, p. 39.

Ricks, Christopher. New Statesman, 7 June 1962, p. 870.

Jarrett's Jade: A Novel

Best Sellers, 1 May 1972, p. 72.

Judas, My Brother: The Story of the Thirteenth Disciple

Best Sellers, 1 January 1969, p. 408.

Kirkus, 1 September 1968, p. 1006.

Negro Digest 18 (April 1969): 80.

New York Times, 4 March 1969, p. 41.

Publishers' Weekly, 16 September 1968, p. 69; 18 May 1970, p. 40.

An Odor of Sanctity

Kirkus, 1 October 1965, p. 1058.

Linehan, E. J. Best Sellers, 15 December 1965, p. 365.

Times Literary Supplement, 28 July 1966, p. 656.

The Old Gods Laugh: A Modern Romance

Graff, G. Books Today, 21 June 1964, p. 9.

Pride's Castle

Bell, Lisle. New York Herald Tribune Weekly Book Review, 12 June 1949, p. 17.

Kirkus, 15 March 1949, p. 154.

Litten, F. N. Chicago Sun, 17 May 1949.

Rivette, Marc. San Francisco Chronicle, 8 May 1949, p. 19.

Saturday Review of Literature, 18 June 1949, p. 33.

Sherman, Beatrice. New York Times Book Review, 15 May 1949, p. 21.

A Rose for Ana Maria

Best Sellers 36 (September 1976): 188.

Kirkus, 15 March 1976, p. 349.

Publishers' Weekly, 29 March 1976, p. 48.

Saracen Blade

Chubb, T. C. New York Times Book Review, 6 April 1952, p. 30.

Fitzgerald, E. J. Saturday Review of Literature, 10 May 1952, p. 36.

Kirkus, 1 April 1952, p. 238.

New York Herald Tribune Book Review, 21 September 1952, p. 18.

Publishers' Weekly, 13 November 1967, p. 81.

Time, 7 April 1952, p. 113.

Yates, William. Chicago Sunday Tribune, 6 April 1952, p. 5.

The Serpent and the Staff

Best Sellers, 1 May 1972, p. 72.

Kane, H. T. Chicago Sunday Tribune, 21 September 1958, p. 8.

Match, Richard. New York Times Book Review, 12 October 1958, p. 33.

Publishers' Weekly, 18 July 1966, p. 78.

Times Literary Supplement, 27 March 1959, p. 173.

Speak Now: A Modern Novel

Best Sellers, 1 January 1970, p. 384.

Kirkus, 15 September 1969, p. 1032.

Library Journal, 15 November 1969, p. 4159.
Negro Digest 19 (February 1970): 79.
New York Times Book Review, 30 November 1969, p. 67.
Publishers' Weekly, 22 September 1969, p. 84.

Tobias and the Angel
Booklist, 1 June 1975, p. 991.
Kirkus, 15 March 1975, p. 332.
Library Journal, 1 April 1975, p. 692.
Pemberton, Gayle R. Third Press Review I (September/October 1975): 22-23, 70-71.
Publishers' Weekly, 7 April 1975, p. 80; 8 November 1976, p. 48.

The Treasure of Pleasant Valley
Best Sellers, 1 April 1973, p. 23.

The Vixens
Best Sellers, 1 May 1972, p. 72.
James, Edith. San Francisco Chronicle, 4 May 1947, p. 12.
Kane, H. T. Chicago Sun Book Week, 27 April 1947, p. 3.
Kent, George. Phylon 37 (March 1976): 100-115.
Kingery, R. E. Library Journal, 15 April 1947, p. 639.
Kirkus, 1 March 1947, p. 132.
MacBride, James. New York Times Book Review, 4 May 1947, p. 22.
Rico, Jennings. New York Herald Tribune Weekly Book Review, 4 May 1947, p. 10.
Wright, Marion T. Journal of Negro Education 16 (Fall 1947): 562.

The Voyage Unplanned
Kirkus, 15 February 1974, p. 211.
Library Journal, 15 May 1974, p. 1410.
Publishers' Weekly, 11 February 1974, p. 62.

A Woman Called Fancy
Fitzgerald, E. J. Saturday Review of Literature, 23 June 1951, p. 39.
Hughes, Riley. Catholic World 174 (October 1951): 74.
New York Herald Tribune Book Review, 15 July 1951, p. 7.
San Francisco Chronicle, 15 July 1951, p. 17.
Watson, Wilbur. New York Times Book Review, 6 May 1951, p. 16.
Yates, William. Chicago Sunday Tribune, 20 May 1951, p. 4.

YOUNG, Al (Albert James Young)

Novels

Sitting Pretty. New York: Holt, Rinehart & Winston, 1976.
Snakes. New York: Holt, Rinehart & Winston, 1970; New York: Dell, 1972; excerpts in Nickel Review, 11 May 1970; Reed, 19 Necromancers from Now.
Who is Angelina? New York: Holt, Rinehart & Winston, 1975; excerpt in Yardbird Reader 2 (1973): 1-9.

Short Fiction

"Chicken Hawk's Dream." In Chapman, New Black Voices; Haupt,
    Man in the Fictional Mode: Book 4.
"Introduction." Iowa Review 6 (Spring 1975): 42-44.

Biography and Criticism

Bolling, Douglass. "Artistry and Theme in Al Young's Snakes."
    Negro American Literature Forum 8 (1974): 223-225.
Contemporary Authors, 29/32.
O'Brien, John. Interviews with Black Writers. New York: Live-
    right, 1973.
Reilly, John M. In Contemporary Novelists. Edited by James Vin-
    son. New York: St. Martin's Press, 1976.
Rush, Theressa Gunnels, Carol Fairbanks Myers, and Esther Spring
    Arata. Black American Writers Past and Present. Metuchen,
    N.J.: Scarecrow Press, 1975.
Schmitz, Neil. "Al Young's Snakes: Words to Music." Paunch 35
    (1974): 3-9.
Schraufnagel, Noel. From Apology to Protest, The Black American
    Novel. DeLand, Fla.: Everett/Edwards, 1973.

Reviews

Sitting Pretty
    Choice 13 (Summer 1976): 832.
    Hudson Review 29 (Summer 1976): 270.
    Mtosha, Nashira. San Francisco Review of Books 2 (July-
        August 1976): 11-12.
    National Observer, 24 July 1976, p. 19.
Snakes
    Booklist, 1 November 1970, p. 215; 15 November 1970, p. 265;
        1 April 1971, p. 655.
    Books and Bookmen 16 (August 1971): 34.
    Davis, L. J. Book World, 17 May 1970, p. 8.
    English Journal 63 (January 1974): 66.
    Hendin, Josephine. Saturday Review of Literature, 22 August
        1970, p. 55.
    Kirkus, 15 February 1970, p. 204; 15 March 1970, p. 335.
    Kuehl, Linda. Commonweal, 23 October 1970, p. 106.
    Levin, Martin. New York Times Book Review, 17 May 1970,
        p. 38.
    Publishers' Weekly, 9 February 1970, p. 76.
    Sissman, L. E. New Yorker, 11 July 1970, p. 77.
    Time, 29 June 1970, p. 76.
    Times Literary Supplement, 30 July 1971, p. 881.
    Top of the News 27 (April 1971): 309.
    Weisenberg, C. M. Library Journal, 15 April 1970, p. 1505.
Who Is Angelina?
    Best Sellers 35 (April 1975): 6.
    Christian Science Monitor, 6 March 1975, p. 9.
    Hartford (Conn.) Courant, 17 March 1975; Newsbank--Literature

(May-June 1975):   Card 13:   B8-12.
Kent, George.   Phylon 37 (March 1976):   100-115.
Kirkus, 15 August 1974, p. 902; 15 November 1974, p. 1223.
Lentz, Perry.   Michigan Quarterly Review 15 (Spring 1976):
    235-239.
Library Journal, 1 December 1974, p. 3148.
New York Times, 23 January 1975, p. 31.
New York Times Book Review, 9 February 1975, p. 10.
Palm, Roberta.   Black World 24 (September 1975):   88-89.
Publishers' Weekly, 11 November 1974, p. 42.

GENERAL BIBLIOGRAPHY

Abcarian, Richard and M. Klotz, eds. Literature: The Human
Experience. New York: St. Martin's Press, 1973.

Abels, Cyrilly and Margarita G. Smith, eds. 40 Best Stories from
Mademoiselle, 1935-1960. New York: Harper & Row, 1960.

Abrahams, William, ed. Fifty Years of the American Short Story:
From the O. Henry Awards, 1919-1970. Garden City, N. Y.:
Doubleday, 1970.

_____. Prize Stories: The O. Henry Awards. Garden City,
N. Y.: Doubleday, 1967, 1970, 1971, 1973, 1974, 1975.

Adams, Bruce Payton. "The White Negro: The Image of the Pas-
sable Mulatto Character in Black Novels, 1853-1954." Ph. D.
Dissertation, University of Kansas, 1975.

Adoff, Arnold, ed. Brothers and Sisters: Modern Stories by
Black Americans. New York: Macmillan, 1970.

Albrecht, R. C., ed. The World of Short Fiction. New York:
Free Press, 1969.

Alexander, Margaret Walker. "Some Aspects of the Black Aesthetic." Freedomways 16 (Second Quarter 1976): 95-102.

Alhamisi, Ahmed and Harun Kofi Wangara, eds. Black Arts: An
Anthology of Black Creations. Detroit: Black Arts, 1969.

Allen, Donald M. and Robert Creeley, eds. New American Story.
New York: Grove Press, 1965.

Allison, Leonard, Leonard Jenkin and Robert Perrault, eds. Survival Printout: Total Effect. New York: Random House, 1973.

Anderson, Jo Ann. "Beyond the Stereotypes." Freedomways 16
(Third Quarter 1976): 192-194.

Angus, Douglas and Sylvia Angus. Contemporary American Short
Stories. Greenwich, Conn.: Fawcett, 1967.

Angus, S. L., ed. The Trouble Is: Stories of Social Dilemma.

Encino, Ca.: Dickenson, 1973.

Antico, John and Meredith K. Hazelrigg, eds. Insight Through Fiction: Dealing Effectively with the Short Story. Menlo Park, Ca.: Cummings, 1970.

Arden, Eugene. "The Early Harlem Novel." Phylon 20 (Spring 1959): 25-31.

Armstrong, Gregory, ed. Life at the Bottom. New York: Bantam Books, 1971.

Ashour, Radwa M. "The Search for a Black Poetics: A Study of Afro-American Critical Writings." Ph.D. Dissertation, University of Massachusetts, 1975.

Asimov, Isaac, ed. The Hugo Winners. Garden City, N.Y.: Doubleday, 1971.

Austin, Lettie J., Lewis W. Fenderson and Sophia P. Nelson, eds. The Black Man and the Promise of America. Glenview, Ill.: Scott, Foresman, 1970.

Avery, Evelyn. "Hungry Hearts: Women in Black and Jewish Literature." Paper presented at the MLA meeting, New York City, December 1976.

Baker, Donald G. "Black Images: The Afro-American in Popular Novels, 1900-1945." Journal of Popular Culture 7 (Fall 1973): 327-346.

_____. "From Apartheid to Invisibility: Black Americans in Popular Fiction, 1900-1960." Midwest Quarterly 13 (July 1972): 365-385.

Baker, Houston A., Jr. Singers of Daybreak: Studies in Black American Literature. Washington, D.C.: Howard University Press, 1974.

Ball, Jane Eklund, ed. Designs for Reading: Short Stories. Boston: Houghton Mifflin, 1969.

Bambara, Toni Cade, ed. Tales and Stories for Black Folks. Garden City, N.Y.: Doubleday, 1971.

Barcus, F. Earle and Jack Levin. "Role Distance in Negro and Majority Fiction." Journalism Quarterly 43 (Winter 1966): 709-714.

Barksdale, Richard K. "Alienation and the Anti-Hero in Recent American Fiction." CLA Journal 10 (September 1966): 1-10.

_____. "Black America and the Mask of Comedy." In The

Comic Imagination in American Literature, pp. 349-360. Edited by Louis D. Rubin, Jr. New Brunswick, N.J.: Rutgers University Press, 1973.

_____ and Keneth Kinnamon, eds. Black Writers of America: A Comprehensive Anthology. New York: Macmillan, 1972.

Baro, Gene, ed. After Appomattox: The Image of the South in Its Fiction, 1865-1900. New York: Corinth Books, 1963.

Bayliss, John Francis. "Novels of Black Americans Passing as Whites." Ph.D. Dissertation, Indiana University, 1976.

Beaty, Jerome, ed. The Norton Introduction to Literature: Fiction. New York: Norton, 1973.

Beck, Warren A. and Miles L. Clowers, eds. Understanding American History Through Fiction, vol. 2. New York: McGraw-Hill 1975.

Beier, Ulli, ed. Black Orpheus: An Anthology of African and Afro-American Prose. Nigeria: Longmans of Nigeria, 1964.

Beja, Morris. "It Must Be Important: Negroes in Contemporary American Fiction." Antioch Review 24 (Fall 1964): 323-336.

Bell, Bernard W. "Literary Sources of the Early Afro-American Novel." CLA Journal 18 (September 1974): 29-43.

Bennett, Stephen B. and William W. Nichols. "Violence in Afro-American Fiction: An Hypothesis." Modern Fiction Studies 17 (Summer 1971): 221-228.

Berkley, S. G., ed. The Short Story Reader, 3rd ed. Indianapolis: Bobbs-Merrill, 1973.

Bigsby, C. W. E., ed. The Black American Writer, 2 vols. De-Land, Florida: Everett/Edwards, 1969.

_____. "From Protest to Paradox: The Black Writer at Mid-Century." In In the Fifties, pp. 217-240. Edited by Norman Podhoretz. New York: Farrar, Straus, 1964.

Billingsley, Ronald G. "The Burden of the Hero in Modern Afro-American Fiction." Black World 25 (December 1975): 38-45, 66-73.

Bland, Edward. "Social Forces Shaping the Negro Novel." Negro Quarterly 1 (Fall 1942): 241-248.

Bluestein, Gene. "Blues as a Literary Theme." Massachusetts Review 8 (Autumn 1967): 593-617.

Bone, Robert. Down Home: A History of Afro-American Short
   Fiction from Its Beginnings to the End of the Harlem Renaissance. New York: G. P. Putnam's, 1975.

_____. The Negro Novel in America. New Haven: Yale Uni-
   versity Press, 1966.

Bontemps, Arna, ed. The Harlem Renaissance Remembered. New
   York: Dodd, Mead, 1972.

Bowen, James K. and Richard Van Der Beets, eds. American Short
   Fiction: Readings and Criticism. Indianapolis: Bobbs-Merrill,
   1970.

Boynton, Robert W. and Maynard Mack, eds. Introduction to the
   Short Story, rev. ed. Rochelle Park, N.J.: Hayden, 1972.

Bradford, Ernest Marvin. "Biblical Metaphors of Bondage and
   Liberation in Black Writing: A Study of the Evolution of Black
   Liberation as Mediated in Writing Based on the Bible." Ph.D.
   Dissertation, The University of Nebraska--Lincoln, 1976.

Brawley, Benjamin. Early Negro American Writers. Freeport,
   N.Y.: Books for Libraries, 1968.

_____. The Negro Genius: A New Appraisal of the Achievement
   of the American Negro in Literature and the Fine Arts. New
   York: Dodd, Mead, 1940.

_____. The Negro in Literature and Art. New York: Duffield,
   1930.

Brewster, Dorothy, ed. Book of Contemporary Short Stories. New
   York: Macmillan, 1936.

Brickel, Herschel, ed. Prize Stories of 1947: The O'Henry
   Awards. Garden City, N.Y.: Doubleday, 1947.

Britwum, Atta. "Black Survival and Culture: Rambling Thoughts
   on Black Aesthetics." Ameska: A Literary Journal of the Cape
   Coast 1 (1974): 99-110.

Brown, Lloyd W. "Black Entitles: Names as Symbols in Afro-
   American Literature." Studies in Black Literature 1 (Spring
   1970): 16-44.

_____. "The Expatriate Consciousness in Black American Lit-
   erature." Studies in Black Literature 3 (Summer 1972): 9-11.

Brown, Martha Hursey. "Images of Black Women: Family Roles
   in Harlem Renaissance Literature." D.A. Dissertation, Carnegie-Mellon University, 1976.

Brown, Sterling A. "A Century of Negro Portraiture in American Literature." Massachusetts Review 7 (Winter 1966): 73-96.

_____, Arthur P. Davis and Ulysses Lee, eds. The Negro Caravan. New York: Arno, 1970.

Burnett, E. W. and Martha Foley, eds. Story in America. New York: Vanguard, 1934.

Burnett, Whit, ed. Black Hands on a White Face: A Timepiece of Experiences in a Black and White America; an Anthology. New York: Dodd, Mead, 1971.

_____, ed. Seas of Gold: Great Stories of the Human Spirit. Philadelphia: Lippincott, 1944.

_____ and Hallie Burnett, eds. Prize College Stories, 1963. New York: Random House, 1963.

_____, eds. The Stone Soldier: Prize College Stories, 1964. New York: Fleet Press, 1964.

_____, eds. Story: The Fiction of the Forties. New York: Dutton, 1949.

_____, eds. Story: The Yearbook of Discovery, 1968. New York: Four Winds, 1968.

_____, eds. Story Jubilee. Garden City, N.Y.: Doubleday, 1965.

_____ and Martha Foley, eds. Story in America, 1933-1934. New York: Vanguard, 1934.

Butcher, Margaret Just. The Negro in American Culture. New York: Mentor, 1971.

Butcher, Philip. "The Younger Novelists and the Urban Negro." CLA Journal 4 (March 1961): 196-203.

Cahill, Tom and Susan Cahill, eds. Big City Stories by Modern American Writers. New York: Bantam, 1971.

Calverton, Victor Francis, ed. Anthology of American Negro Literature. New York: Modern Library, 1929.

Carey, G. O., ed. Quest for Meaning: Modern Short Stories. New York: McKay, 1975.

Carpenter, William and Peter F. Neumeyer, eds. Elements of Fiction: Introduction to the Short Story. Dubuque, Iowa: William C. Brown, 1974.

Carson, Herbert L. and Ada Lou Carson, eds. The Impact of

Fiction. Menlo Park, Ca.: Cummings, 1970.

Cary, Elisabeth L. "A New Element in Fiction." Book Buyer 23 (1901): 26-28.

Casmier, Adam A. and Sally Souder, eds. Coming Together: Modern Stories by Black and White Americans. Encino, Ca.: Dickenson, 1972.

Cassill, R. V., ed. Intro #3. New York: Bantam, 1970.

Casty, Alan H., ed. The Shape of Fiction, 2nd ed. Lexington: Heath, 1975.

Cayton, H. R. "Ideological Forces in the Work of Negro Writers." Negro Digest 15 (July 1966): 53-63.

Certner, Simon and George H. Henry, eds. Short Stories for Our Times. Boston: Houghton Mifflin, 1950.

Chametzky, Jules and Sidney Kaplan, eds. Black and White in American Culture. Amherst: University of Massachusetts Press, 1969.

Chapman, Abraham, ed. Black Voices. New York: New American Library, 1968.

_____, ed. New Black Voices: An Anthology of Contemporary Afro-American Literature. New York: New American Library, 1972.

Chavis, Helen De Lois. "The New Decorum: Moral Perspectives of Black Literature." Ph.D. Dissertation, The University of Wisconsin, 1971.

Clareson, Thomas D., ed. A Spectrum of Worlds. Garden City, N.Y.: Doubleday, 1972.

Clark, W. Bedford. "The Metaphor of Passing: To Be or Not to Be Black." Paper presented at the MLA meeting, New York City, December 1976.

Clarke, John Henrik, ed. American Negro Short Stories. New York: Hill & Wang, 1966.

_____, ed. Harlem: Voices from the Soul of Black America. New York: New American Library, 1970.

_____. "Transition in the American Negro Short Story." Phylon 21 (Winter 1960): 360-366.

Cooke, Gwendolyn. "Reading Literary Works by Black and White Writers: Effects on Students' Attitudes." Journal of Black

Studies 5 (December 1974): 123-133.

Cooke, M. G., ed. Modern Black Novelists. Englewood Cliffs, N.J.: Prentice-Hall, 1971.

Coombs, Orde, ed. What We Must See: Young Black Storytellers. New York: Dodd, Mead, 1971.

Copy, 1927. New York: D. Appleton, 1927.

Corrington, John William and Miller Williams, eds. Southern Writing in the Sixties. Baton Rouge: Louisiana State University Press, 1966.

Cowan, Gregory et al., eds. Three for Show. Philadelphia: Philadelphia Book Co., 1973.

Coyle, William, ed. The Young Man in American Literature: The Initiation Theme. Indianapolis: Odyssey, 1969.

Cromwell, Otelia, Lorenzo Dow Turner, and Eva Beatrice Dykes, eds. Readings from Negro Authors for Schools and Colleges. New York: Harcourt, Brace, 1931.

Cruse, Harold. The Crisis of the Negro Intellectual. New York: Morrow, 1967.

Current-Garcia, Eugene and Walton R. Patrick, eds. What Is the Short Story? Studies in the Development of a Literary Form, rev. ed. Glenview, Ill.: Scott, Foresman, 1974.

Dance, Daryl C. "Black Eve or Madonna? A Study of the Antithetical Views of the Mother in Black American Literature." In Perspectives on Afro-American Women, pp. 103-111. Edited by Willa D. Johnson and Thomas L. Green. Washington, D.C.: ECCA Publications, 1975.

_____. "Contemporary Militant Black Humor." Negro American Literature Forum 8 (1974): 217-222.

_____. "Wit and Humor in Black American Literature." Ph.D. Dissertation, University of Virginia, 1971.

Dashiell, Alfred Sheppard, ed. Editor's Choice. New York: G. P. Putnam's, 1934.

Davis, Arthur P. From the Dark Tower: Afro-American Writers from 1900 to 1960. Washington, D.C.: Howard University Press, 1974.

_____ and J. Saunders Redding, eds. Cavalcade: Negro American Writing from 1760 to the Present. Boston: Houghton Mifflin, 1971.

_____ and Michael W. Peplow, eds. The New Negro Renaissance. New York: Holt, Rinehart & Winston, 1975.

Davis, Robert Gorham, ed. Ten Modern Masters, 3rd ed. New
York: Harcourt Brace Jovanovich, 1972.

Daykin, Walter I. "Social Thought in Negro Novels." Sociological
and Social Research 19 (1935): 247-252.

Demarest, David P. and Lois S. Lamdin, eds. The Ghetto Reader.
New York: Random House, 1970.

Deodene, Frank and William P. French. Black American Fiction
Since 1952. Chatham, N.J.: Chatham Bookseller, 1970.

The Dial: an Annual of Fiction. New York: Dial Press, 1962.

Dietrich, R. F. and R. H. Sundell, eds. The Art of Fiction: An
Anthology, 2nd ed. New York: Holt, Rinehart & Winston,
1974.

Dolan, Paul J. and Joseph T. Bennett, eds. Introduction to Fiction.
New York: John Wiley, 1974.

Dreer, Herman, ed. American Literature by Negro Authors. New
York: Macmillan, 1950.

Edwards, Sister Ann. "Three Views on Blacks: The Black Woman
in American Literature." CEA Critic 37 (May 1975): 14-16.

Elder, Carol E. "'The Discovery of America': Literary Nationalism
in the Criticism of Black American Literature." Ph.D. Dissertation, University of Pittsburgh, 1972.

Ellison, Ralph. Shadow and Act. New York: Random House, 1972.

Emanual, James A. and Theodore L. Gross, eds. Dark Symphony:
Negro Literature in America. New York: Free Press, 1968.

Emerson, O. B. "Cultural Nationalism in Afro-American Literature." In The Cry of Home, pp. 211-244. Edited by H. Ernest
Lewald. Knoxville: University of Tennessee Press, 1972.

Engle, Paul, ed. Prize Stories 1959: The O. Henry Awards.
New York: Doubleday, 1959.

Everett, Chestyn. "'Tradition' in Afro-American Literature."
Black World 25 (December 1975): 20-35.

Exum, Pat. "Contemporary Black Women Writers." DeLand, Florida: Everett/Edwards, n.d. (Cassette.)

_____, ed. Keeping the Faith: Writings by Contemporary Black
Women. Greenwich, Conn.: Fawcett, 1974.

Fabricant, Noah Daniel and Heinz Werner, eds. Caravan of Music Stories, by the World's Great Authors. New York: Fell, 1947.

Faderman, Lillian and Barbara Bradshaw, eds. Speaking for Ourselves: American Ethnic Writing. Glenview, Ill.: Scott, Foresman, 1969.

Fagin, Nathan Bryllion, ed. America Through the Short Story. Boston: Little, Brown, 1936.

Farrison, W. Edward. "Much Ado About Negro Fiction: A Review Essay." CLA Journal 19 (September 1975): 90-100. (Review of Roger Rosenblatt's Black Fiction.)

Felgar, Robert. "Black Content, White Form." Studies in Black Literature 5 (Spring 1974): 28-31.

Fenton, Charles A., ed. Best Short Stories of World War II. New York: Viking Press, 1957.

Ferguson, Alfred R. "The Abolition of Blacks in Abolitionist Fiction, 1830-1860." Journal of Black Studies 5 (December 1974): 134-156.

Ferguson, Mary A., ed. Images of Women in Literature. Boston: Houghton Mifflin, 1973.

Ferman, Edward L., ed. The Best from Fantasy and Science Fiction. 17th Series. New York: Ace Books, 1966.

Ferris, Helen Josephine, comp. Girls, Girls, Girls: Stories of Love, Courage and the Quest for Happiness. New York: Franklin Watts, 1956.

Fiedler, Leslie. Love and Death in the American Novel, rev. ed. New York: Stein & Day, 1966.

Fleming, Robert. "Playing the Dozens in the Black Novel." Studies in Black Literature 3 (Autumn 1972): 17-22.

Flower, Dean, ed. Counterparts: Classic and Contemporary American Short Stories. Greenwich, Conn.: Fawcett, 1971.

Foley, Martha, ed. Best American Short Stories, 1946, 1972, 1973. Boston: Houghton Mifflin, 1946, 1972, 1973.

_____, ed. Fifty Best American Short Stories 1915-1965. Boston: Houghton Mifflin, 1965.

_____, ed. Two Hundred Years of Great American Short Stories. Boston: Houghton Mifflin, 1975.

_____ and David Burnett, eds. Best American Short Stories, 1959-1971, 1973, 1974. Boston: Houghton Mifflin, 1959-1974.

Foley, Mary C. and Ruth Graeme Gentles, eds. America in Story: A Collection of Short Stories for High Schools. New York: Harper, 1932.

Ford, Nick Aaron, ed. Black Insights: Significant Literature by Black Americans, 1760 to the Present. Waltham, Mass.: Ginn, 1971.

_____. The Contemporary Negro Novel: A Study in Race Relations. Boston: Meador, 1936.

_____. "The Negro Novel as a Vehicle of Propaganda." Quarterly Review of Higher Education Among Negroes 9 (1941): 135-139.

_____ and H. L. Faggett, eds. Best Short Stories by Afro-American Writers, 1924-1950. Boston: Meador, 1950.

Fuller, Hoyt W. "Contemporary Negro Fiction." Southwest Review 50 (1965): 321-335.

Gable, Sister Mariella, ed. Many-Colored Fleece. New York: Sheed & Ward, 1950.

Gaer, Joseph, ed. Our Lives: American Labor Stories. New York: Boni & Gaer, 1948.

Gasarch, Pearl and Ralph Gasarch, eds. Fiction: The Universal Elements. New York: Van Nostrand Reinhold, 1972.

Gates, Skip. "Of Negroes Old and New." Transition No. 46 (1974): 44-57.

Gayle, Addison, Jr., ed. The Black Aesthetic. Garden City, N.Y.: Doubleday, 1971.

_____. "The Black Aesthetic 10 Years Later." Black World 23 (September 1974): 20-29.

_____, ed. Black Expression: Essays by and about Black Americans in the Creative Arts. New York: Weybright & Talley, 1969.

_____. "Strangers in a Strange Land." Southern Exposure 3 no. 1 (1975): 4-7.

Gerald, John Bart and George Blecher, eds. Survival Prose: An Anthology of New Writing. New York: Bobbs-Merrill, 1971.

Gerard, Albert. "Humanism and Negritude: Notes on the Contemporary Afro-American Novel." Diogenes No. 37 (Spring 1962): 115-133.

Gibson, Donald B., ed. Five Black Writers: Essays on Wright, Ellison, Baldwin, Hughes and Jones. New York: New York University Press, 1970.

_____ and Carol Anselment, eds. Black and White: Stories of American Life. New York: Washington Square Press, 1971.

Gilkes, Lillian Barnard, ed. Short Story Craft: An Introduction to Short Story Writing. New York: Macmillan, 1949.

Girodias, Maurice, ed. The Olympia Reader. New York: Grove Press, 1965.

Glicksberg, Charles I. "The Negro Cult of the Primitive." Antioch Review 4 (Spring 1944): 47-55.

_____. "Negro Fiction in America." South Atlantic Quarterly 45 (1946): 477-488.

Gloster, Hugh M. Negro Voices in American Fiction. Chapel Hill: University of North Carolina Press, 1948.

Gold, Don, ed. The Human Commitment: An Anthology of Contemporary Short Fiction. Philadelphia: Chilton, 1967.

Gold, Herbert, ed. Fiction of the Fifties: A Decade of American Writing. Garden City, N.Y.: Doubleday, 1959.

_____ and David L. Stevenson, eds. Stories of Modern America. New York: St. Martin's 1961.

Gold, Robert S., ed. Point of Departure: Youth and Discovery. New York: Dell, 1967.

Goldstone, Herbert, ed. Points of Departure: A Collection of Short Fiction. Englewood Cliffs, N.J.: Prentice-Hall, 1971.

Gordon, Eugene. "Negro Novelists and the Negro Masses." New Masses 8 (July 1933): 16-20.

Gordon, John and L. Rust Hills, eds. New York: New York: The City 'as Seen by Masters of Art and Literature. New York: Showcrest, 1965.

Grimes, Alan and Janet Owen. "Civil Rights and the Race Novel." Chicago Jewish Forum 15 (1956): 12-15.

Gross, Seymour L. "Stereotype to Archetype: The Negro in American Literary Criticism." In Images of the Negro in American Literature, pp. 1-26. Edited by Seymour L. Gross and John

Edward Hardy. Chicago: University of Chicago Press, 1966.

Gross, Theodore L., ed. A Nation of Nations: Ethnic Literature in America. New York: Free Press, 1971.

Guilford, Virginia N. Brown. "The Black Contemporary Novel: Social Index." D. A. Dissertation, Carnegie-Mellon University, 1974.

Gulassa, Cyril M., ed. The Fact of Fiction: Social Relevance in the Short Story. San Francisco: Canfield Press, 1972.

Haberly, David T. "The Literature of an Invisible Nation." Journal of Black Studies 7 (December 1976): 133-150.

Hagopian, John V. "Mau-Mauing the Literary Establishment." Studies in the Novel 3 (Summer 1971): 135-147.

Hall, James B., ed. The Realm of Fiction: 65 Short Stories, 2nd ed. New York: McGraw Hill, 1970.

Hamalian, Leo and Edmond L. Volpe, eds. Eleven Modern Short Novels. New York: G. P. Putnam's Sons, 1970.

Hardy, J. E., ed. The Modern Talent. New York: Holt, Rinehart & Winston, 1964.

Hart, J., et al. Discovery and Response: The Strategies of Fiction. Cambridge, Mass.: Winthrop, 1972.

Hart, Nina and Edna Maude Perry, comps. Representative Short Stories. New York: Macmillan, 1930.

Hayashi, Susanna. "Dark Odyssey: Descent into the Underworld in Black American Fiction." Ph. D. Dissertation, Indiana University, 1971.

Hayden, Robert, David J. Burrows and Frederick R. Lapides, eds. Afro-American Literature: An Introduction. New York: Harcourt Brace Jovanovich, 1971.

Hayman, David and Eric S. Rabkin, eds. Form in Fiction: An Introduction to the Analysis of Narrative Prose. New York: St. Martin's Press, 1974.

Heermance, J. Noel. "The Modern Negro Novel." Negro Digest 13 (May 1964): 66-76.

Hemenway, Robert, ed. The Black Novelist. Columbis: Charles E. Merrill, 1970.

Heydrick, Benjamin Alexander, ed. Americans All: Stories of American Life of To-Day. New York: Harcourt, 1920.

Hibbard, Addison, ed. Stories of the South: Old and New. Chapel Hill: University of North Carolina Press, 1931.

Hicks, Jack, ed. Cutting Edges: Young American Fiction for the Seventies. New York: Holt, Rinehart & Winston, 1973.

Hill, Herbert, ed. Anger, and Beyond: The Negro Writer in the United States. New York: Harper & Row, 1966.

_____, ed. Soon, One Morning: New Writing by American Negroes, 1940-1962. New York: Knopf, 1968.

Hills, Penny Chapin and L. Rust Hills, eds. How We Live: Contemporary Life in Contemporary Fiction, 2 vols. New York: Collier, 1968.

Himber, David K., ed. Toward Theme in Short Fiction. Boston: Holbrook Press, 1973.

Hollander, John, ed. American Short Stories Since 1945. New York: Harper & Row, 1968.

Hondius, Katherine, ed. Identity: Stories for This Generation. Glencoe, Ill.: Scott, Foresman, 1966.

Houston, Helen Ruth. "The Afro-American Novel 1965-1975: A Descriptive Bibliography of Primary and Secondary Material." D.A. Dissertation, Middle Tennessee State University, 1976.

Howe, Irving. A World More Attractive. Freeport, N.Y.: Books for Libraries, 1963.

Howes, Barbara and Gregory Jay Smith, eds. The Sea-Green Horse: A Collection of Short Stories. New York: Macmillan, 1970.

Huggins, Kathryn. "Aframerican Fiction." Southern Literary Messenger 3 (1941): 315-320.

Huggins, Nathan Irvin. Harlem Renaissance. New York: Oxford University Press, 1971.

_____, ed. Voices from the Harlem Renaissance. New York: Oxford University Press, 1976.

Hughes, Carl M. The Negro Novelist: A Discussion of the Writings of American Negro Novelists, 1940-1950. New York: Citadel Press, 1953.

Hughes, Langston, ed. The Best Short Stories by Negro Writers: An Anthology from 1899 to the Present. Boston: Little, Brown, 1967.

Hurtik, Emil and Robert Yarber, eds. An Introduction to Short

Fiction and Criticism. New York: John Wiley, 1971.

Isani, Mukhtar Ali. "The Exotic and Protest in Earlier Black Literature: The Use of Alien Setting and Character." Studies in Black Literature 5 (Summer 1974): 9-14.

Jackson, Blyden. "A Golden Mean for the Negro Novel." CLA Journal 3 (December 1959): 81-87.

_____. "The Negro's Image of the Universe as Reflected in His Fiction." CLA Journal 4 (September 1960): 22-31.

_____. "The Negro's Negro in Negro Literature." Michigan Quarterly Review 4 (October 1965): 290-295.

_____. The Waiting Years: Essays on American Negro Literature. Baton Rouge: Louisiana State University Press, 1976.

Jackson, Esther Merle. "The American Negro and the Image of the Absurd." Phylon 23 (Winter 1962): 359-371.

James, Charles L. From the Roots: Short Stories by Black Americans. New York: Dodd, Mead, 1970.

Jarrett, Thomas. "Recent Fiction by Negroes." College English 16 (November 1954): 85-91.

_____. "Toward Unfettered Creativity: A Note on the Negro Novelist's Coming of Age." Phylon 11 (Fourth Quarter 1950): 313-317.

Johnson, Charles S., ed. Ebony and Topaz: A Collectanea. New York: National Urban League, 1927.

Jones, Norma Ramsay. "The Image of the 'White Liberal' in Black American Fiction and Drama." Ph.D. Dissertation, Bowling Green State University, 1973.

Karl, Frederick R. and Leo Hamalian, eds. the naked i: fiction for the seventies. New York: Fawcett, 1971.

Karlin, Wayne, Basil T. Paquet and Larry Rottmann, eds. Free Fire Zone: Short Stories by Vietnam Veterans. New York: McGraw-Hill, 1973.

Kendricks, Ralph and Claudette Levitt, eds. Afro-American Voices: 1770's-1970's. New York: Oxford Book Co., 1970.

Kent, George E. Blackness and the Adventure of Western Culture. Chicago: Third World Press, 1972.

Kielty, B., ed. A Treasury of Short Stories. New York: Simon & Schuster, 1947.

Killens, John O. "The Image of Black Folk in American Literature." Black Scholar 6 (June 1975): 45-52.

Killinger, John. The Fragile Presence: Transcendence in Modern Literature. Philadelphia: Fortress Press, 1973.

Kilson, Martin. "The Black Aesthetic: Ideology or Aesthetics?" Harvard Advocate 107 no. 4 (1974): 36-37.

King, Woodie, ed. Black Short Story Anthology. New York: New American Library, 1972.

Kissin, Eva H., comp. Stories in Black and White. Philadelphia: Lippincott, 1970.

Klein, Marcus and Robert Pack, eds. Short Stories: Classic, Modern, Contemporary. Boston: Little, Brown, 1967.

Klinkowitz, Jerome. "Black Superfiction." North American Review 259 (Winter 1974): 69-74.

_____. Literary Disruptions: The Making of a Post-Contemporary American Fiction. Urbana: University of Illinois Press, 1975.

Klotman, Phyllis Rauch. Another Man Gone: The Black Runner in Contemporary Afro-American Literature. Port Washington, N.Y.: Kennikat Press, 1976.

_____. "The White Bitch Archetype in Contemporary Black Fiction." Bulletin of the Midwest Modern Language Association 6 (Spring 1973): 96-110.

Knight, Etheridge, ed. Black Voices from Prison. New York: Pathfinder, 1970.

Knox, George. "The Negro Novelist's Sensibility and the Outsider Theme." Western Humanities Review 11 (Spring 1957): 137-148.

Kostelanetz, Richard, ed. The Young American Writers: Fiction, Poetry, Drama, and Criticism. New York: Funk & Wagnalls, 1967.

Kreymborg, Alfred, Lewis Mumford and Paul Rosenfeld, eds. New American Caravan: A Yearbook of American Literature. New York: Macaulay, 1929.

_____, eds. The Second American Caravan: A Yearbook of American Literature. New York: Macaulay, 1928.

Larson, Charles R., ed. Prejudice: 20 Tales of Oppression and Liberation. New York: New American Library, 1971.

Lehan, Richard. "Existentialism in Recent American Fiction: The Demonic Quest." Texas Studies in Literature and Language 1 (1959): 181-202.

Lindberg, J. "Black Aesthetic: Minority or Mainstream?" North American Review 260 (Winter 1975): 48-52.

Littlejohn, David. Black on White: A Critical Survey of Writing by American Negroes. New York: Grossman, 1966.

Locke, Alain, ed. The New Negro: An Interpretation. New York: Albert Charles Boni, 1925.

Loggins, Vernon. The Negro Author: His Development in America to 1900. Port Washington, N.Y.: Kennikat, 1964.

Lomax, Micahel L. "Fantasies of Affirmation: The 1920's Novel of Negro Life." CLA Journal 16 (December 1972): 232-246.

Long, Richard A. and Eugenia W. Collier, eds. Afro-American Writing: An Anthology of Prose and Poetry. New York: New York University Press, 1972.

Love, Theresa R. "The Black Woman in Afro-American Literature." Paper presented at the Midwest Modern Language Association Meeting, Chicago, November 1975. (Mimeographed.)

McConnell, Frank D. "Black Words and Black Becoming." Yale Review 63 (Winter 1974): 193-210.

Macebuh, Stanley. "The Way of the Old World." Third Press Review 1 (September/October 1975): 33, 55, 68-69.

Major, Clarence. The Dark and Feeling: Reflections on Black American Writing. New York: Third Press, 1974.

Marcus, Steven. "The American Negro in Search of Identity." Commentary 16 (November 1953): 456-463.

Margolies, Edward. Native Sons: A Critical Study of Twentieth-Century Negro American Authors. Philadelphia: J. B. Lippincott, 1970.

_____, ed. A Native Sons Reader. Philadelphia: J. B. Lippincott, 1970.

Martin, S. Rudolph, Jr. "A New Mind: Black Consciousness, 1950-1970." Ph.D. Dissertation, Washington State University, 1974.

Matthews, Jack, ed. Archetypal Themes in the Modern Story. New York: St. Martin's, 1973.

Maund, Alfred. "The Negro Novelist and the Contemporary American Scene." Chicago Jewish Forum 13 (Fall 1954): 28-34.

May, John R., S. J. "Images of Apocalypse in the Black Novel." Renascence 23 (Autumn 1970): 31-45.

Mayfield, Julian, ed. Ten Times Black: Stories from the Black Experience. New York: Bantam, 1972.

Mays, Benjamin E. The Negro's God as Reflected in His Literature. Boston: Grimes & Chapman, 1938.

Meier, August. "Some Reflections on the Negro Novel." CLA Journal 2 (March 1959): 168-177.

Mellard, James M., ed. Four Modes: A Rhetoric of Modern Fiction. New York: Macmillan, 1973.

Miller, Ruth, ed. Blackamerican Literature: 1760-Present. Beverly Hills, Calif.: Glencoe Press, 1971.

Mills, Nicolaus, ed. Comparisons: A Short Story Anthology. New York: McGraw-Hill, 1972.

Minot, Stephen and Robley Wilson, eds. Three Stances of Modern Fiction: A Critical Anthology of the Short Story. Cambridge, Mass.: Winthrop, 1972.

Mizener, Arthur, ed. Modern Short Stories: The Uses of the Imagination, 3rd ed. New York: Norton, 1971.

Moon, Bucklin. "A Literature of Protest." Reporter, 6 December 1949): 35-37.

_____, ed. Primer for White Folks. Garden City, N.Y.: Doubleday, 1946.

Morris, Alton C., Biron Walker, and Philip Bradshaw, eds. Imaginative Literature, 2nd ed. New York: Harcourt Brace Jovanovich, 1973.

Morse, Donald, ed. The Choices of Fiction. Cambridge, Mass.: Winthrop, 1974.

Mphahlele, Ezekiel. "From the Black American World." Okike 4 (1973): 51-61; 5 (1974): 62-69.

_____. "The Function of Literature at the Present Time: The Ethnic Imperative." Transition 45 (1974): 47-53.

Murray, Albert. The Omni-Americans: New Perspectives on Black Experience and American Culture. New York: Outerbridge & Dienstfrey, 1970.

_____. "Something Different, Something More." In Anger, and Beyond, pp. 112-137. Edited by Herbert Hill. New York: Harper & Row, 1966.

Murray, Alma and Robert Thomas, eds. The Journey. New York: Scholastic Book Services, 1970.

_____, eds. Major Black Writers. New York: Scholastic Book Services, 1971.

_____, eds. The Scene. New York: Scholastic Book Services, 1971.

Musgrave, Marian E. "Patterns of Violence and Non-Violence in Pro-Slavery and Anti-Slavery Fiction. CLA Journal 16 (June 1973): 426-437.

Nagel, James, ed. Vision and Value: A Thematic Introduction to the Short Story. Encino, Calif.: Dickenson, 1975.

New, W. H. and H. J. Rosengarten, eds. Modern Stories in English. New York: T. Y. Crowell, 1975.

New World Writing, vol. 2. New York: New American Library, 1952.

Newman, Katherine D., ed. Ethnic American Short Stories. New York: Washington Square Press, 1975.

North, Joseph. New Masses: An Anthology of the Rebel Thirties. New York: International, 1969.

O'Brien, Edward J., ed. Best American Short Stories, 1923, 1925, 1926. Boston: Houghton Mifflin, 1923, 1925, 1926.

Olsen, James and Laurence Swinburne, eds. Dreamers of Dreams. New York: Noble & Noble, 1970.

_____, eds. He Who Dares. New York: Noble & Noble, 1970.

_____, eds. Love's Blues. New York: Noble & Noble, 1970.

_____, eds. Me, Myself, and I. New York: Noble & Noble, 1970.

Palmer, Paul, ed. World's Best Short Stories of 1928. New York: Minton, 1928.

Palosaari, Ronald Gerald. "The Image of the Black Minister in the Black Novel from Dunbar to Baldwin." Ph.D. Dissertation, University of Minnesota, 1970.

The Paris Review. Best Stories from the Paris Review. New

York: E. P. Dutton, 1959.

Parker, Bettye J. "Black Literature Teachers: Torch-Bearers of European Myths?" Black World 25 (December 1975): 61-65.

Parker, John W. "The Emergence of Negro Fiction." Negro History Bulletin 12 (October 1948): 12, 18.

Parks, Carole A. "Symposium on Black Criticism." Black World 24 (July 1975): 64-65, 97.

Patterson, Lindsay, ed. An Introduction to Black Literature in America from 1746 to the Present. Cornwell Heights, Pa.: Publisher's Agency, 1968.

Peavy, Charles D. "The Black Revolutionary Novel, 1899-1969." Studies in the Novel 3 (Summer 1971): 180-189.

Peden, William. The American Short Story: Continuity and Change 1940-1975. Boston: Houghton Mifflin, 1975.

_____, ed. Short Fiction: Shape and Substance. Boston: Houghton Mifflin, 1971.

Perkins, George, ed. Realistic American Short Fiction. Glenview, Ill.: Scott, Foresman, 1972.

Perrine, Laurence, ed. Story and Structure, 4th ed. New York: Harcourt Brace Jovanovich, 1974.

Perry, Robert L. "The Afro-American Intellectual of the 1920's: The Sociological Implications of the Harlem Renaissance." Paper presented at the MLA Meeting, New Yori City, December 1976.

Petesch, Donald A. "The Role of Folklore in the Modern Black Novel." Kansas Quarterly 7 (Summer 1975): 99-100.

Pfeiffer, John. "Black American Speculative Literature: A Checklist." Extrapolation 17 (December 1975): 35-43.

Pickering, James H., ed. Fiction 100: An Anthology of Short Stories. New York: Macmillan, 1974.

Potter, Vilma R. "New Politics, New Mothers." CLA Journal 16 (December 1972): 247-255.

Roscoe, Burton. "Negro Novel and White Reviewers." African Methodist Review 50 (1940): 113-117.

Ravitz, Abe C., ed. The American Disinherited: A Profile in Fiction. Belmont, Calif.: Dickenson, 1970.

Reddick, L. D. "No Kafka in the South." Phylon 11 (Fourth Quarter 1950): 380-383.

Reed, Ishmael, ed. 19 Necromancers from Now: An Anthology of Original American Writing for the 70's. Garden City, N.Y.: Doubleday, 1970.

Rideout, Walter B. The Radical Novel in the United States, 1900-1954. Cambridge: Harvard University Press, 1956.

Robinson, Anna T. "Race Consciousness and Survival Techniques Depicted in Harlem Renaissance Fiction." Ph.D. Dissertation, Pennsylvania State University, 1973.

Robinson, William H., ed. Nommo: An Anthology of Modern African and Black American Literature. New York: Macmillan, 1972.

Rollin, Roger B., ed. Hero/Anti-Hero. New York: Webster Division McGraw-Hill, 1973.

Rosenblatt, Roger. Black Fiction. Cambridge: Harvard University Press, 1974.

Rotter, Pat, ed. Bitches and Sad Ladies: An Anthology of Fiction by and about Women. New York: Harper's Magazine Press, 1975.

Rubin, Louis D., Jr. and C. Hugh Holman, eds. Southern Literary Study: Problems and Possibilities. Chapel Hill: University of North Carolina Press, 1975.

Rush, Theressa Gunnels, Carol Fairbanks Myers, and Esther Spring Arata. Black American Writers Past and Present: A Biographical and Bibliographical Dictionary. Metuchen, N.J.: Scarecrow Press, 1975.

Sanchez, Sonia, ed. Three Hundred Sixty Degrees of Blackness Comin at You: An Anthology of the Sonia Sanchez Writers Workshop at Countee Cullen Library in Harlem. New York: 5X Publishing Co., 1971.

_____, ed. We Be Word Sorcerers: 25 Stories by Black Americans. New York: Bantam, 1973.

Schneider, Elisabeth, et al., eds. The Range of Literature: Fiction, 3rd ed. New York: Van Nostrand, 1973.

Schneiderman, Beth Kline, ed. By and About Women. New York: Harcourt Brace Jovanovich, 1973.

Scholes, Robert, ed. Some Modern Writers: Essays and Fiction by Conrad, Dinesen, Lawrence, Orwell, Faulkner, and Ellison. New York: Oxford University Press, 1971.

Schraufnagel, Noel. From Apology to Protest: Black American Novel. DeLand, Florida: Everett/Edwards, 1973.

Schulberg, Budd. "Black Phoenix: An Introduction." Antioch Review 27 (Fall 1967): 277-284.

_____, ed. From the Ashes: Voices of Watts. New York: New American Library, 1967.

Schulman, L. M. , ed. The Loners: Short Stories about the Young and Alienated. New York: Macmillan, 1970.

_____, ed. Travelers. New York: Macmillan, 1972.

Scott, Elaine. "Black Women Writers and the Critical Establishment." Paper presented at the MLA Meeting, New York City, December 1976.

Scott, Nathan A. , Jr. "Judgment Marked by a Cellar: The American Negro Writer and the Dialectic of Despair." Denver Quarterly 2 (Summer 1967): 5-35.

Scott, Virgil, ed. Studies in the Short Story, alternate ed. New York: Holt, Rinehart & Winston, 1971.

Seaver, Edwin, ed. Cross-Section. New York: Fisher, 1944.

_____, ed. Cross-Section: A Collection of New American Writing. New York: Simon & Schuster, 1947.

Seyersted, Per. "A Survey of Trends and Figures in Afro-American Fiction." American Studies in Scandinavia 6 nos. 1-2 (1973-74): 67-86.

Sherrill, A. and P. Robertson, eds. Four Elements: A Creative Approach to the Short Story. New York: Holt, Rinehart & Winston, 1975.

Shockley, Ann A. and Sue Chandler. Living Black American Authors: A Biographical Dictionary. New York: Bowker, 1973.

Shuman, R. Baird, ed. A Galaxy of Black Writing. Durham, N.C. : Moore, 1970.

Simmons, Gloria M. , and Helen D. Hutchinson, eds. Black Culture: Reading and Writing Black. New York: Holt, Rinehart & Winston, 1972.

Simonson, Harold P. , ed. Quartet: A Book of Stories, Plays, Poems, and Critical Essays. New York: Harper & Row, 1970.

Simpson, Claude M. , ed. The Local Colorists: American Short Stories, 1857-1900. New York: Harper & Row, 1960.

Singh, Amritjit. The Novels of the Harlem Renaissance: Twelve Black Writers 1923-1933. University Park: Pennsylvania State University, 1976.

Singh, Raman K. "The Black Novel and Its Tradition." Colorado Quarterly 20 (Summer 1971): 23-29.

_____ and Peter Fellowes, eds. Black Literature in America: A Casebook. New York: T. Y. Crowell, 1970.

Skeeter, Sharyn J. "Black Women Writers." Essence 4 (May 1973): 58-59.

Smart, William, ed. Women & Men, Men & Women: An Anthology of Short Stories. New York: St. Martin's 1975.

Smith, Bernard, ed. Democratic Spirit: A Collection of American Writings from the Earliest Times to the Present Day. New York: Knopf, 1941.

Solotaroff, Theodore, ed. American Review 16. New York: Bantam, 1973.

Somer, John, ed. Narrative Experience: The Private Voice. Glenview, Ill.: Scott, Foresman, 1970.

Somerville, Rose M., ed. Intimate Relationships: Marriage, Family, and Lifestyles Through Literature. Englewood Cliffs, N.J.: Prentice-Hall, 1975.

Stadler, Quandra Prettyman, ed. Out of Our Lifes: A Selection of Contemporary Black Fiction. Washington, D.C.: Howard University Press, 1975.

Stanford, Barbara Dodds, ed. I, Too, Sing America: Black Voices in American Literature. New York: Hayden, 1971.

Stansbury, Donald L., ed. Impact: Short Stories for Pleasure. Englewood Cliffs, N.J.: Prentice-Hall, 1971.

Statements: New Fiction from the Fiction Collection. New York: George Braziller, 1975.

Stegner, Wallace and Richard Scowcroft, eds. Stanford Short Stories, 1960. Stanford: Stanford University Press, 1960.

Stein, Allen F. and Thomas N. Walters. The Southern Experience in Short Fiction. Glencoe, Ill.: Scott, Foresman, 1971.

Steinberg, Erwin R., Nan Hohenstein, and Harriet S. Panetta, eds. Insight: The Literature of Imagination. New York: Noble & Noble, 1969.

Stetson, Earlene. "The Mulatto Motif in Black Fiction." Ph.D. Dissertation, State University of New York at Buffalo, 1976.

Storm, Hans Otto, et al., eds. American Writing. Prairie City, Ill.: Decker, 1940.

Takai, Ronald T. Violence in the Black Imagination: Essays and Documents. New York: G. P. Putnam's, 1972.

Taylor, J. Chesley, ed. The Short Story: Fiction in Transition, 2nd ed. New York: Scribner's, 1973.

Thomas, Will. "Negro Writers of Pulp Fiction." Negro Digest 8 (July 1950): 81-84.

Thune, Ensaf and Ruth Prigozye, eds. Short Stories: A Critical Anthology. New York: Macmillan, 1973.

Timko, Michael, ed. 29 Short Stories: An Introductory Anthology. New York: Knopf, 1975.

Turner, Darwin T., ed. Black American Literature: Fiction. Columbus, Ohio: Charles E. Merrill, 1969.

_____. "The Negro Novel in America: In Rebuttal." CLA Journal 10 (December 1966): 122-134.

_____. "The Negro Novelist and the South." Southern Humanities Review 1 (Winter 1967): 21-29.

Tytell, John and Harold Jaffe, eds. Affinities: A Short Story Anthology. New York: T. Y. Crowell, 1970.

Wagenknecht, Edward Charles, ed. Fireside Book of Christmas Stories. New York: Bobbs, 1945.

Waldmeir, J., ed. Recent American Fiction: Some Critical Views. Boston: Houghton Mifflin, 1963.

Walker, Alice. "In Search of Our Mothers' Gardens: Honoring the Creativity of the Black Woman." Jackson State Review 6 (1974): 44-53.

Walser, Richard Gaither, ed. North Carolina in the Short Story. Chapel Hill: University of North Carolina Press, 1948.

_____, ed. Short Stories from the Old North State. Chapel Hill: University of North Carolina Press, 1959.

Waniek, Marilyn Nelson. "The Space Where Sex Should Be: Toward a Definition of the Black American Literary Tradition." Studies in Black Literature 6 (Fall 1975): 7-13.

Ward, Jerry W. "N. J. Loftis' Black Anima: A Problem in Aesthetics." Journal of Black Studies 7 (December 1976): 195-210.

Ward, Theodore. "Five Negro Novelists: Revolt and Retreat." Mainstream 1 (Winter 1947): 100-110.

Warfel, Harry Redcay. American Novelists of Today. Westport, Conn.: Greenwood, 1951.

_____ and George Harrison Orians, eds. American Local-Color Stories. New York: American Book Co., 1941.

Warren, Robert Penn and Albert Erskine, eds. A New Southern Harvest, New York: Dell, 1957.

Washington, Mary Helen. "The Black Woman as Suppressed Artist in Fiction." Paper presented at the MLA Meeting, New York City, December 1976.

_____. "Black Women Image Makers." Black World 23 (August 1974): 10-18.

_____, ed. Black-Eyed Susans: Classic Stories By and About Black Women. Garden City, N.Y.: Doubleday, 1975.

_____. "The Contemporary Black Woman Writer: Sources and Influences." Paper presented at the MLA Meeting, San Francisco, December 1975.

Watkins, Mel, ed. Black Review No. 1, No. 2. New York: William Morrow, 1971, 1972.

Watkins, Mel and Jay David, eds. To Be a Black Woman: Portraits in Fact and Fiction. New York: William Morrow, 1970.

Watson, Robert and Gibbons Ruark, eds. The Greensboro Reader. Chapel Hill: University of North Carolina Press, 1968.

Weimer, David R., ed. Modern American Classics: An Anthology of Short Fiction. New York: Random House, 1969.

Welburn, Ron. "Nationalism and Internationalism in Black Literature: The Afro-American Scene." Greenfield Review 3 no. 4 (1974): 60-72.

White, Walter. "Negro Literature." In American Writers on American Literature, pp. 442-451. Edited by John Macy. New York: Horace Liveright, 1931.

Whiteman, Maxwell. A Century of Fiction by American Negroes, 1853-1952: A Descriptive Bibliography. Philadelphia: Press of Maurice Jacobs, 1955.

Whitlow, Roger. Black American Literature: A Critical History. Chicago: Nelson Hall, 1973.

_____. "Black Literature and American Innocence." Studies in Black Literature 5 (Summer 1974): 1-4.

_____. "A Socio-Critical History of Nineteenth-Century Fiction Written by Black Americans." Ph.D. Dissertation, Saint Louis University, 1975.

Williams, Blanche C., ed. Prize Stories of 1926: The O. Henry Memorial Award Prize. Garden City, N.Y.: Doubleday, 1926.

Williams, John A. and Charles F. Harris, eds. Amistad 1, 2. New York: Vintage Books, 1970, 1971.

Williams, Ora. American Black Women in the Arts and Social Sciences: A Bibliographic Survey. Metuchen, N.J.: Scarecrow Press, 1973.

Williams, Sherley Ann. Give Birth to Brightness: A Thematic Study in Neo-Black Literature. New York: Dial, 1972.

Winslow, Henry. "Two Visions of Reality." Negro Digest 16 (May 1967): 36-39.

Willheim, Donald A., ed. Ace Science Fiction Reader. New York: Ace Books, 1971.

_____ and Terry Carr, eds. World's Best Science Fiction, Fourth Series. New York: Ace Books, 1968.

_____, eds. World's Best Science Fiction, 1969. New York: Ace Books, 1969.

Yellin, Jean Fagan. The Intricate Knot: The Negro in American Literature, 1776-1863. New York: New York University Press, 1971.

Young, Carlene, ed. Black Experience: Analysis and Synthesis. San Rafael, Calif.: Leswing Press, 1972.

Young, James O. Black Writers of the Thirties. Baton Rouge: Louisiana State University Press, 1973.